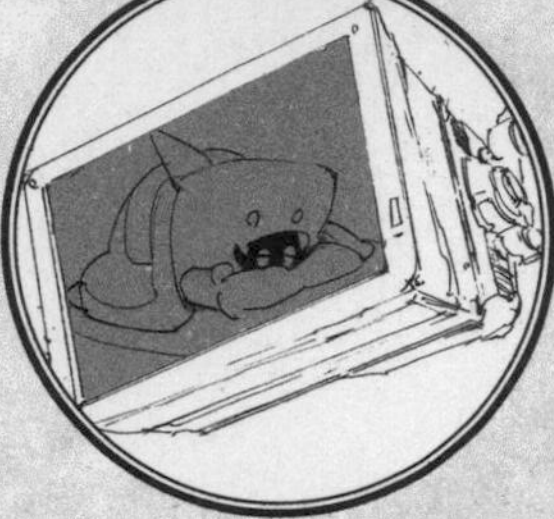

POSUKA DEMIZU

I'm so excited about the underground shelter! The water is good! The food is good! And the small space is also good! Being frugal with resources and using the garden to manage is very good!

But after a month—no, after even a week—anyone would probably start wanting sunlight.

I wonder how long the young children are going to spend underground.

Hoping they can run around in the green gardens again, they quietly wait for Emma and Ray to return. To be continued soon in volume 8.

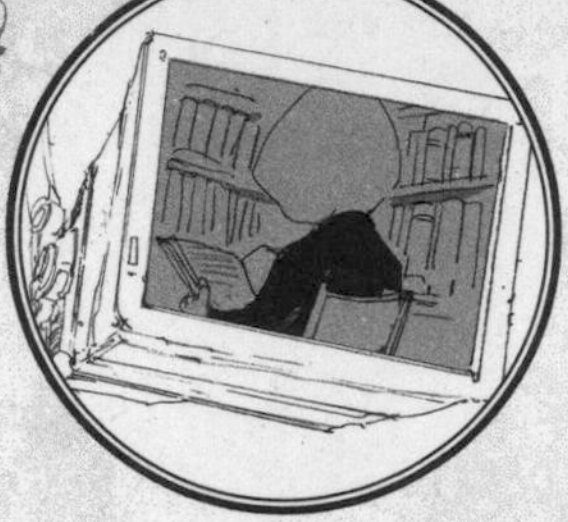

KAIU SHIRAI

These were things I found when I reviewed my early notes.

• Norman isn't the knight, he's the shining armor.

• Krone has an amazing bod under her clothes. (*Probably talking about muscle)

• The geezer is the type of horrible adult who throws poo at you.

What the heck? These are pretty...out there.

Anyway, please enjoy the volume!

Posuka Demizu debuted as a manga artist with the 2013 *CoroCoro* series *Oreca Monster Bouken Retsuden*. A collection of illustrations, *The Art of Posuka Demizu*, was released in 2016 by PIE International.

Kaiu Shirai debuted in 2015 with *Ashley Gate no Yukue* on the *Shonen Jump+* website. Shirai first worked with Posuka Demizu on the two-shot *Poppy no Negai*, which was released in February 2016.

THE PROMISED NEVERLAND

VOLUME 7
SHONEN JUMP Manga Edition

STORY BY KAIU SHIRAI
ART BY POSUKA DEMIZU

Translation/Satsuki Yamashita
Touch-Up Art & Lettering/Mark McMurray
Design/Julian [JR] Robinson
Editor/Alexis Kirsch

Printed in the U.S.A.

Published by VIZ Media, LLC
P.O. Box 77010
San Francisco, CA 94107

10 9 8 7 6 5 4 3 2
First printing, December 2018
Second printing, April 2019

PARENTAL ADVISORY
THE PROMISED NEVERLAND is rated T+
and is recommended for ages 16 and up.
This volume contains fantasy violence and
adult themes.

viz.com

shonenjump.com

THE PROMISED NEVERLAND

7

Decision

STORY	KAIU SHIRAI
ART	POSUKA DEMIZU

SHONENJUMP MANGA

The Children of Grace Field House

They aim to free all of the children who are trapped in Grace Field House within two years.

CHARACTERS

EMMA

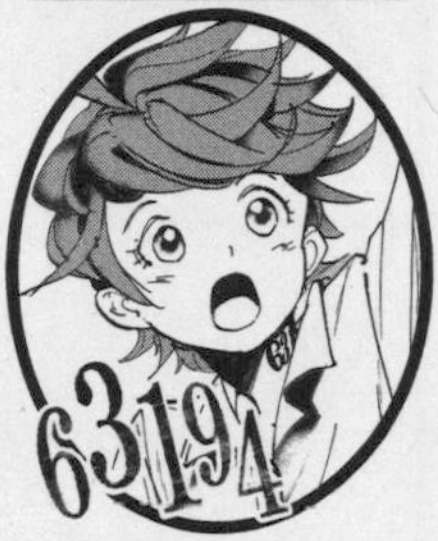
63194

An enthusiastic and optimistic girl with superb athletic and learning abilities.

RAY

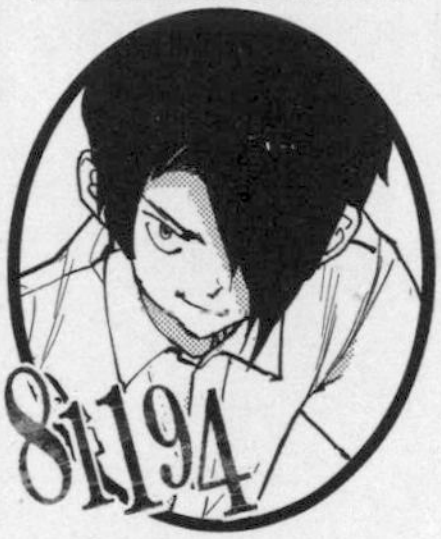
81194

The only one among the Grace Field House children who could match wits with Norman.

NORMAN

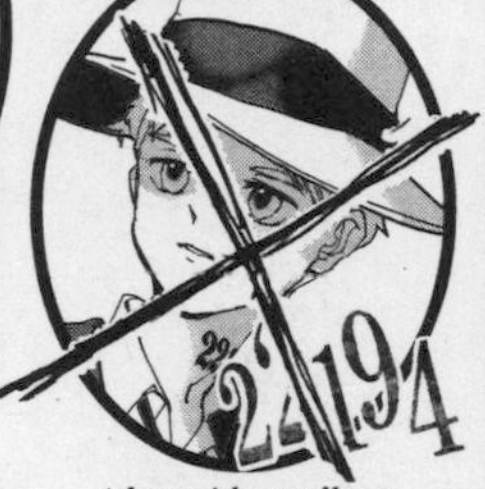
22194

A boy with excellent analytical and decision-making capabilities. He was the smartest child at Grace Field House.

PHIL

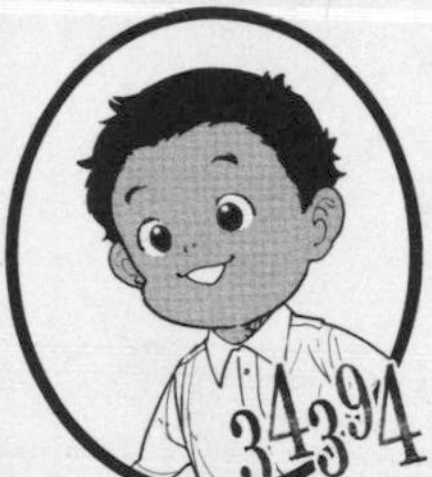
34394

A bighearted boy who loves Emma. He is always full of energy.

GILDA

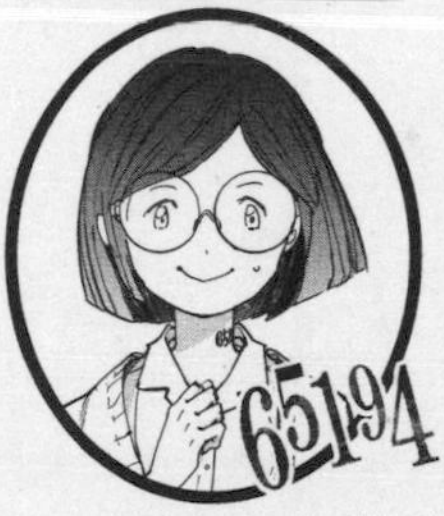
65194

A clever girl who has great insight and acts accordingly.

DON

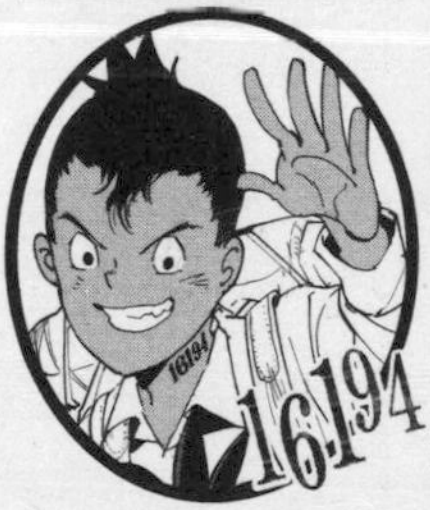
16194

A carefree boy who is cheerful but competitive.

LANNION

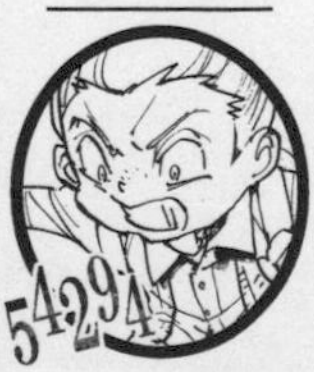
54294

A boy who is always with his best buddy, Thoma.

THOMA

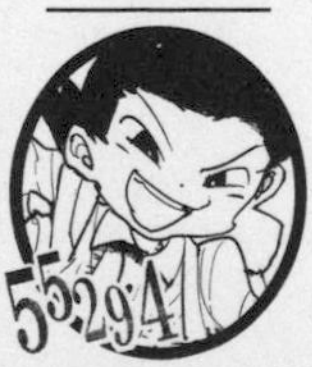
55294

A boy who is always with his best buddy, Lannion.

NAT

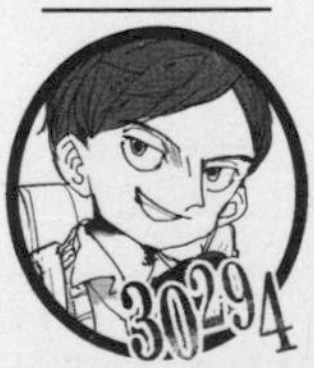
30294

A slightly narcissistic boy who is a bit of a scaredy-cat.

ANNA

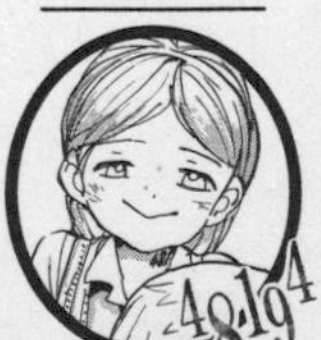
48194

A quiet but strong-willed girl who is kind to everyone.

???

WILLIAM MINERVA

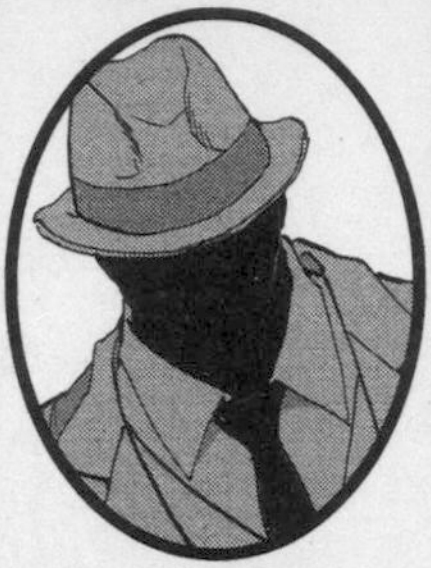

A mysterious figure who leaves various items that seem to help the children.

MUJIKA

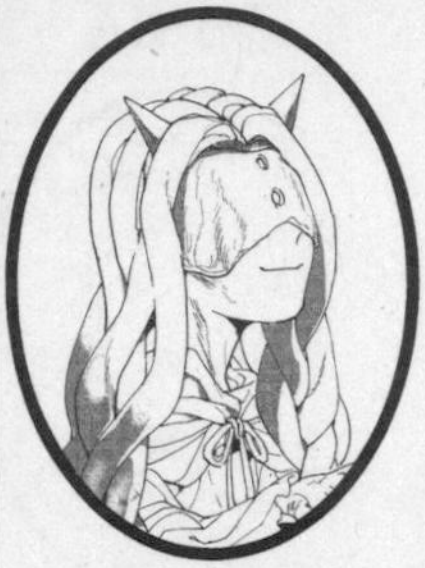

A petite demon who travels with Sonju.

SONJU

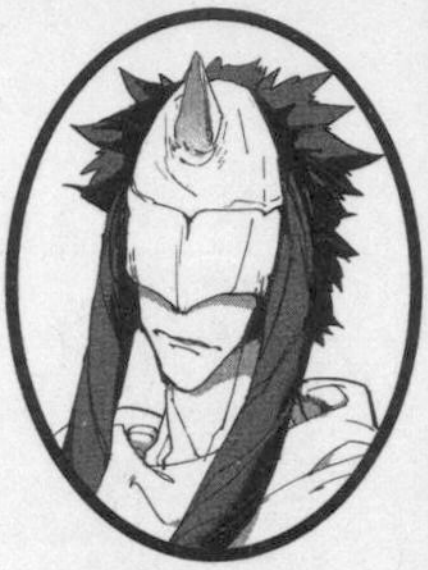

For religious reasons he does not eat humans bred in farms.

The Adult of Grace Field House

ISABELLA

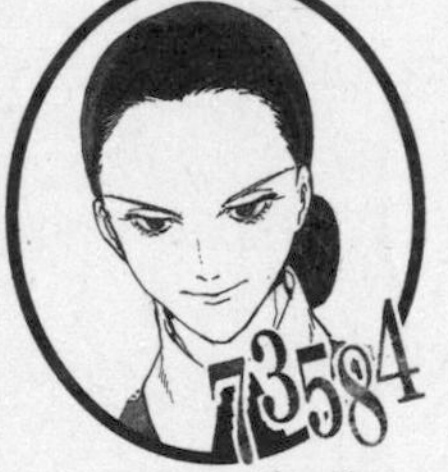
73584

A competent handler who raised Emma and the other children.

Demons of Grace Field House

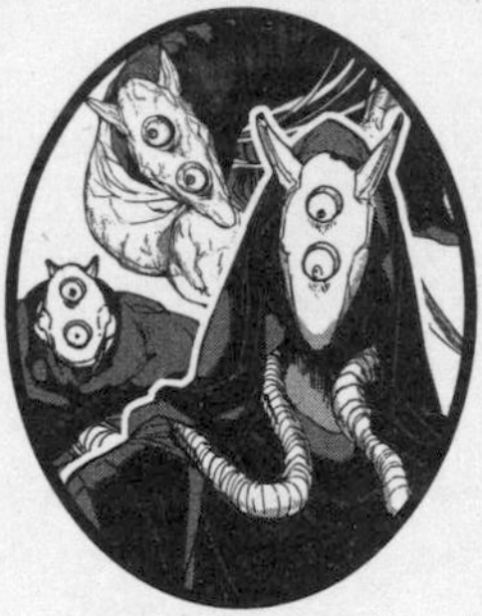

They raise human children to eat their developed brains.

The Story So Far

Emma is living happily at Grace Field House with her foster siblings. One day, she realizes that they are being bred as food for demons and decides to escape with everyone. Their first mission is to reach point B06-32, a place indicated in a pen left by a supposed collaborator named William Minerva. Leaving the younger children under the age of four behind, Emma and the other kids succeed in escaping. Outside, they meet demons Sonju and Mujika and learn that the humans and demons agreed to a promise about 1,000 years ago to split their world into two. Despite a seemingly desperate situation, the children find hope and learn the skills to survive. They finally reach B06-32, where a man is waiting for them...

THE PROMISED NEVERLAND 7

Decision

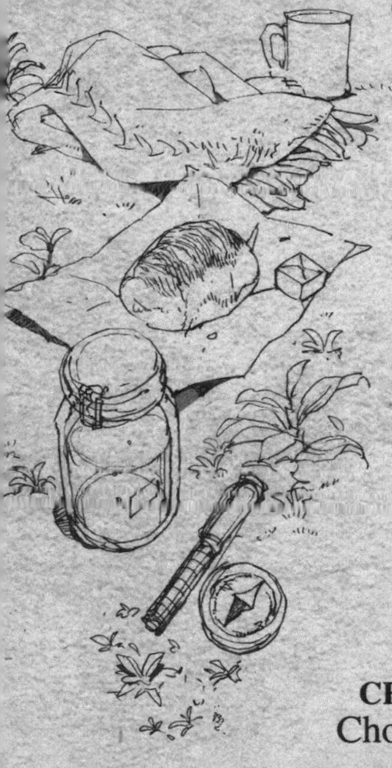

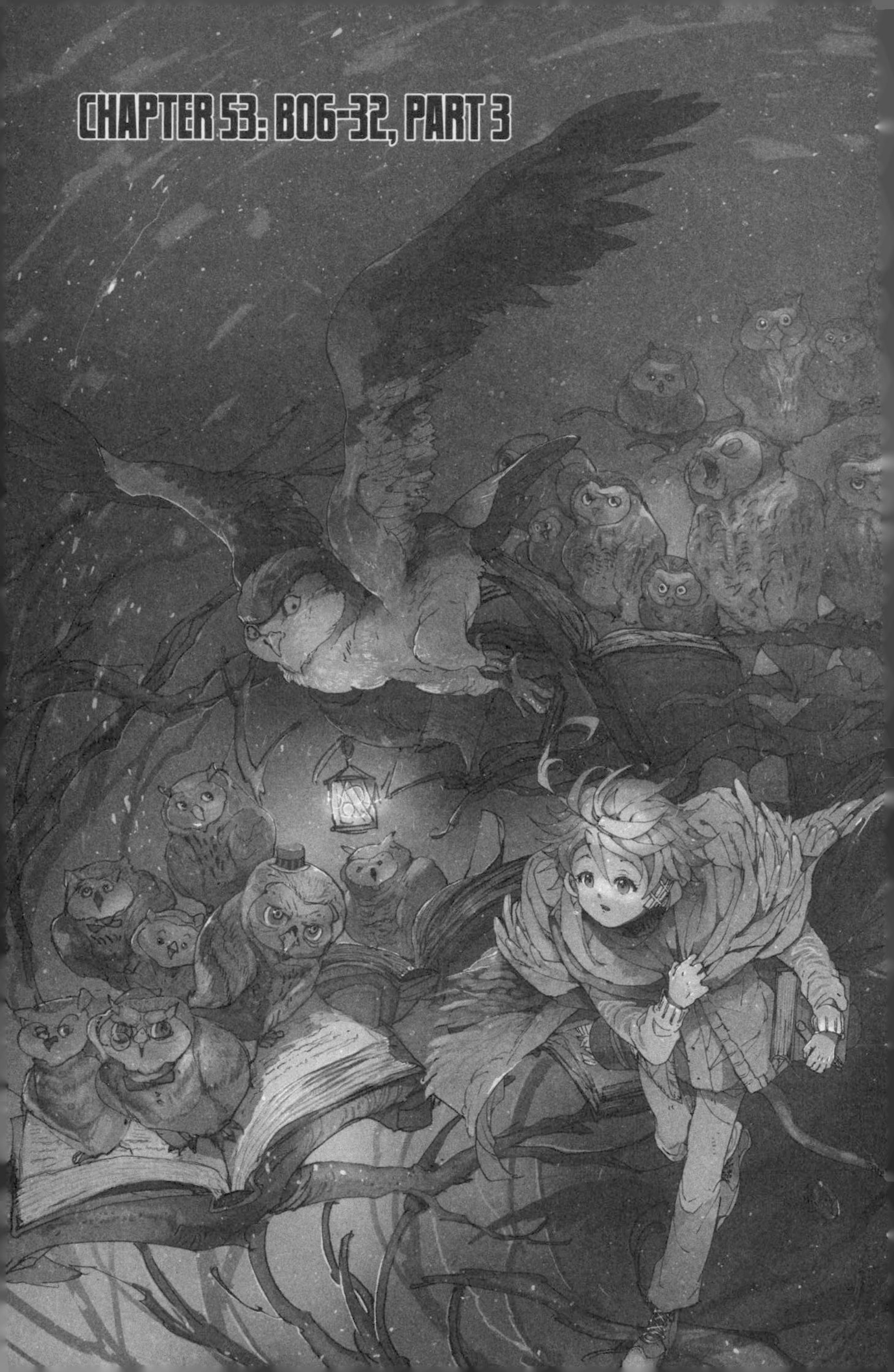
CHAPTER 53: B06-32, PART 3

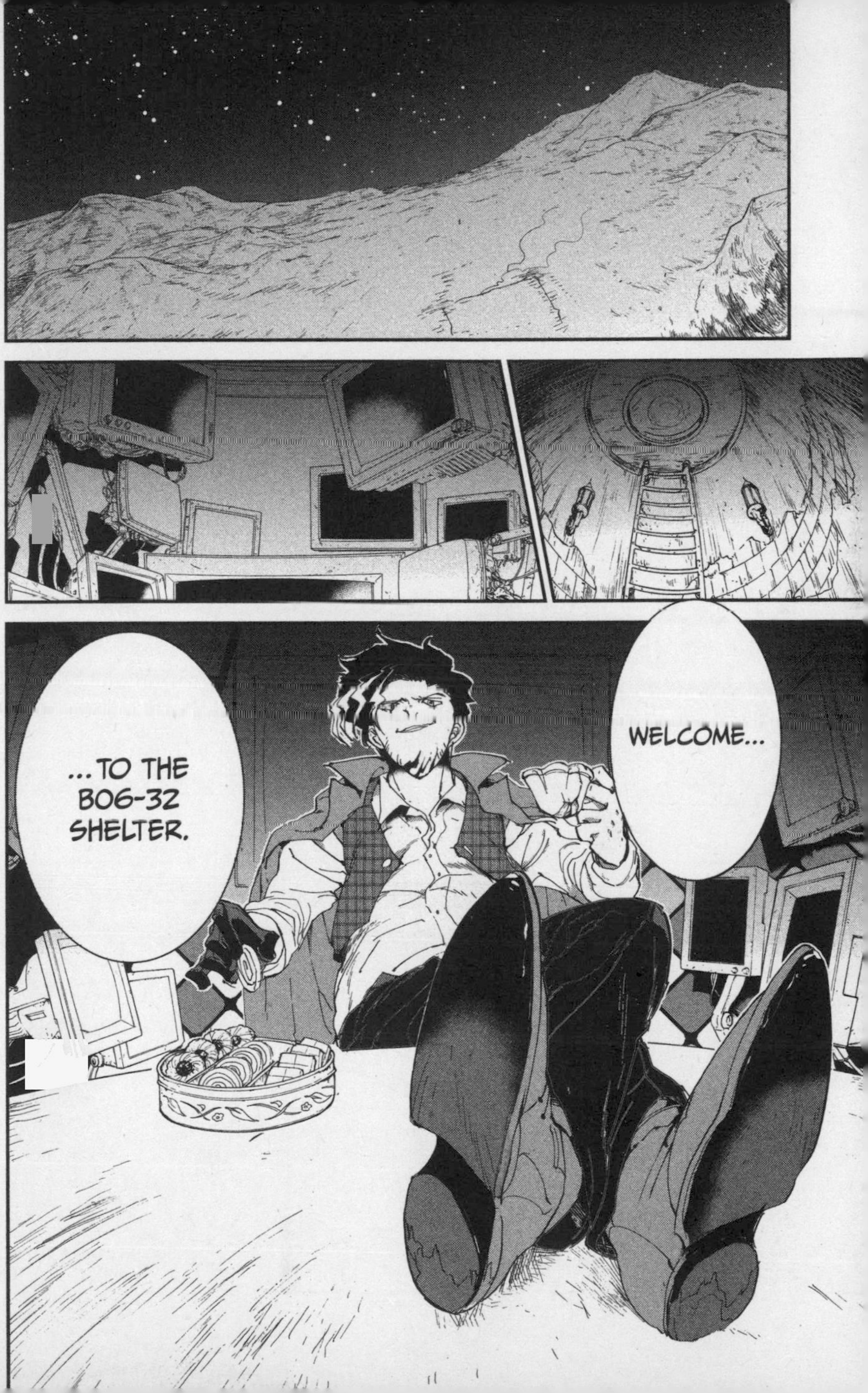
WELCOME...
...TO THE B06-32 SHELTER.

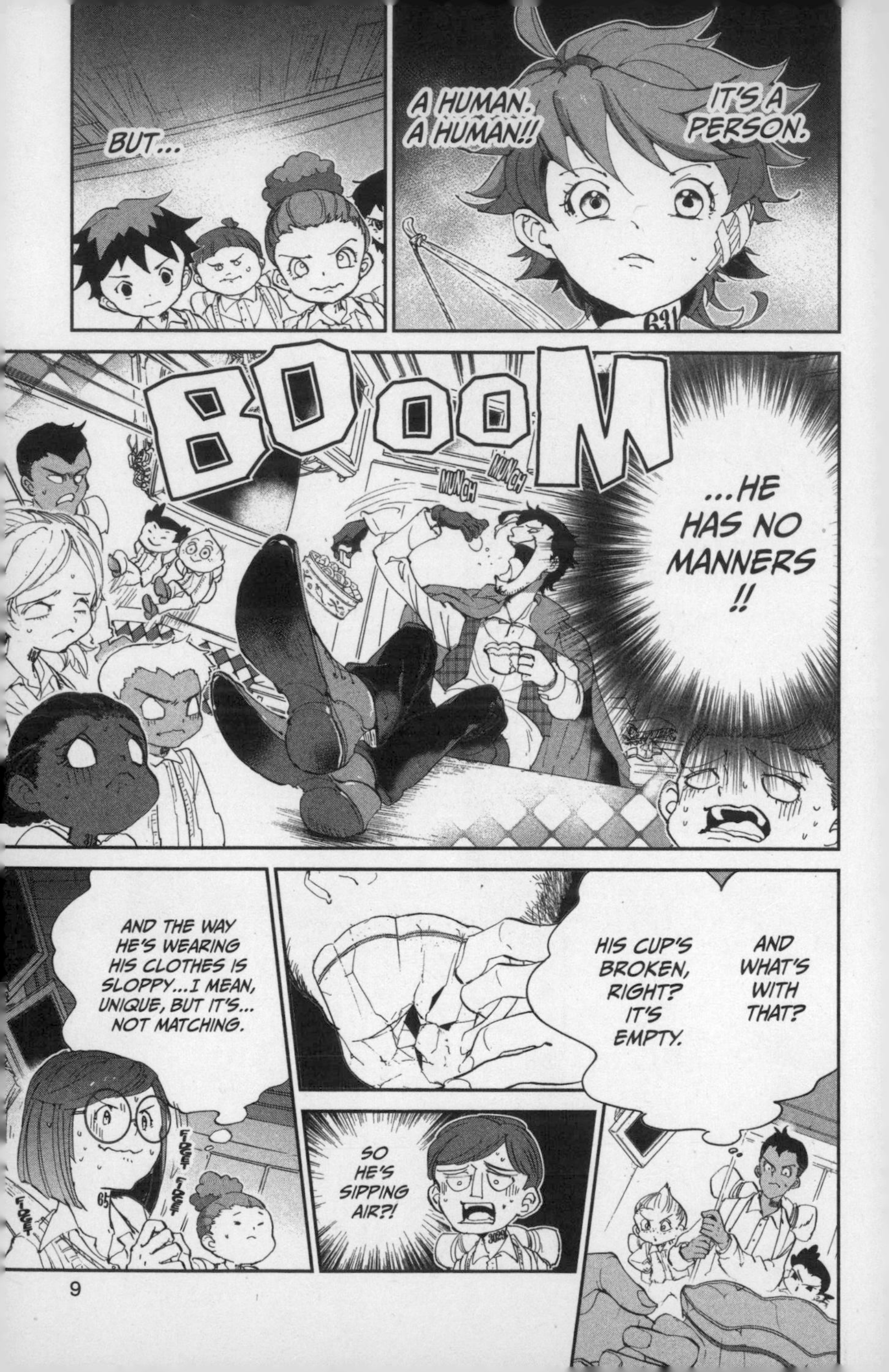
IT'S A PERSON.
A HUMAN. A HUMAN!!
BUT...
BOOOM
MUNCH
MUNCH
...HE HAS NO MANNERS!!
AND WHAT'S WITH THAT?
HIS CUP'S BROKEN, RIGHT? IT'S EMPTY.
SO HE'S SIPPING AIR?!
AND THE WAY HE'S WEARING HIS CLOTHES IS SLOPPY...I MEAN, UNIQUE, BUT IT'S... NOT MATCHING.
FIDGET
FIDGET
FIDGET

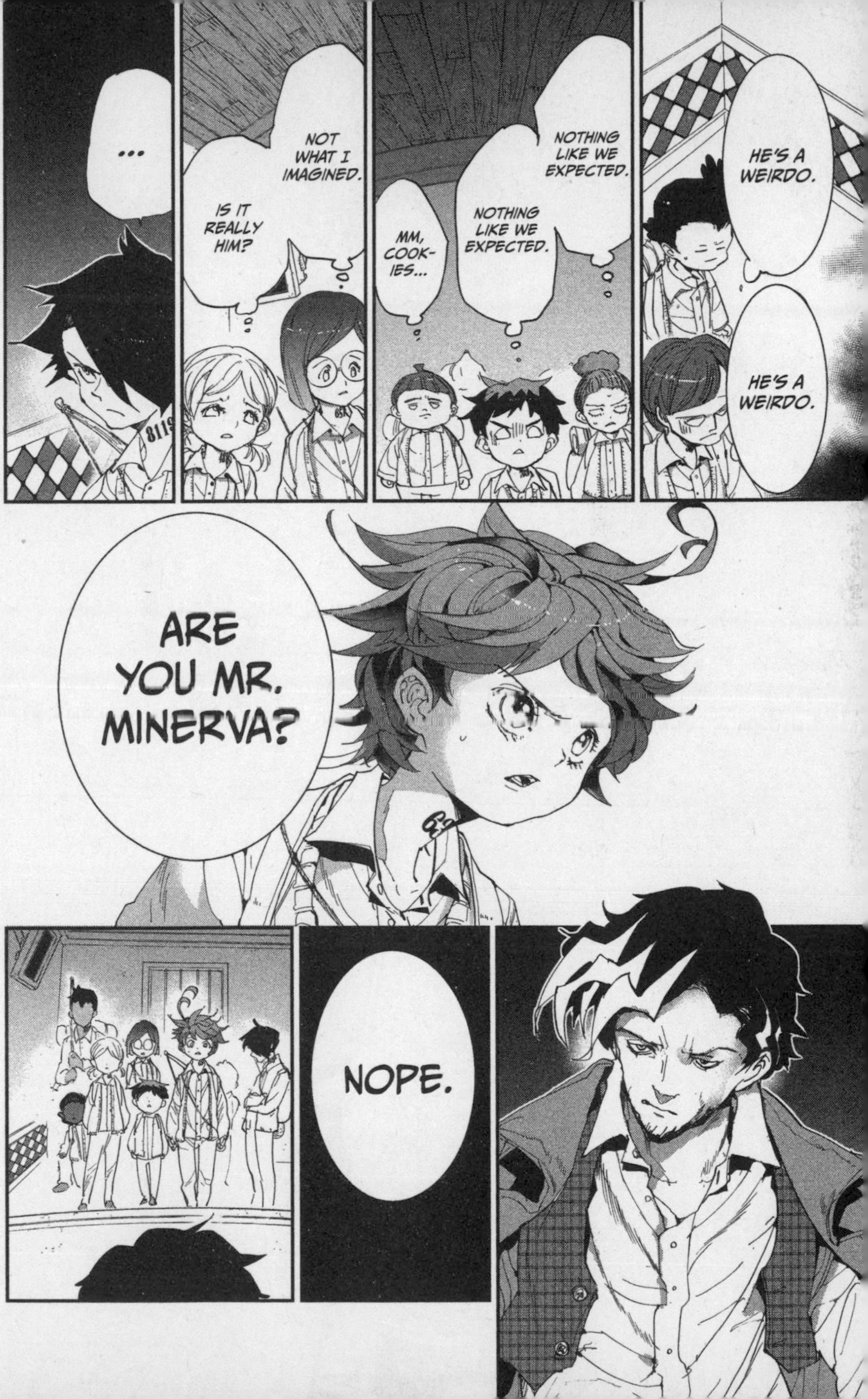
HE'S A WEIRDO.
HE'S A WEIRDO.
NOTHING LIKE WE EXPECTED.
NOTHING LIKE WE EXPECTED.
MM, COOKIES...
NOT WHAT I IMAGINED.
IS IT REALLY HIM?
...
ARE YOU MR. MINERVA?
NOPE.

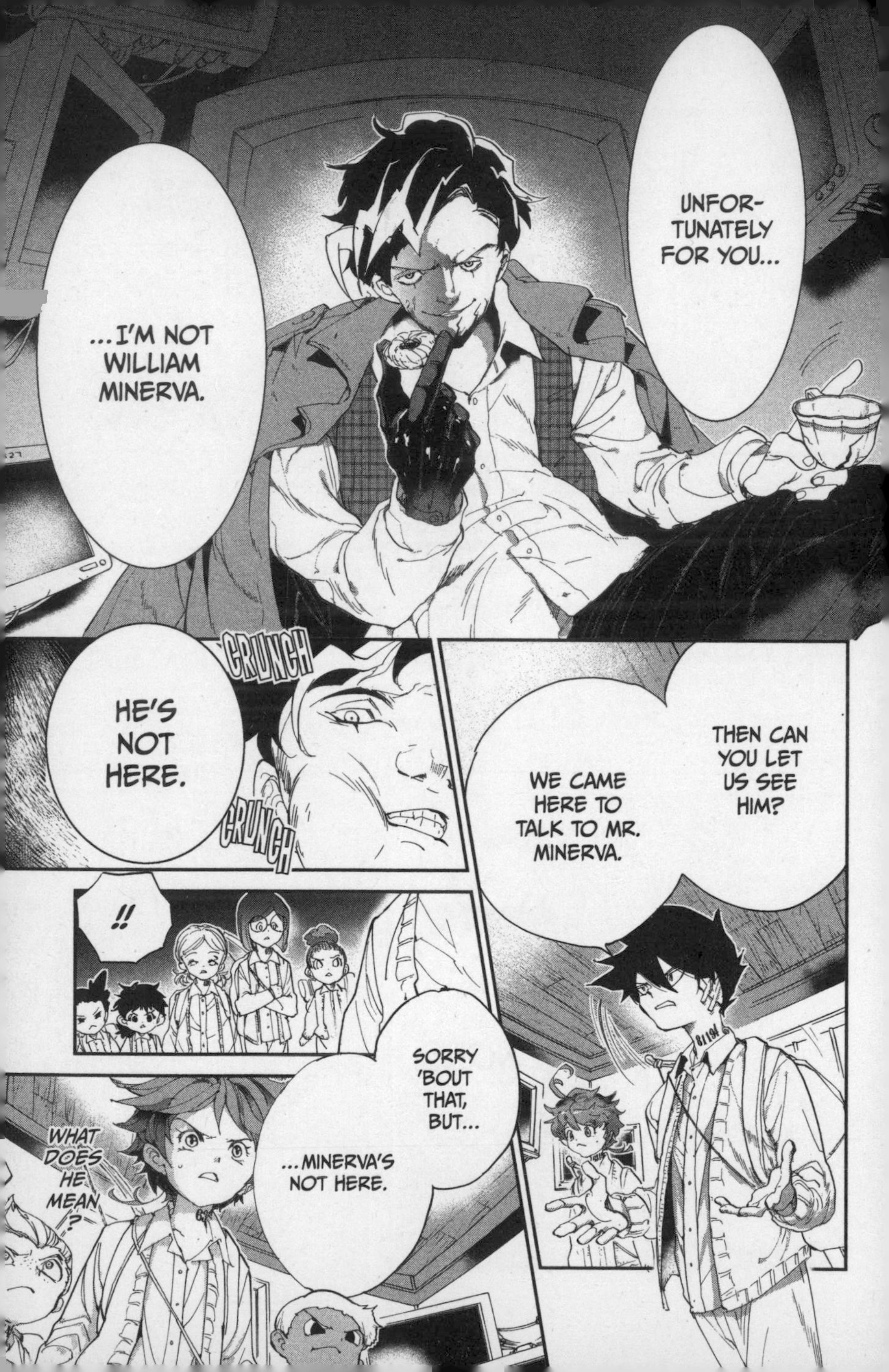
UNFOR-TUNATELY FOR YOU...
...I'M NOT WILLIAM MINERVA.
THEN CAN YOU LET US SEE HIM?
WE CAME HERE TO TALK TO MR. MINERVA.
CRUNCH
CRUNCH
HE'S NOT HERE.
!!
SORRY 'BOUT THAT, BUT...
...MINERVA'S NOT HERE.
WHAT DOES HE MEAN?

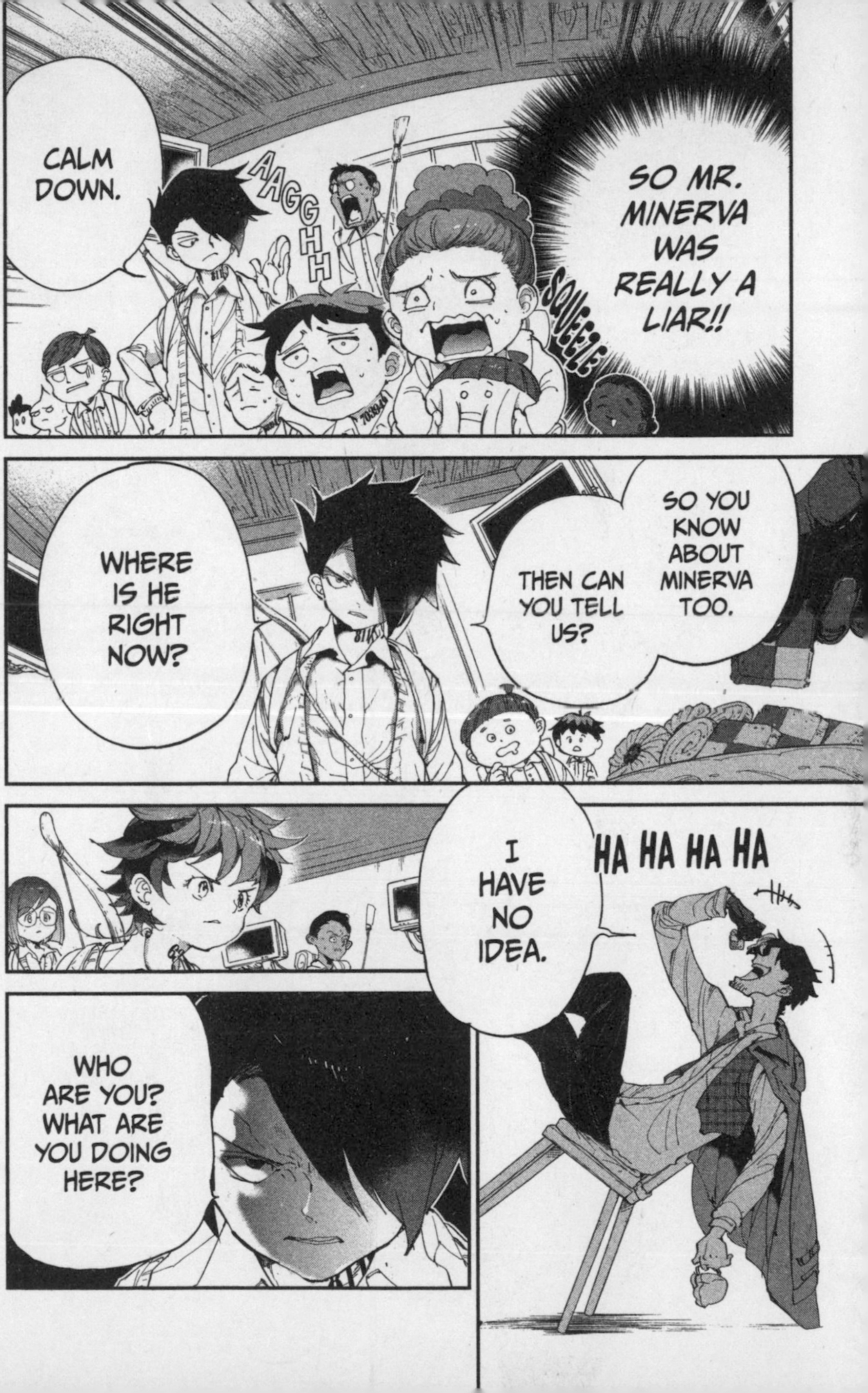
SO MR. MINERVA WAS REALLY A LIAR!!
SQUEEZE
AAGGHH
CALM DOWN.
SO YOU KNOW ABOUT MINERVA TOO.
THEN CAN YOU TELL US?
WHERE IS HE RIGHT NOW?
HA HA HA HA
I HAVE NO IDEA.
WHO ARE YOU? WHAT ARE YOU DOING HERE?

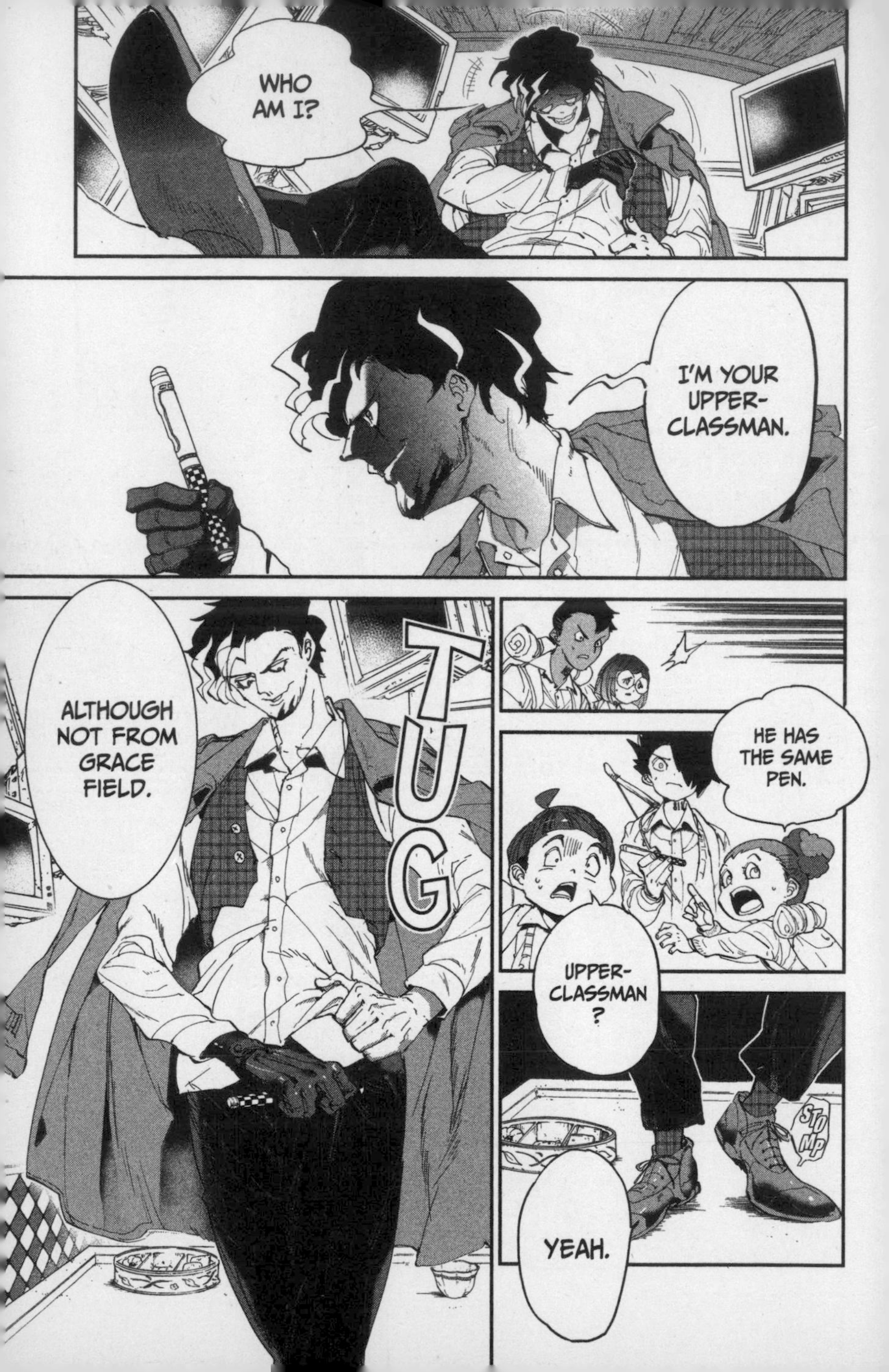
WHO AM I?
I'M YOUR UPPER-CLASSMAN.
HE HAS THE SAME PEN.
UPPER-CLASSMAN?
STOMP
YEAH.
ALTHOUGH NOT FROM GRACE FIELD.
TUG

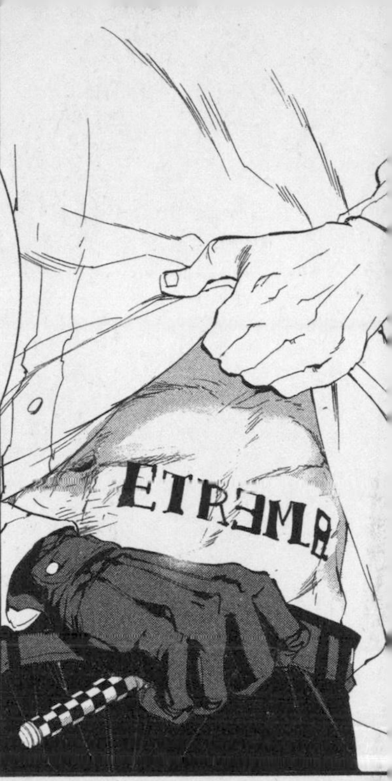

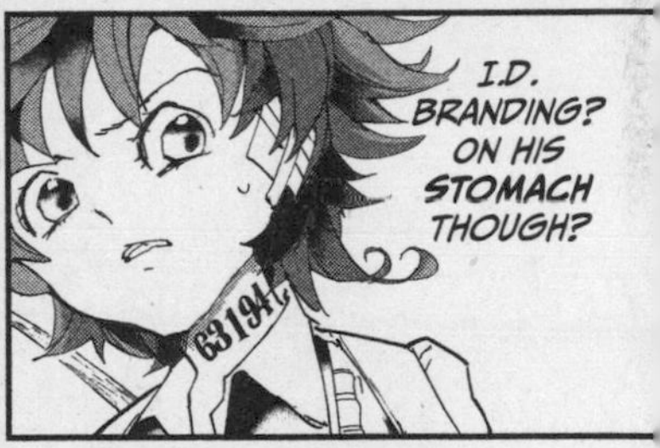
I.D. BRANDING? ON HIS STOMACH THOUGH?
63194

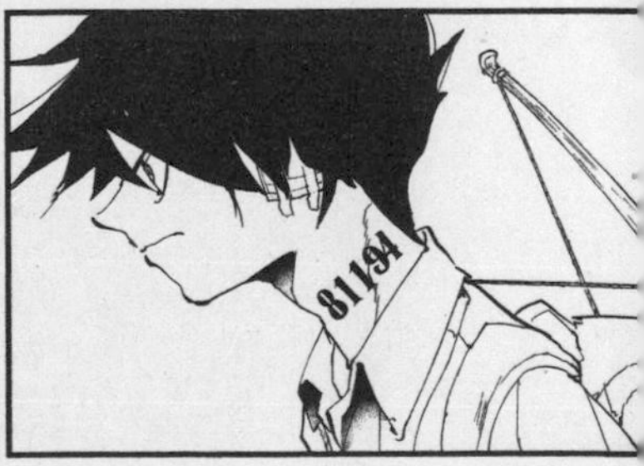
81194

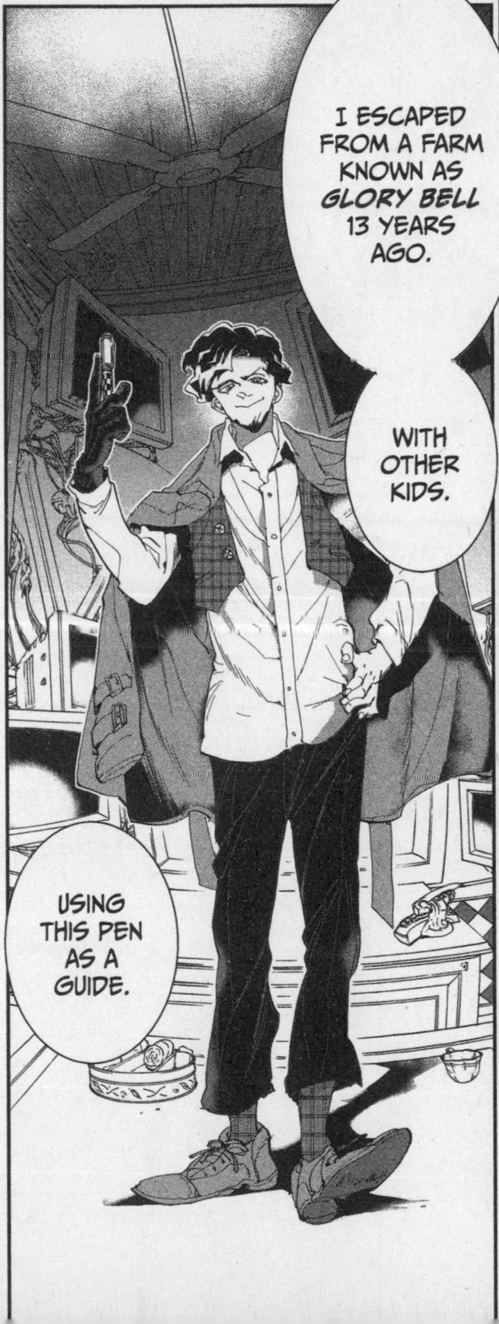
I ESCAPED FROM A FARM KNOWN AS GLORY BELL 13 YEARS AGO.
WITH OTHER KIDS.
USING THIS PEN AS A GUIDE.

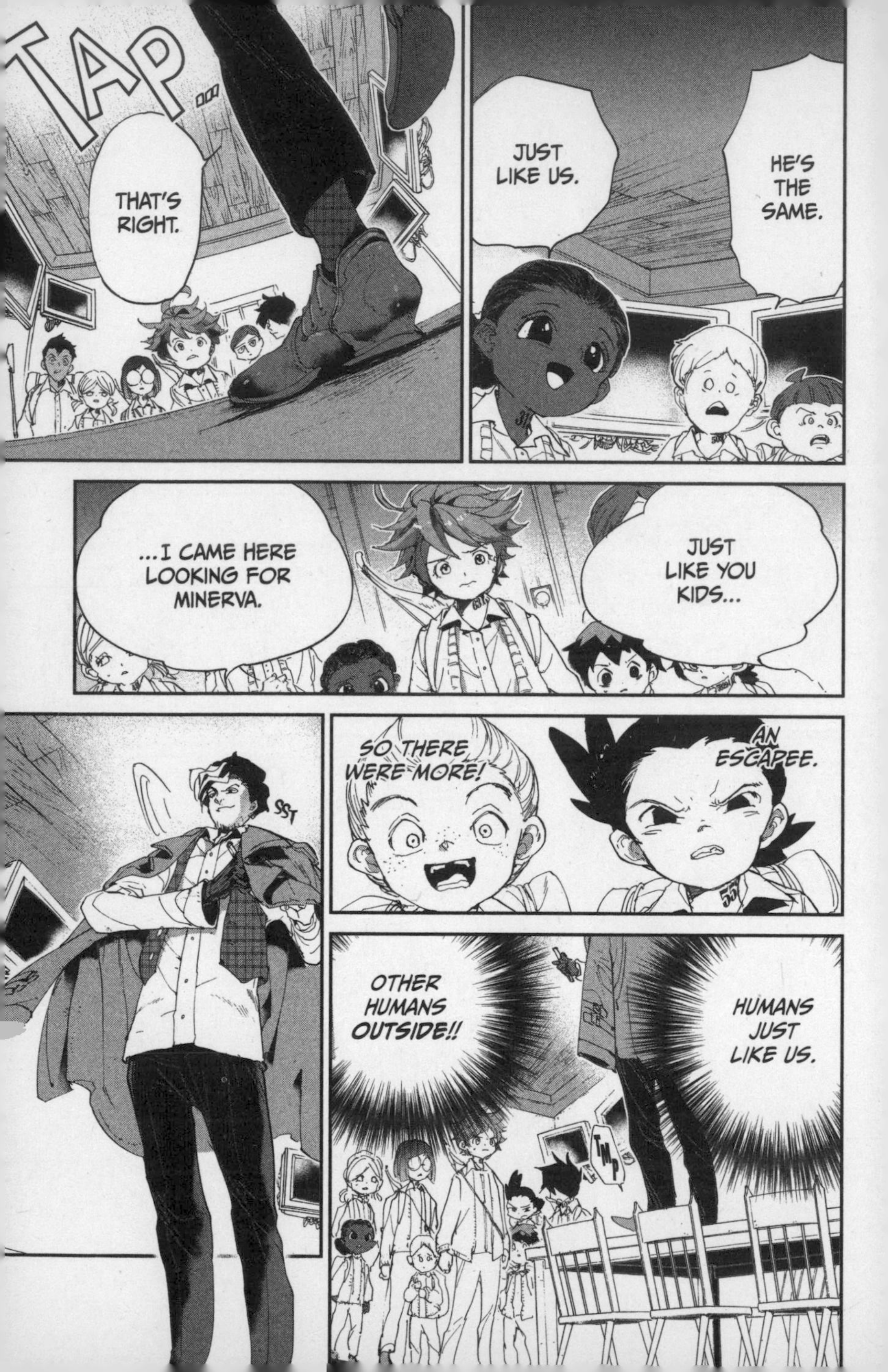
HE'S THE SAME.
JUST LIKE US.
TAP
THAT'S RIGHT.
JUST LIKE YOU KIDS...
...I CAME HERE LOOKING FOR MINERVA.
AN ESCAPEE.
SO THERE WERE MORE!
HUMANS JUST LIKE US.
OTHER HUMANS OUTSIDE!!
TMP
SST

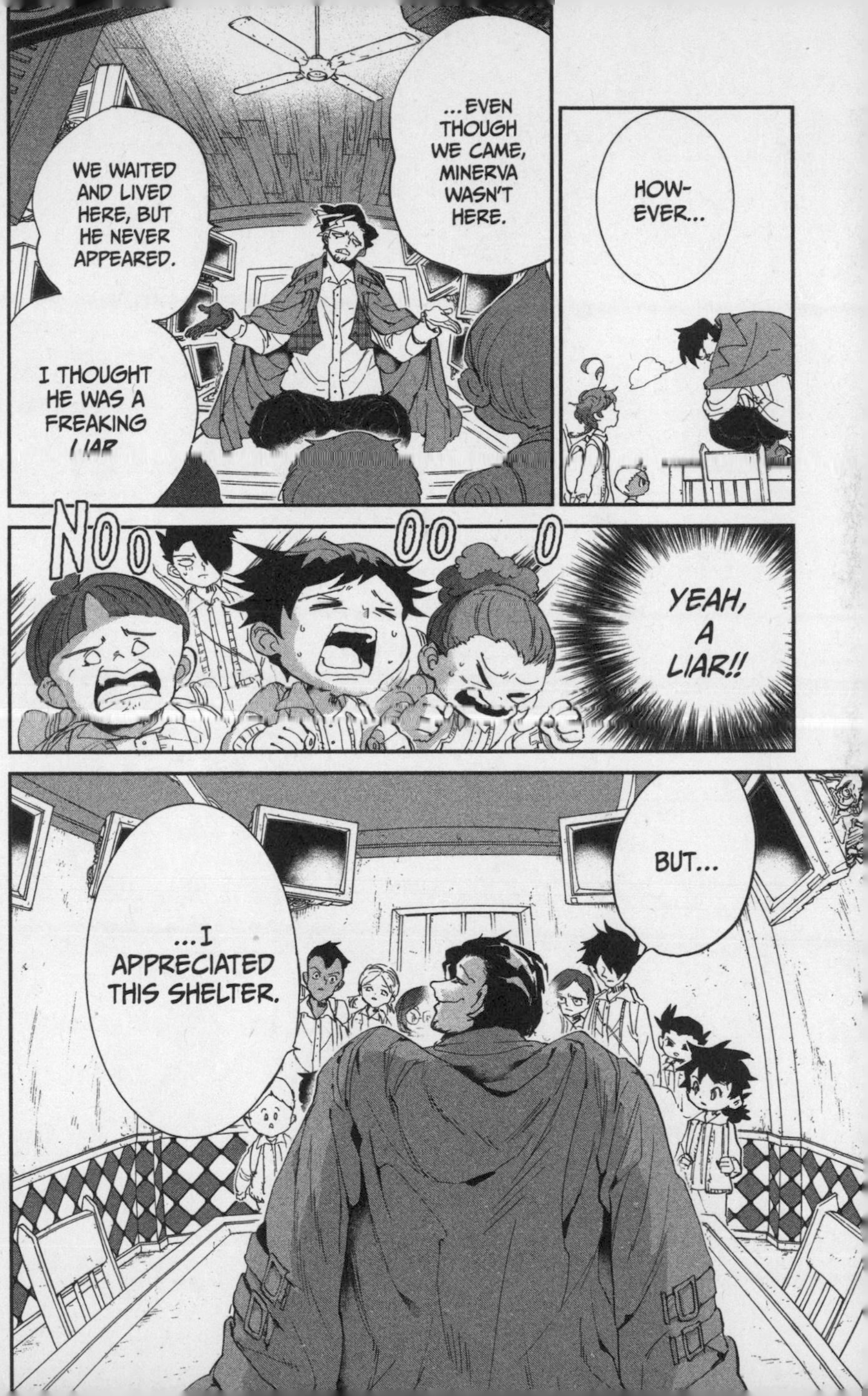
HOW-EVER...
...EVEN THOUGH WE CAME, MINERVA WASN'T HERE.
WE WAITED AND LIVED HERE, BUT HE NEVER APPEARED.
I THOUGHT HE WAS A FREAKING LIAR
YEAH, A LIAR!!
NOOOOO
BUT...
...I APPRECIATED THIS SHELTER.

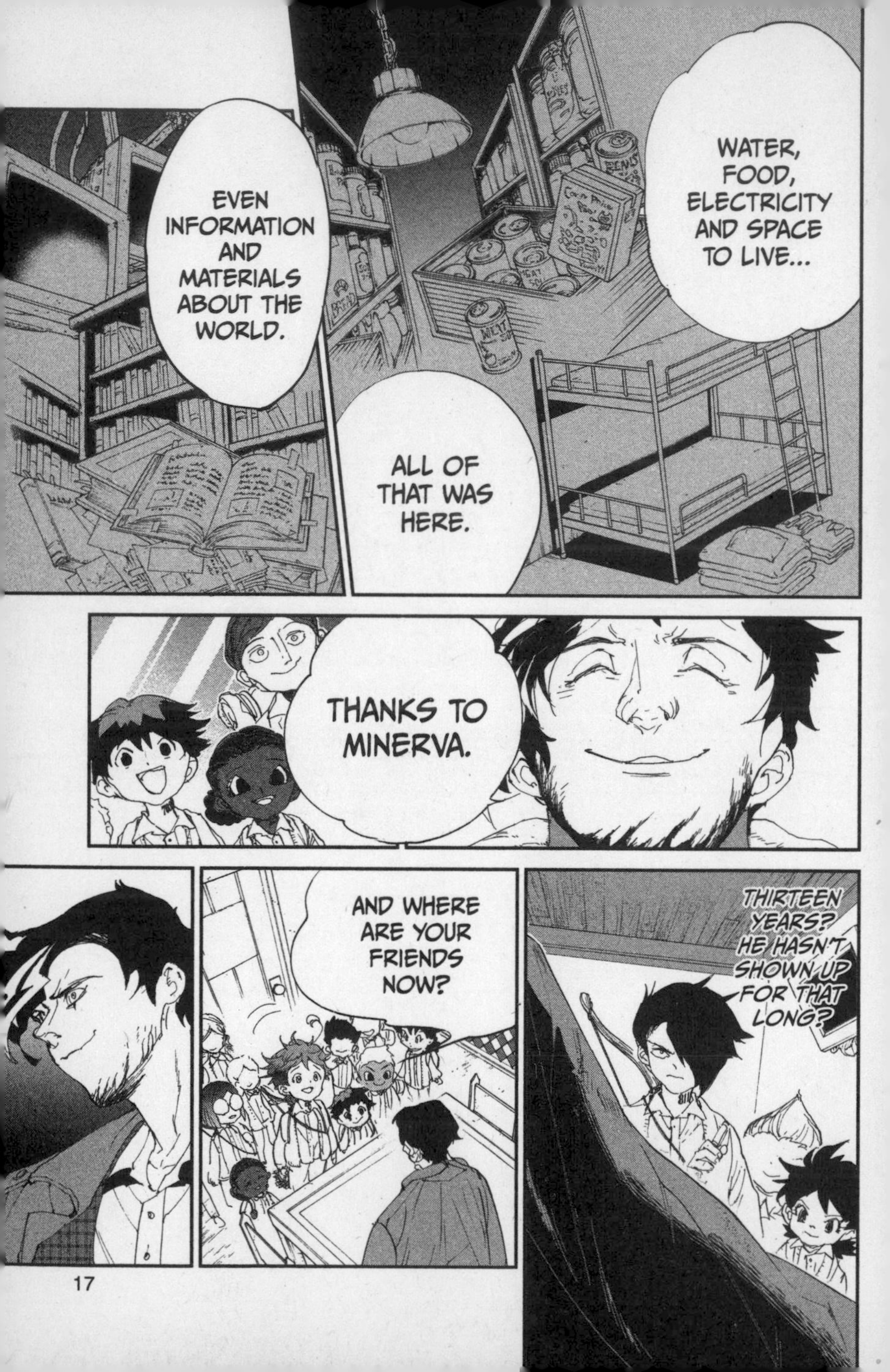
WATER, FOOD, ELECTRICITY AND SPACE TO LIVE...
EVEN INFORMATION AND MATERIALS ABOUT THE WORLD.
ALL OF THAT WAS HERE.
THANKS TO MINERVA.
THIRTEEN YEARS? HE HASN'T SHOWN UP FOR THAT LONG?
AND WHERE ARE YOUR FRIENDS NOW?

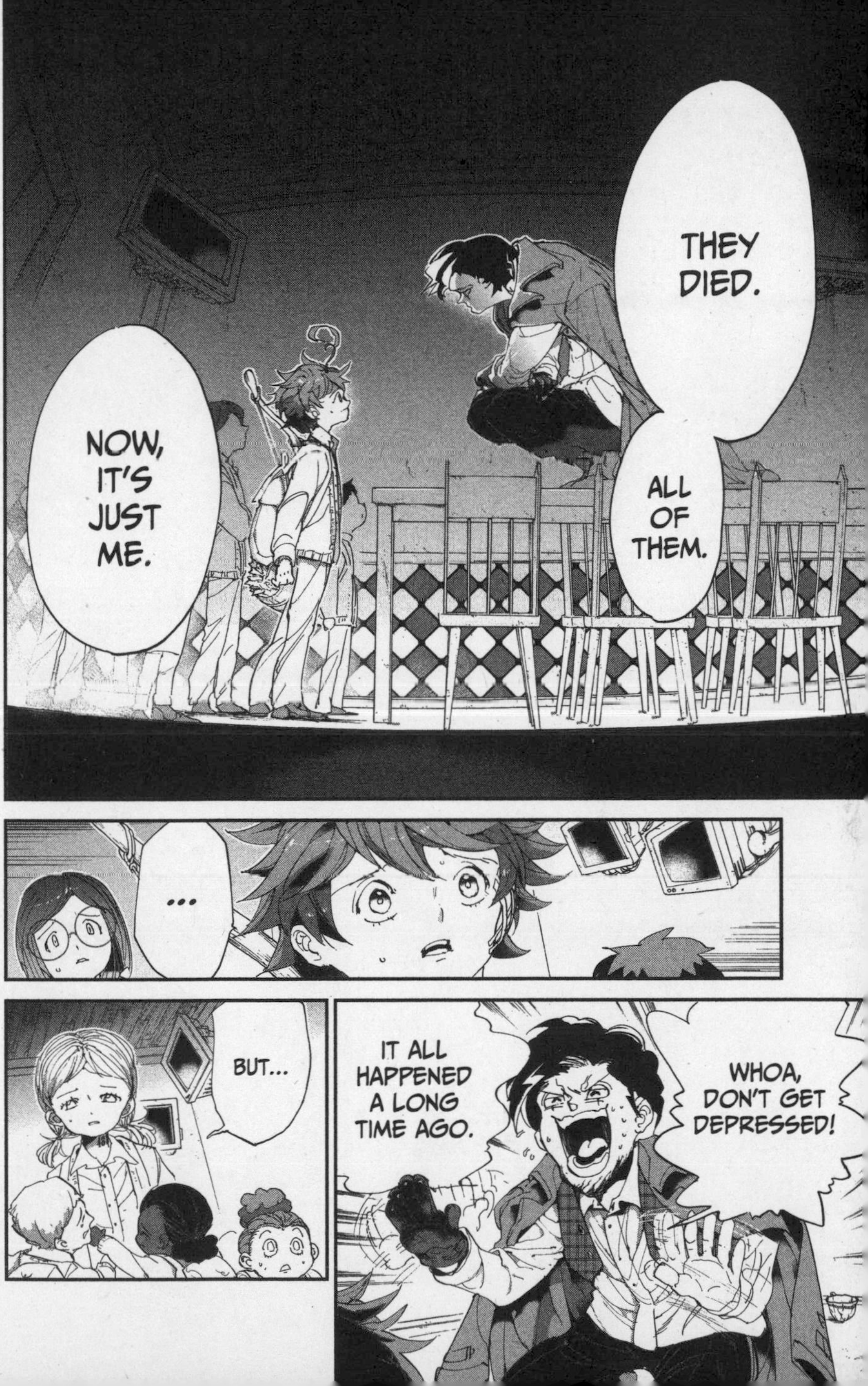
THEY DIED.
ALL OF THEM.
NOW, IT'S JUST ME.
...
WHOA, DON'T GET DEPRESSED!
IT ALL HAPPENED A LONG TIME AGO.
BUT...

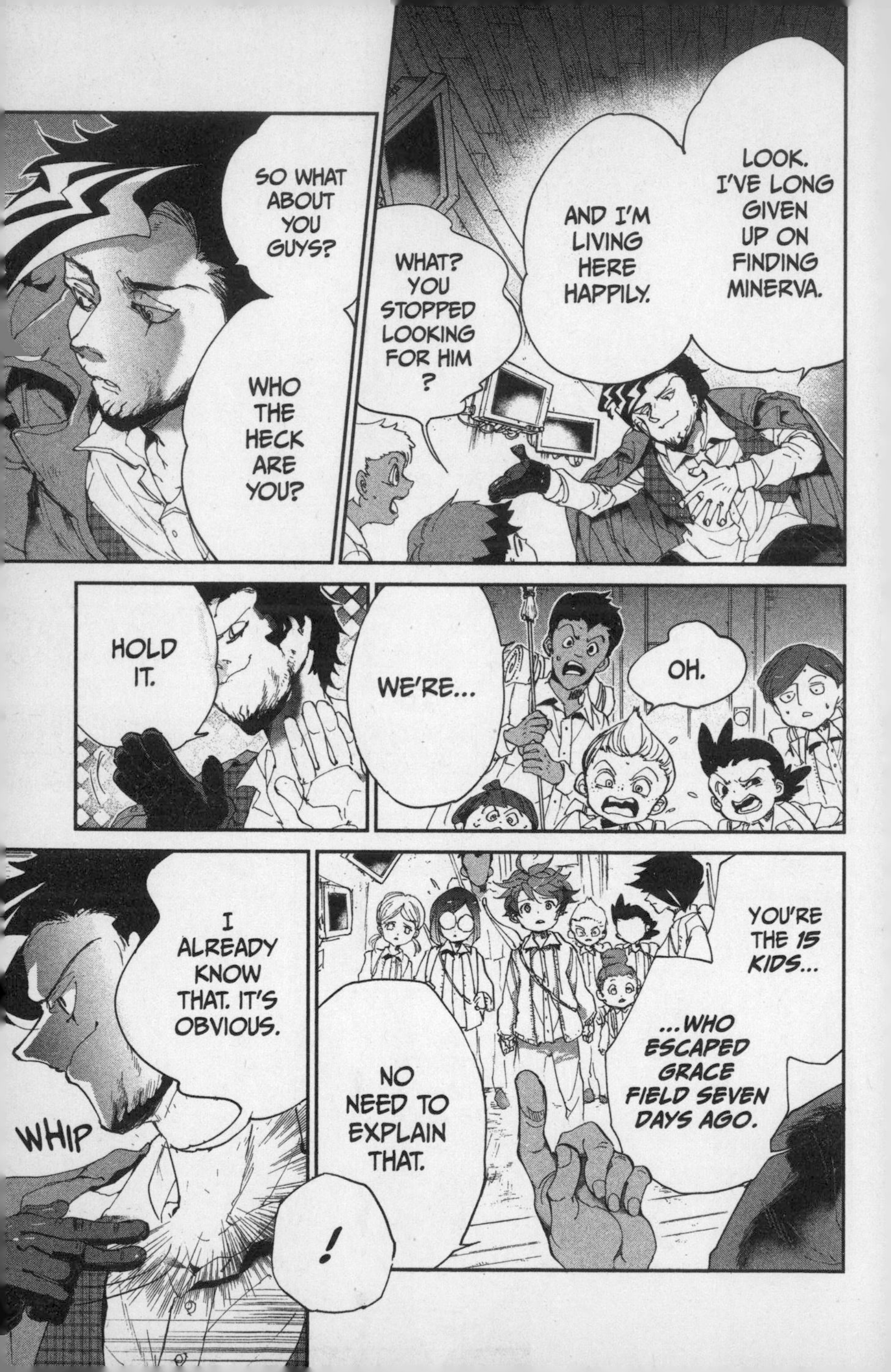
LOOK. I'VE LONG GIVEN UP ON FINDING MINERVA.
AND I'M LIVING HERE HAPPILY.
WHAT? YOU STOPPED LOOKING FOR HIM ?
SO WHAT ABOUT YOU GUYS?
WHO THE HECK ARE YOU?
OH.
WE'RE...
HOLD IT.
YOU'RE THE 15 KIDS...
...WHO ESCAPED GRACE FIELD SEVEN DAYS AGO.
NO NEED TO EXPLAIN THAT.
!
I ALREADY KNOW THAT. IT'S OBVIOUS.
WHIP

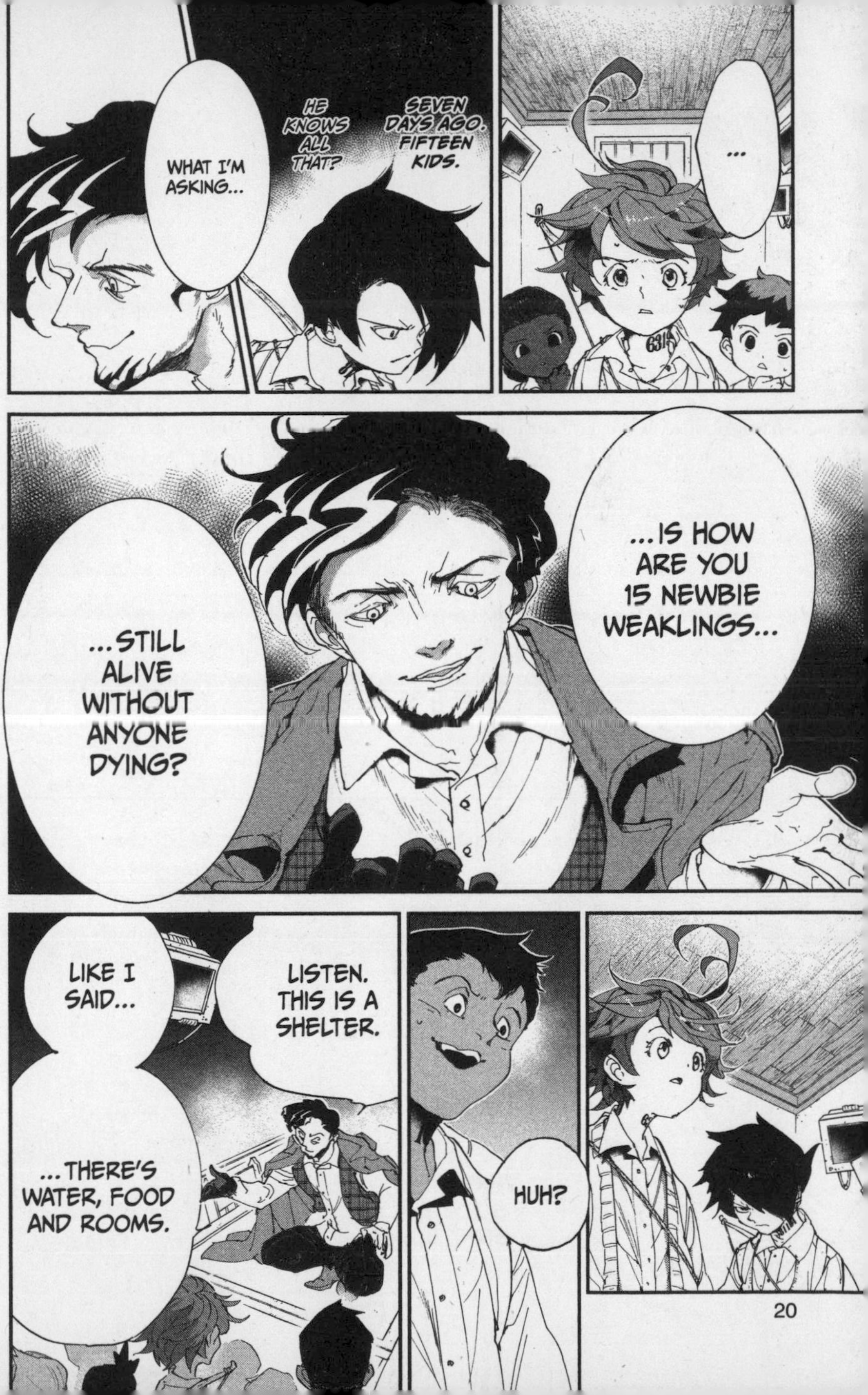
...
SEVEN DAYS AGO. FIFTEEN KIDS.
HE KNOWS ALL THAT?
WHAT I'M ASKING...
...IS HOW ARE YOU 15 NEWBIE WEAKLINGS...
...STILL ALIVE WITHOUT ANYONE DYING?
HUH?
LISTEN. THIS IS A SHELTER.
LIKE I SAID...
...THERE'S WATER, FOOD AND ROOMS.

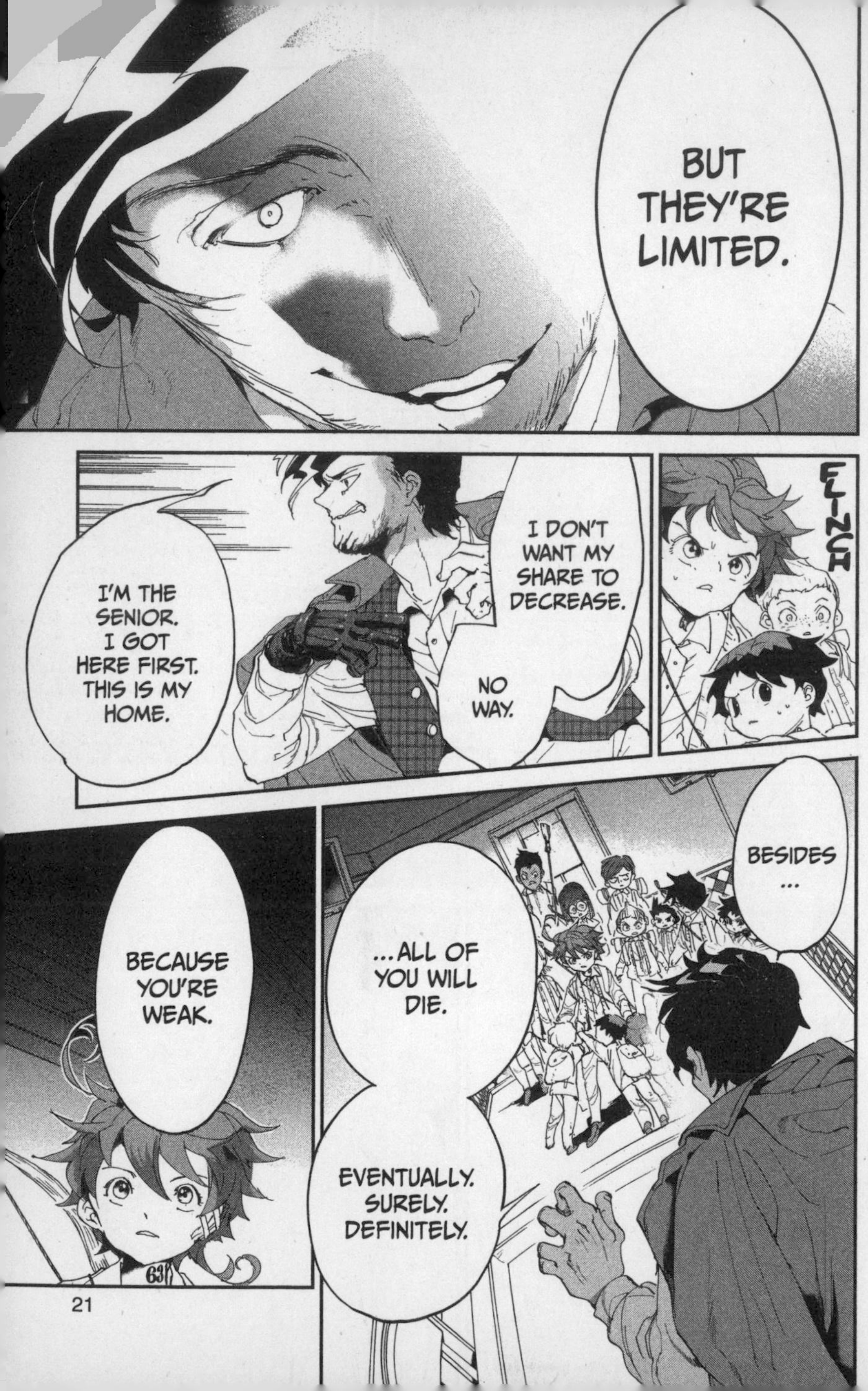
BUT THEY'RE LIMITED.
FLINCH
I DON'T WANT MY SHARE TO DECREASE.
NO WAY.
I'M THE SENIOR. I GOT HERE FIRST. THIS IS MY HOME.
BESIDES ...
...ALL OF YOU WILL DIE.
EVENTUALLY. SURELY. DEFINITELY.
BECAUSE YOU'RE WEAK.

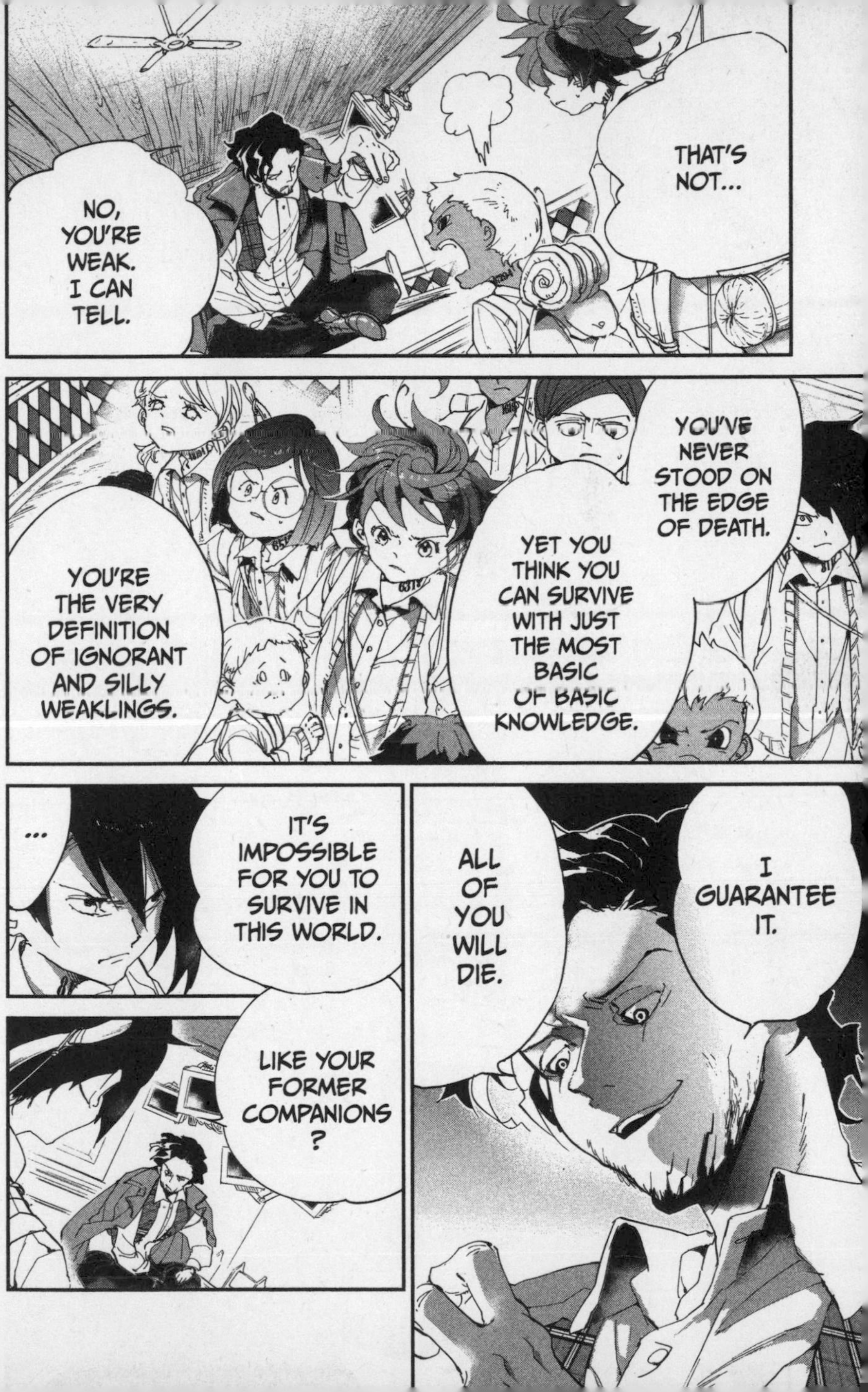
THAT'S NOT...
NO, YOU'RE WEAK. I CAN TELL.
YOU'VE NEVER STOOD ON THE EDGE OF DEATH.
YET YOU THINK YOU CAN SURVIVE WITH JUST THE MOST BASIC OF BASIC KNOWLEDGE.
YOU'RE THE VERY DEFINITION OF IGNORANT AND SILLY WEAKLINGS.
I GUARANTEE IT.
ALL OF YOU WILL DIE.
IT'S IMPOSSIBLE FOR YOU TO SURVIVE IN THIS WORLD.
...
LIKE YOUR FORMER COMPANIONS ?

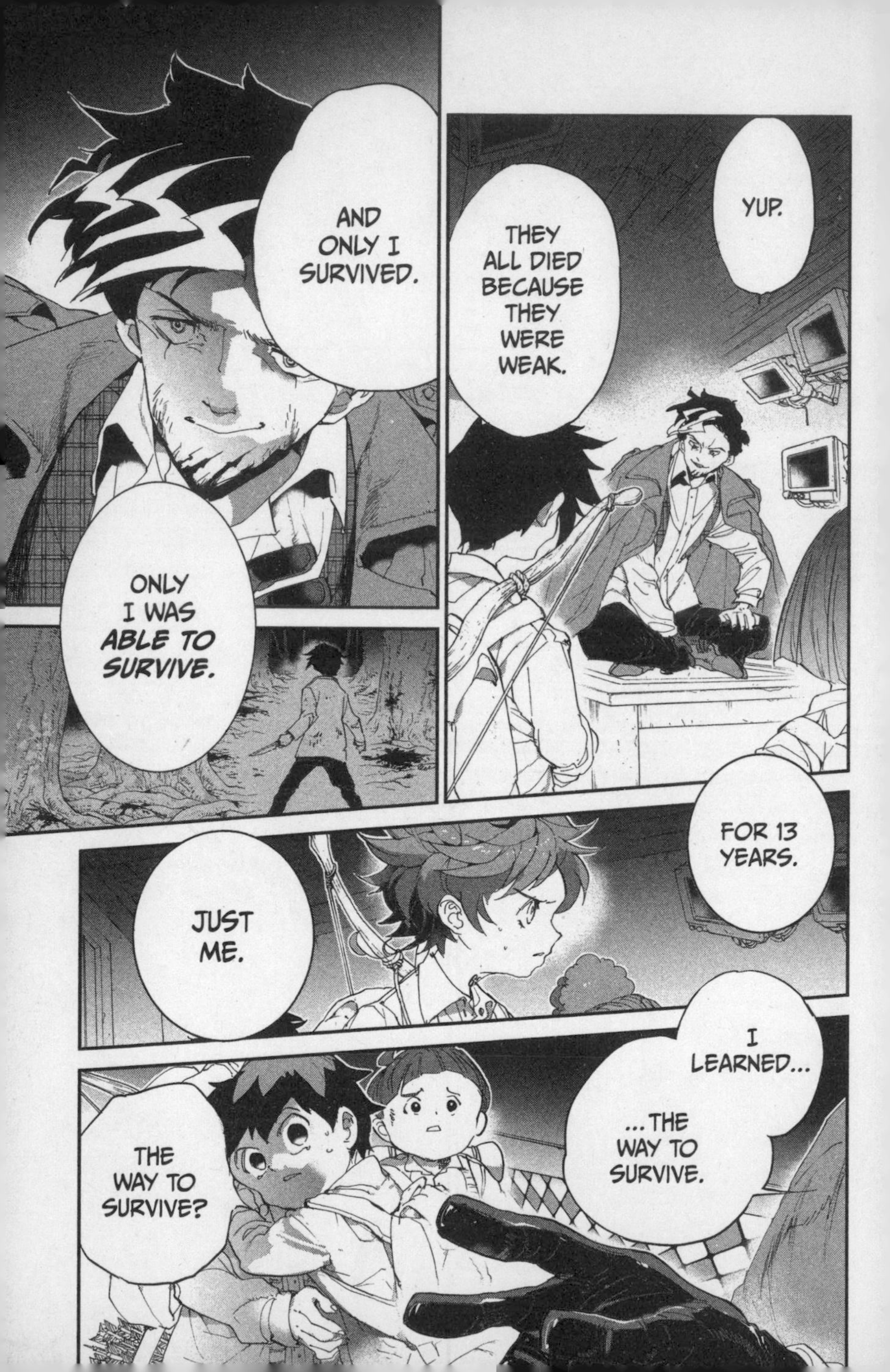
YUP.
THEY ALL DIED BECAUSE THEY WERE WEAK.
AND ONLY I SURVIVED.
ONLY I WAS ABLE TO SURVIVE.
FOR 13 YEARS.
JUST ME.
I LEARNED...
...THE WAY TO SURVIVE.
THE WAY TO SURVIVE?

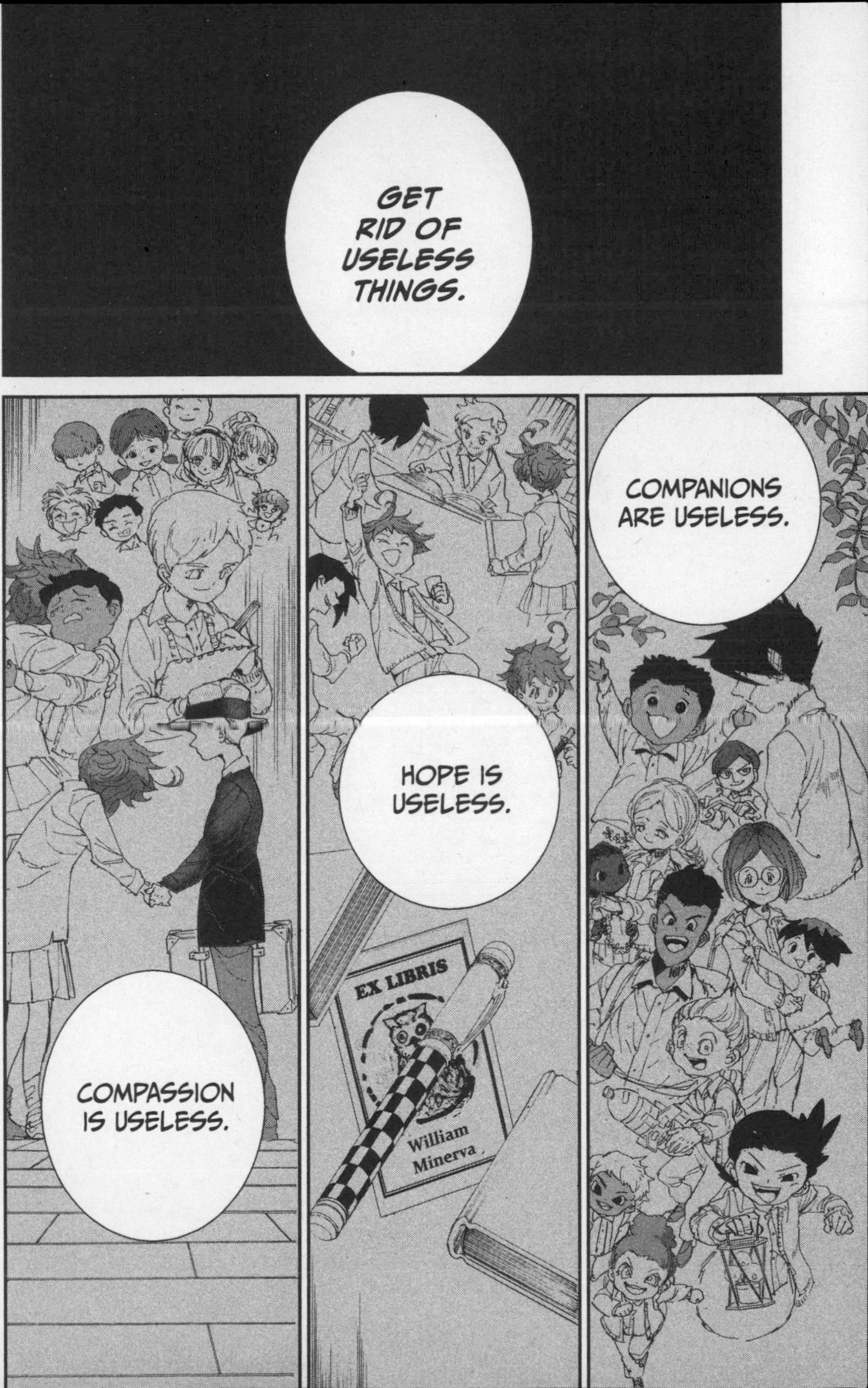
GET RID OF USELESS THINGS.
COMPANIONS ARE USELESS.
HOPE IS USELESS.
EX LIBRIS
William Minerva
COMPASSION IS USELESS.

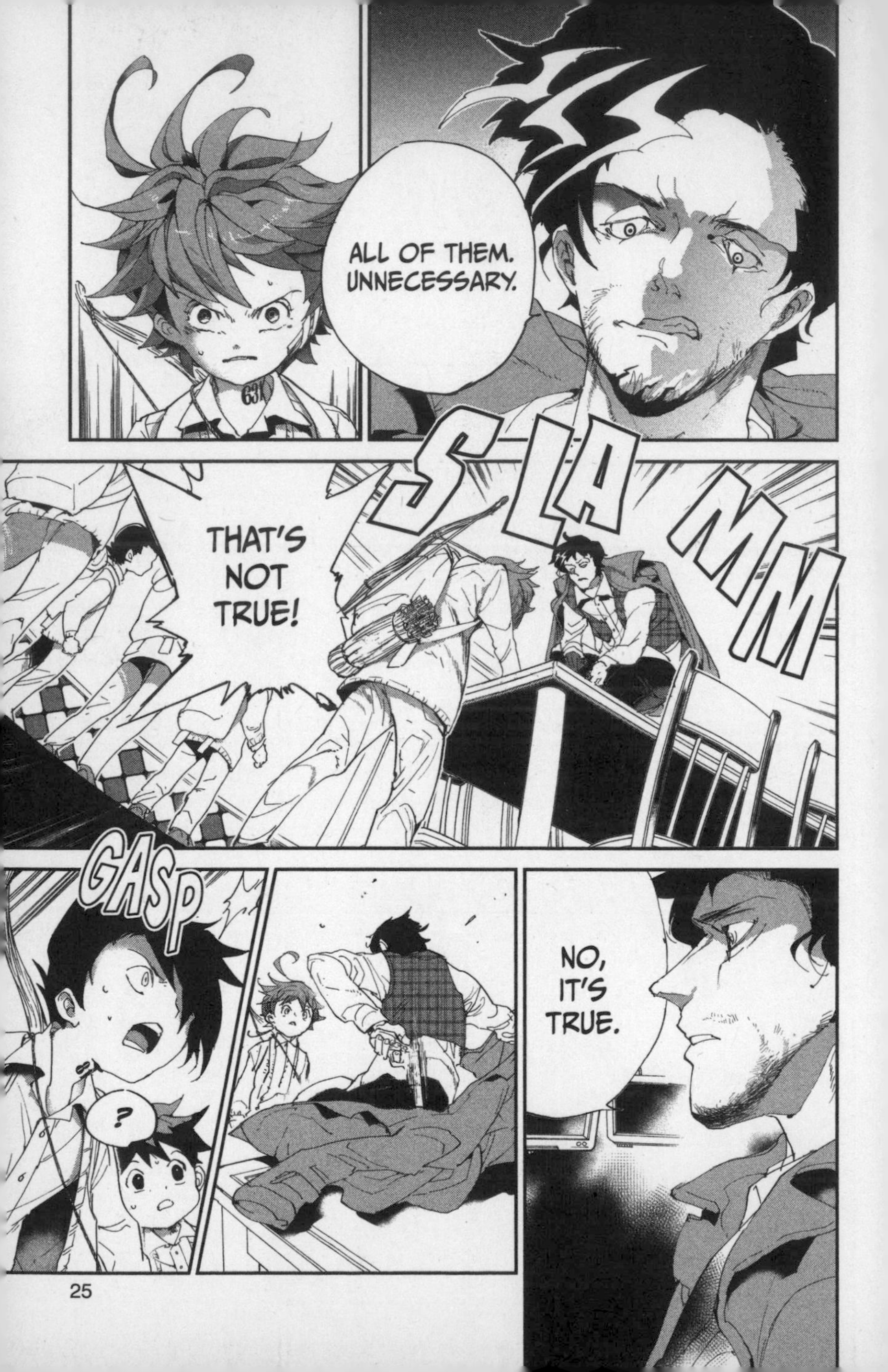
ALL OF THEM. UNNECESSARY.
SLAMM
THAT'S NOT TRUE!
NO, IT'S TRUE.
GASP
?

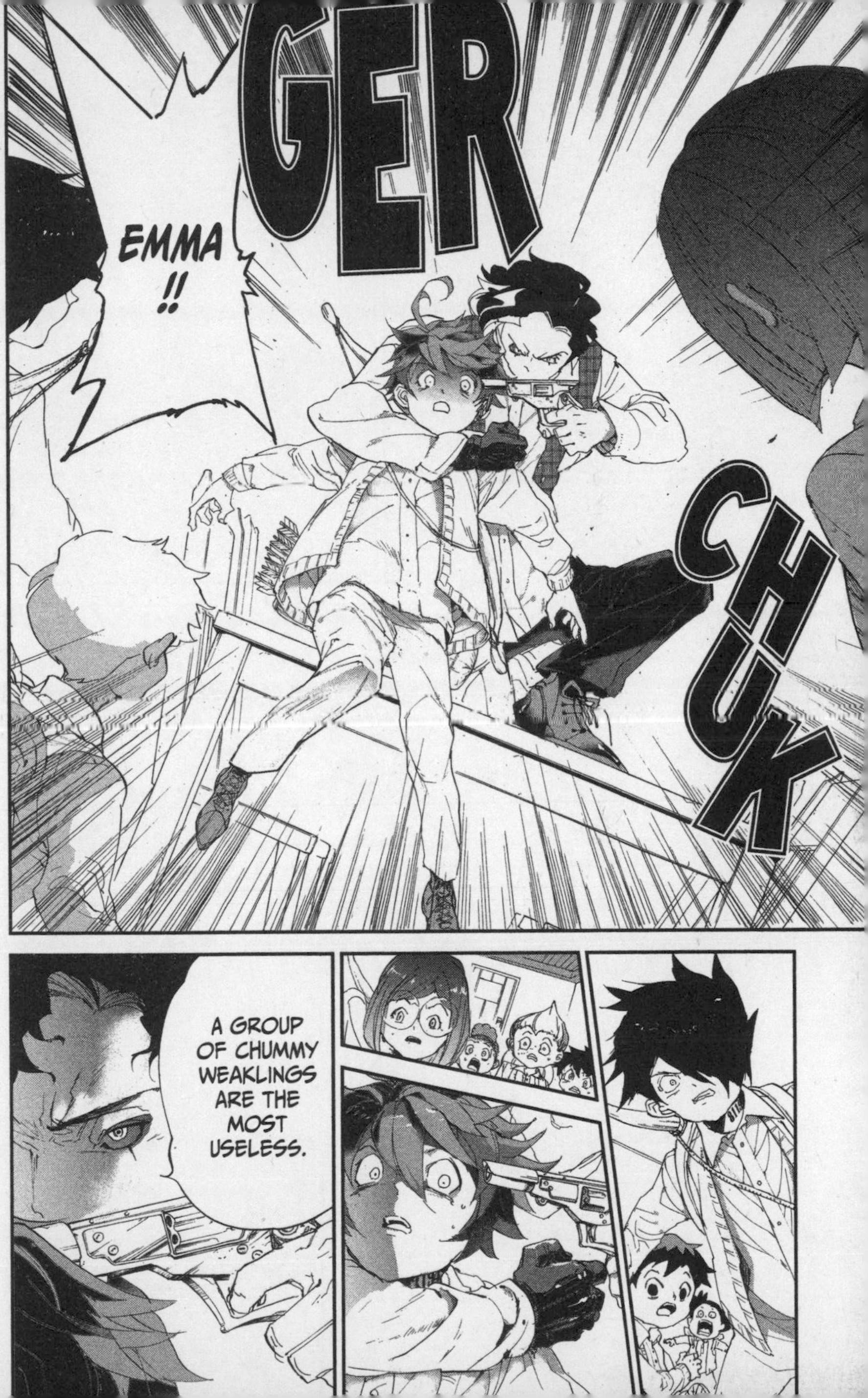
GER
EMMA !!
CHUK
A GROUP OF CHUMMY WEAKLINGS ARE THE MOST USELESS.

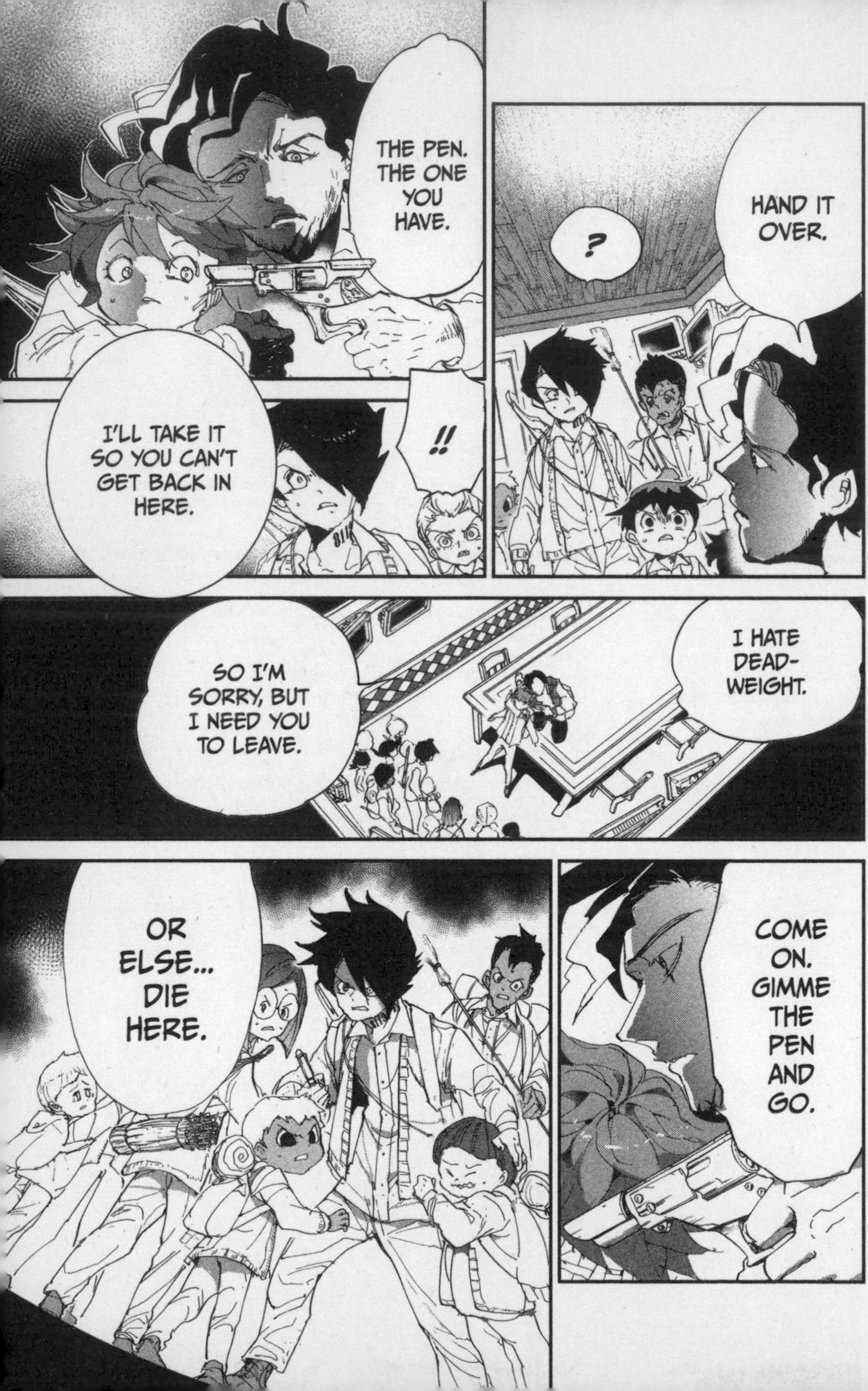
HAND IT OVER.
?
THE PEN. THE ONE YOU HAVE.
!!
I'LL TAKE IT SO YOU CAN'T GET BACK IN HERE.
I HATE DEAD-WEIGHT.
SO I'M SORRY, BUT I NEED YOU TO LEAVE.
COME ON. GIMME THE PEN AND GO.
OR ELSE... DIE HERE.

Cookie

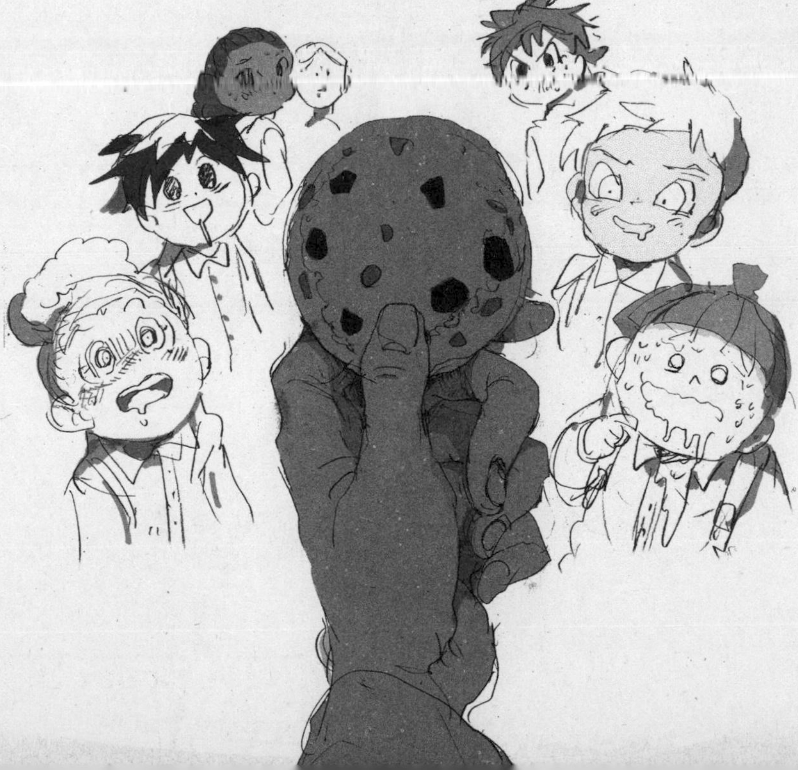

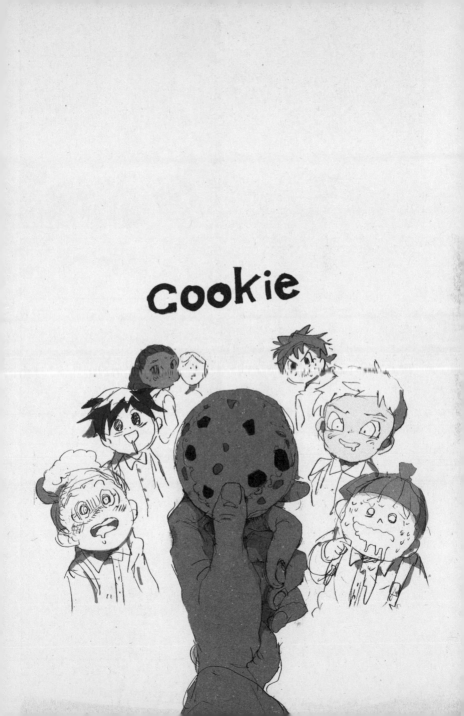

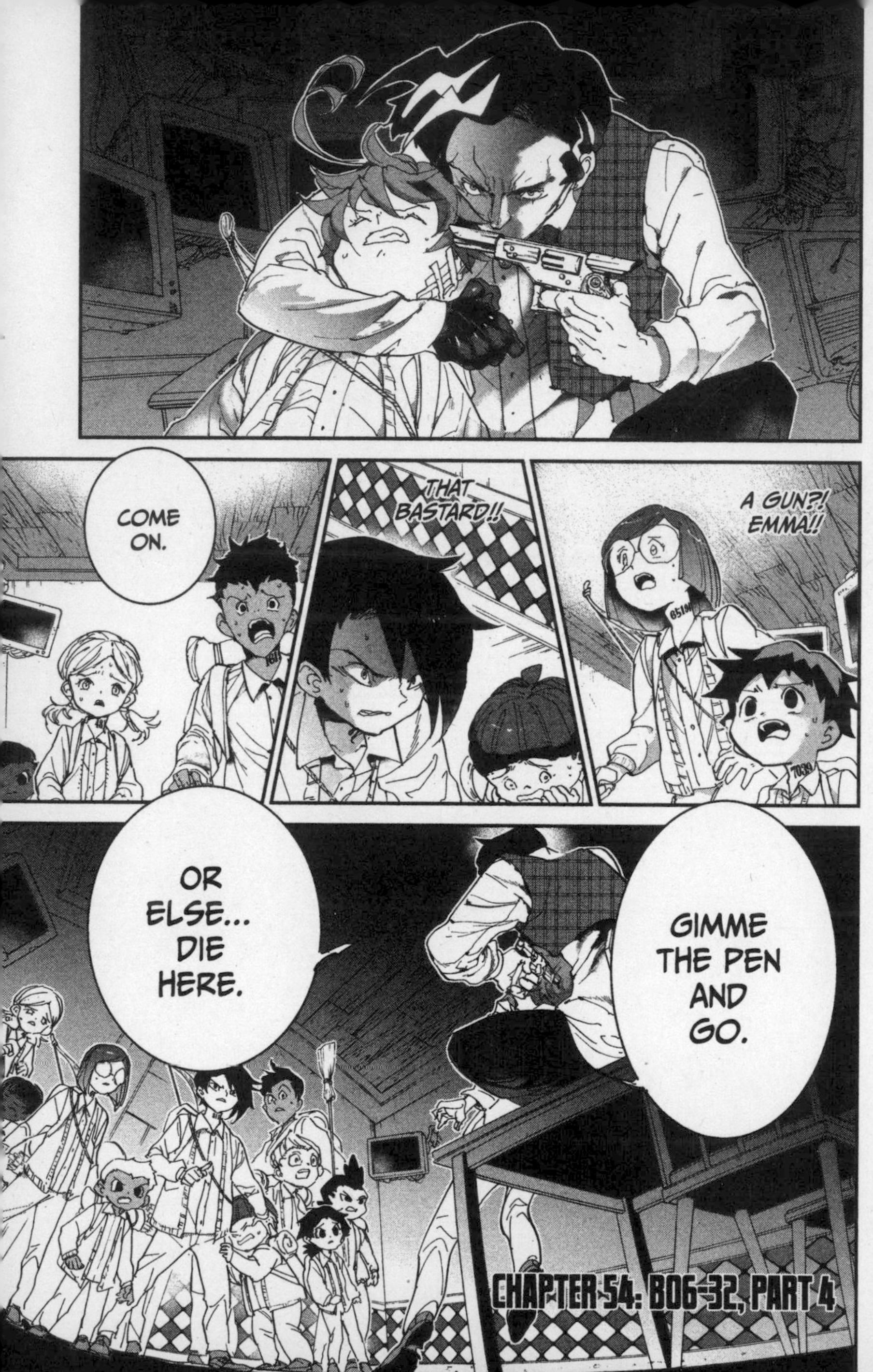
A GUN?! EMMA!!
THAT BASTARD!!
COME ON.
GIMME THE PEN AND GO.
OR ELSE... DIE HERE.
CHAPTER 54: B06-32, PART 4

CHAPTER 54: B06-32, PART 4

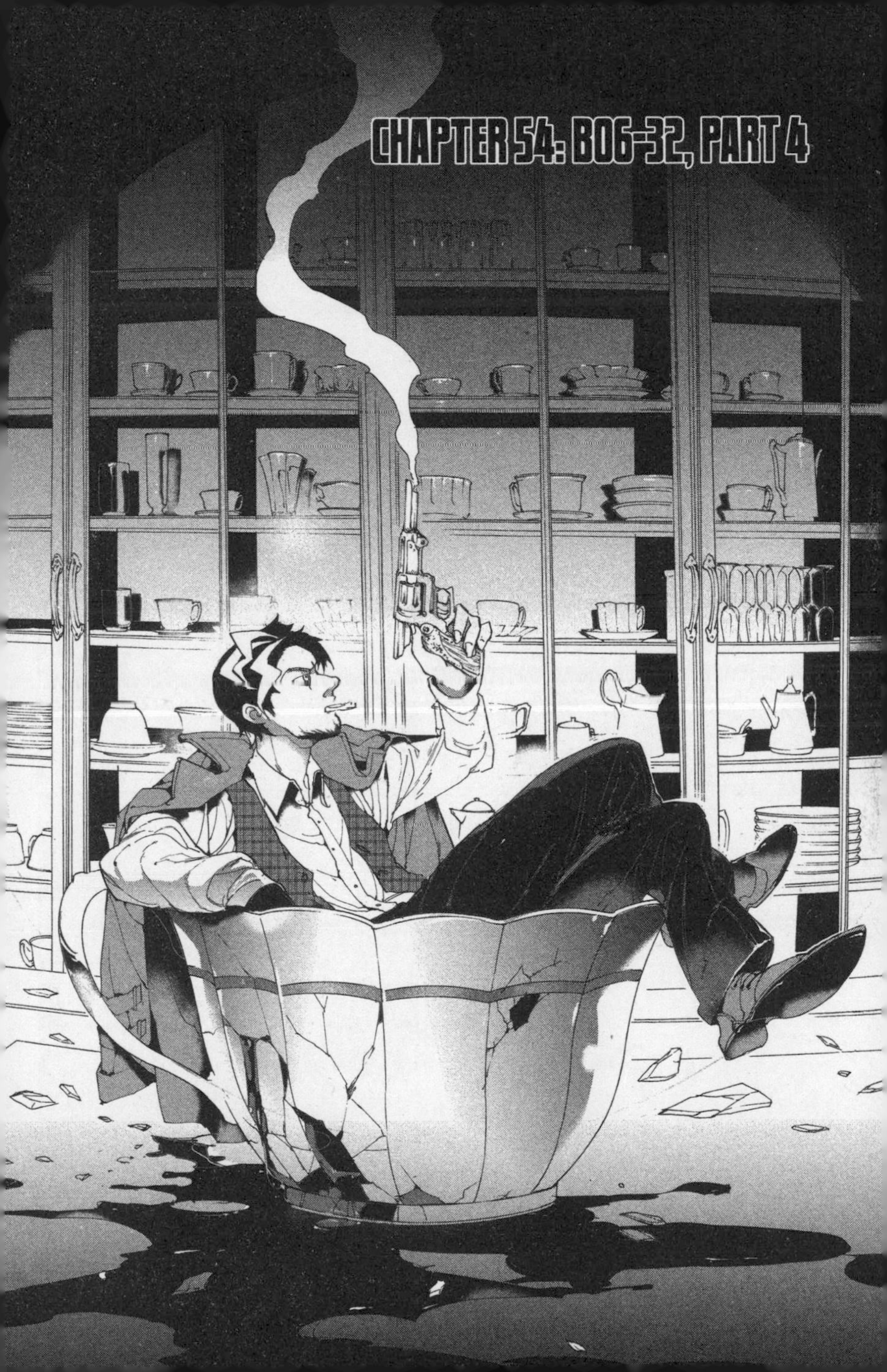

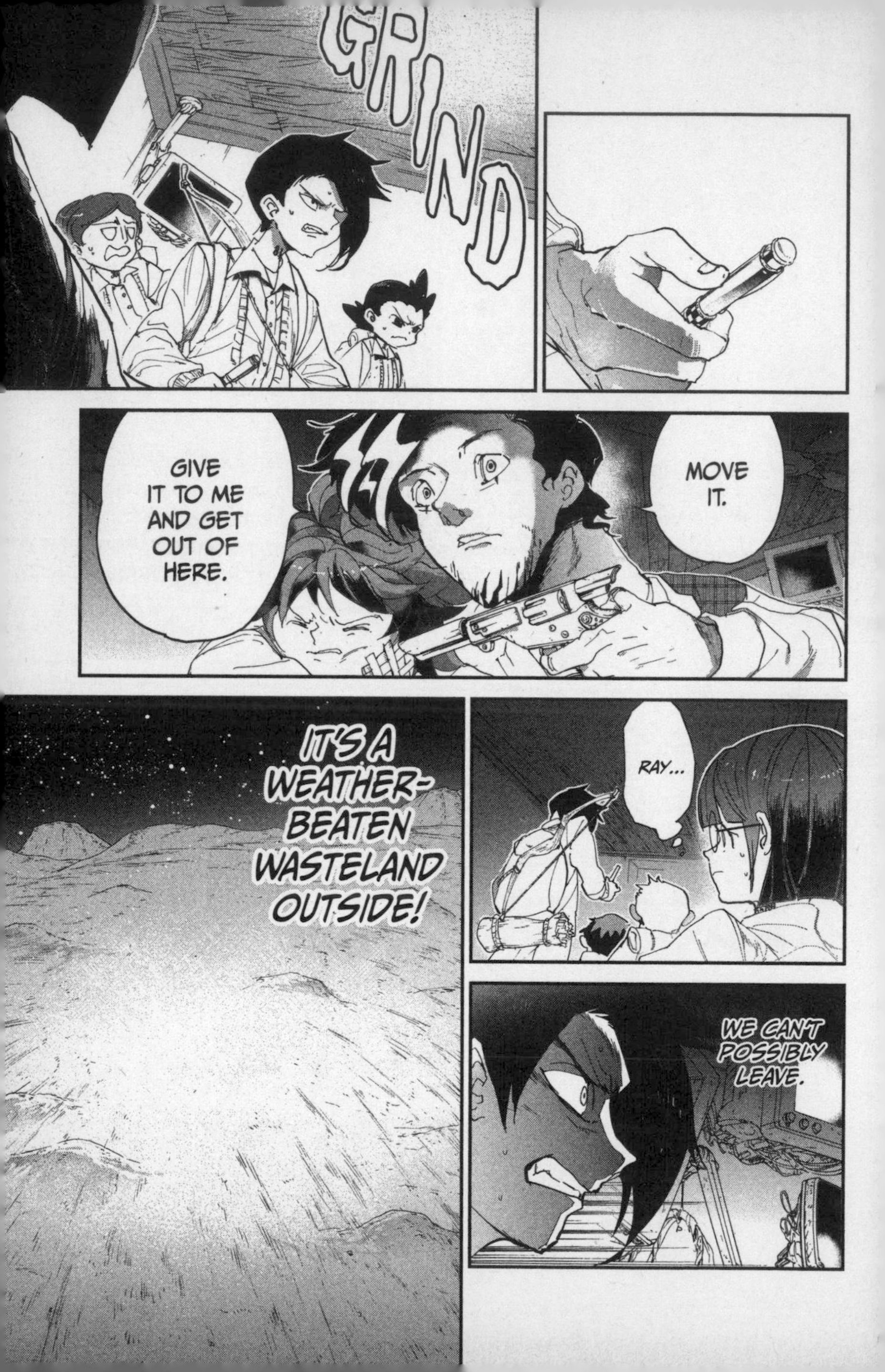
GRIND
MOVE IT.
GIVE IT TO ME AND GET OUT OF HERE.
RAY...
WE CAN'T POSSIBLY LEAVE.
IT'S A WEATHER-BEATEN WASTELAND OUTSIDE!

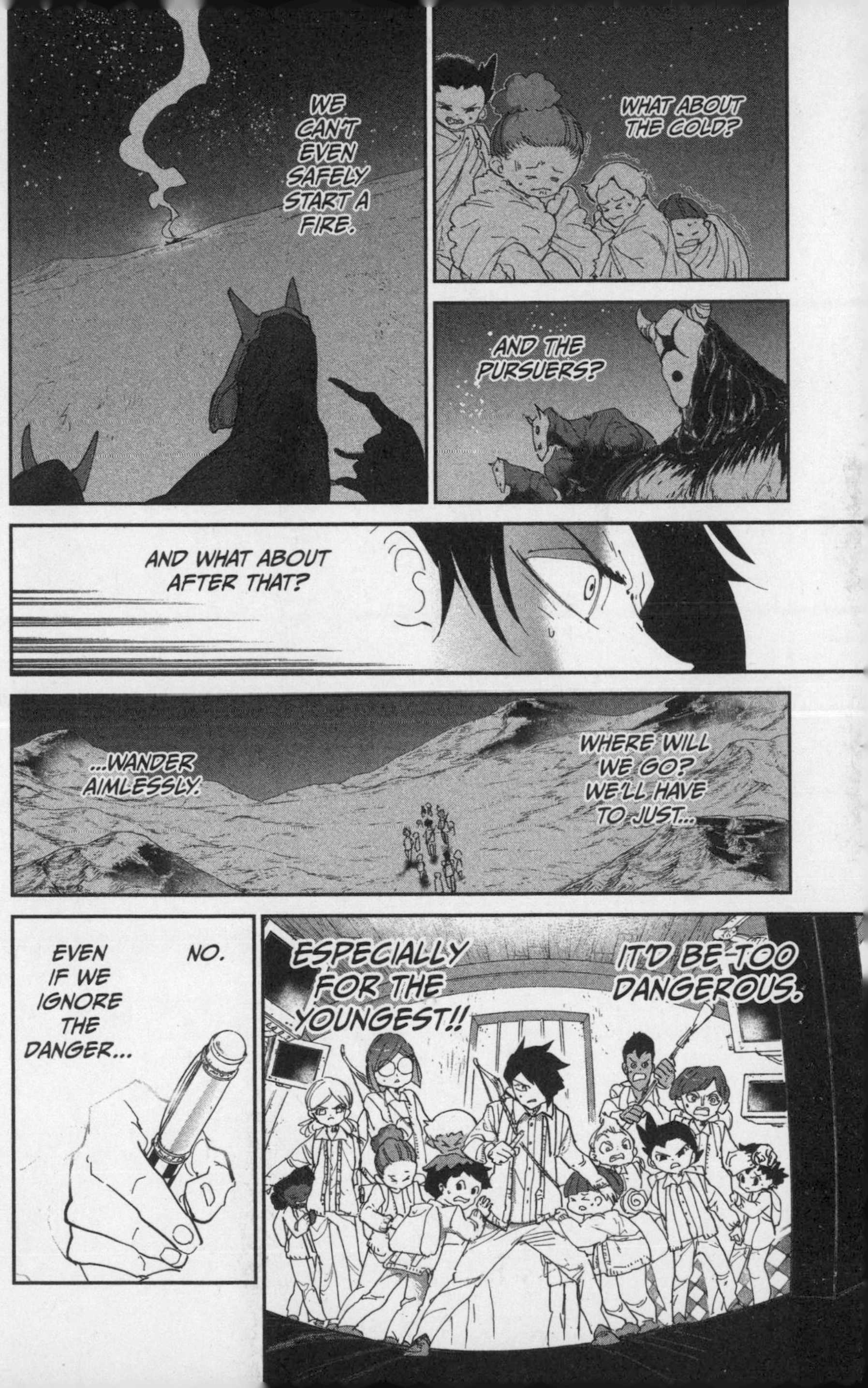
WHAT ABOUT THE COLD?
AND THE PURSUERS?
WE CAN'T EVEN SAFELY START A FIRE.
AND WHAT ABOUT AFTER THAT?
WHERE WILL WE GO? WE'LL HAVE TO JUST...
...WANDER AIMLESSLY.
IT'D BE TOO DANGEROUS.
ESPECIALLY FOR THE YOUNGEST!!
NO.
EVEN IF WE IGNORE THE DANGER...

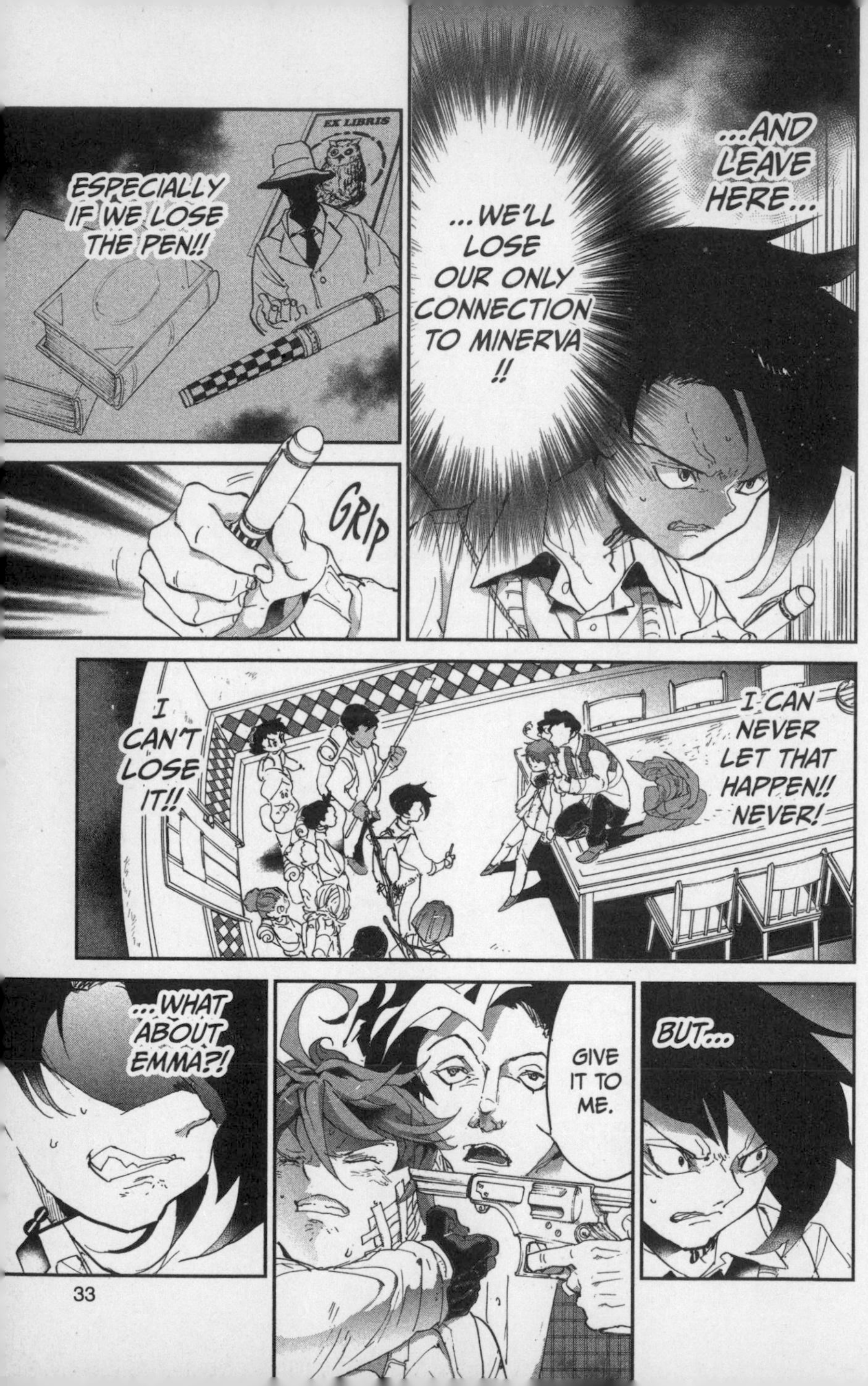
...AND LEAVE HERE...
...WE'LL LOSE OUR ONLY CONNECTION TO MINERVA !!
ESPECIALLY IF WE LOSE THE PEN!!
EX LIBRIS
GRIP
I CAN NEVER LET THAT HAPPEN!! NEVER!
I CAN'T LOSE IT!!
BUT...
GIVE IT TO ME.
...WHAT ABOUT EMMA?!

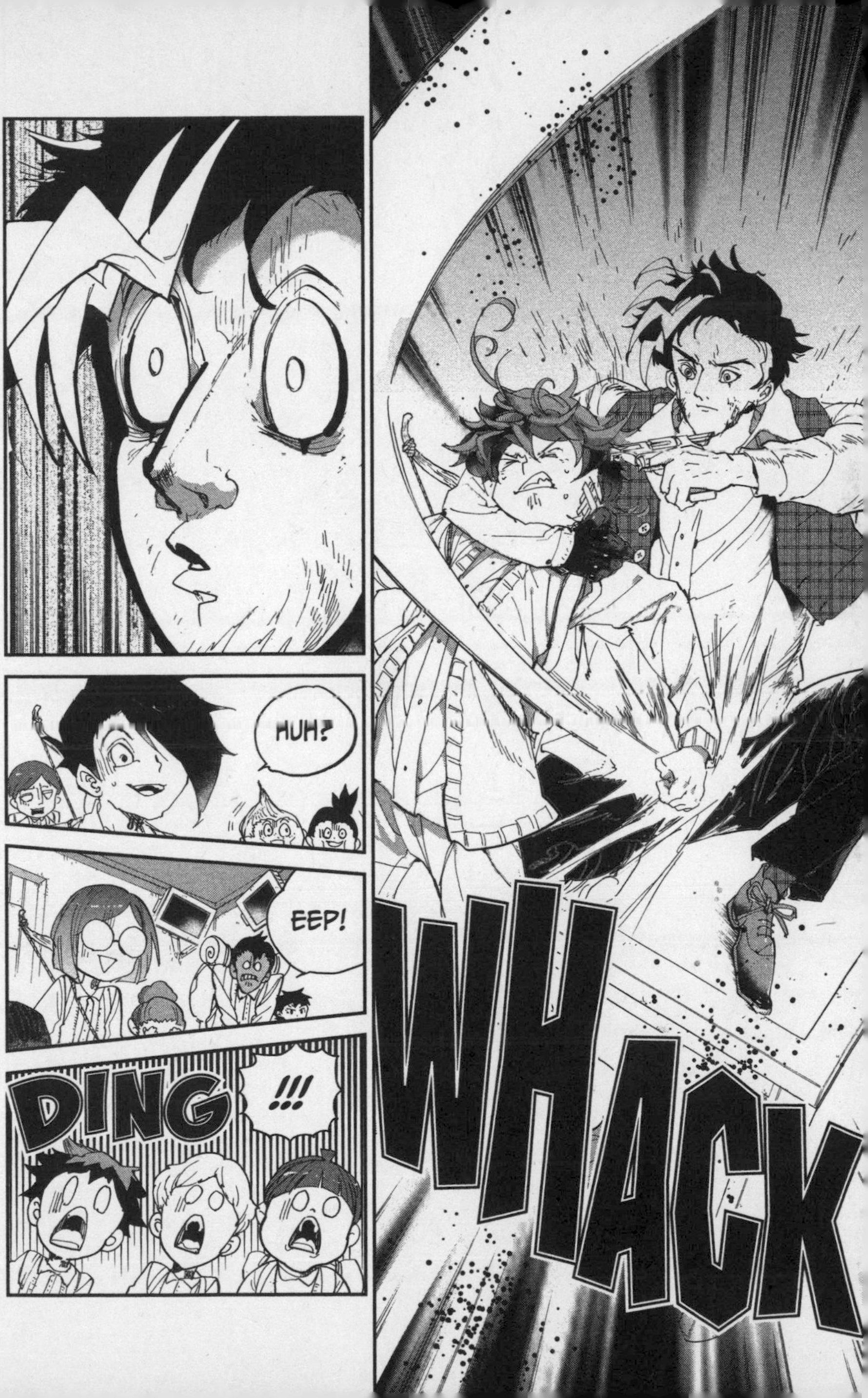
WHACK
HUH?
EEP!
DING
!!!

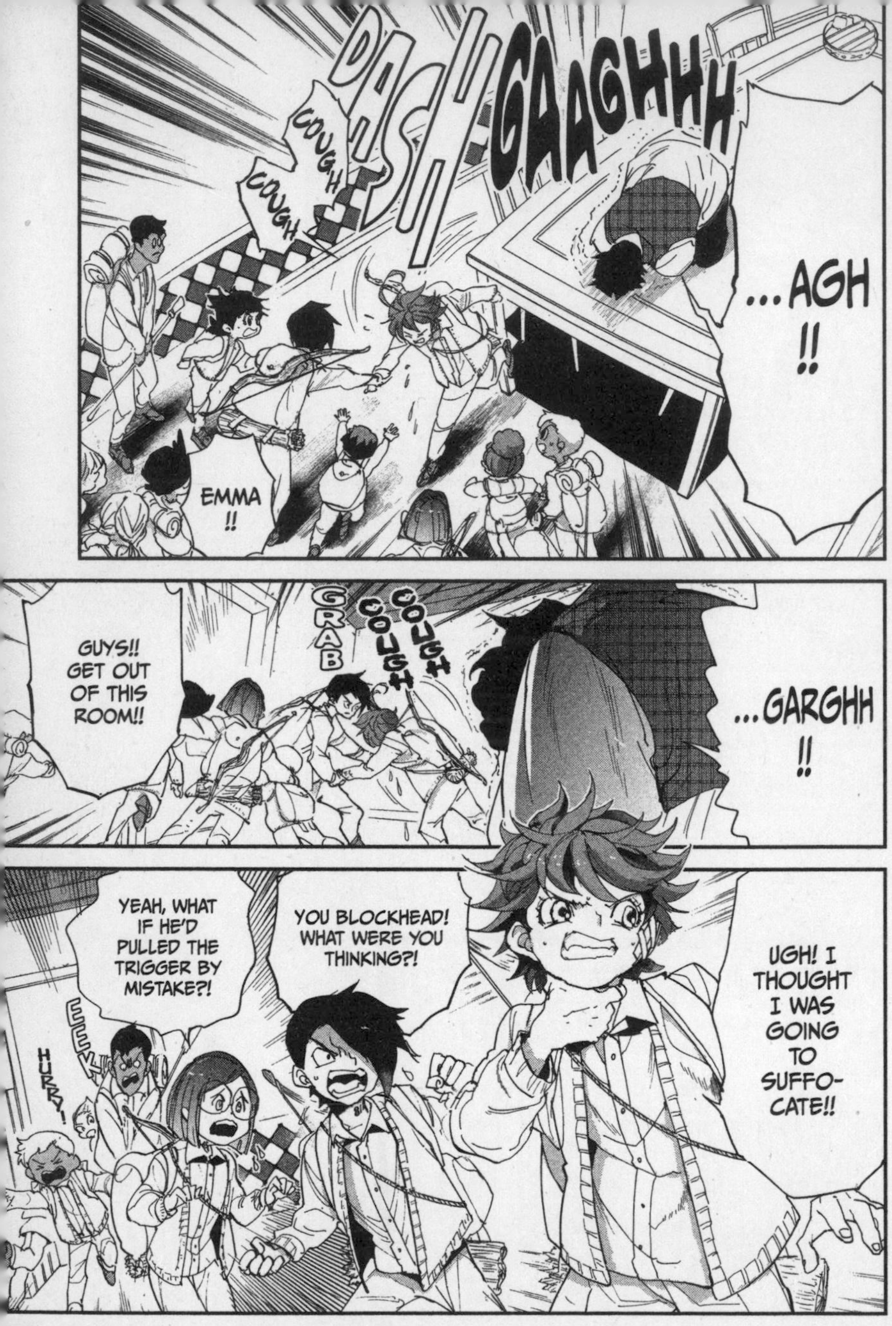
...AGH !!
GAGHHH
DASH
COUGH
COUGH
EMMA !!
...GARGHH !!
COUGH
COUGH
GRAB
GUYS!! GET OUT OF THIS ROOM!!
UGH! I THOUGHT I WAS GOING TO SUFFO-CATE!!
YOU BLOCKHEAD! WHAT WERE YOU THINKING?!
YEAH, WHAT IF HE'D PULLED THE TRIGGER BY MISTAKE?!
HURRY!

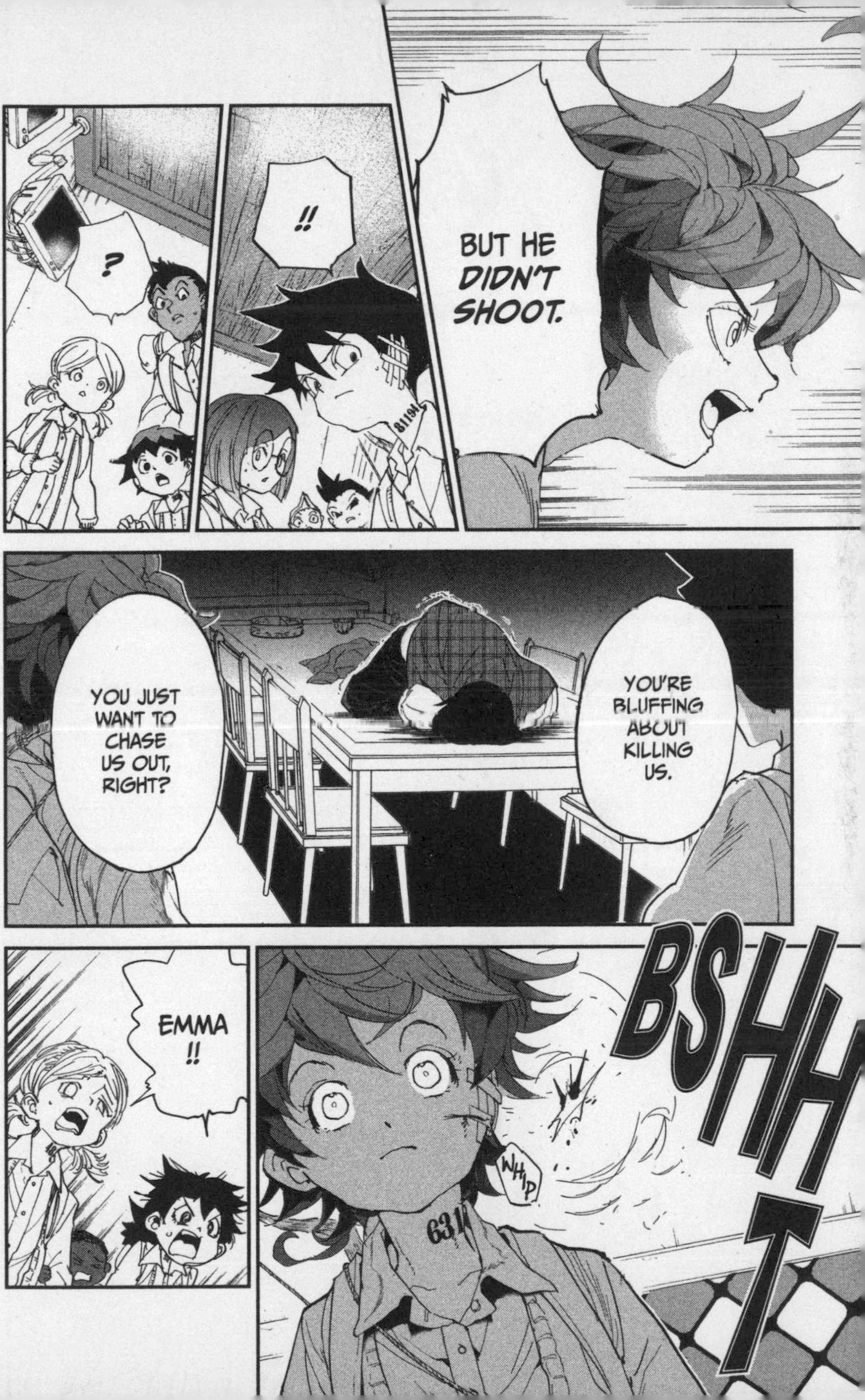
BUT HE DIDN'T SHOOT.
!!
?
YOU'RE BLUFFING ABOUT KILLING US.
YOU JUST WANT TO CHASE US OUT, RIGHT?
BSHHT
WHIP
EMMA!!

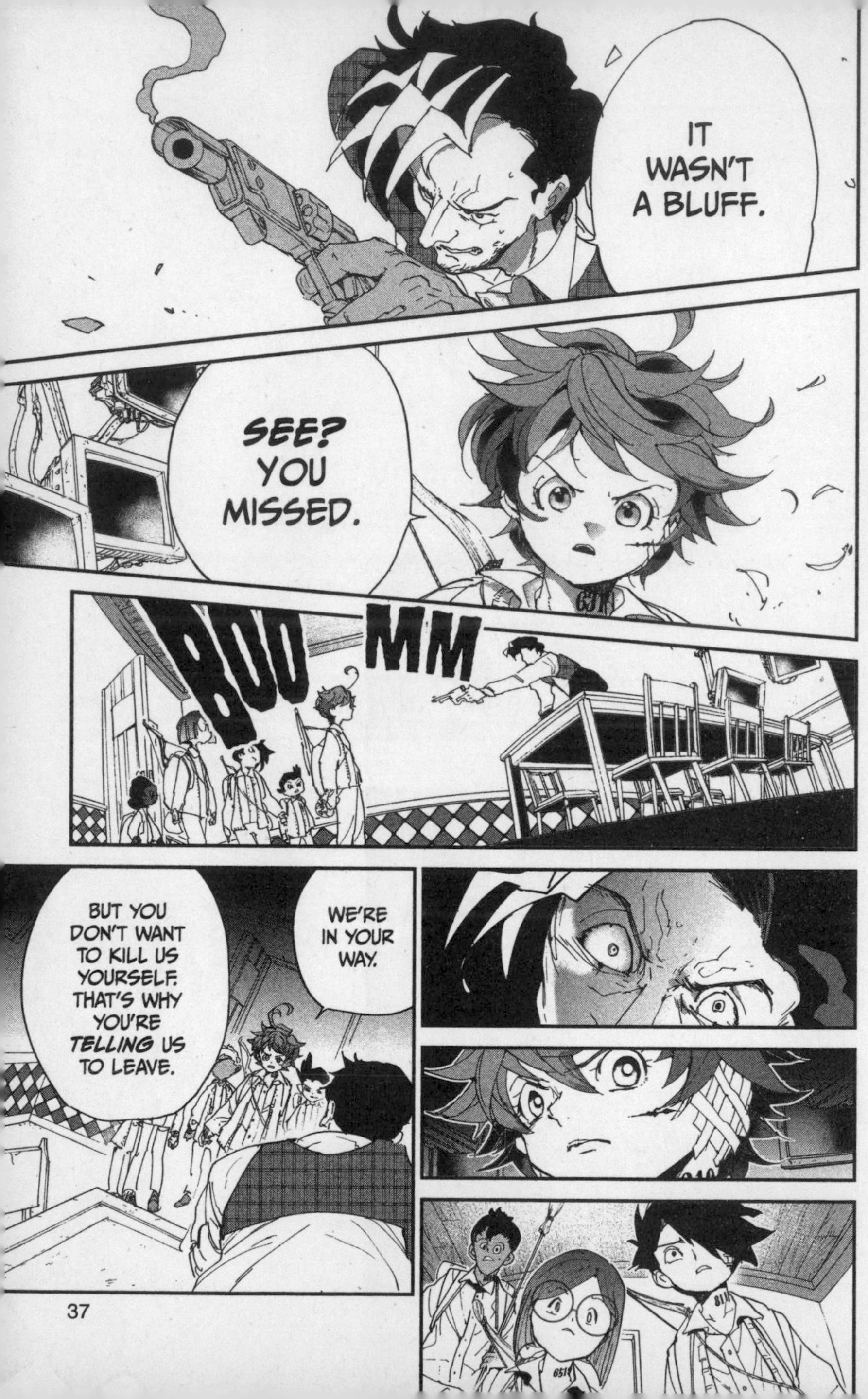
IT WASN'T A BLUFF.
SEE? YOU MISSED.
BOOMM
WE'RE IN YOUR WAY.
BUT YOU DON'T WANT TO KILL US YOURSELF. THAT'S WHY YOU'RE *TELLING* US TO LEAVE.

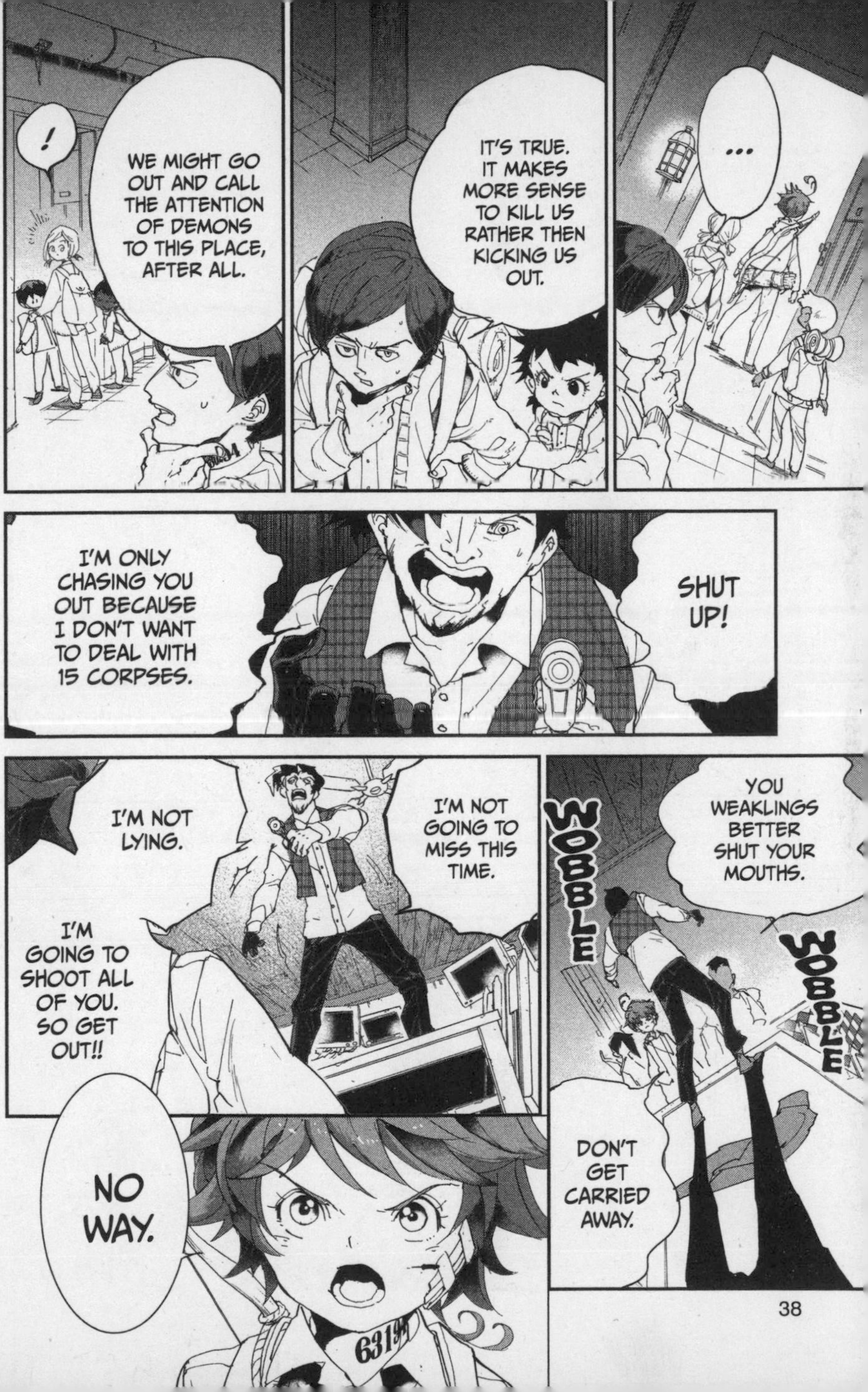
...
IT'S TRUE. IT MAKES MORE SENSE TO KILL US RATHER THEN KICKING US OUT.
WE MIGHT GO OUT AND CALL THE ATTENTION OF DEMONS TO THIS PLACE, AFTER ALL.
!
SHUT UP!
I'M ONLY CHASING YOU OUT BECAUSE I DON'T WANT TO DEAL WITH 15 CORPSES.
YOU WEAKLINGS BETTER SHUT YOUR MOUTHS.
WOBBLE
WOBBLE
DON'T GET CARRIED AWAY.
I'M NOT GOING TO MISS THIS TIME.
I'M NOT LYING.
I'M GOING TO SHOOT ALL OF YOU. SO GET OUT!!
NO WAY.

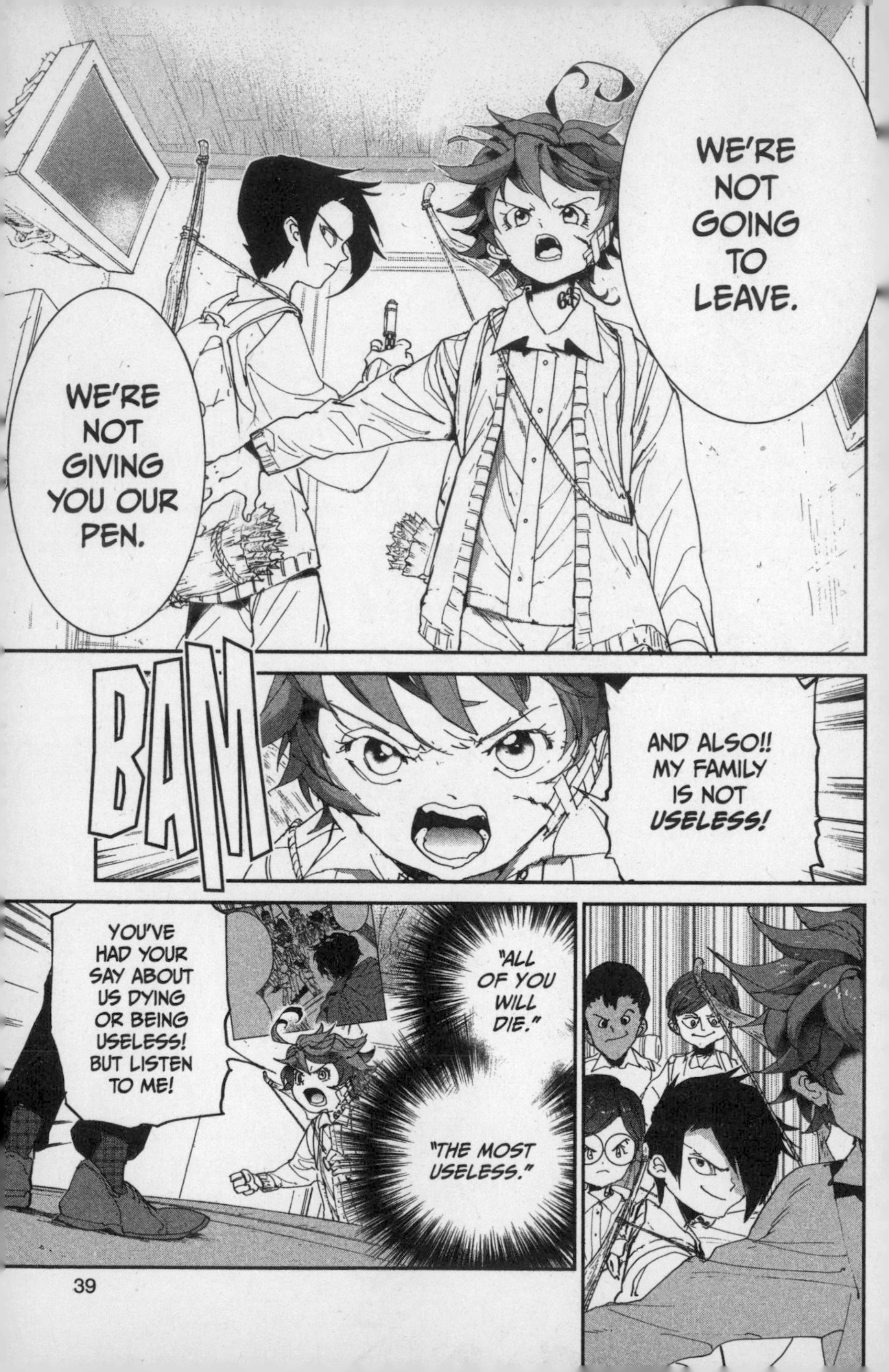
WE'RE NOT GOING TO LEAVE.
WE'RE NOT GIVING YOU OUR PEN.
AND ALSO!! MY FAMILY IS NOT USELESS!
BAM
"ALL OF YOU WILL DIE."
"THE MOST USELESS."
YOU'VE HAD YOUR SAY ABOUT US DYING OR BEING USELESS! BUT LISTEN TO ME!

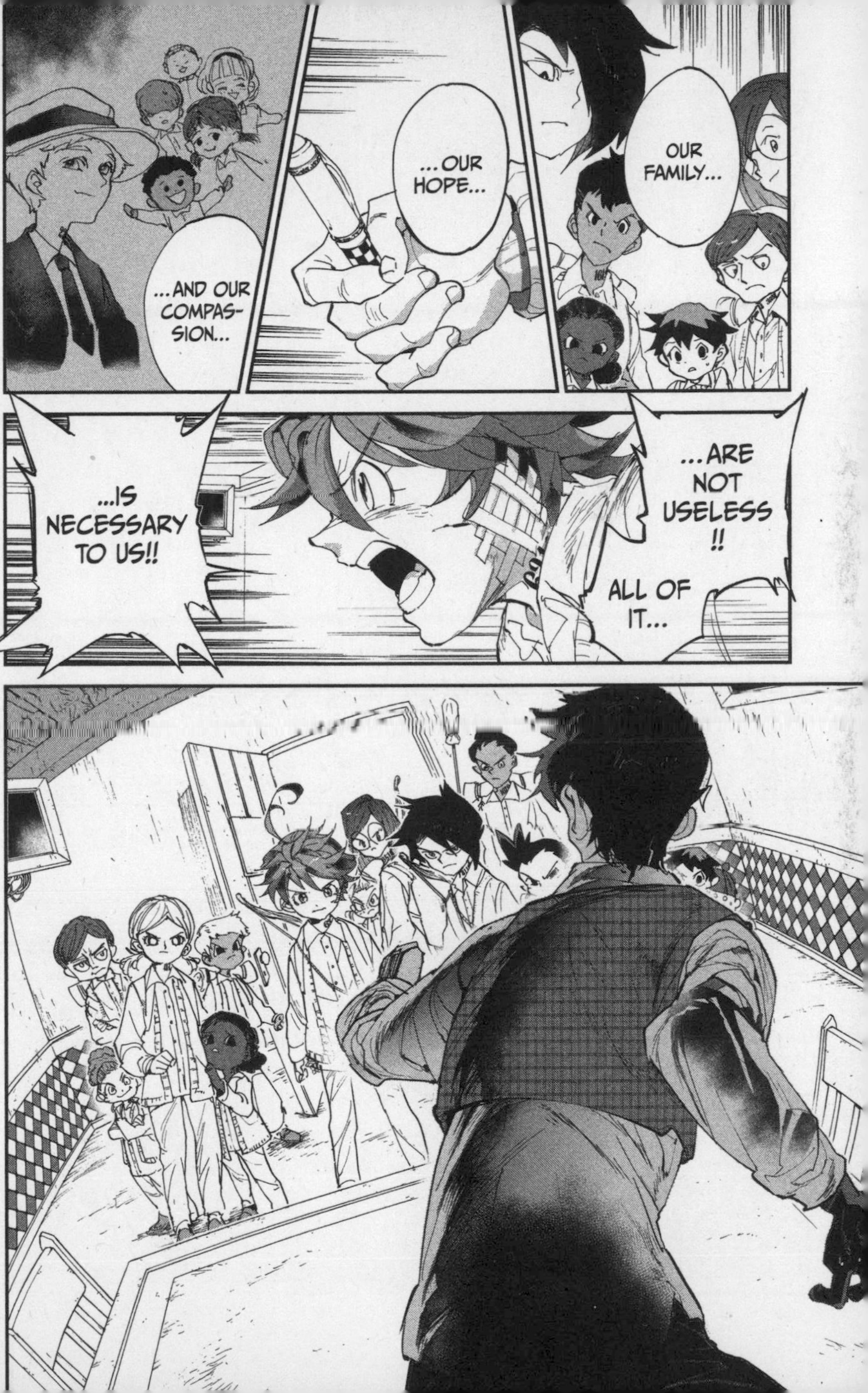
OUR FAMILY...
...OUR HOPE...
...AND OUR COMPASSION...
...ARE NOT USELESS!!
ALL OF IT...
...IS NECESSARY TO US!!

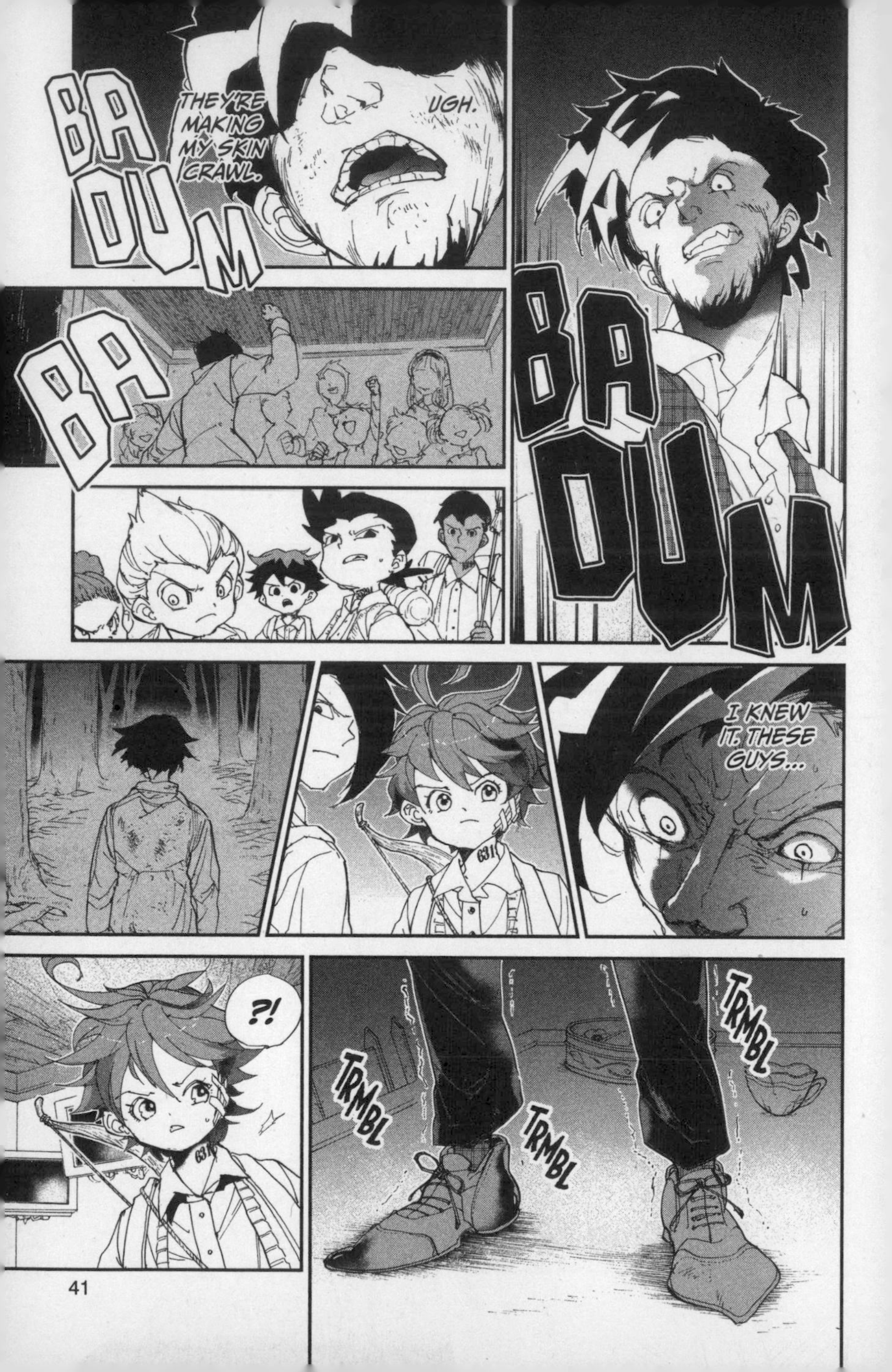
BA DUM
UGH.
THEY'RE MAKING MY SKIN CRAWL.
BA DUM
BA
I KNEW IT. THESE GUYS...
TRMBL
TRMBL
TRMBL
?!

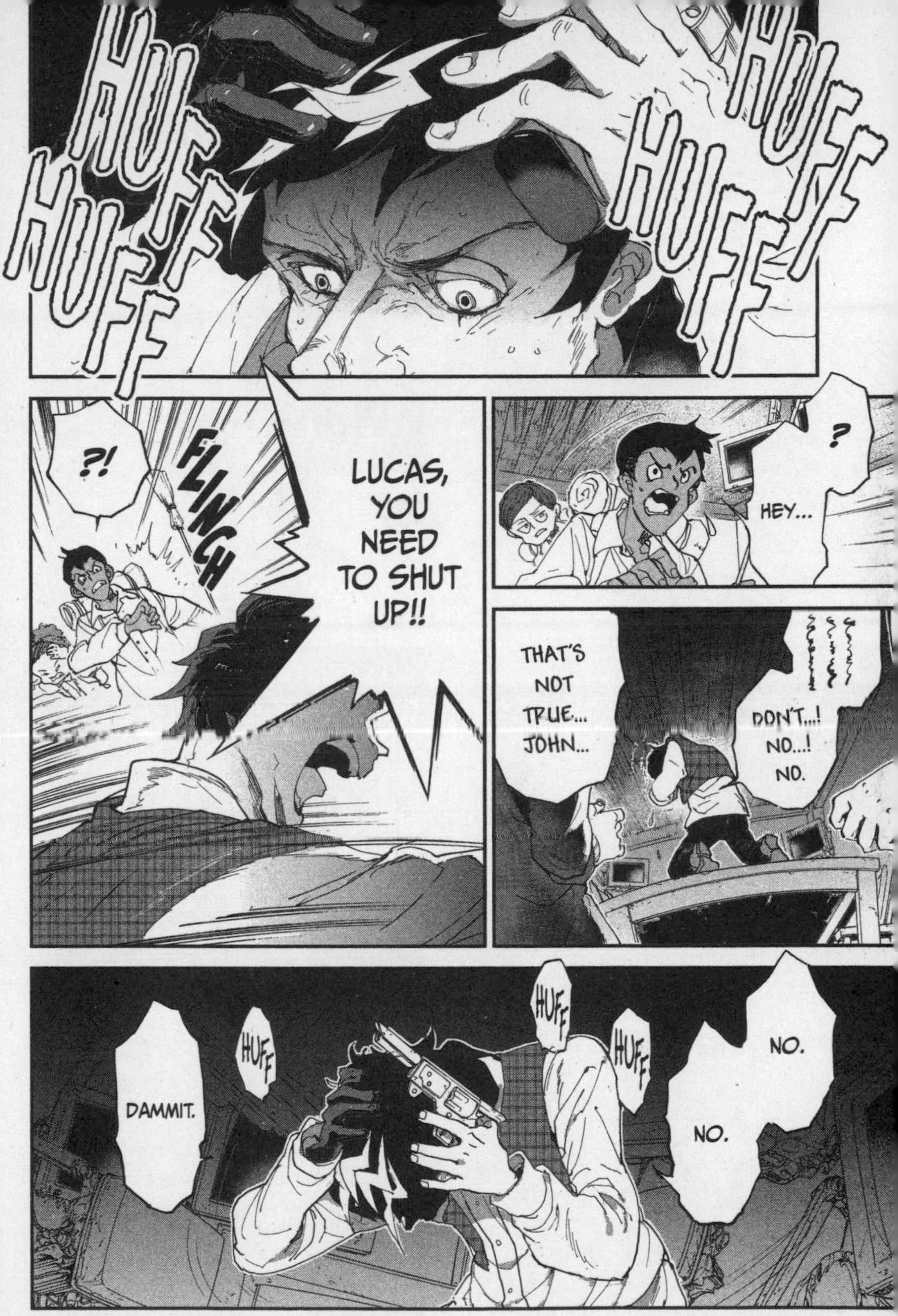
HUFF HUFF
HUFF HUFF
?
HEY...
DON'T...! NO...! NO.
THAT'S NOT TRUE... JOHN...
?!
FLINCH
LUCAS, YOU NEED TO SHUT UP!!
NO.
NO.
HUFF
HUFF
HUFF
DAMMIT.

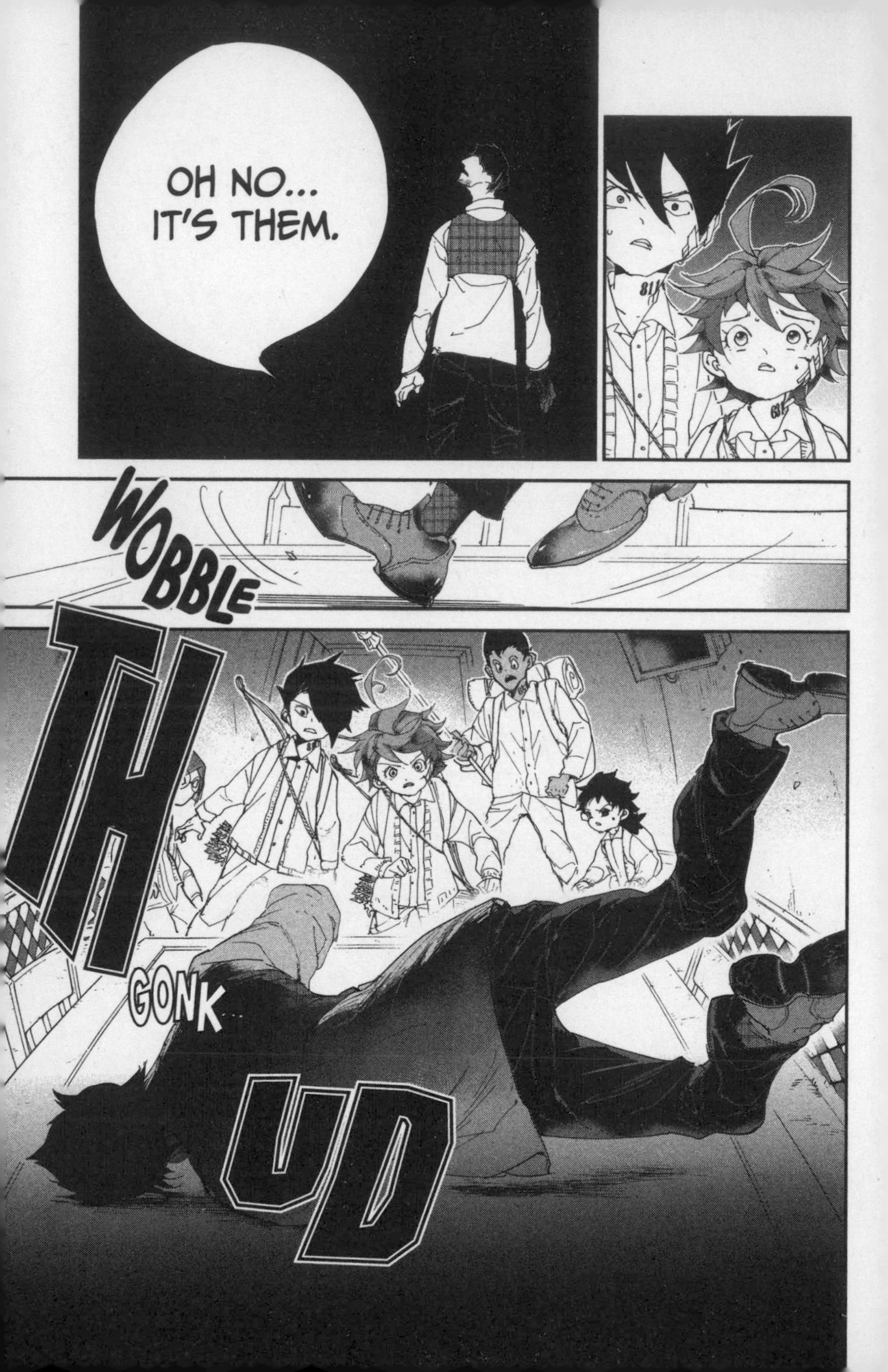
OH NO... IT'S THEM.
WOBBLE
THUD
GONK...

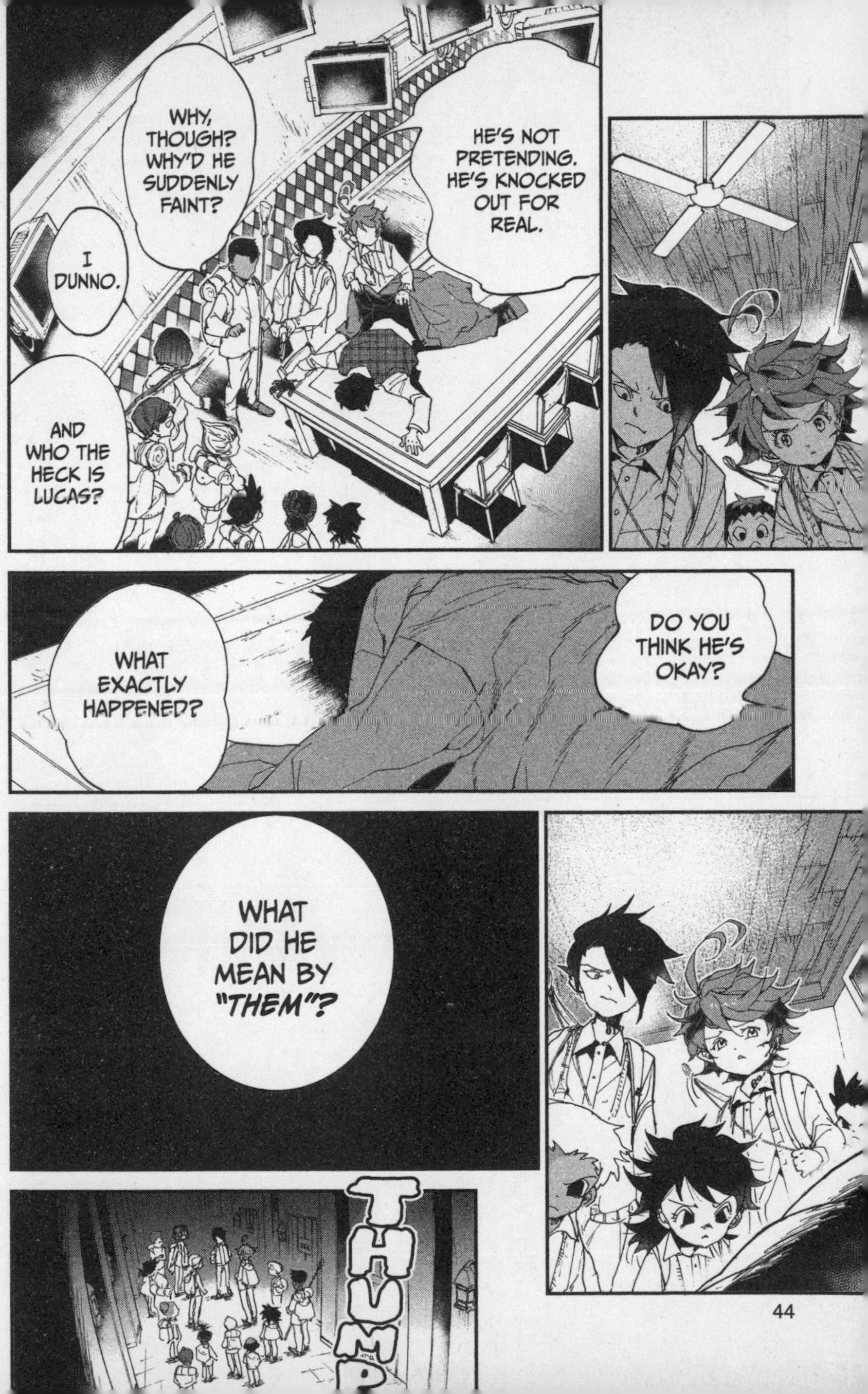
HE'S NOT PRETENDING. HE'S KNOCKED OUT FOR REAL.
WHY, THOUGH? WHY'D HE SUDDENLY FAINT?
I DUNNO.
AND WHO THE HECK IS LUCAS?
DO YOU THINK HE'S OKAY?
WHAT EXACTLY HAPPENED?
WHAT DID HE MEAN BY "THEM"?
THUMP

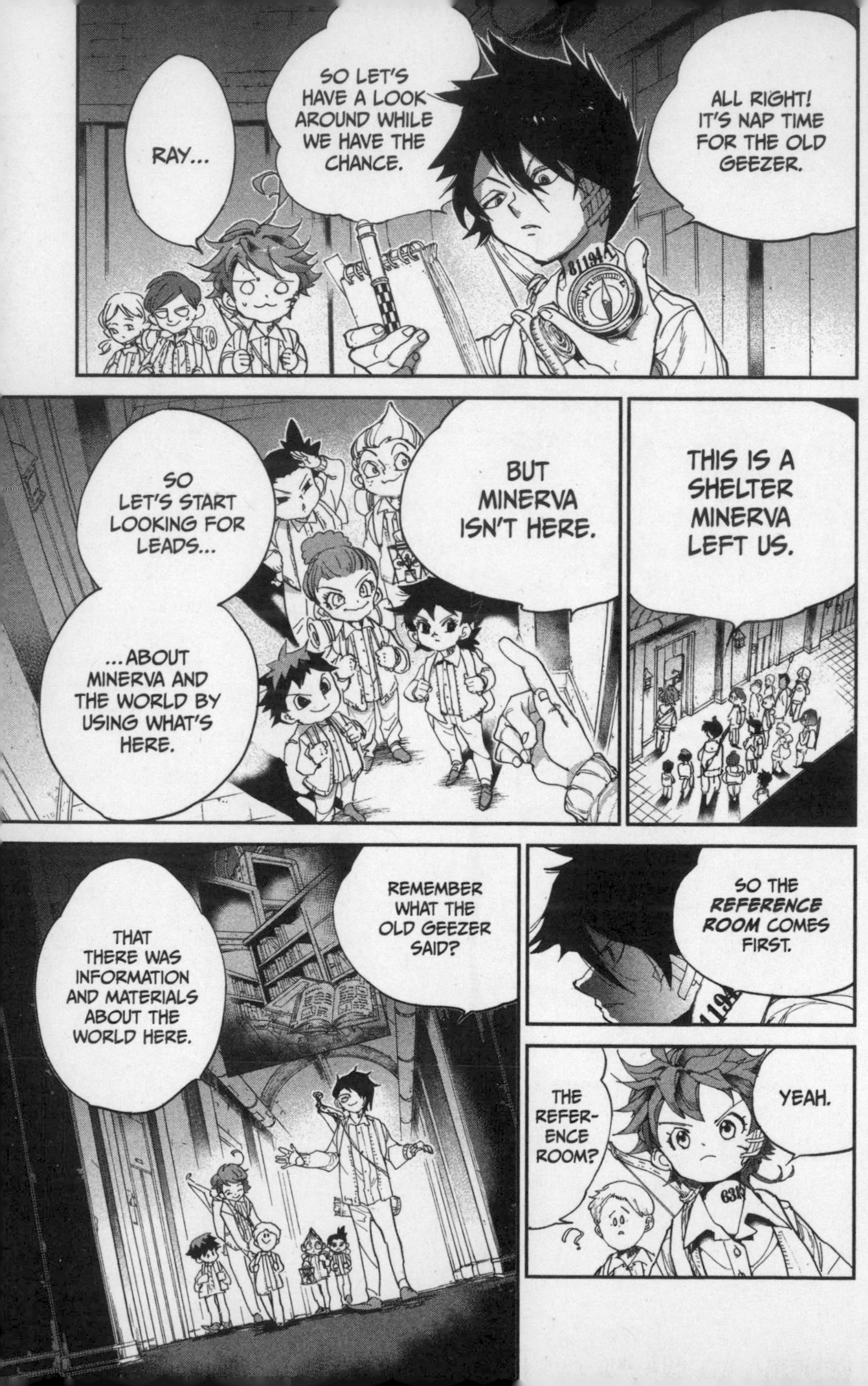
ALL RIGHT! IT'S NAP TIME FOR THE OLD GEEZER.
SO LET'S HAVE A LOOK AROUND WHILE WE HAVE THE CHANCE.
RAY...
THIS IS A SHELTER MINERVA LEFT US.
BUT MINERVA ISN'T HERE.
SO LET'S START LOOKING FOR LEADS...
...ABOUT MINERVA AND THE WORLD BY USING WHAT'S HERE.
SO THE REFERENCE ROOM COMES FIRST.
YEAH.
THE REFER-ENCE ROOM?
REMEMBER WHAT THE OLD GEEZER SAID?
THAT THERE WAS INFORMATION AND MATERIALS ABOUT THE WORLD HERE.

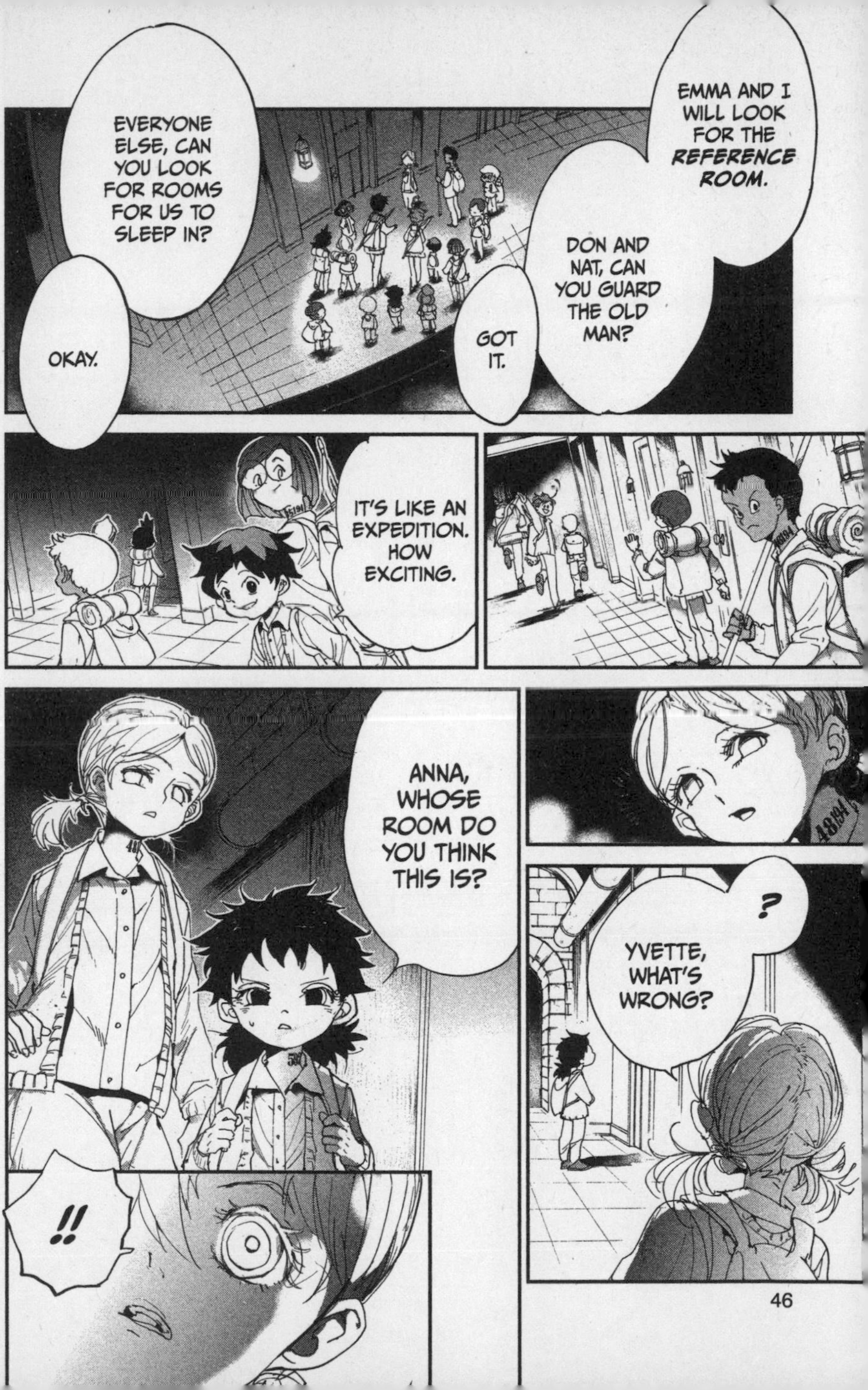
EMMA AND I WILL LOOK FOR THE *REFERENCE ROOM.*
DON AND NAT, CAN YOU GUARD THE OLD MAN?
GOT IT.
EVERYONE ELSE, CAN YOU LOOK FOR ROOMS FOR US TO SLEEP IN?
OKAY.
IT'S LIKE AN EXPEDITION. HOW EXCITING.
?
YVETTE, WHAT'S WRONG?
ANNA, WHOSE ROOM DO YOU THINK THIS IS?
!!

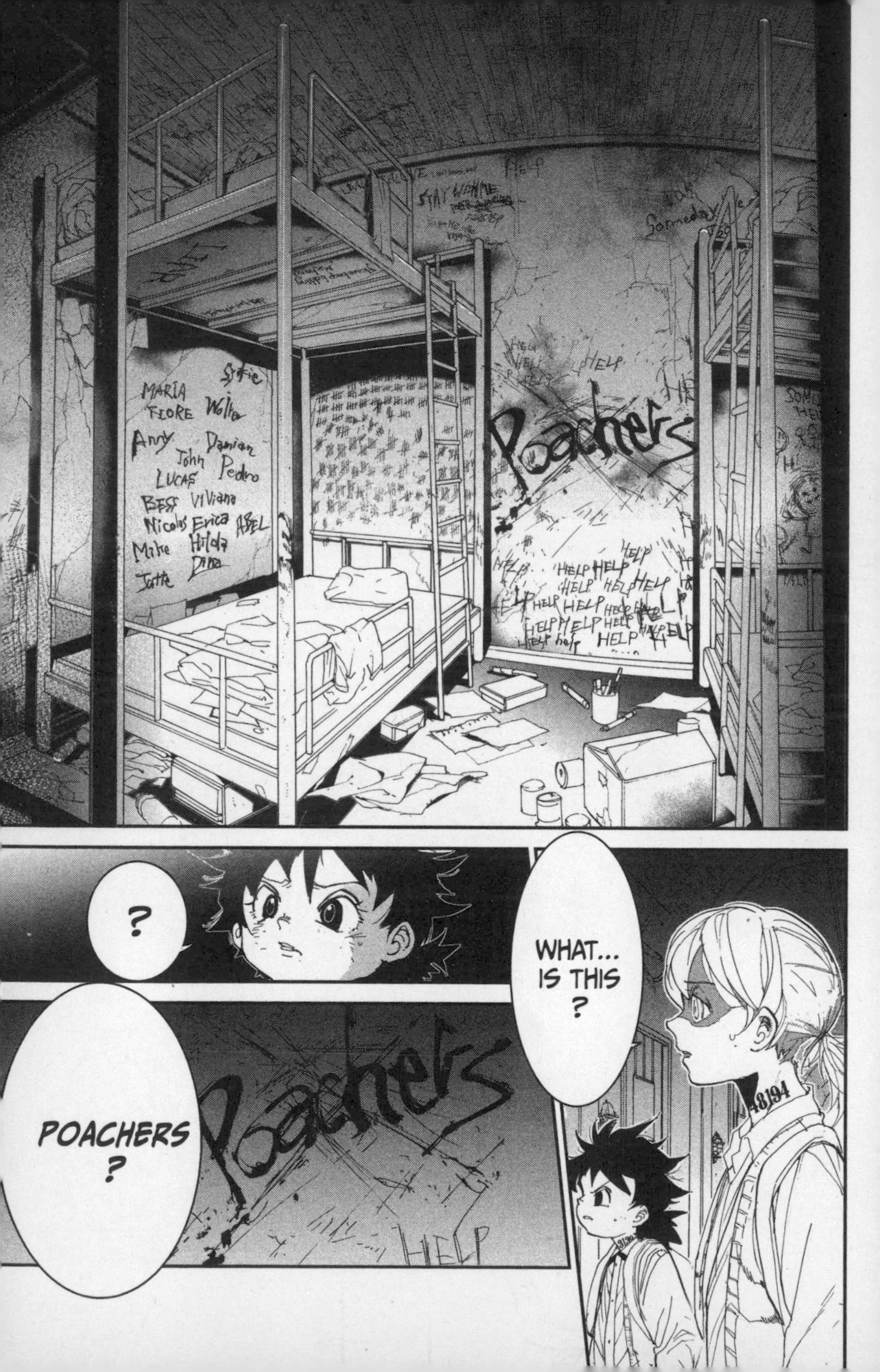
Poachers
WHAT... IS THIS ?
?
POACHERS ?

THE PROMISED NEVERLAND SIDE SCENE 011

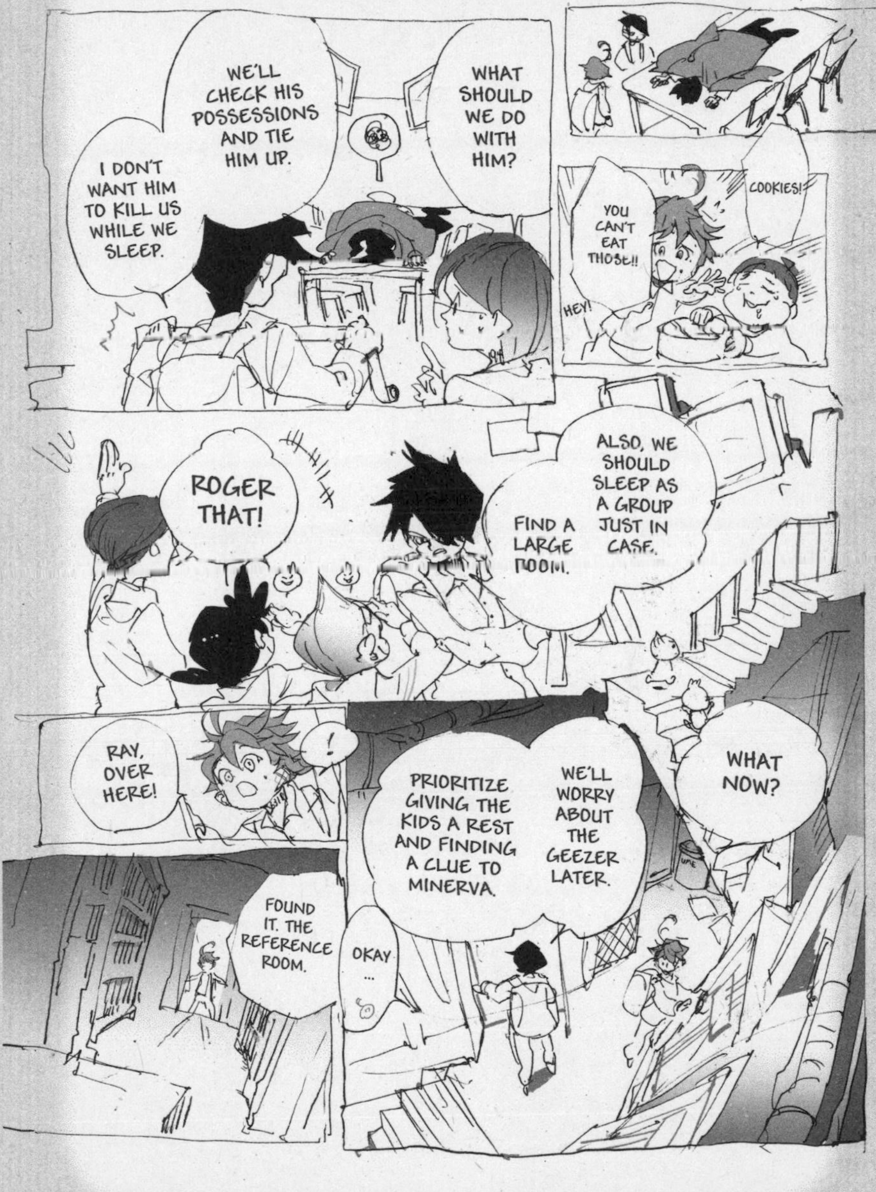
COOKIES!
YOU CAN'T EAT THOSE!!
HEY!
WHAT SHOULD WE DO WITH HIM?
WE'LL CHECK HIS POSSESSIONS AND TIE HIM UP.
I DON'T WANT HIM TO KILL US WHILE WE SLEEP.
ALSO, WE SHOULD SLEEP AS A GROUP JUST IN CASE.
FIND A LARGE ROOM.
ROGER THAT!
WHAT NOW?
WE'LL WORRY ABOUT THE GEEZER LATER.
PRIORITIZE GIVING THE KIDS A REST AND FINDING A CLUE TO MINERVA.
OKAY...
RAY, OVER HERE!
FOUND IT. THE REFERENCE ROOM.

CHAPTER 55: B06-32, PART 5

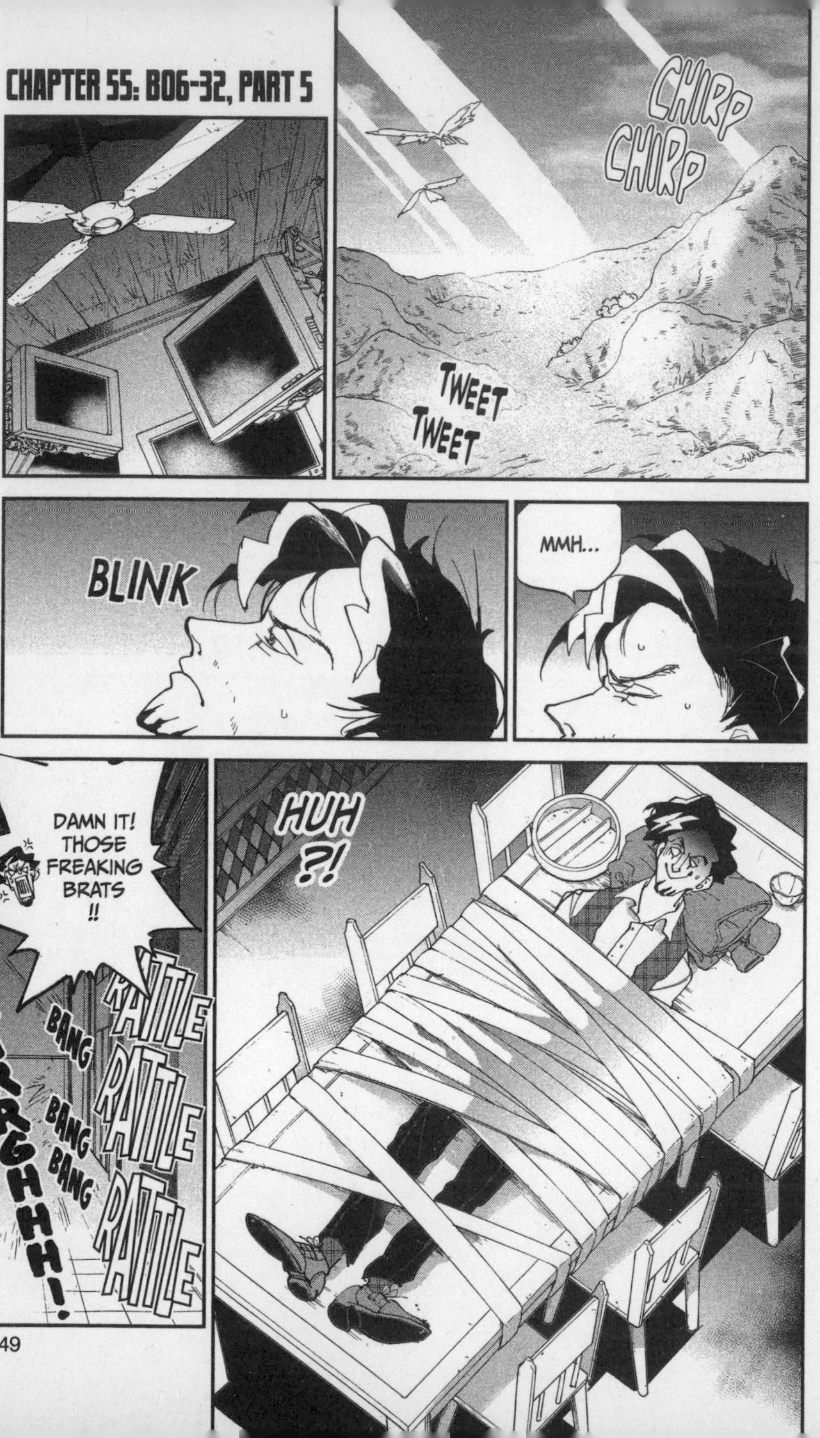
CHIRP CHIRP
TWEET TWEET
MMH...
BLINK
HUH ?!
DAMN IT! THOSE FREAKING BRATS !!
RATTLE RATTLE RATTLE RATTLE
BANG BANG BANG BANG
AARRGHHH!

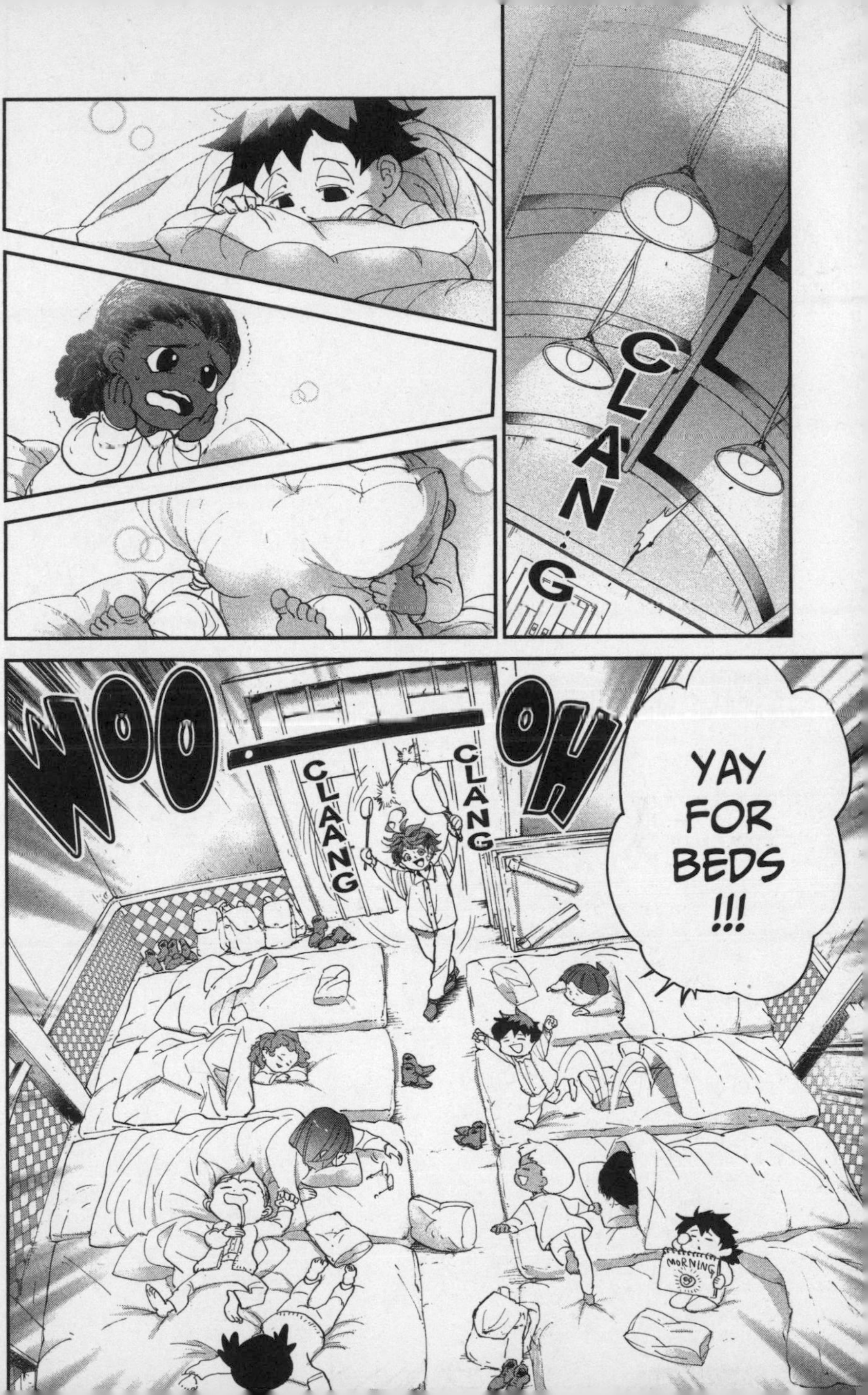
CLANG
YAY FOR BEDS !!!
WOO—OH
CLANG
CLANG
MORNING

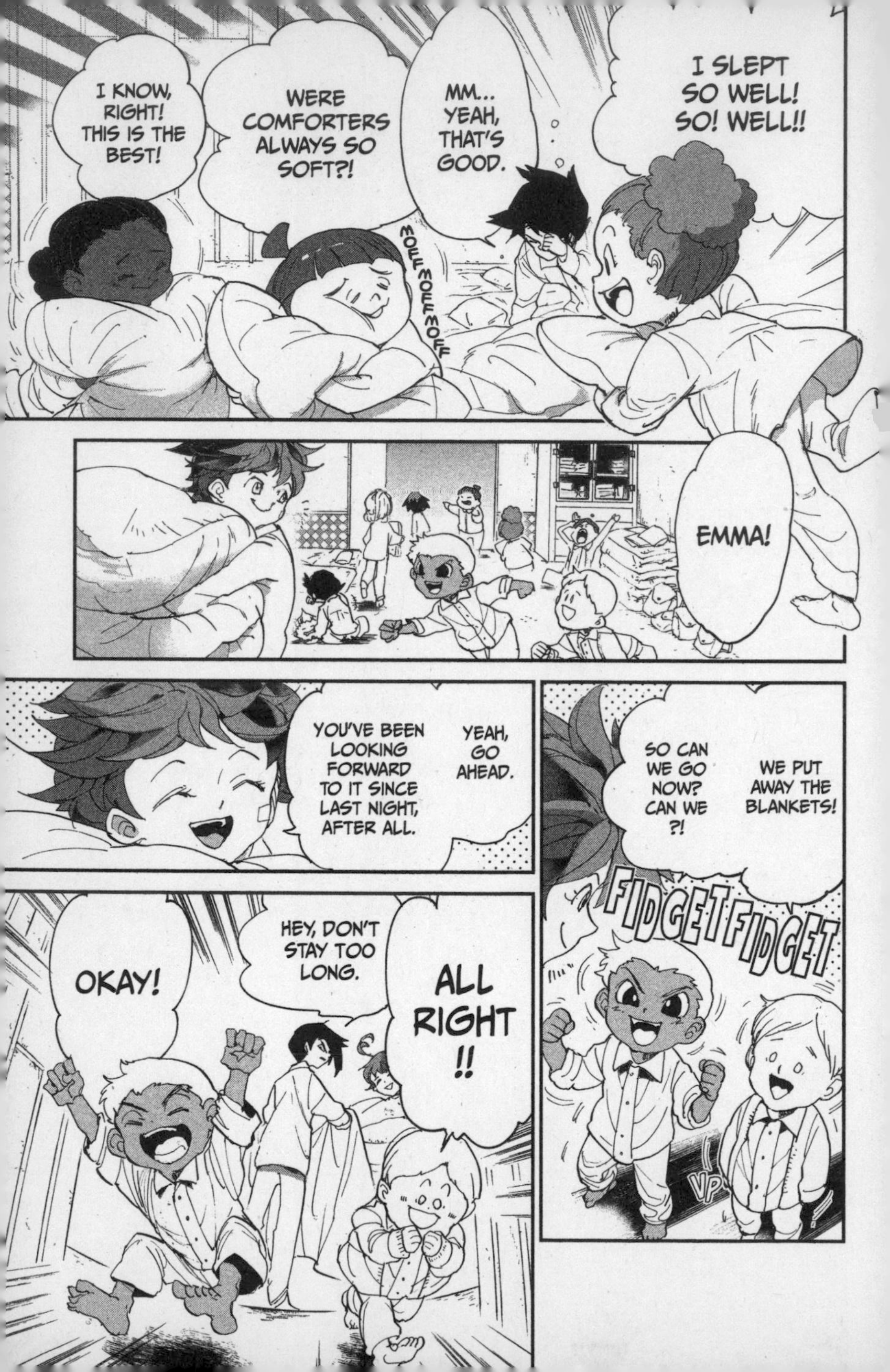
I SLEPT SO WELL! SO! WELL!!
MM... YEAH, THAT'S GOOD.
MOFF MOFF MOFF MOFF
WERE COMFORTERS ALWAYS SO SOFT?!
I KNOW, RIGHT! THIS IS THE BEST!
EMMA!
WE PUT AWAY THE BLANKETS!
SO CAN WE GO NOW? CAN WE ?!
FIDGET FIDGET
VP
YEAH, GO AHEAD.
YOU'VE BEEN LOOKING FORWARD TO IT SINCE LAST NIGHT, AFTER ALL.
ALL RIGHT !!
HEY, DON'T STAY TOO LONG.
OKAY!

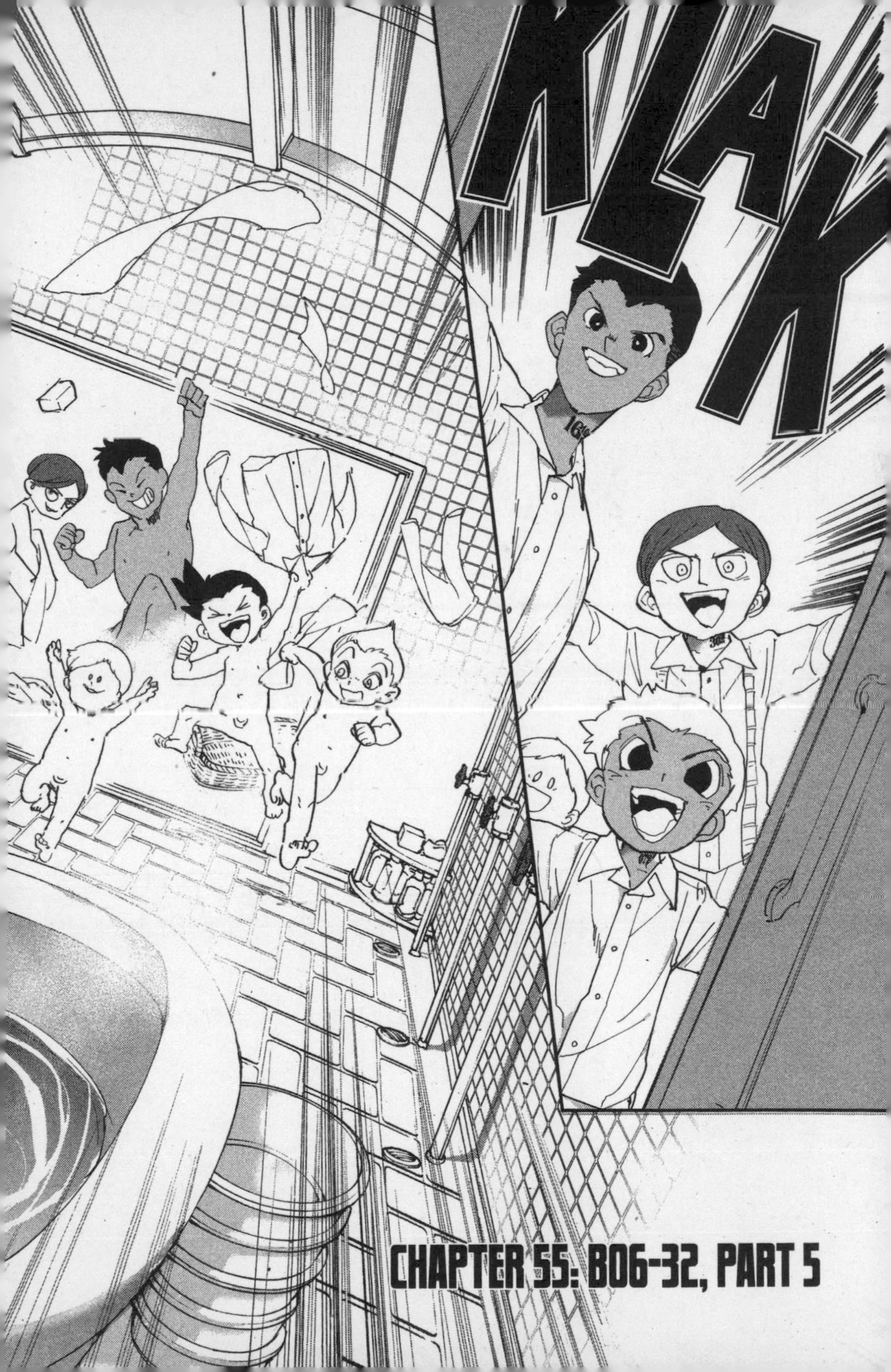
KLAK
CHAPTER 55: B06-32, PART 5

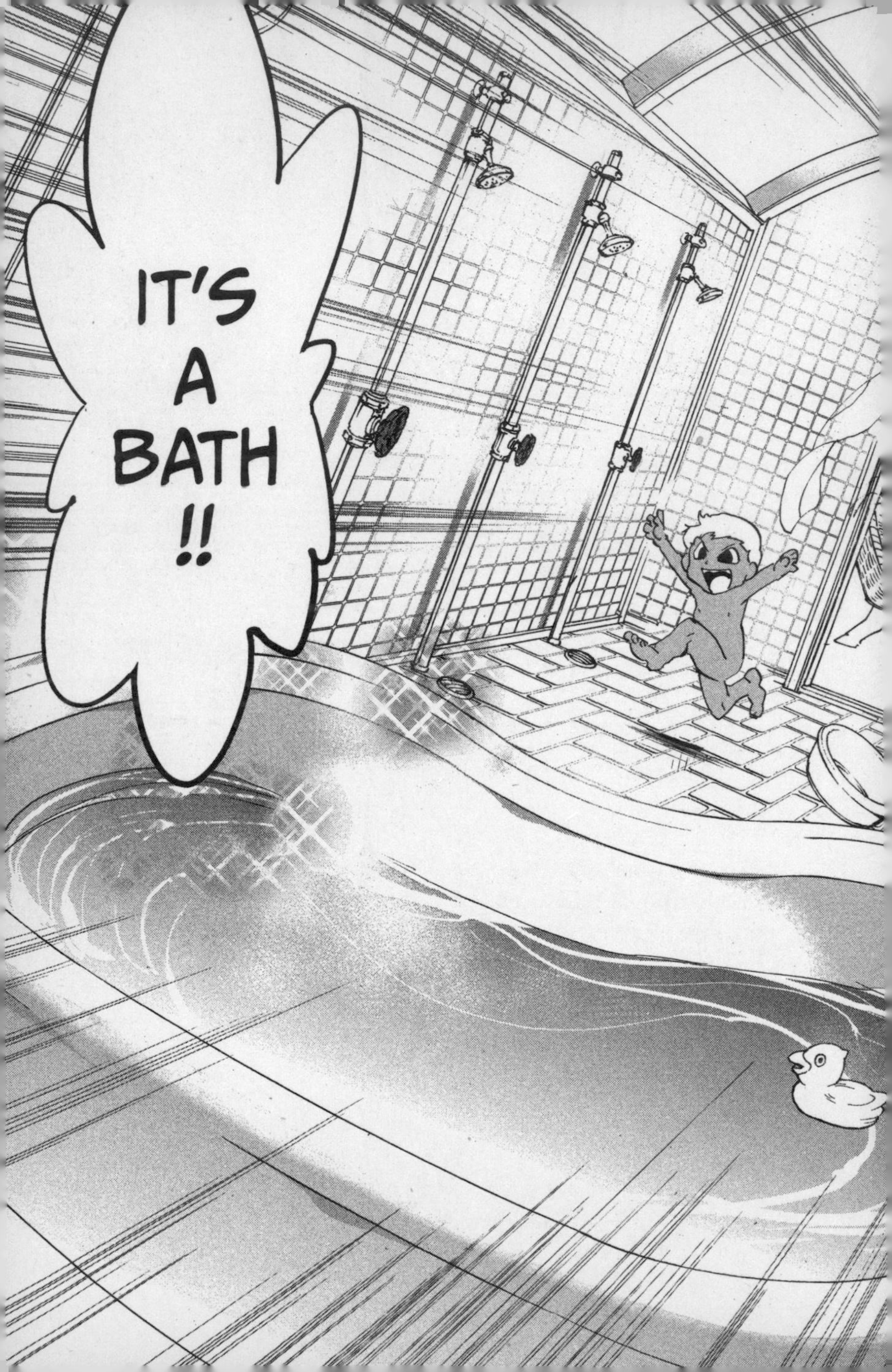
IT'S A BATH!!

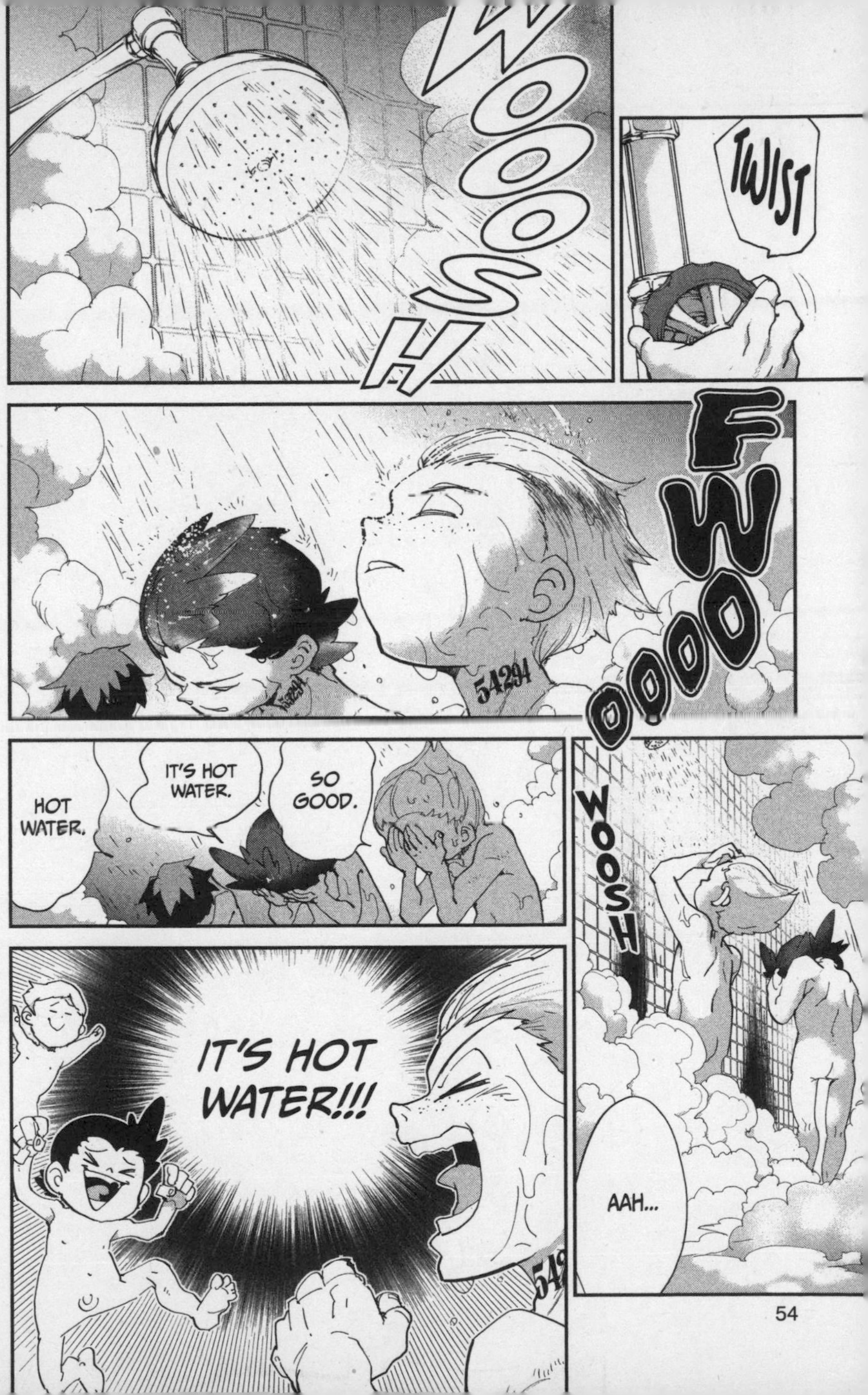
TWIST
WOOOOSH
FWOOOOO
54294
WOOSH
AAH...
SO GOOD.
IT'S HOT WATER.
HOT WATER.
IT'S HOT WATER!!!

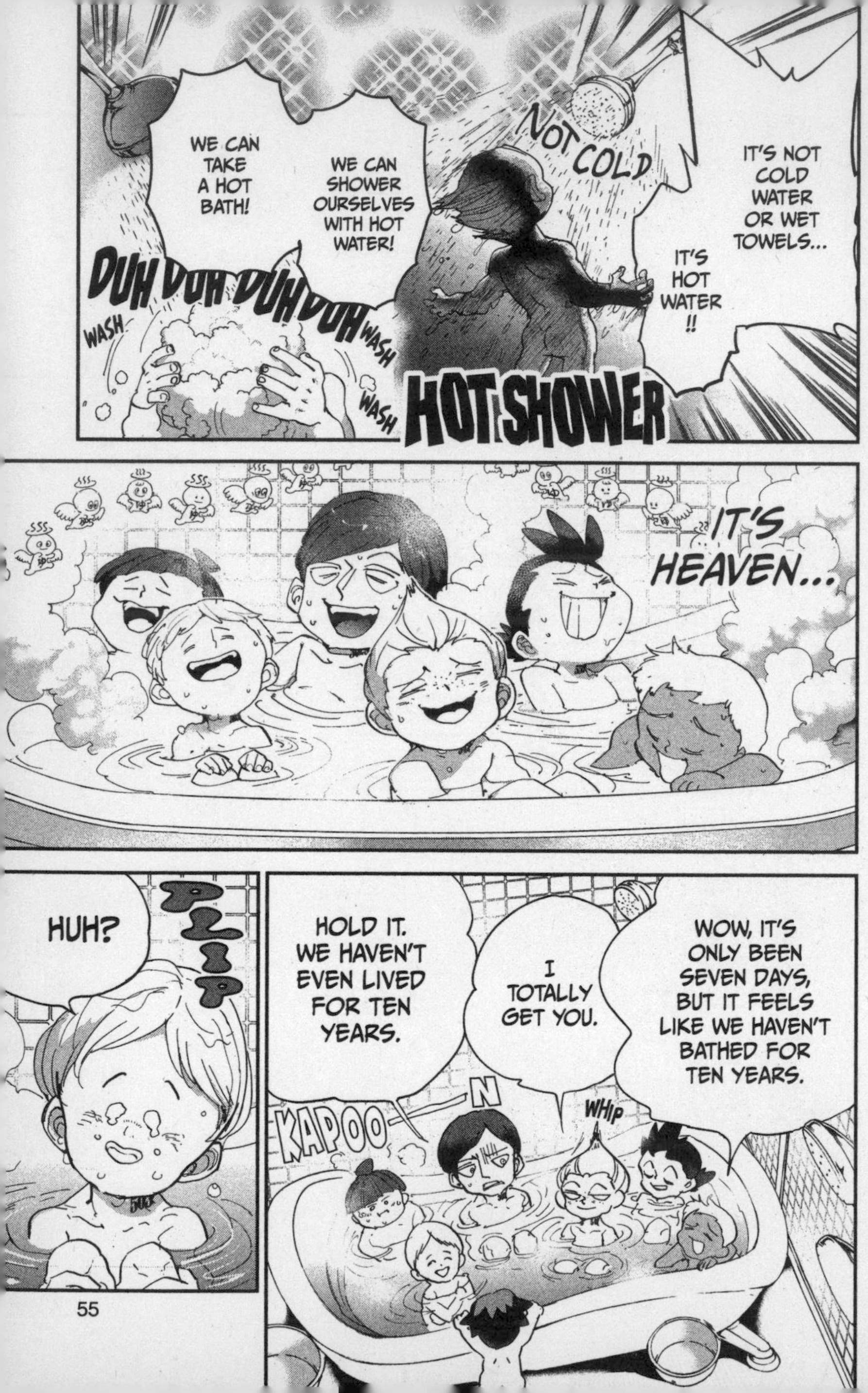
IT'S NOT COLD WATER OR WET TOWELS...
NOT COLD
IT'S HOT WATER !!
WE CAN SHOWER OURSELVES WITH HOT WATER!
WE CAN TAKE A HOT BATH!
HOT SHOWER
WASH
WASH
DUH DUH DUH DUH
WASH
IT'S HEAVEN...
WOW, IT'S ONLY BEEN SEVEN DAYS, BUT IT FEELS LIKE WE HAVEN'T BATHED FOR TEN YEARS.
I TOTALLY GET YOU.
WHIP
HOLD IT. WE HAVEN'T EVEN LIVED FOR TEN YEARS.
KAPOO—N
PLIP
HUH?

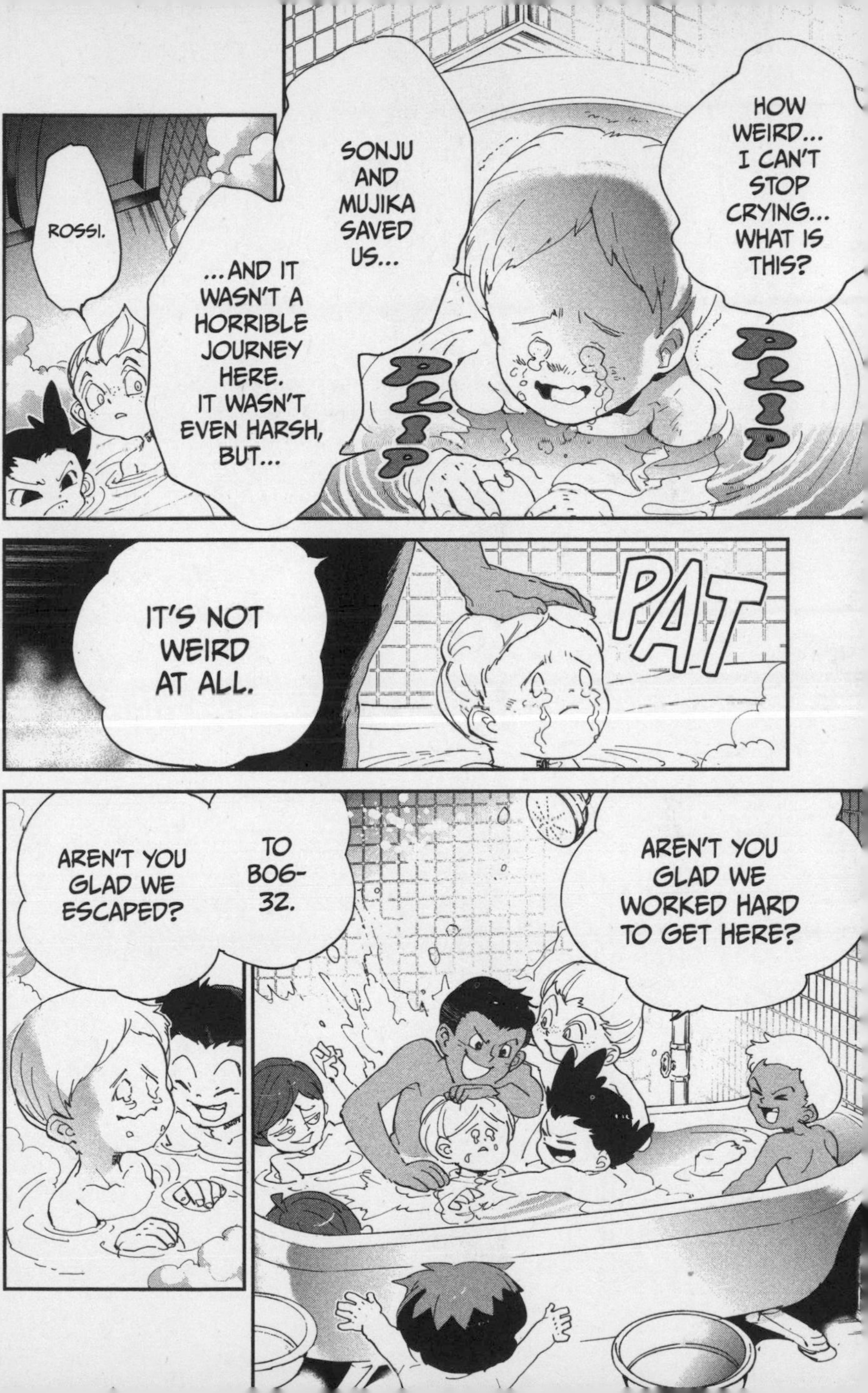
HOW WEIRD... I CAN'T STOP CRYING... WHAT IS THIS?
PLIP
PLIP
SONJU AND MUJIKA SAVED US...
...AND IT WASN'T A HORRIBLE JOURNEY HERE. IT WASN'T EVEN HARSH, BUT...
ROSSI.
PAT
IT'S NOT WEIRD AT ALL.
AREN'T YOU GLAD WE WORKED HARD TO GET HERE?
AREN'T YOU GLAD WE ESCAPED? TO B06-32.

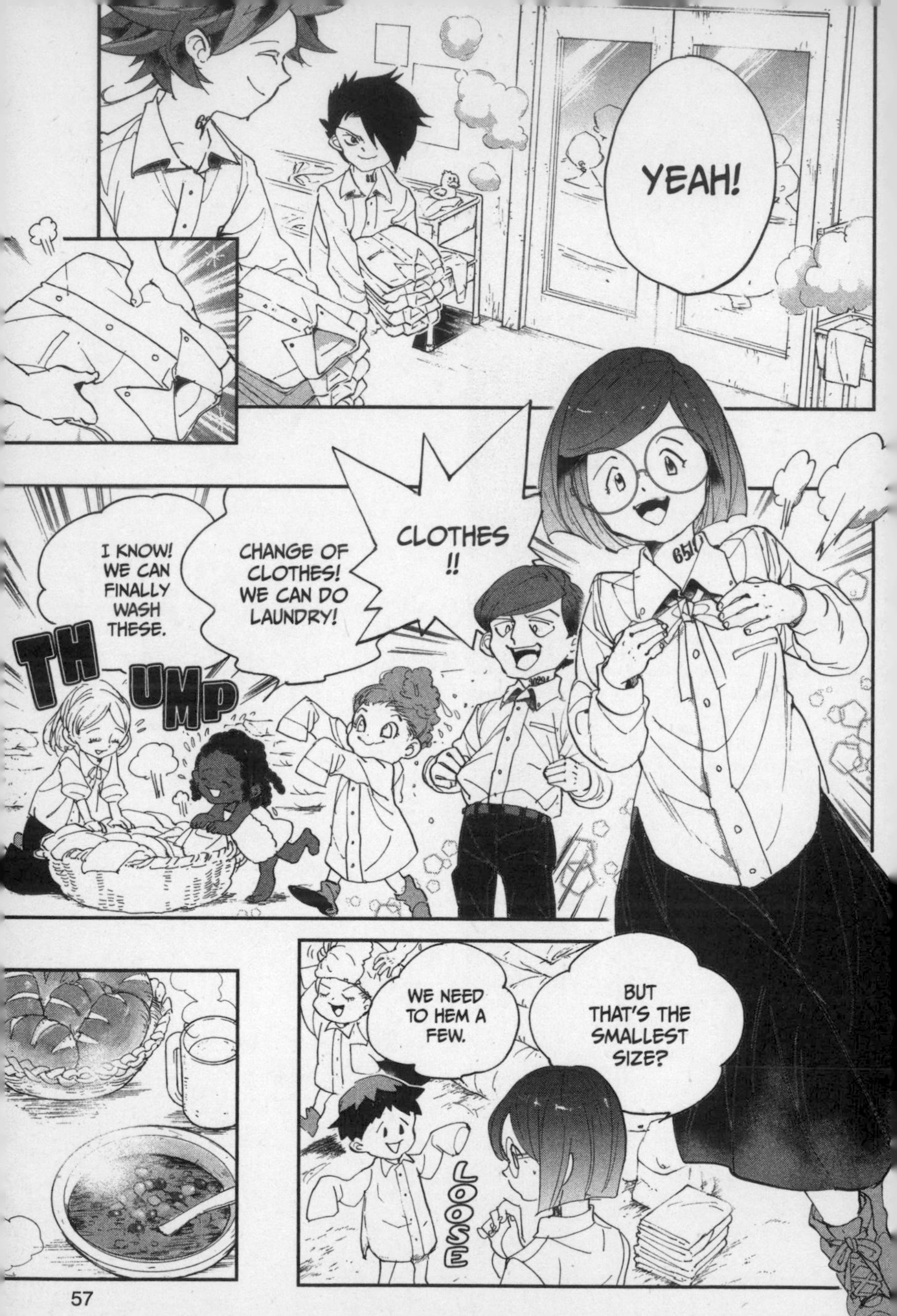
YEAH!
CLOTHES !!
CHANGE OF CLOTHES! WE CAN DO LAUNDRY!
I KNOW! WE CAN FINALLY WASH THESE.
THUMP
BUT THAT'S THE SMALLEST SIZE?
WE NEED TO HEM A FEW.
LOOSE

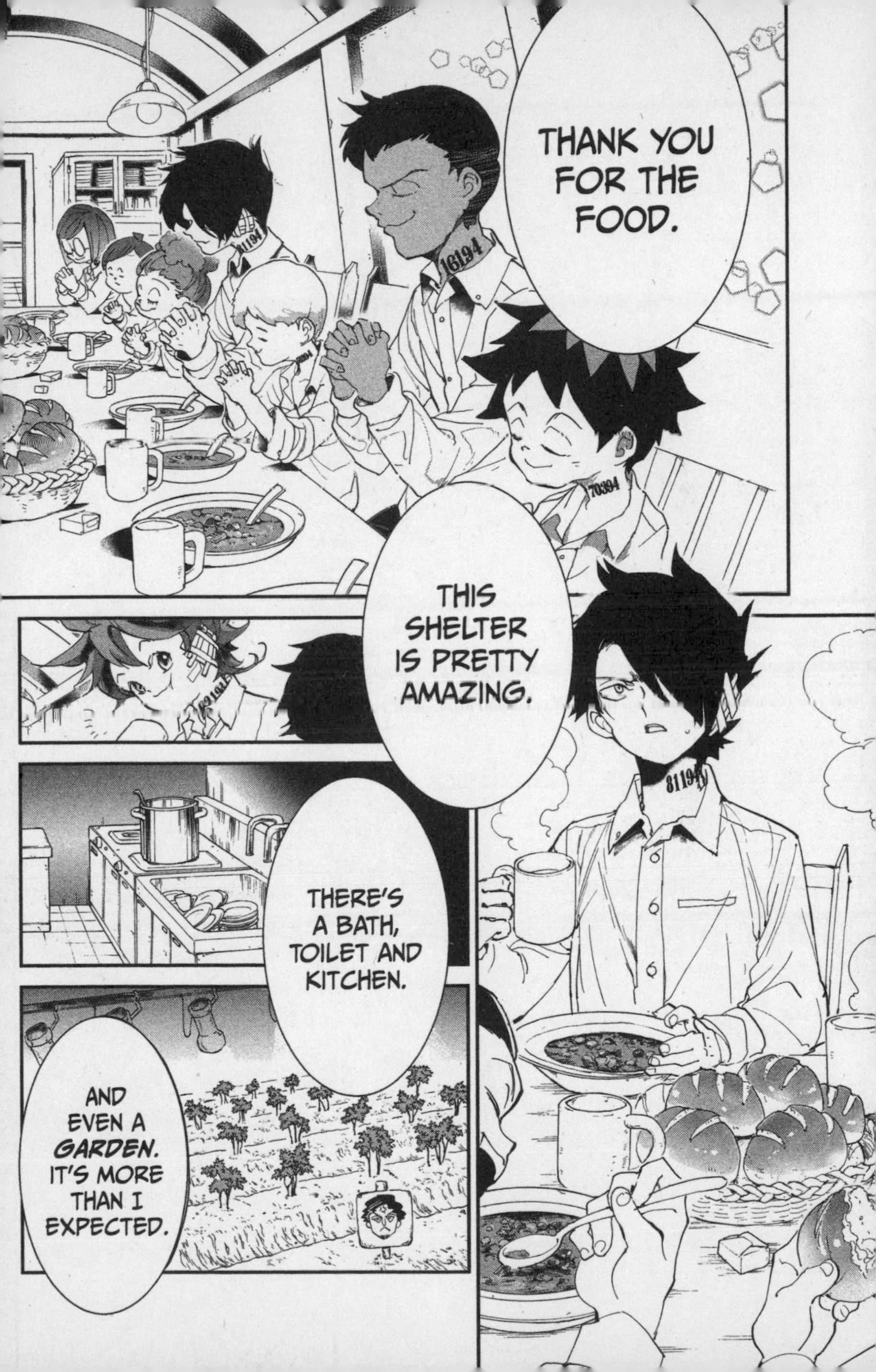
THANK YOU FOR THE FOOD.
THIS SHELTER IS PRETTY AMAZING.
THERE'S A BATH, TOILET AND KITCHEN.
AND EVEN A *GARDEN*. IT'S MORE THAN I EXPECTED.

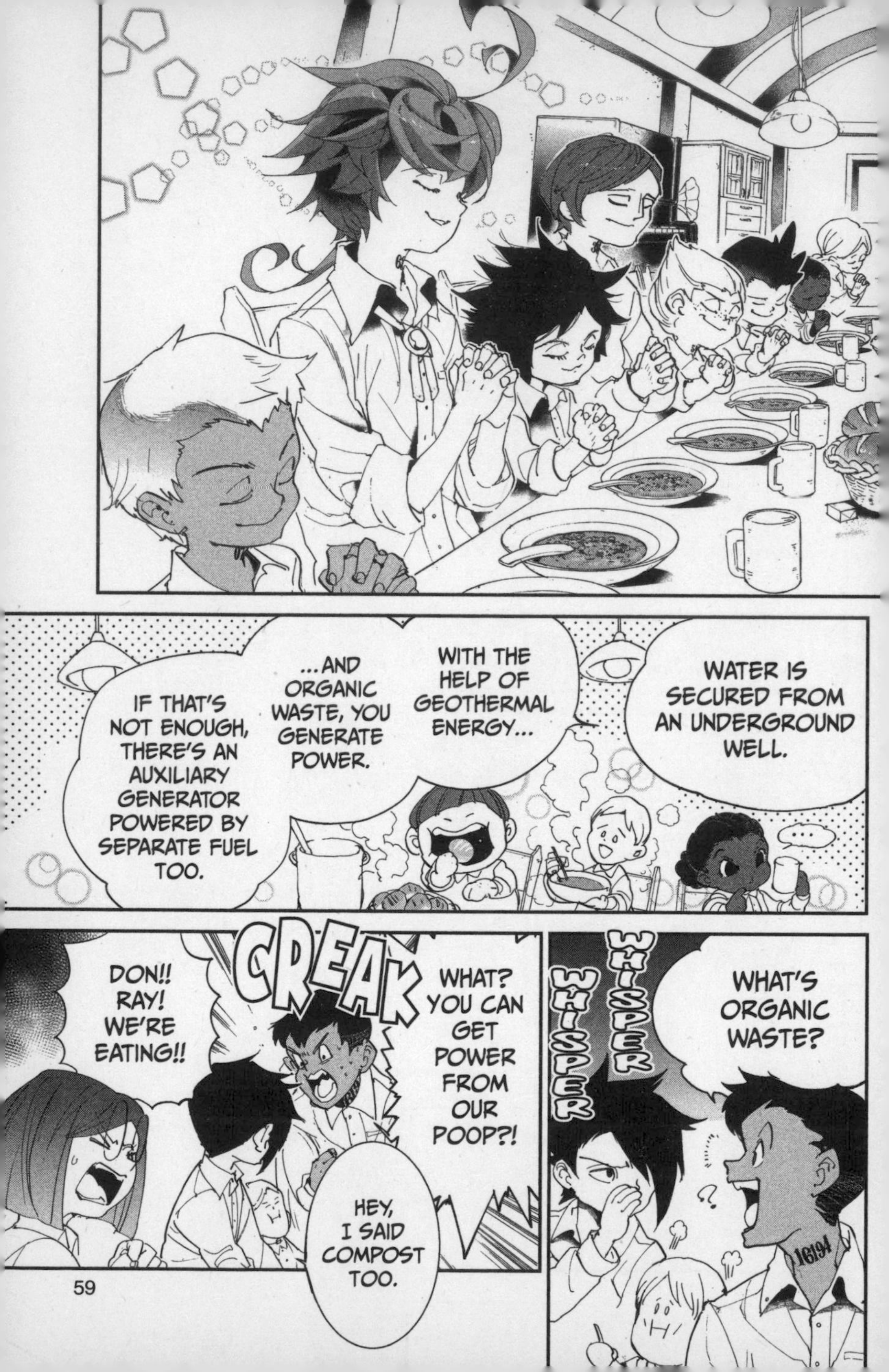
WATER IS SECURED FROM AN UNDERGROUND WELL.
...
WITH THE HELP OF GEOTHERMAL ENERGY...
...AND ORGANIC WASTE, YOU GENERATE POWER.
IF THAT'S NOT ENOUGH, THERE'S AN AUXILIARY GENERATOR POWERED BY SEPARATE FUEL TOO.
WHAT'S ORGANIC WASTE?
WHISPER
WHISPER
WHAT? YOU CAN GET POWER FROM OUR POOP?!
CREAK
DON!! RAY! WE'RE EATING!!
HEY, I SAID COMPOST TOO.

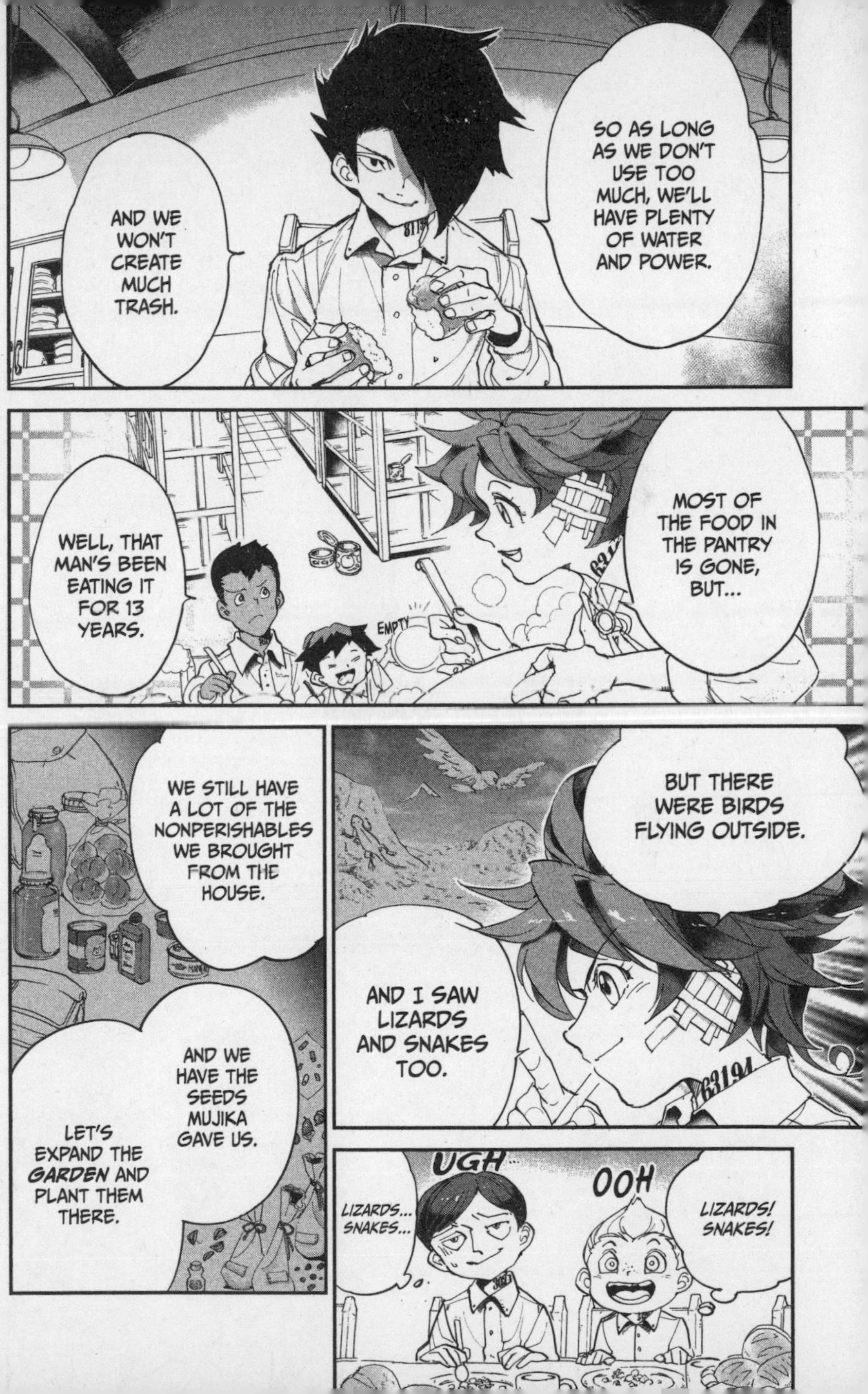
SO AS LONG AS WE DON'T USE TOO MUCH, WE'LL HAVE PLENTY OF WATER AND POWER.
AND WE WON'T CREATE MUCH TRASH.
MOST OF THE FOOD IN THE PANTRY IS GONE, BUT...
EMPTY
WELL, THAT MAN'S BEEN EATING IT FOR 13 YEARS.
BUT THERE WERE BIRDS FLYING OUTSIDE.
AND I SAW LIZARDS AND SNAKES TOO.
OOH
LIZARDS! SNAKES!
UGH...
LIZARDS... SNAKES...
WE STILL HAVE A LOT OF THE NONPERISHABLES WE BROUGHT FROM THE HOUSE.
AND WE HAVE THE SEEDS MUJIKA GAVE US.
LET'S EXPAND THE *GARDEN* AND PLANT THEM THERE.

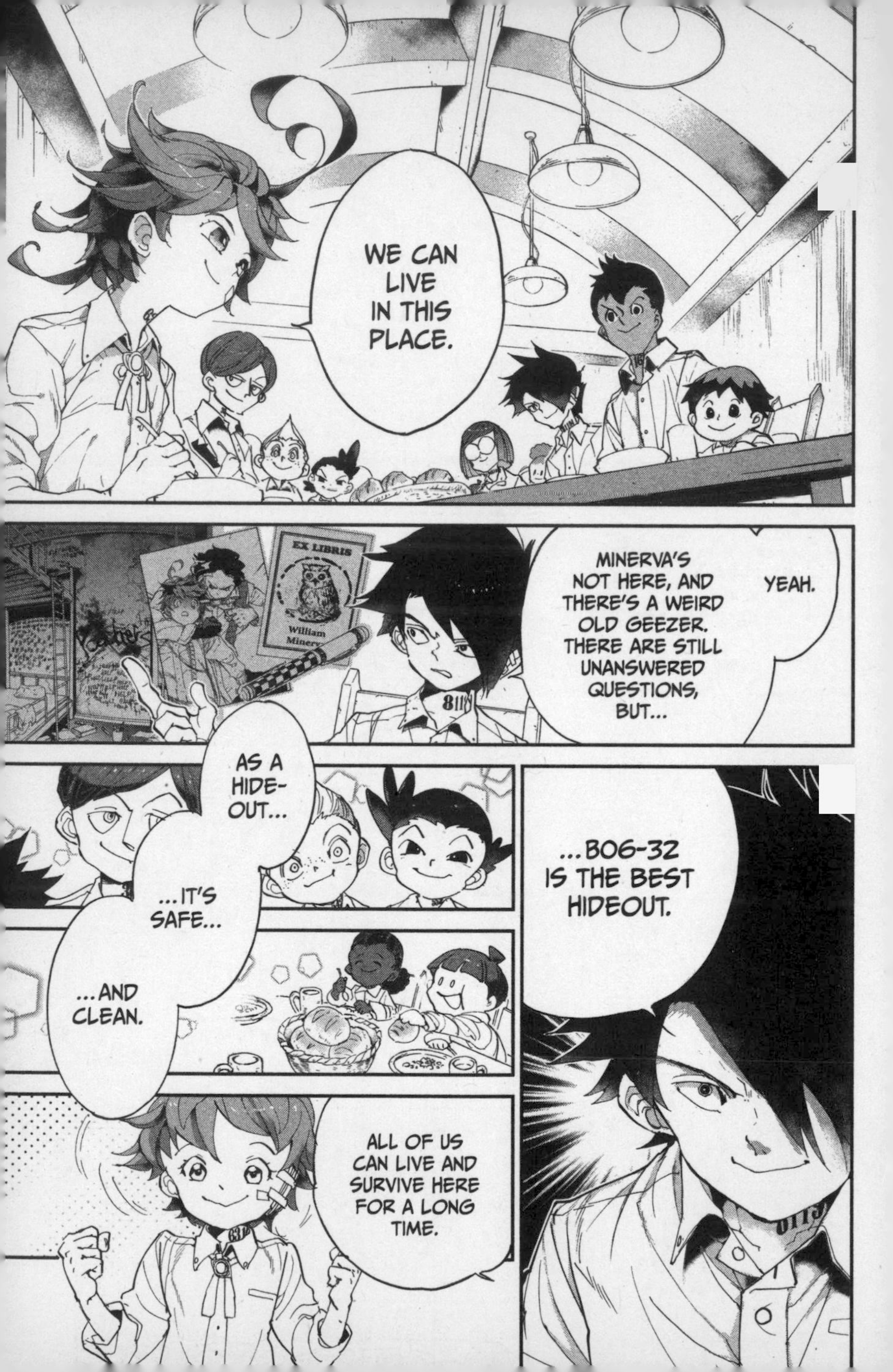
WE CAN LIVE IN THIS PLACE.
YEAH.
MINERVA'S NOT HERE, AND THERE'S A WEIRD OLD GEEZER. THERE ARE STILL UNANSWERED QUESTIONS, BUT...
EX LIBRIS
William Minerva
...B06-32 IS THE BEST HIDEOUT.
AS A HIDE-OUT...
...IT'S SAFE...
...AND CLEAN.
ALL OF US CAN LIVE AND SURVIVE HERE FOR A LONG TIME.

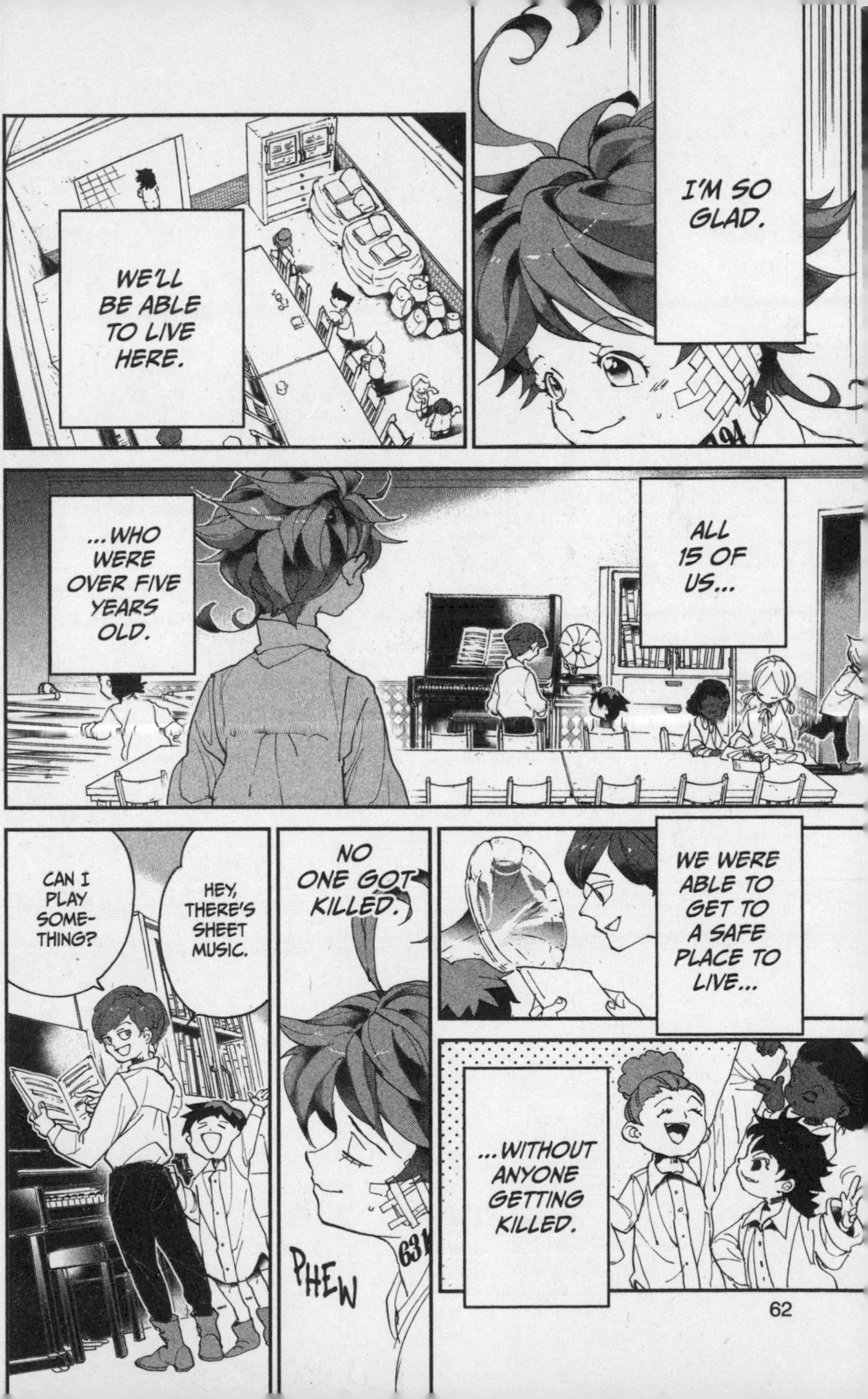
I'M SO GLAD.
WE'LL BE ABLE TO LIVE HERE.
ALL 15 OF US...
...WHO WERE OVER FIVE YEARS OLD.
WE WERE ABLE TO GET TO A SAFE PLACE TO LIVE...
...WITHOUT ANYONE GETTING KILLED.
NO ONE GOT KILLED.
PHEW
HEY, THERE'S SHEET MUSIC.
CAN I PLAY SOMETHING?

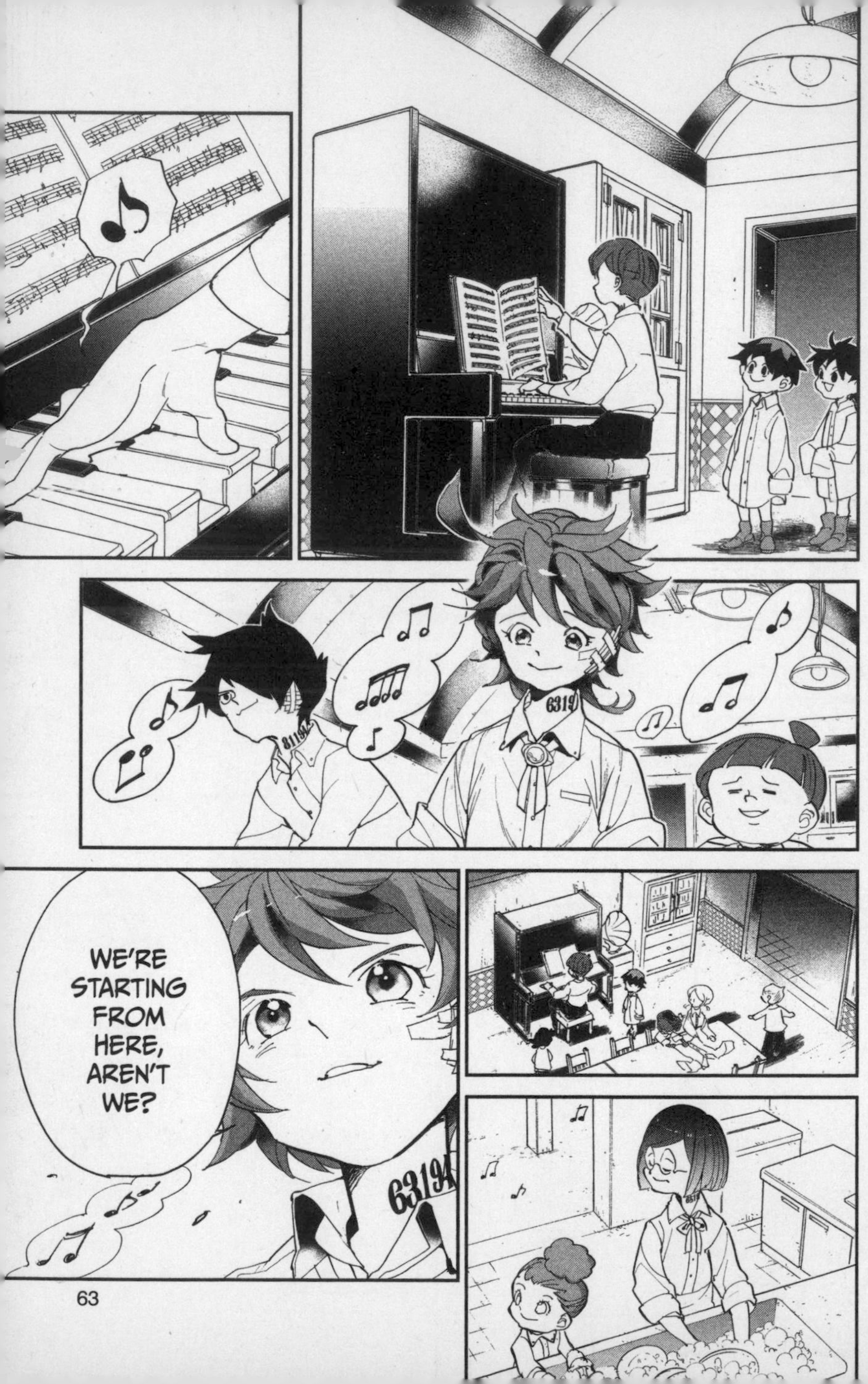
WE'RE STARTING FROM HERE, AREN'T WE?

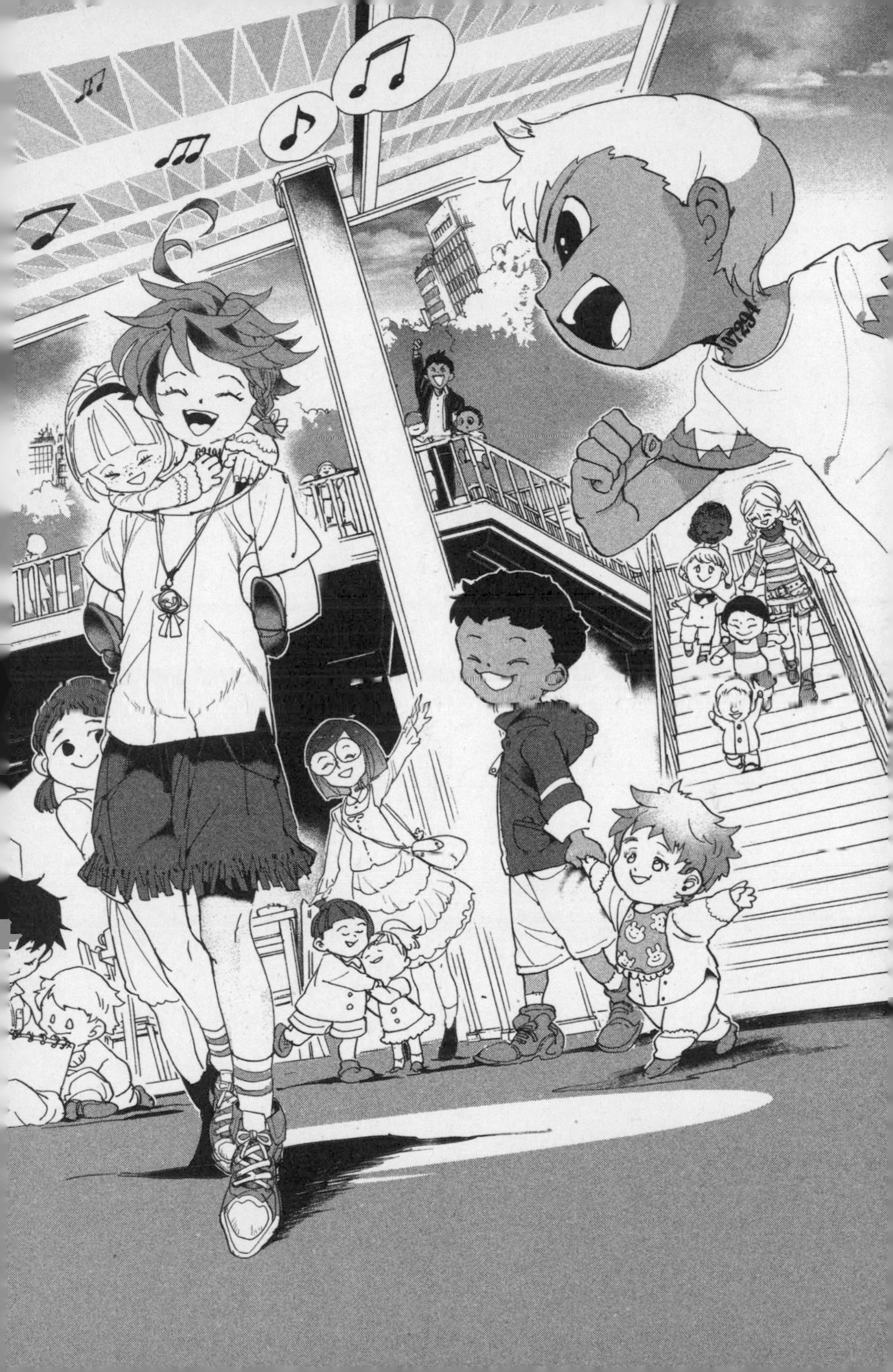

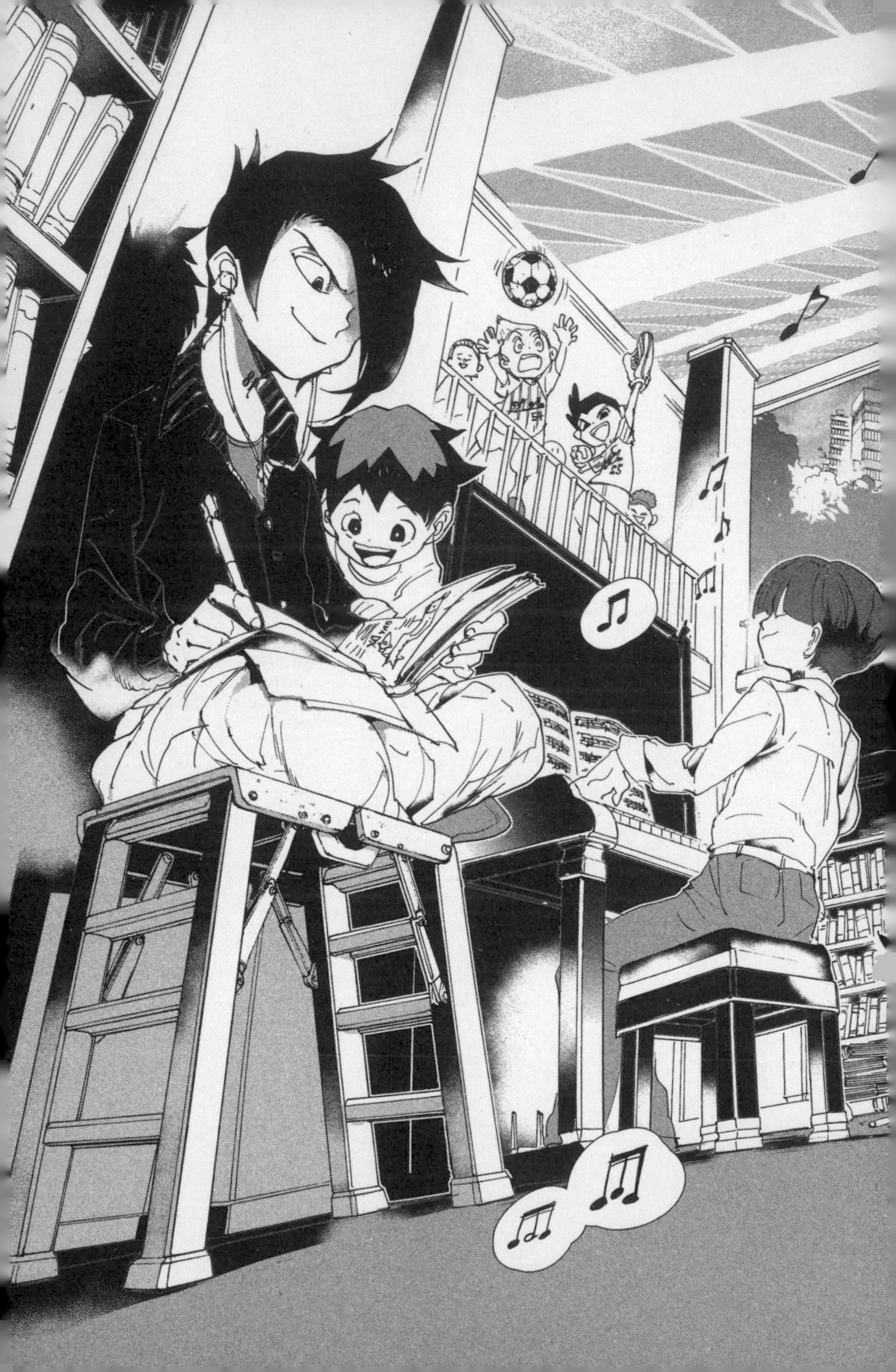

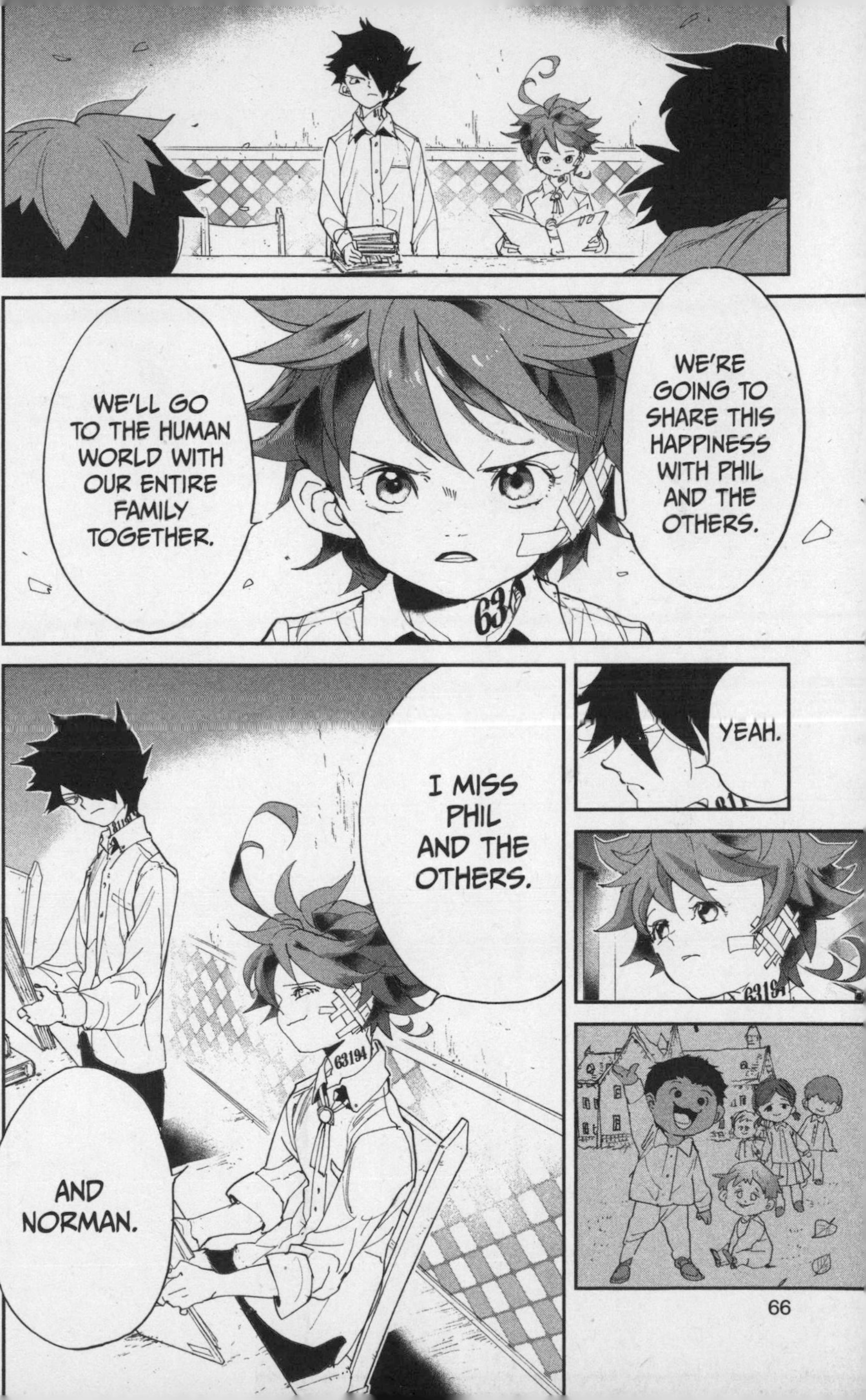
WE'RE GOING TO SHARE THIS HAPPINESS WITH PHIL AND THE OTHERS.
WE'LL GO TO THE HUMAN WORLD WITH OUR ENTIRE FAMILY TOGETHER.
YEAH.
I MISS PHIL AND THE OTHERS.
AND NORMAN.

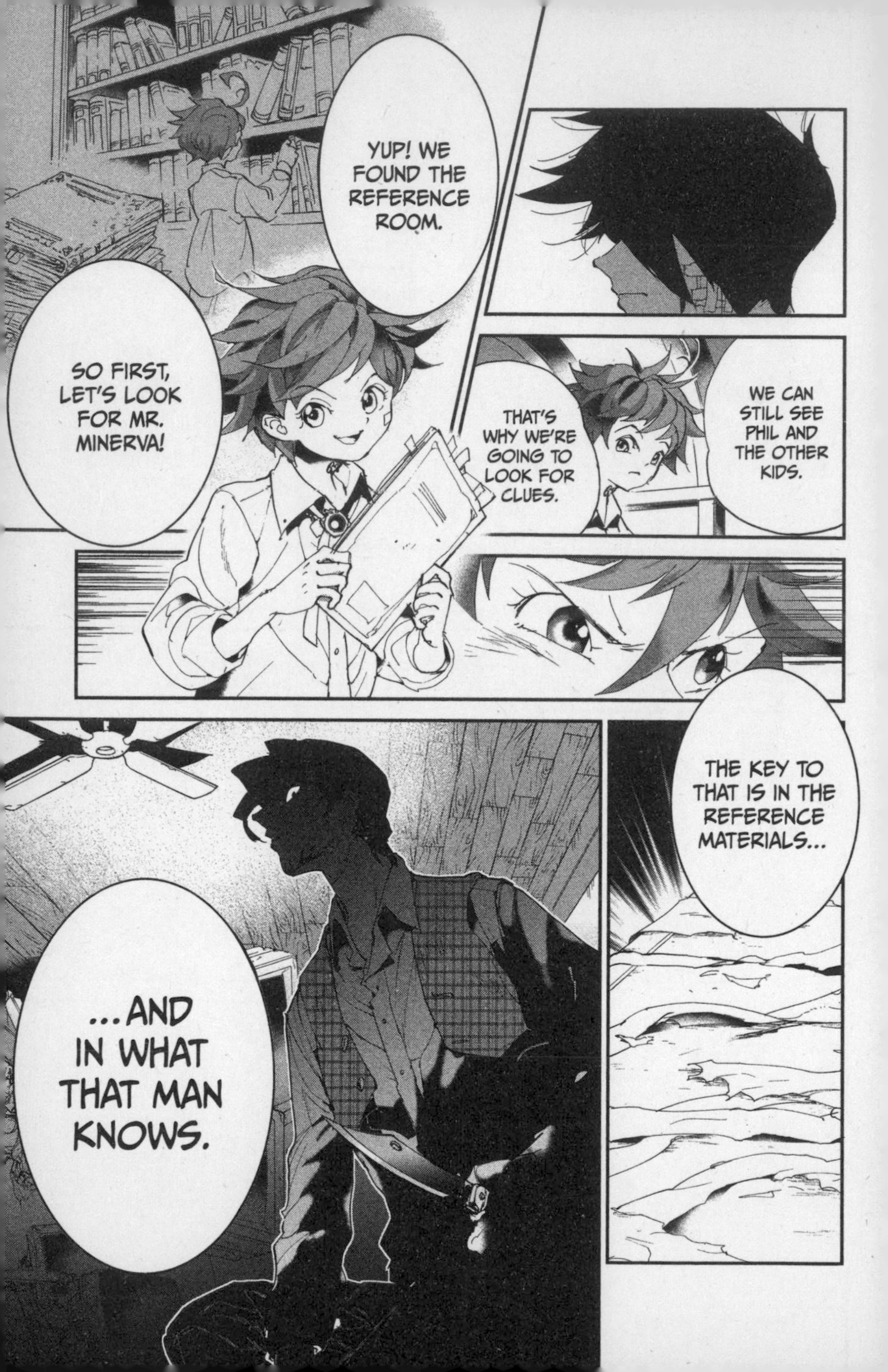
WE CAN STILL SEE PHIL AND THE OTHER KIDS.
THAT'S WHY WE'RE GOING TO LOOK FOR CLUES.
YUP! WE FOUND THE REFERENCE ROOM.
SO FIRST, LET'S LOOK FOR MR. MINERVA!
THE KEY TO THAT IS IN THE REFERENCE MATERIALS...
...AND IN WHAT THAT MAN KNOWS.

THE PROMISED NEVERLAND SIDE SCENE 012

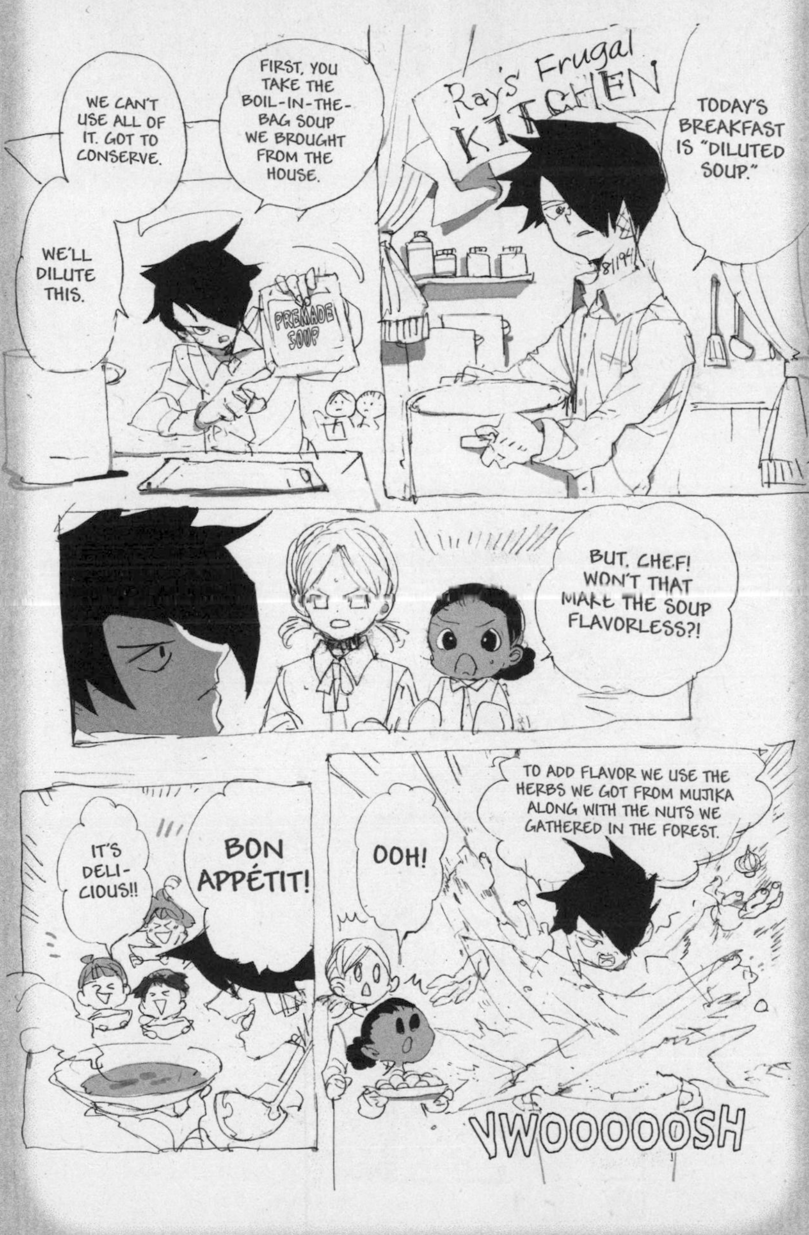
Ray's Frugal KITCHEN
TODAY'S BREAKFAST IS "DILUTED SOUP."
81194
FIRST, YOU TAKE THE BOIL-IN-THE-BAG SOUP WE BROUGHT FROM THE HOUSE.
WE CAN'T USE ALL OF IT. GOT TO CONSERVE.
WE'LL DILUTE THIS.
PREMADE SOUP
BUT, CHEF! WON'T THAT MAKE THE SOUP FLAVORLESS?!
TO ADD FLAVOR WE USE THE HERBS WE GOT FROM MUJIKA ALONG WITH THE NUTS WE GATHERED IN THE FOREST.
OOH!
VWOOOOOOSH
BON APPÉTIT!
IT'S DELI-CIOUS!!

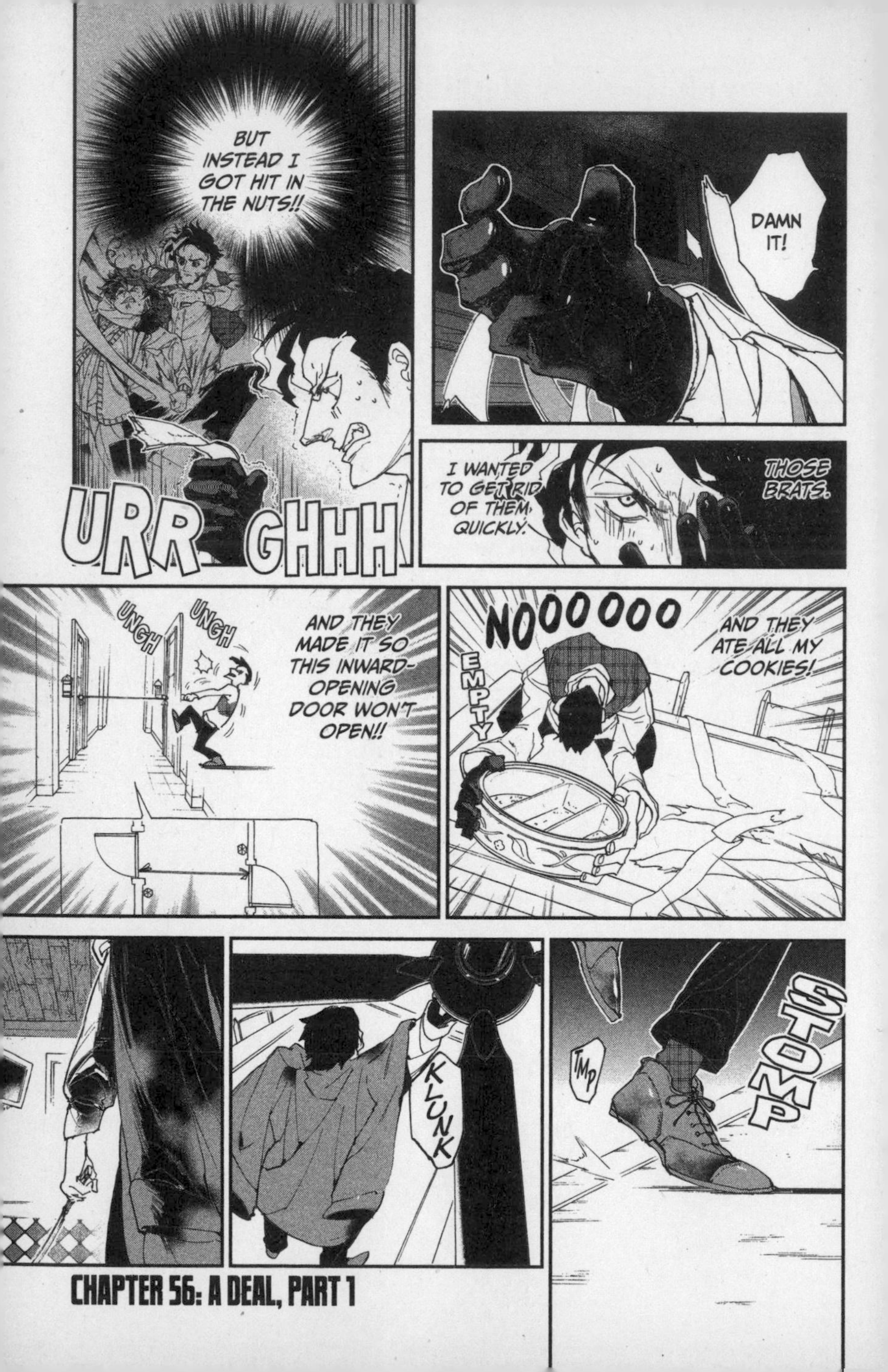
DAMN IT!
THOSE BRATS.
I WANTED TO GET RID OF THEM QUICKLY.
BUT INSTEAD I GOT HIT IN THE NUTS!!
URRGHHH
NOOOOOO
AND THEY ATE ALL MY COOKIES!
EMPTY
AND THEY MADE IT SO THIS INWARD-OPENING DOOR WON'T OPEN!!
UNGH
UNGH
STOMP
TMP
KLUNK

CHAPTER 56: A DEAL, PART 1

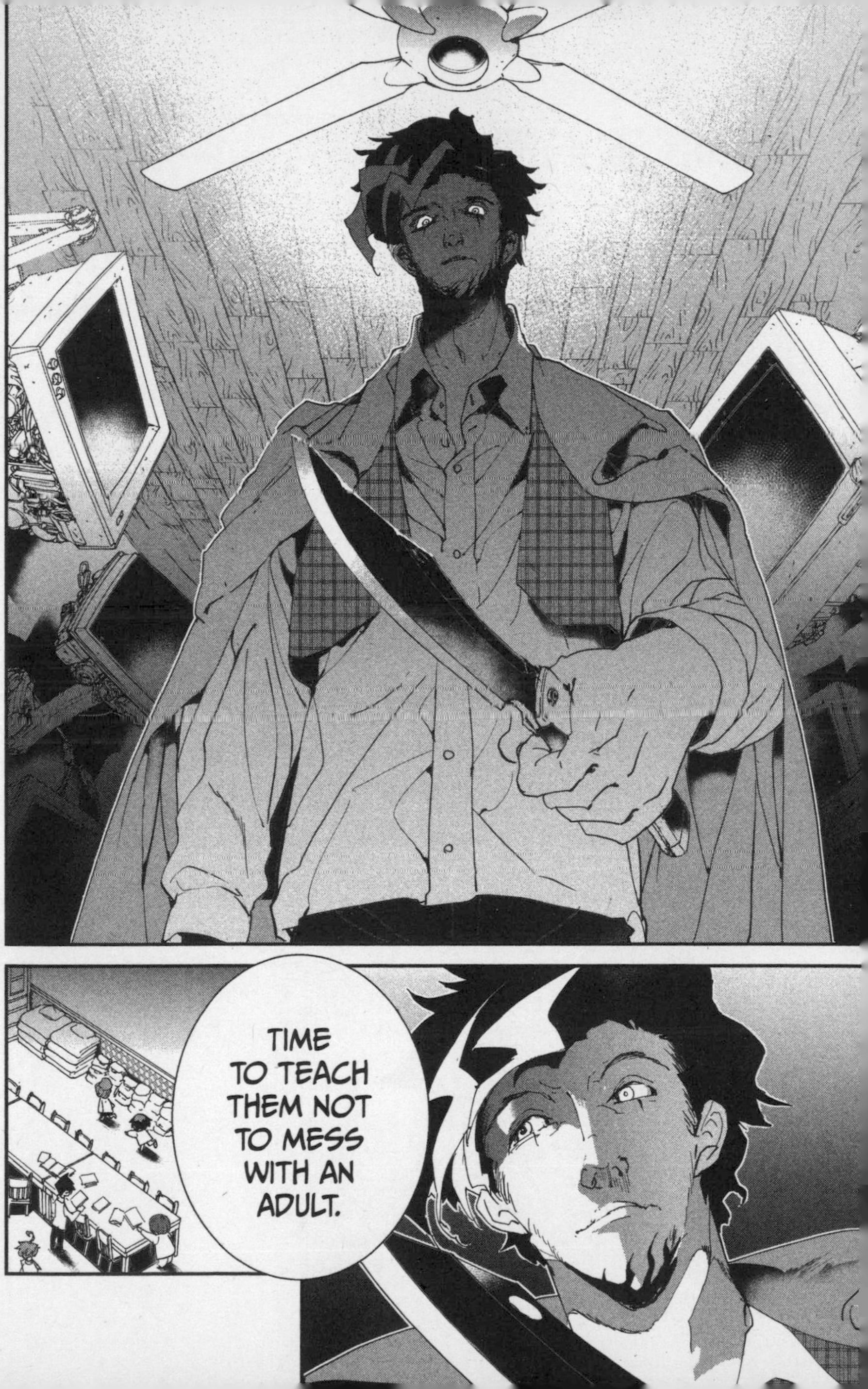
TIME TO TEACH THEM NOT TO MESS WITH AN ADULT.

CHAPTER 56: A DEAL, PART 1

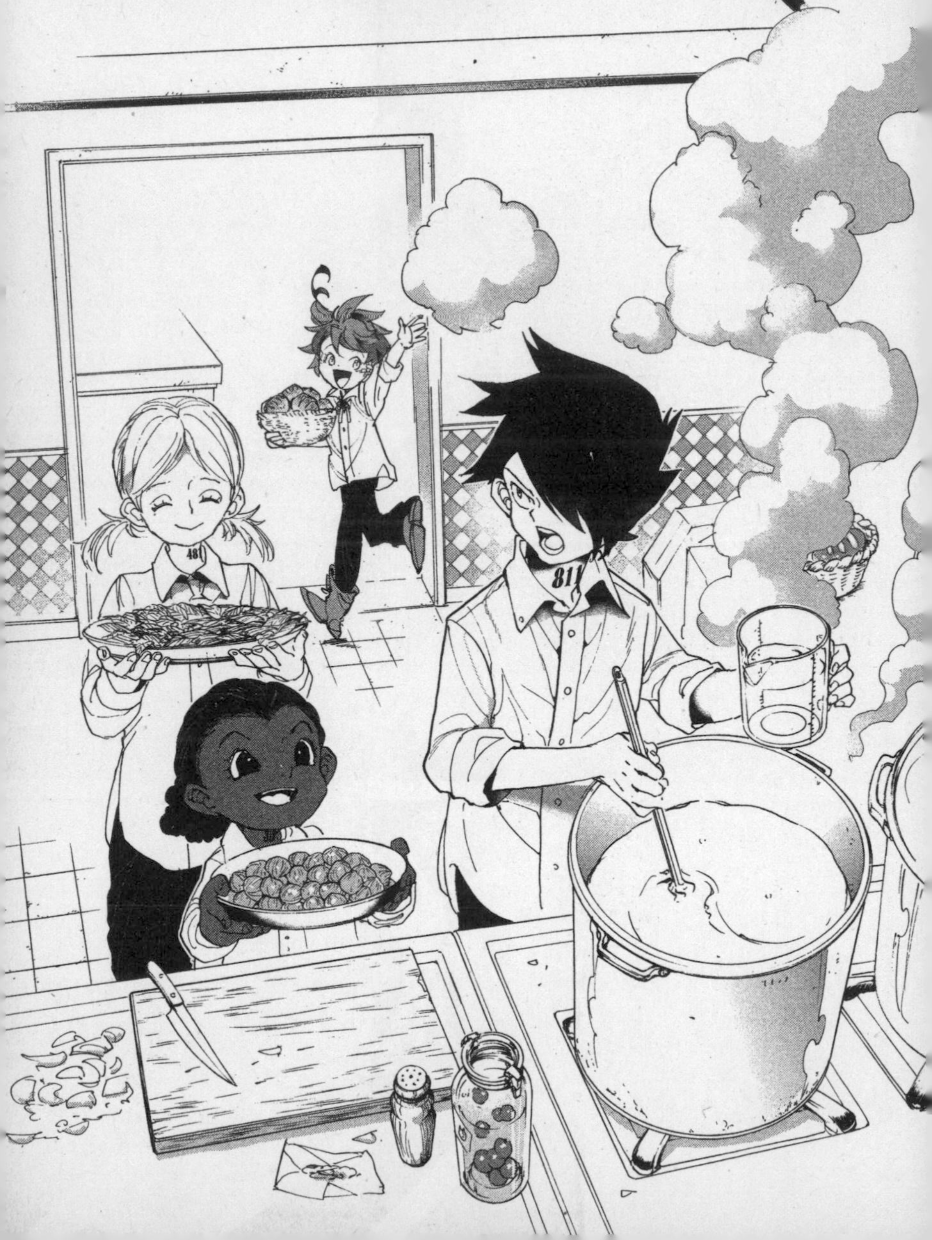

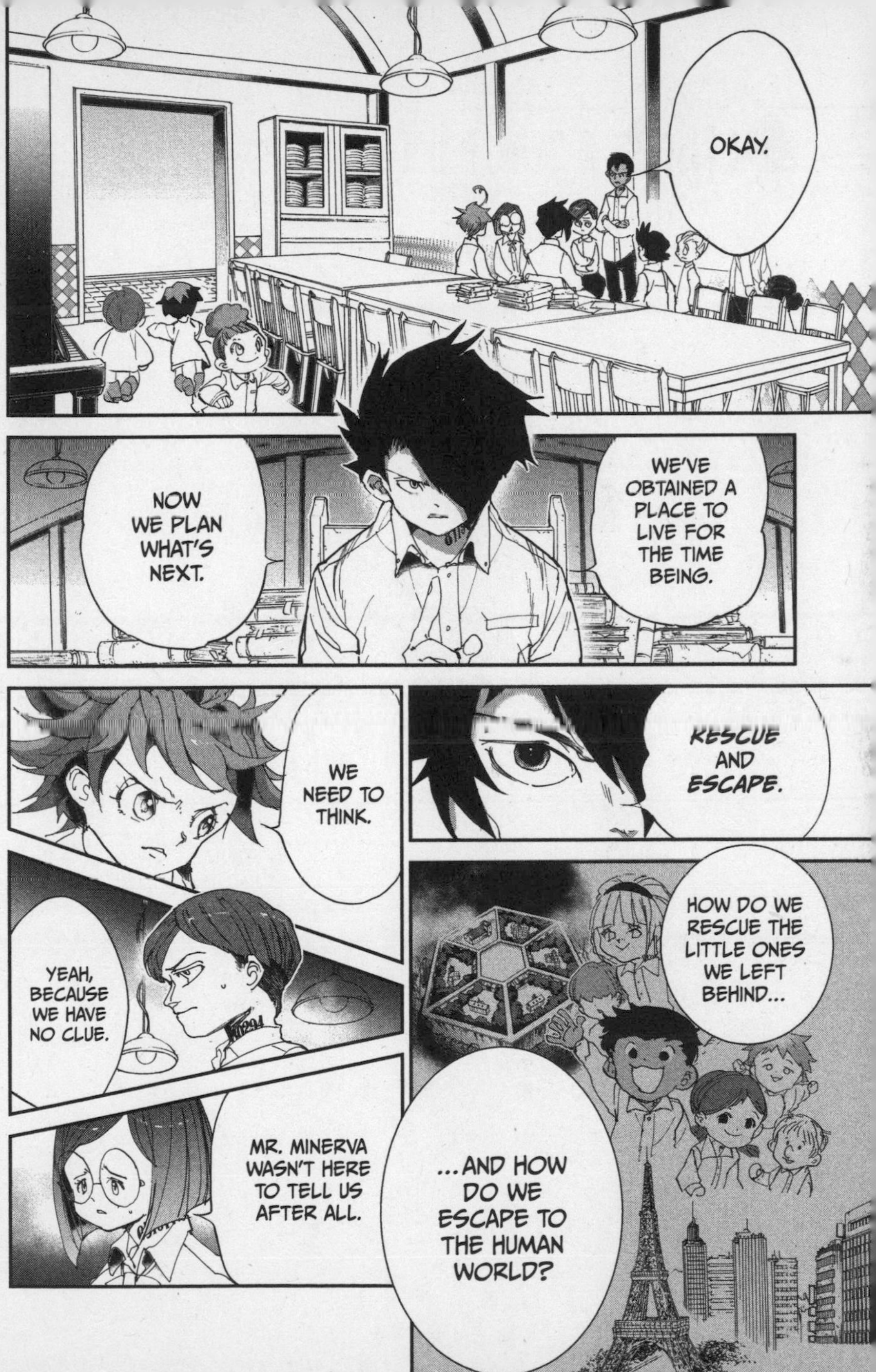
OKAY.
WE'VE OBTAINED A PLACE TO LIVE FOR THE TIME BEING.
NOW WE PLAN WHAT'S NEXT.
RESCUE AND ESCAPE.
HOW DO WE RESCUE THE LITTLE ONES WE LEFT BEHIND...
...AND HOW DO WE ESCAPE TO THE HUMAN WORLD?
WE NEED TO THINK.
YEAH, BECAUSE WE HAVE NO CLUE.
MR. MINERVA WASN'T HERE TO TELL US AFTER ALL.

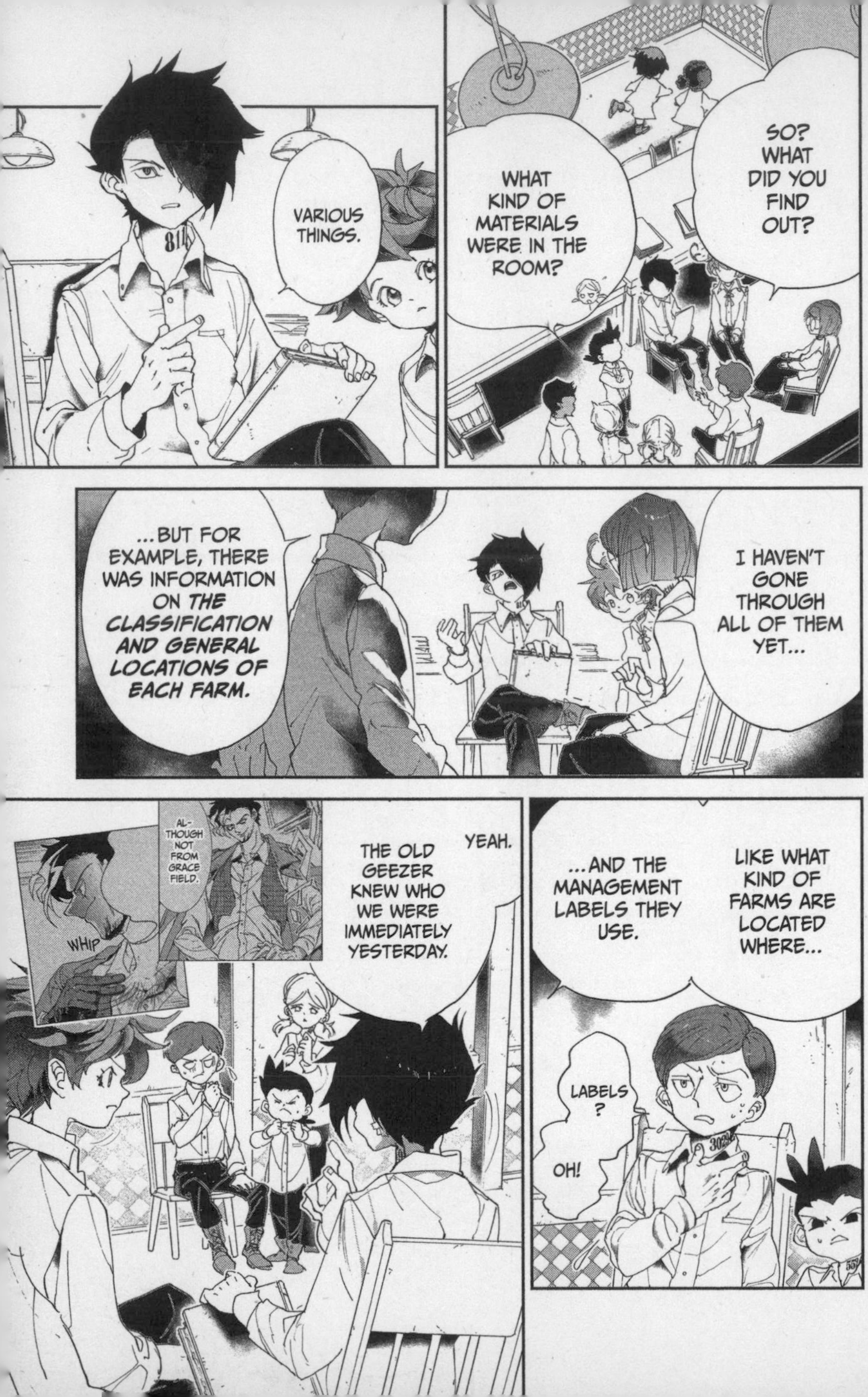
SO? WHAT DID YOU FIND OUT?
WHAT KIND OF MATERIALS WERE IN THE ROOM?
VARIOUS THINGS.
I HAVEN'T GONE THROUGH ALL OF THEM YET...
...BUT FOR EXAMPLE, THERE WAS INFORMATION ON THE CLASSIFICATION AND GENERAL LOCATIONS OF EACH FARM.
LIKE WHAT KIND OF FARMS ARE LOCATED WHERE...
...AND THE MANAGEMENT LABELS THEY USE.
LABELS?
OH!
YEAH.
THE OLD GEEZER KNEW WHO WE WERE IMMEDIATELY YESTERDAY.
AL-THOUGH NOT FROM GRACE FIELD.
WHIP

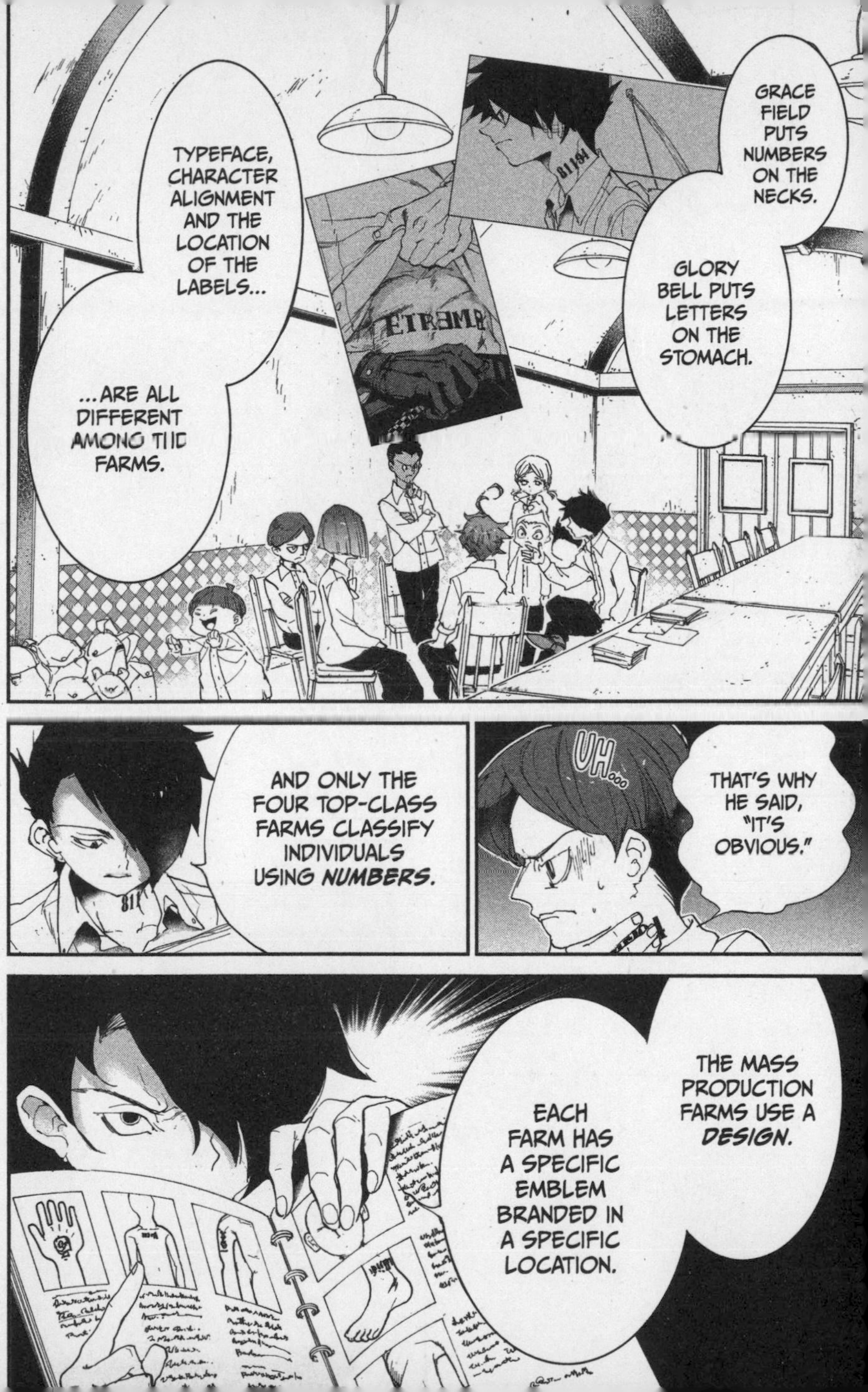
GRACE FIELD PUTS NUMBERS ON THE NECKS.
GLORY BELL PUTS LETTERS ON THE STOMACH.
TYPEFACE, CHARACTER ALIGNMENT AND THE LOCATION OF THE LABELS...
...ARE ALL DIFFERENT AMONG THE FARMS.
UH...
THAT'S WHY HE SAID, "IT'S OBVIOUS."
AND ONLY THE FOUR TOP-CLASS FARMS CLASSIFY INDIVIDUALS USING *NUMBERS*.
THE MASS PRODUCTION FARMS USE A *DESIGN*.
EACH FARM HAS A SPECIFIC EMBLEM BRANDED IN A SPECIFIC LOCATION.

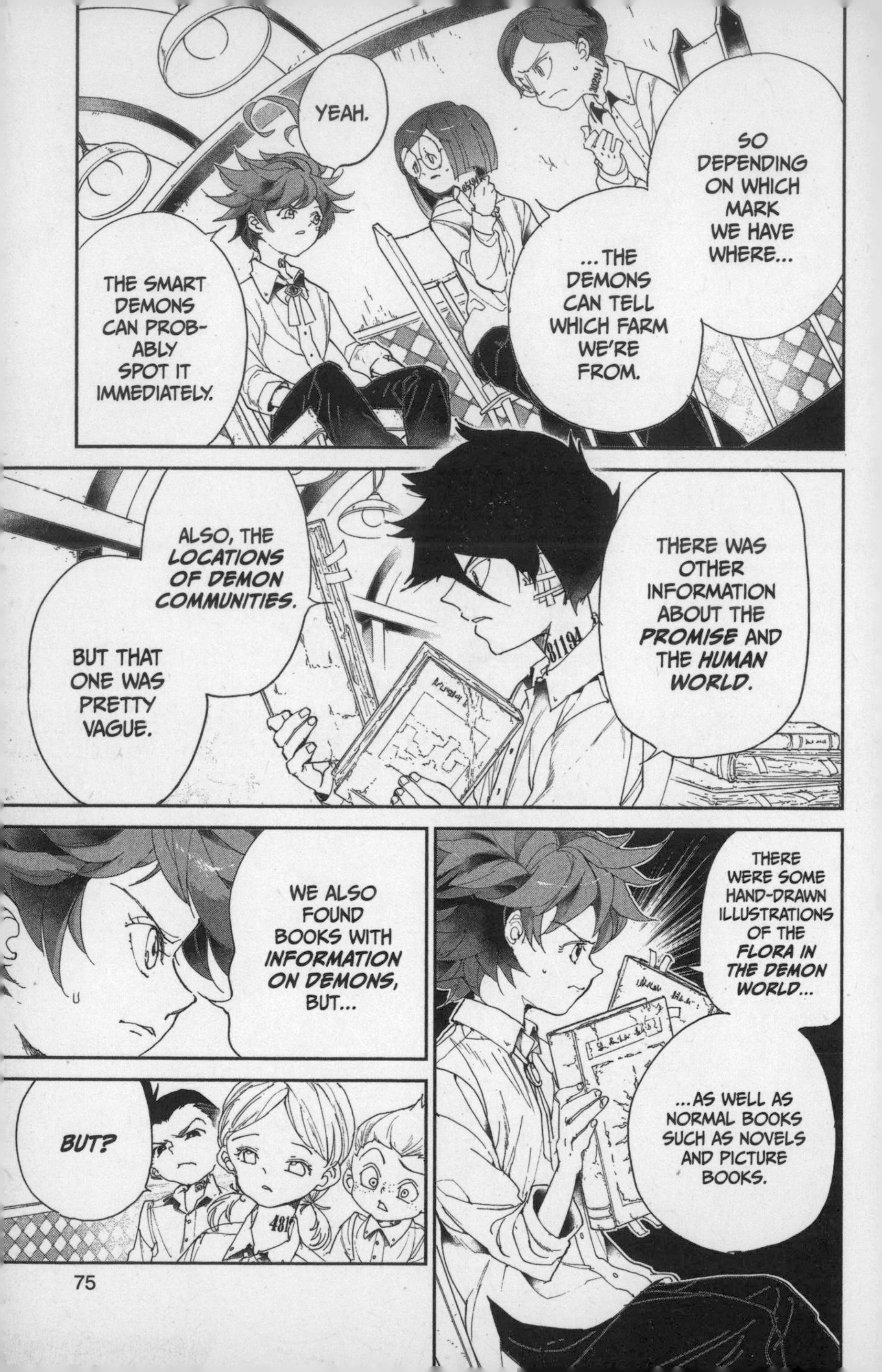
SO DEPENDING ON WHICH MARK WE HAVE WHERE...
...THE DEMONS CAN TELL WHICH FARM WE'RE FROM.
YEAH.
THE SMART DEMONS CAN PROB-ABLY SPOT IT IMMEDIATELY.
THERE WAS OTHER INFORMATION ABOUT THE *PROMISE* AND THE *HUMAN WORLD*.
ALSO, THE *LOCATIONS OF DEMON COMMUNITIES*.
BUT THAT ONE WAS PRETTY VAGUE.
THERE WERE SOME HAND-DRAWN ILLUSTRATIONS OF THE *FLORA IN THE DEMON WORLD*...
...AS WELL AS NORMAL BOOKS SUCH AS NOVELS AND PICTURE BOOKS.
WE ALSO FOUND BOOKS WITH *INFORMATION ON DEMONS*, BUT...
BUT?

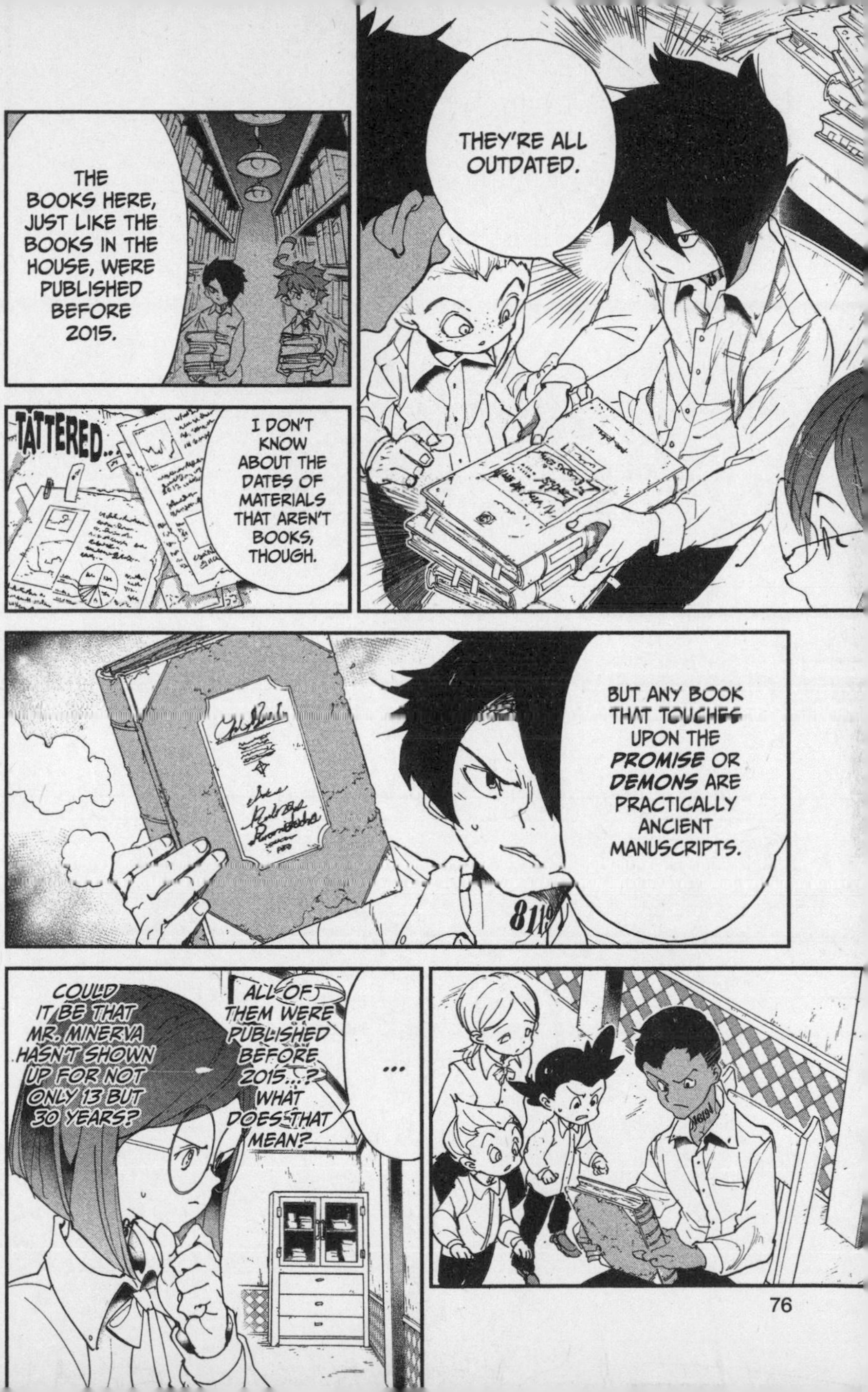

THEY'RE ALL OUTDATED.
THE BOOKS HERE, JUST LIKE THE BOOKS IN THE HOUSE, WERE PUBLISHED BEFORE 2015.
I DON'T KNOW ABOUT THE DATES OF MATERIALS THAT AREN'T BOOKS, THOUGH.
TATTERED...
BUT ANY BOOK THAT TOUCHES UPON THE PROMISE OR DEMONS ARE PRACTICALLY ANCIENT MANUSCRIPTS.
...
ALL OF THEM WERE PUBLISHED BEFORE 2015...? WHAT DOES THAT MEAN?
COULD IT BE THAT MR. MINERVA HASN'T SHOWN UP FOR NOT ONLY 13 BUT 30 YEARS?

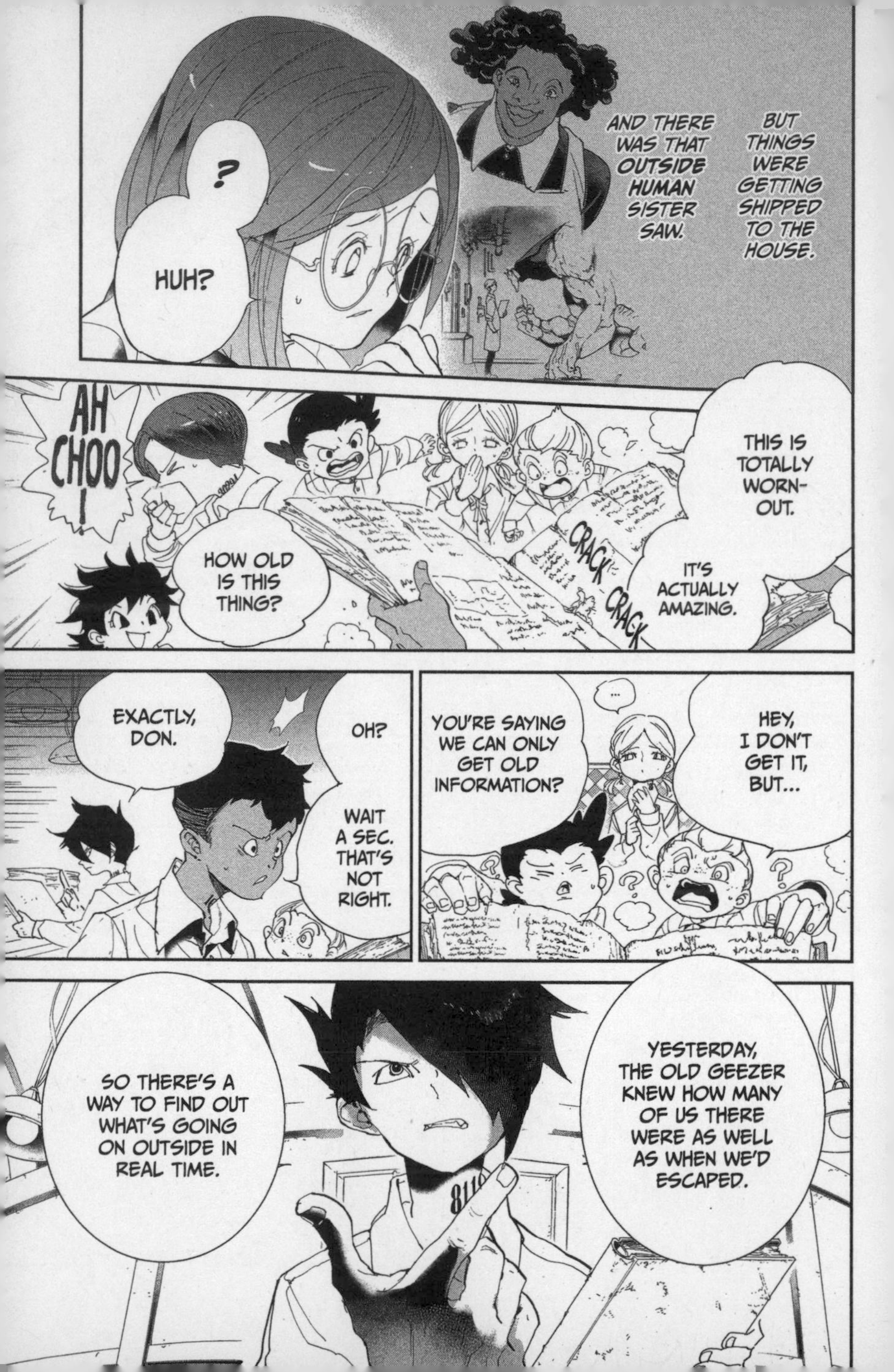
BUT THINGS WERE GETTING SHIPPED TO THE HOUSE.
AND THERE WAS THAT OUTSIDE HUMAN SISTER SAW.
?
HUH?
THIS IS TOTALLY WORN-OUT.
IT'S ACTUALLY AMAZING.
CRACK
CRACK
HOW OLD IS THIS THING?
AH CHOO!
HEY, I DON'T GET IT, BUT...
...
YOU'RE SAYING WE CAN ONLY GET OLD INFORMATION?
EXACTLY, DON.
OH?
WAIT A SEC. THAT'S NOT RIGHT.
YESTERDAY, THE OLD GEEZER KNEW HOW MANY OF US THERE WERE AS WELL AS WHEN WE'D ESCAPED.
SO THERE'S A WAY TO FIND OUT WHAT'S GOING ON OUTSIDE IN REAL TIME.

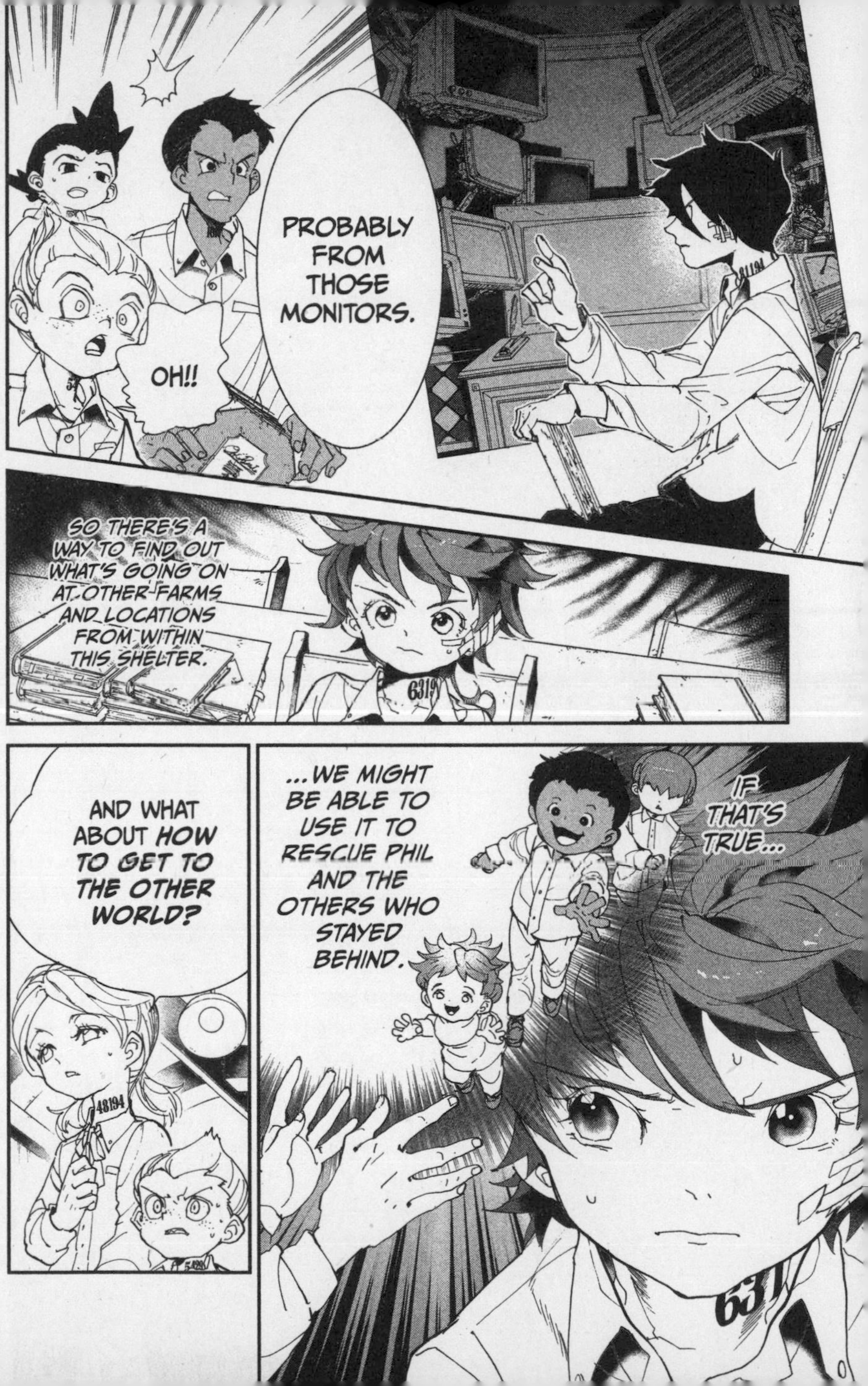
PROBABLY FROM THOSE MONITORS.
OH!!
SO THERE'S A WAY TO FIND OUT WHAT'S GOING ON AT OTHER FARMS AND LOCATIONS FROM WITHIN THIS SHELTER.
IF THAT'S TRUE...
...WE MIGHT BE ABLE TO USE IT TO RESCUE PHIL AND THE OTHERS WHO STAYED BEHIND.
AND WHAT ABOUT HOW TO GET TO THE OTHER WORLD?

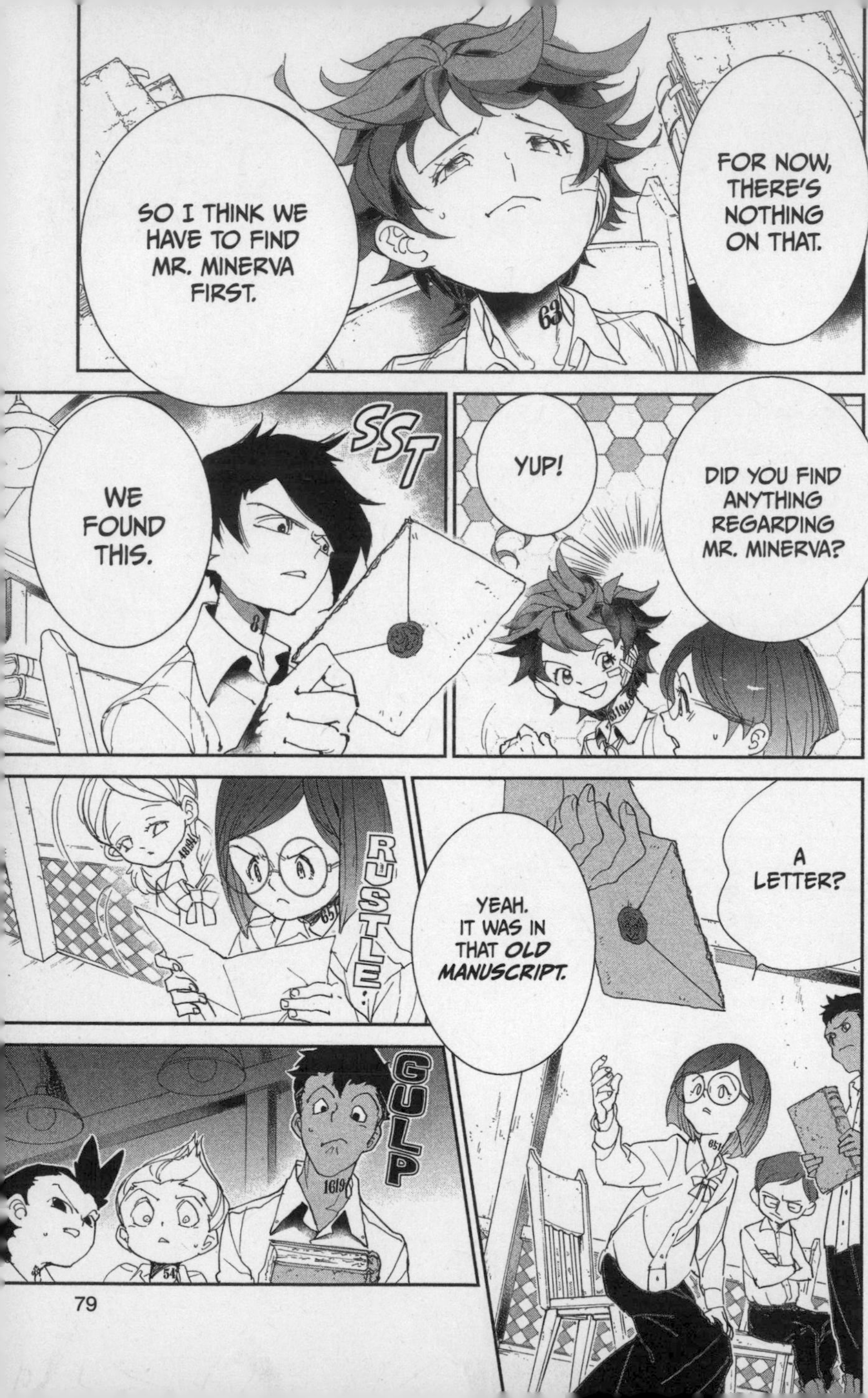
FOR NOW, THERE'S NOTHING ON THAT.
SO I THINK WE HAVE TO FIND MR. MINERVA FIRST.
DID YOU FIND ANYTHING REGARDING MR. MINERVA?
YUP!
SST
WE FOUND THIS.
A LETTER?
YEAH. IT WAS IN THAT *OLD MANUSCRIPT.*
RUSTLE
GULP

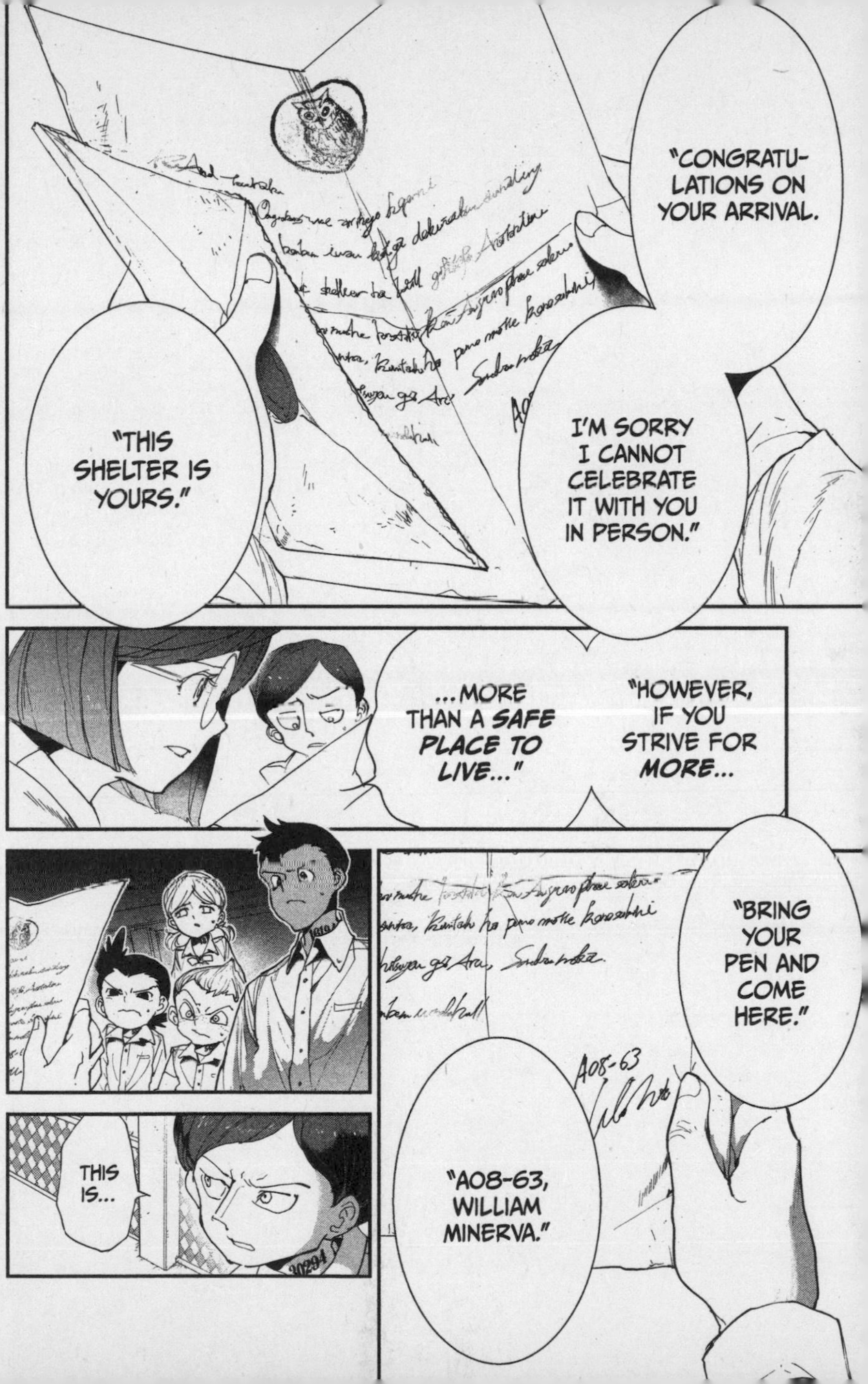

"CONGRATU-LATIONS ON YOUR ARRIVAL.
I'M SORRY I CANNOT CELEBRATE IT WITH YOU IN PERSON."
"THIS SHELTER IS YOURS."
"HOWEVER, IF YOU STRIVE FOR *MORE*...
...MORE THAN A *SAFE PLACE TO LIVE*..."
"BRING YOUR PEN AND COME HERE."
A08-63
"A08-63, WILLIAM MINERVA."
THIS IS...

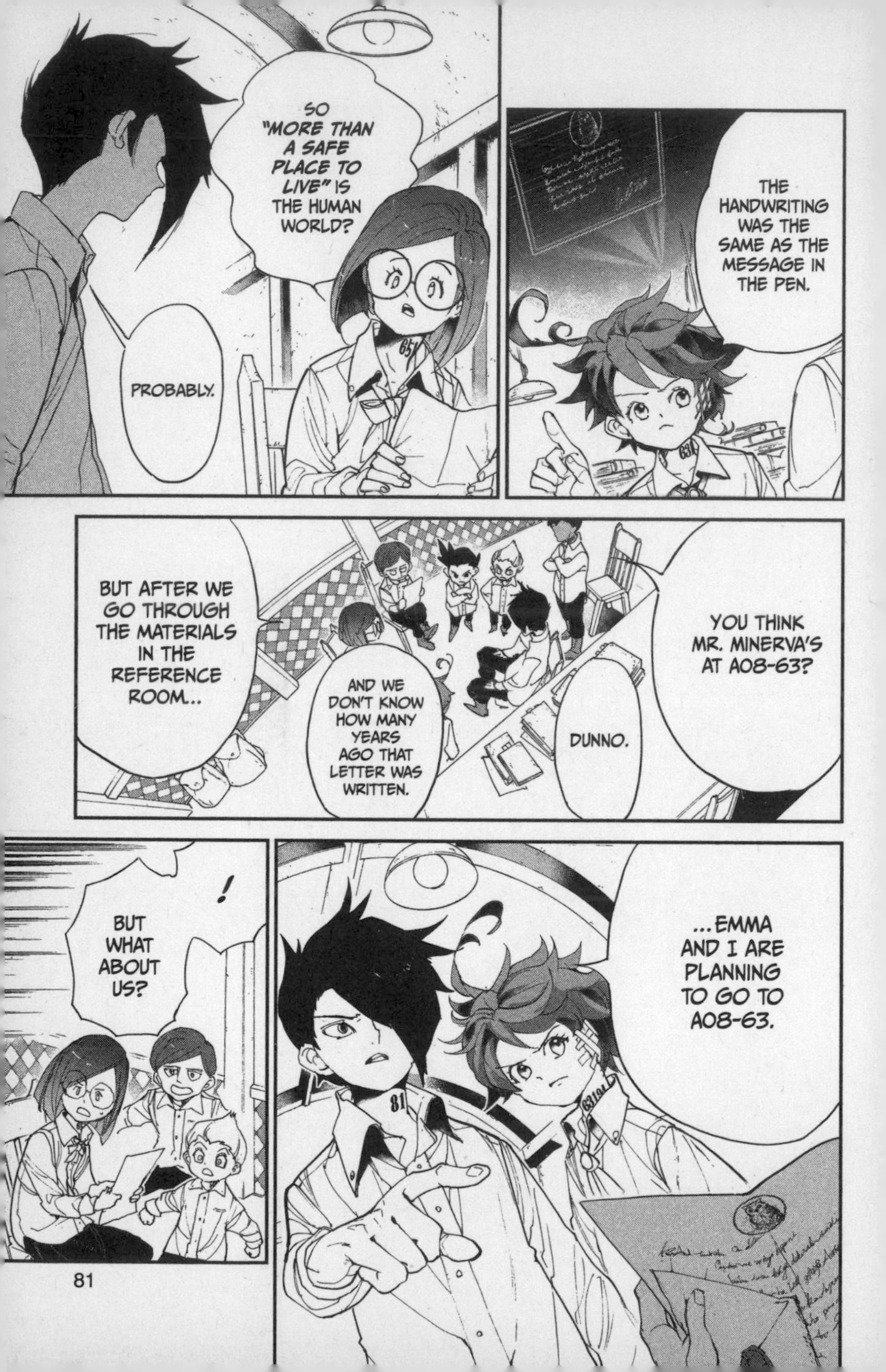
THE HANDWRITING WAS THE SAME AS THE MESSAGE IN THE PEN.
SO *"MORE THAN A SAFE PLACE TO LIVE"* IS THE HUMAN WORLD?
PROBABLY.
YOU THINK MR. MINERVA'S AT A08-63?
DUNNO.
AND WE DON'T KNOW HOW MANY YEARS AGO THAT LETTER WAS WRITTEN.
BUT AFTER WE GO THROUGH THE MATERIALS IN THE REFERENCE ROOM...
...EMMA AND I ARE PLANNING TO GO TO A08-63.
!
BUT WHAT ABOUT US?

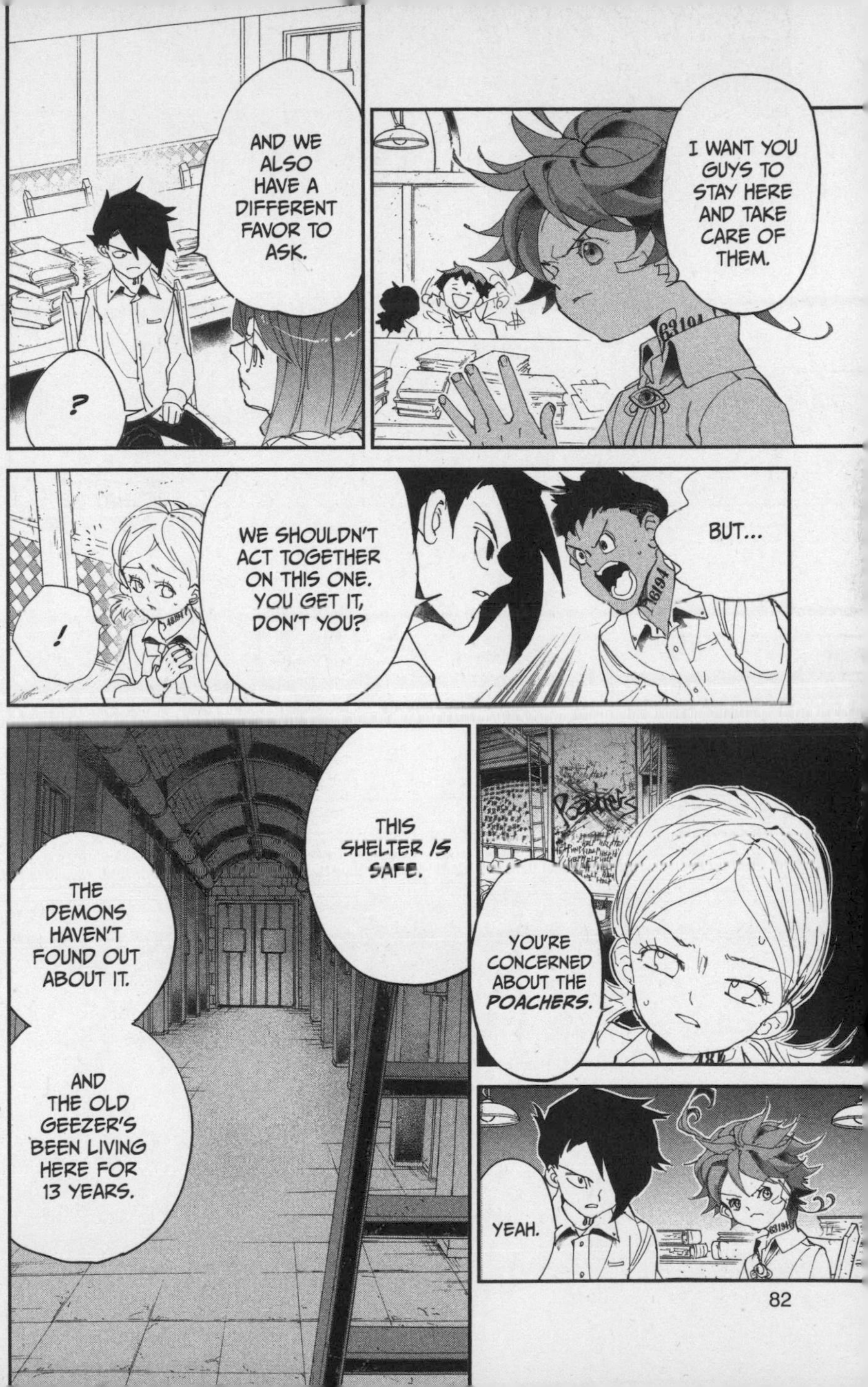
I WANT YOU GUYS TO STAY HERE AND TAKE CARE OF THEM.
AND WE ALSO HAVE A DIFFERENT FAVOR TO ASK.
?
BUT...
WE SHOULDN'T ACT TOGETHER ON THIS ONE. YOU GET IT, DON'T YOU?
!
Poachers
YOU'RE CONCERNED ABOUT THE *POACHERS*.
YEAH.
THIS SHELTER *IS* SAFE.
THE DEMONS HAVEN'T FOUND OUT ABOUT IT.
AND THE OLD GEEZER'S BEEN LIVING HERE FOR 13 YEARS.

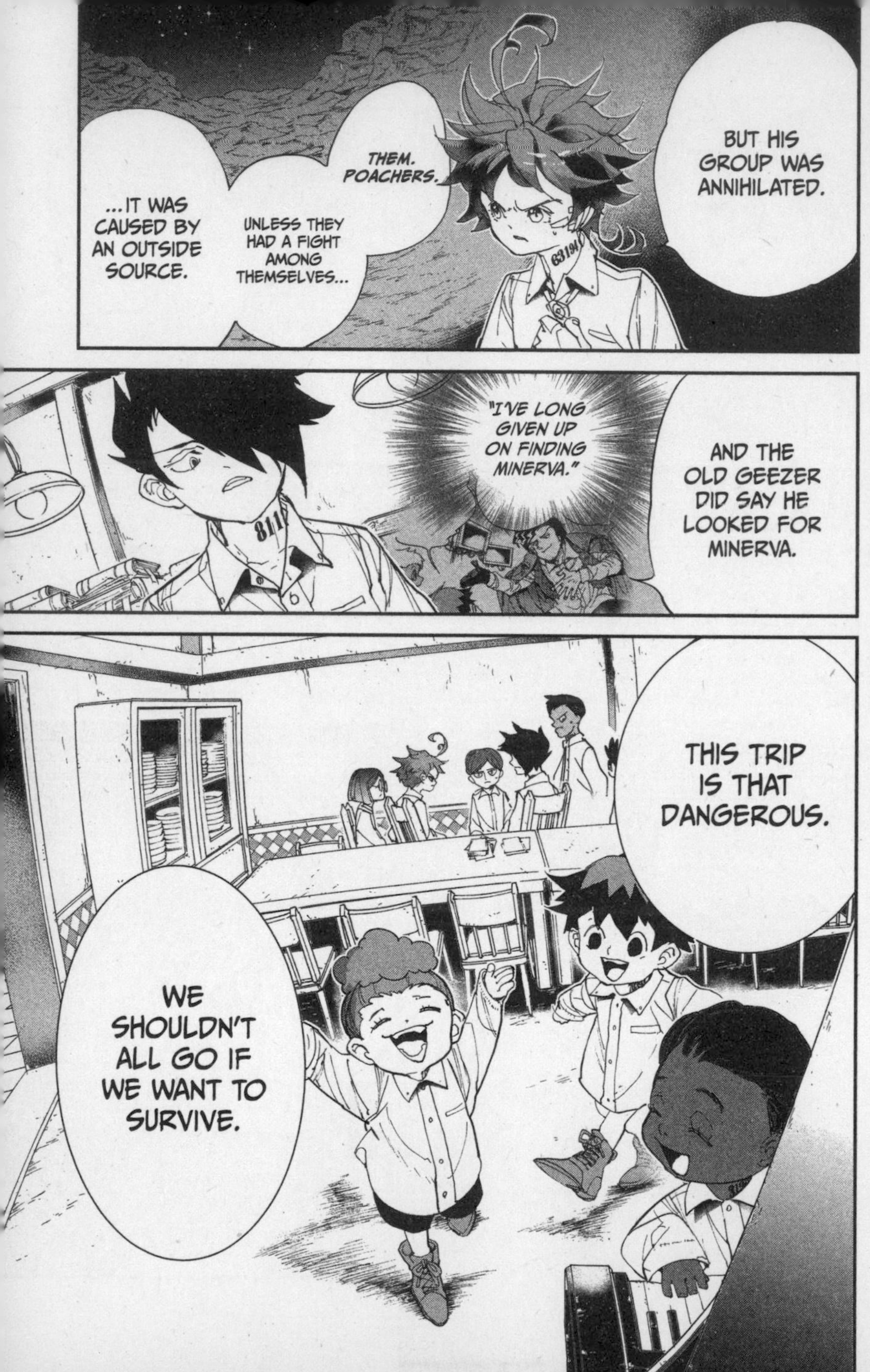
BUT HIS GROUP WAS ANNIHILATED.
UNLESS THEY HAD A FIGHT AMONG THEMSELVES...
...IT WAS CAUSED BY AN OUTSIDE SOURCE.
THEM. POACHERS.
AND THE OLD GEEZER DID SAY HE LOOKED FOR MINERVA.
"I'VE LONG GIVEN UP ON FINDING MINERVA."
THIS TRIP IS THAT DANGEROUS.
WE SHOULDN'T ALL GO IF WE WANT TO SURVIVE.

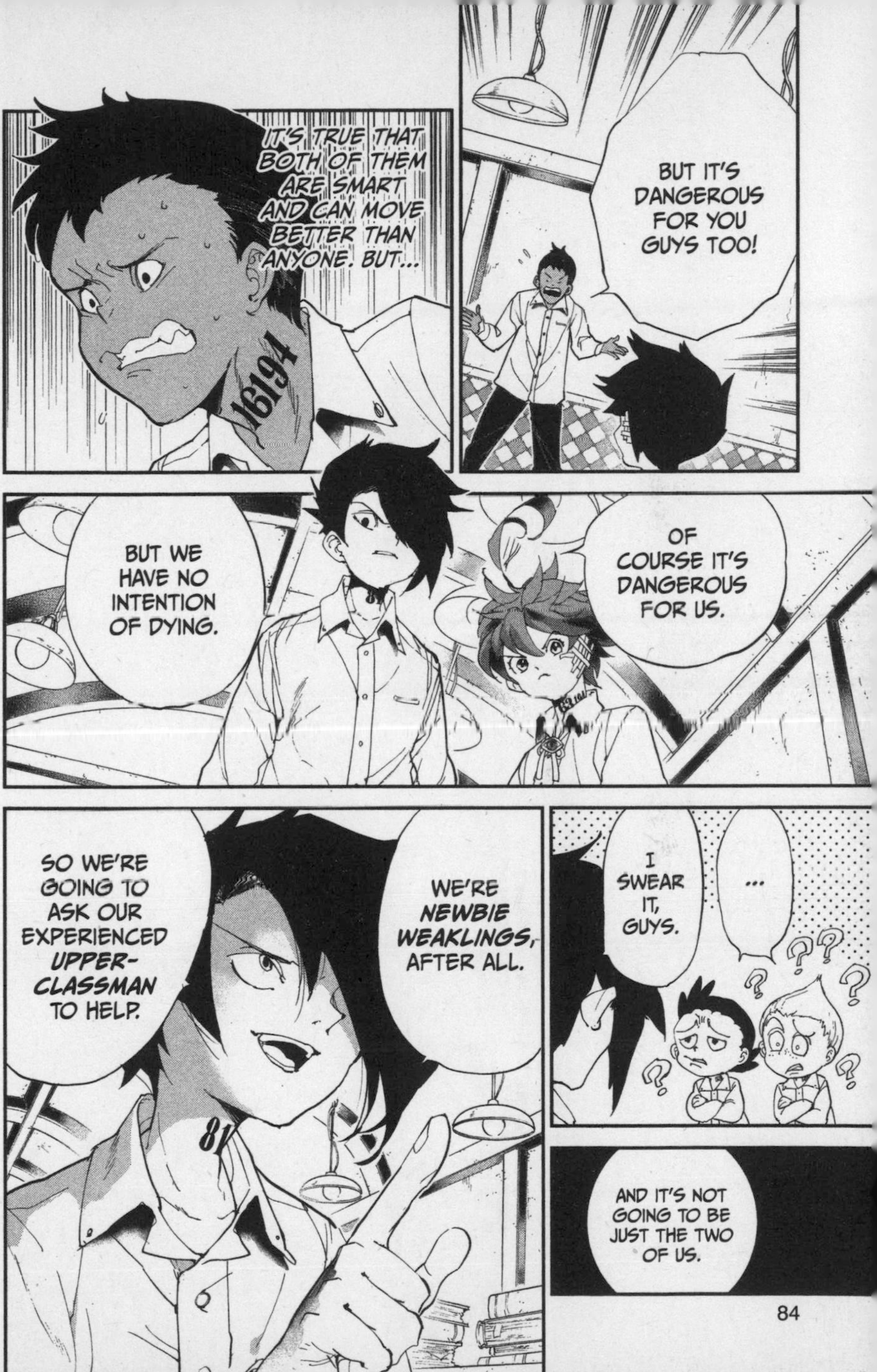
BUT IT'S DANGEROUS FOR YOU GUYS TOO!
IT'S TRUE THAT BOTH OF THEM ARE SMART AND CAN MOVE BETTER THAN ANYONE. BUT...
16194
OF COURSE IT'S DANGEROUS FOR US.
BUT WE HAVE NO INTENTION OF DYING.
...
I SWEAR IT, GUYS.
AND IT'S NOT GOING TO BE JUST THE TWO OF US.
WE'RE NEWBIE WEAKLINGS, AFTER ALL.
SO WE'RE GOING TO ASK OUR EXPERIENCED UPPER-CLASSMAN TO HELP.
81

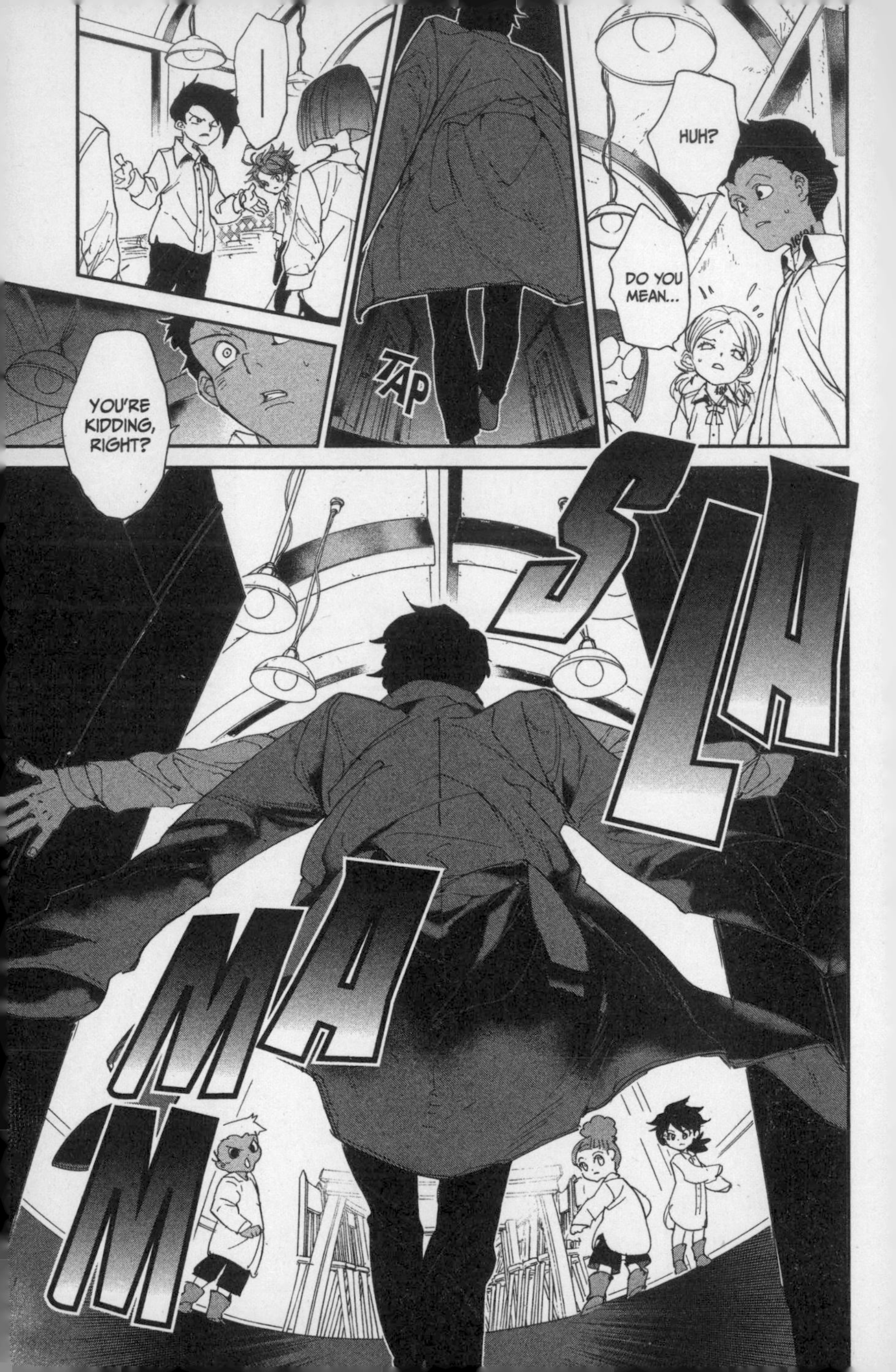
HUH?
DO YOU MEAN...
TAP
YOU'RE KIDDING, RIGHT?

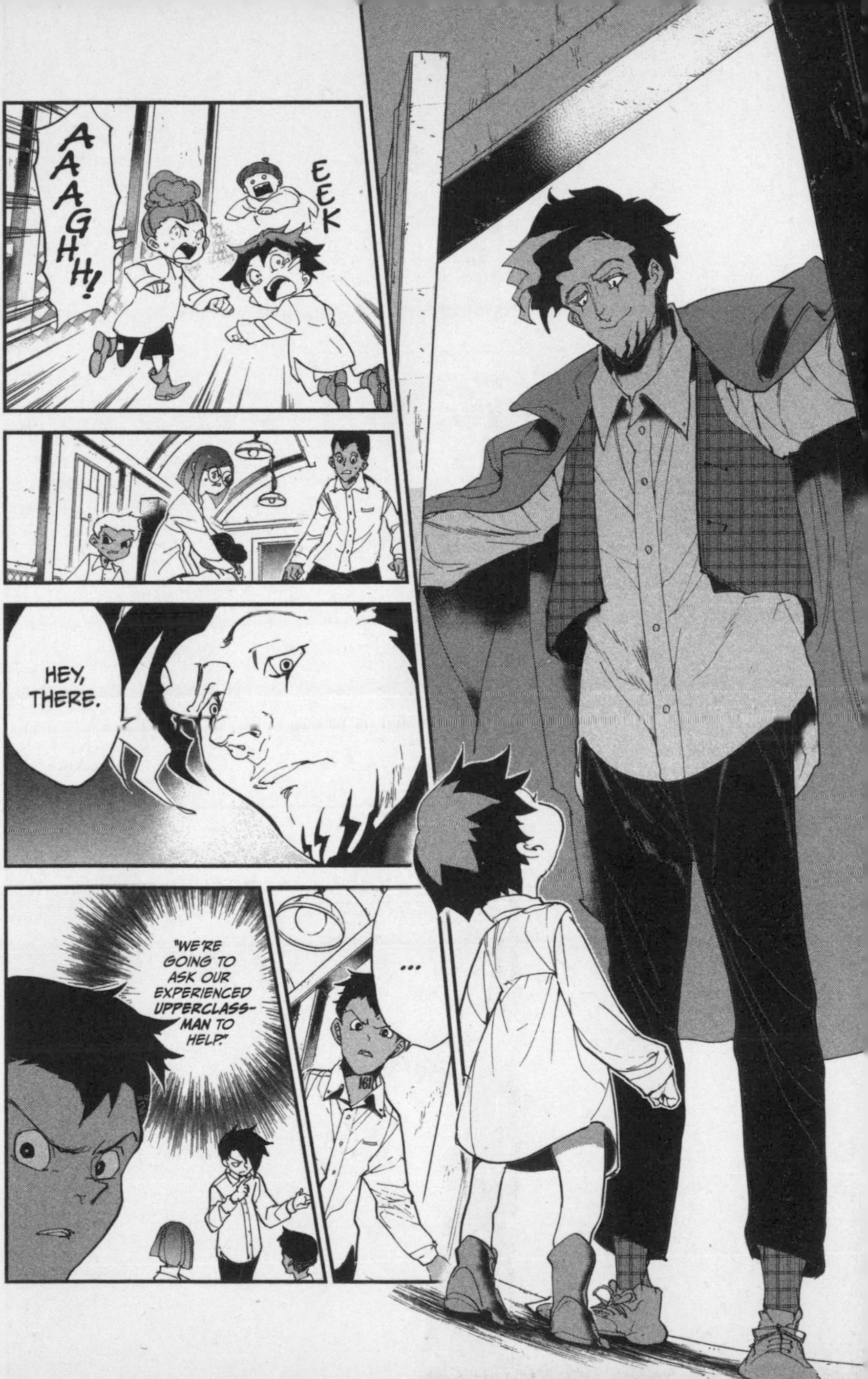
EEK
AAAGHH!
HEY, THERE.
...
"WE'RE GOING TO ASK OUR EXPERIENCED UPPERCLASSMAN TO HELP."

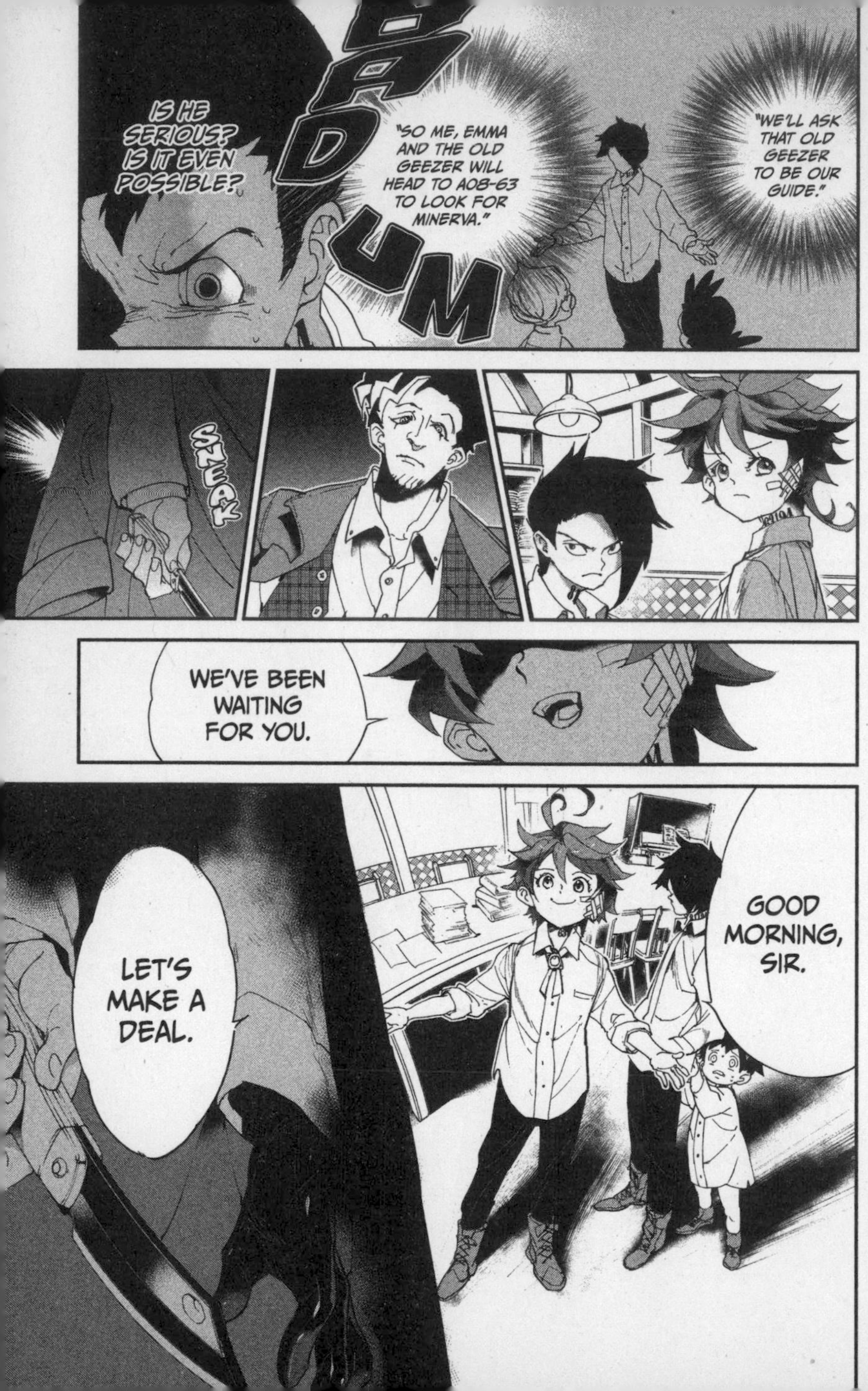
"WE'LL ASK THAT OLD GEEZER TO BE OUR GUIDE."
"SO ME, EMMA AND THE OLD GEEZER WILL HEAD TO A08-63 TO LOOK FOR MINERVA."
BADUM
IS HE SERIOUS? IS IT EVEN POSSIBLE?
SNEAK
WE'VE BEEN WAITING FOR YOU.
GOOD MORNING, SIR.
LET'S MAKE A DEAL.

THE PROMISED NEVERLAND SIDE SCENE 013

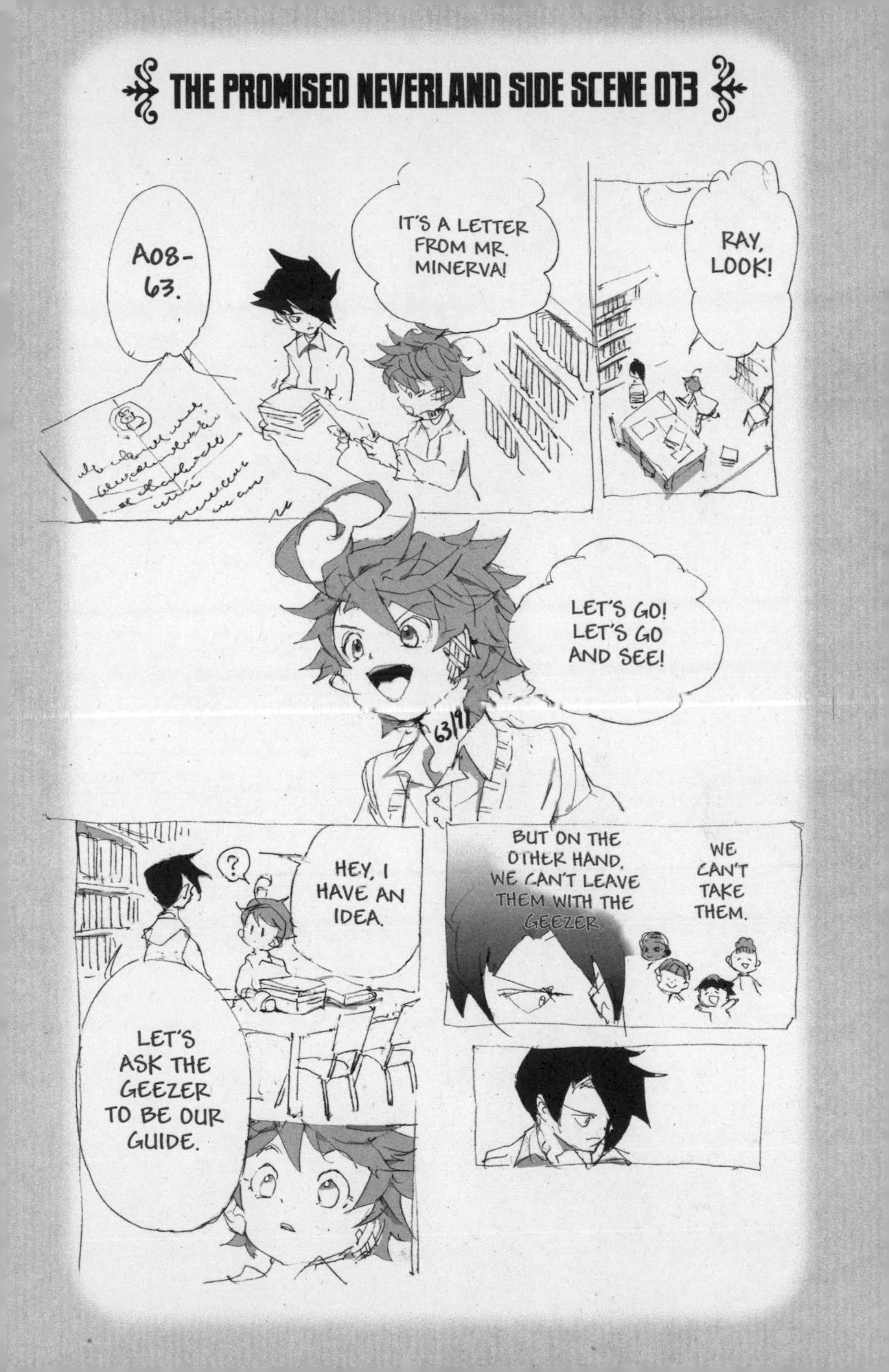

RAY, LOOK!
IT'S A LETTER FROM MR. MINERVA!
A08-63.
LET'S GO! LET'S GO AND SEE!
63194
WE CAN'T TAKE THEM.
BUT ON THE OTHER HAND, WE CAN'T LEAVE THEM WITH THE GEEZER.
HEY, I HAVE AN IDEA.
?
LET'S ASK THE GEEZER TO BE OUR GUIDE.

CHAPTER 57: A DEAL, PART 2

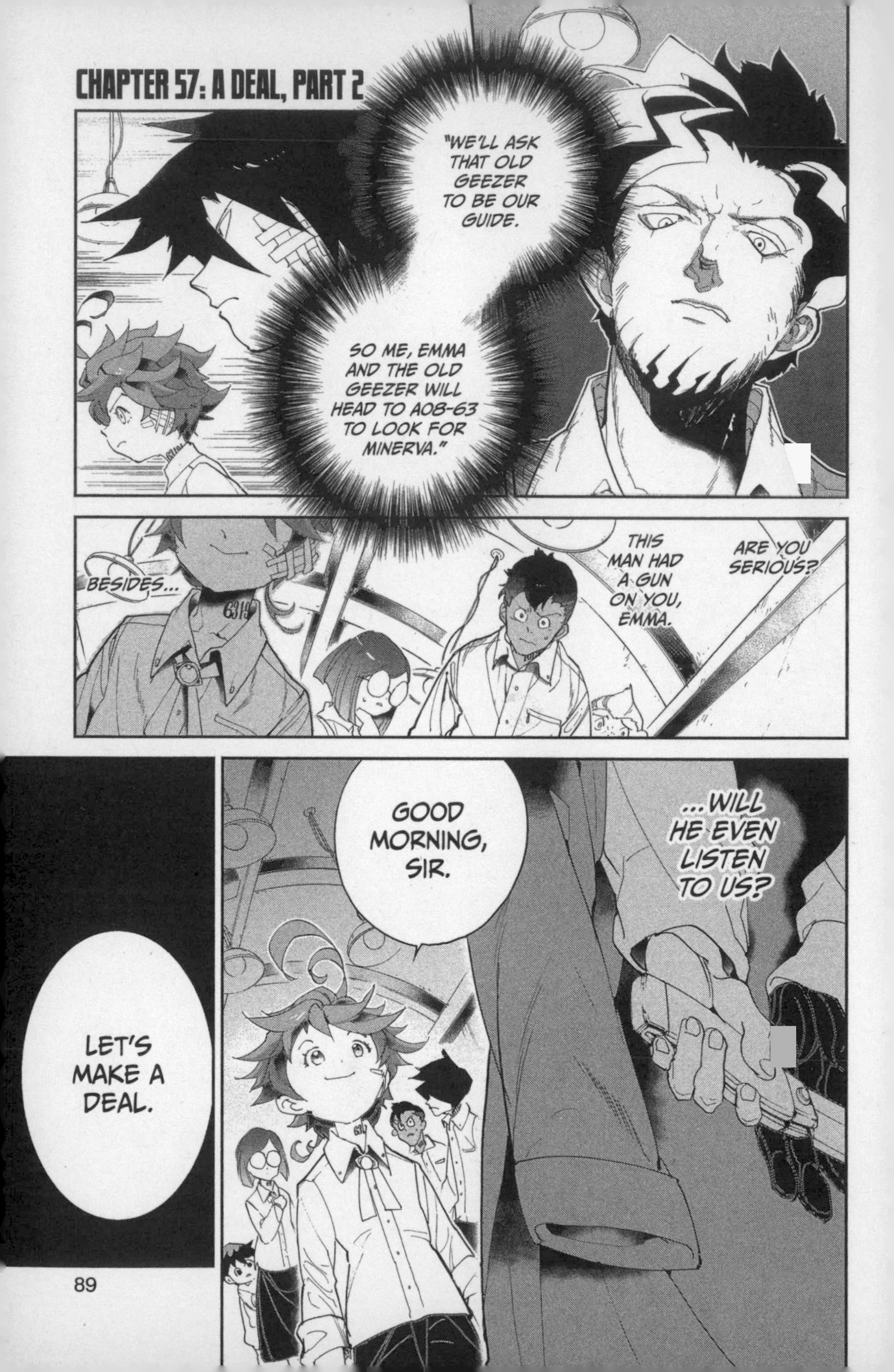

"WE'LL ASK THAT OLD GEEZER TO BE OUR GUIDE.
SO ME, EMMA AND THE OLD GEEZER WILL HEAD TO A08-63 TO LOOK FOR MINERVA."
ARE YOU SERIOUS?
THIS MAN HAD A GUN ON YOU, EMMA.
BESIDES...
...WILL HE EVEN LISTEN TO US?
GOOD MORNING, SIR.
LET'S MAKE A DEAL.

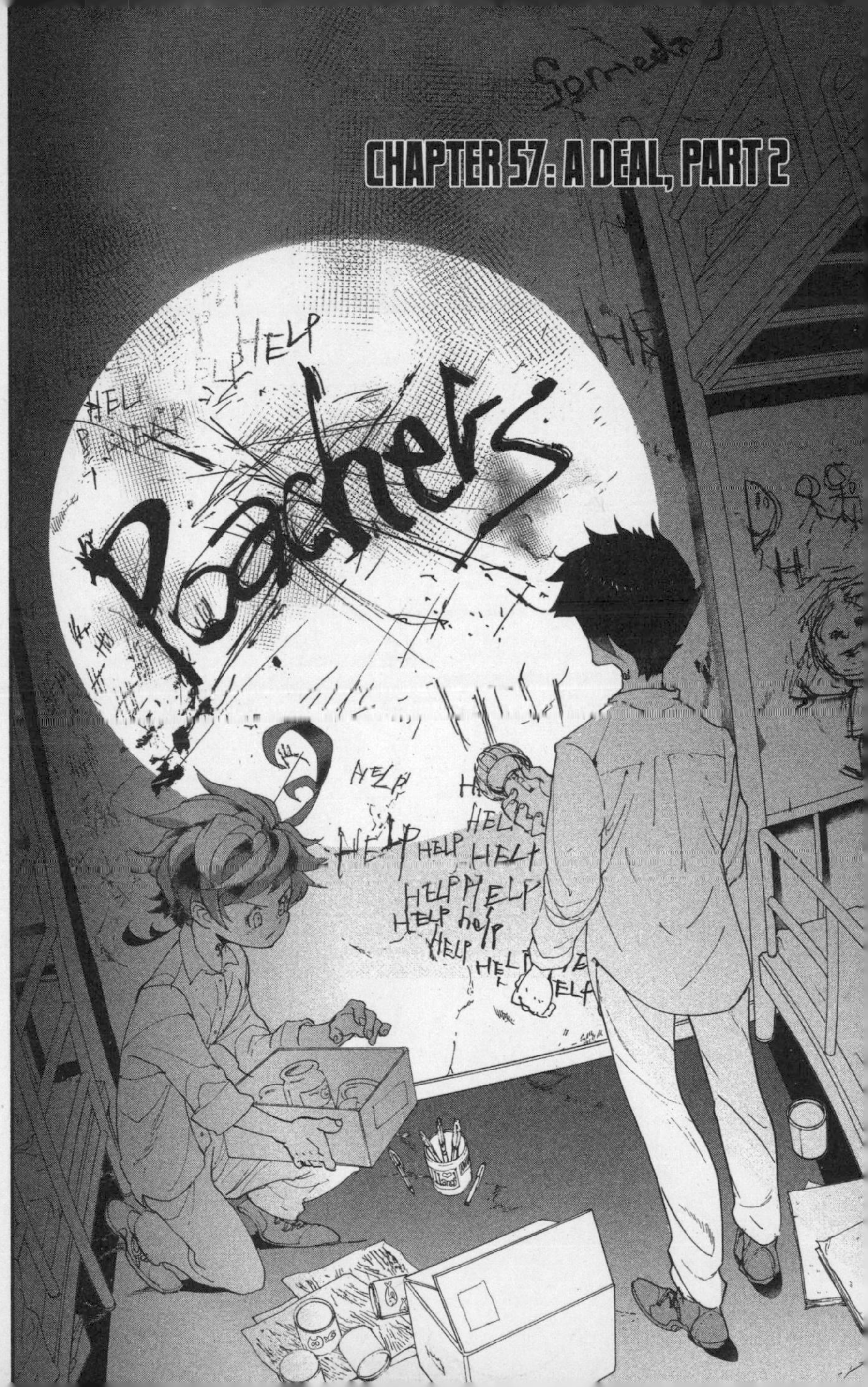
CHAPTER 57: A DEAL, PART 2
Poachers
HELP

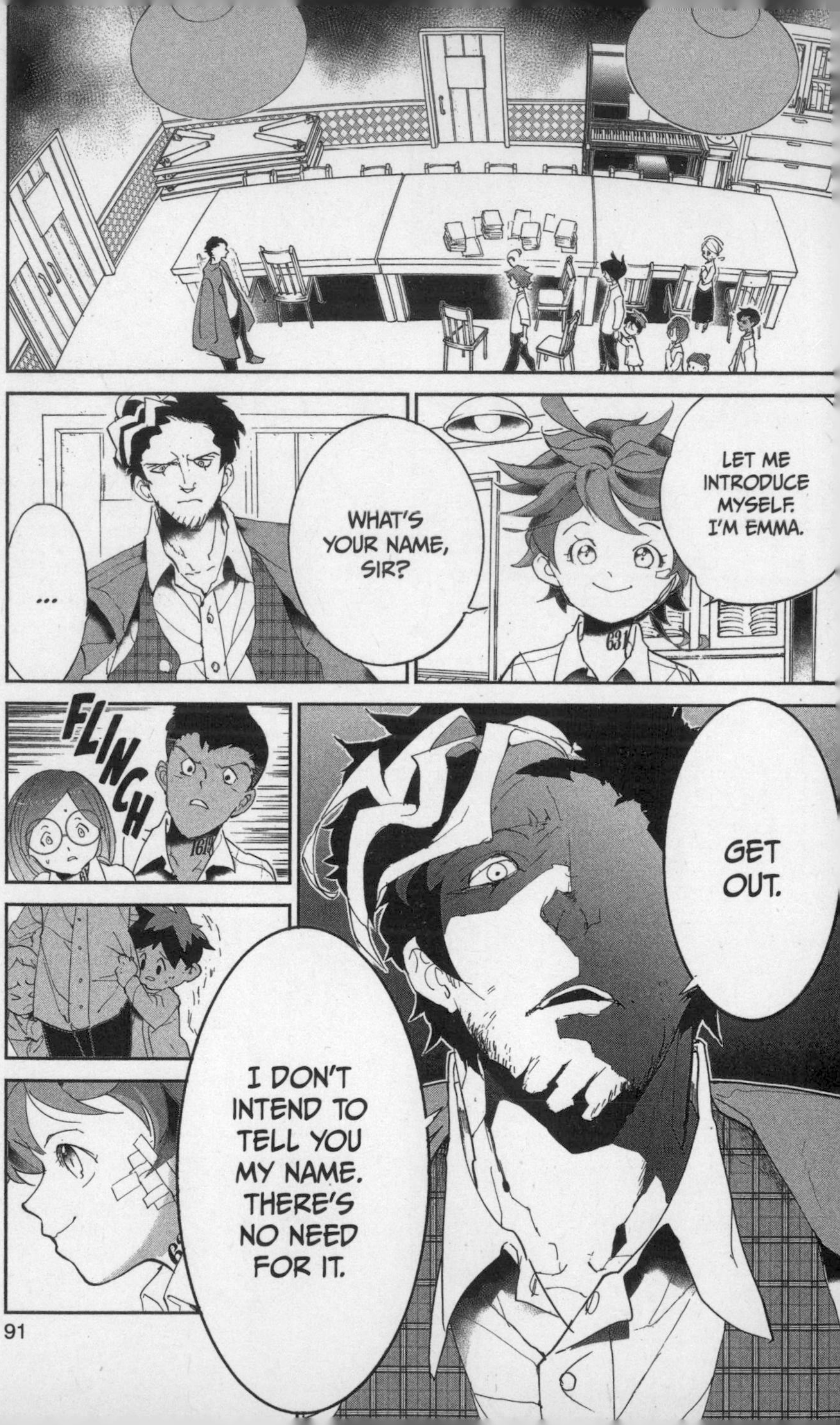
LET ME INTRODUCE MYSELF. I'M EMMA.
WHAT'S YOUR NAME, SIR?
...
GET OUT.
I DON'T INTEND TO TELL YOU MY NAME. THERE'S NO NEED FOR IT.
FLINCH

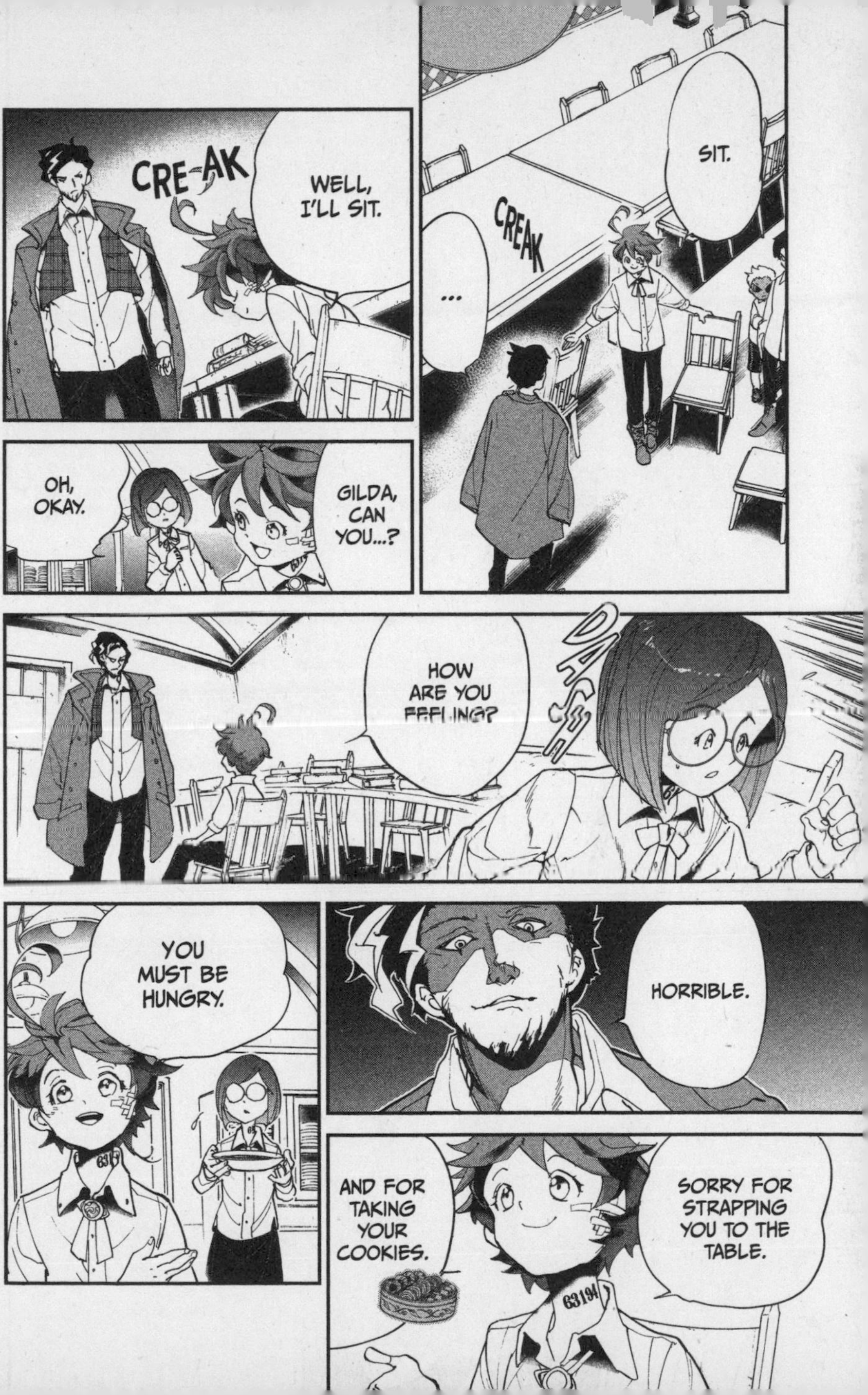
SIT.
CREAK
...
WELL, I'LL SIT.
CRE-AK
GILDA, CAN YOU...?
OH, OKAY.
DASH
HOW ARE YOU FEELING?
HORRIBLE.
SORRY FOR STRAPPING YOU TO THE TABLE.
AND FOR TAKING YOUR COOKIES.
YOU MUST BE HUNGRY.

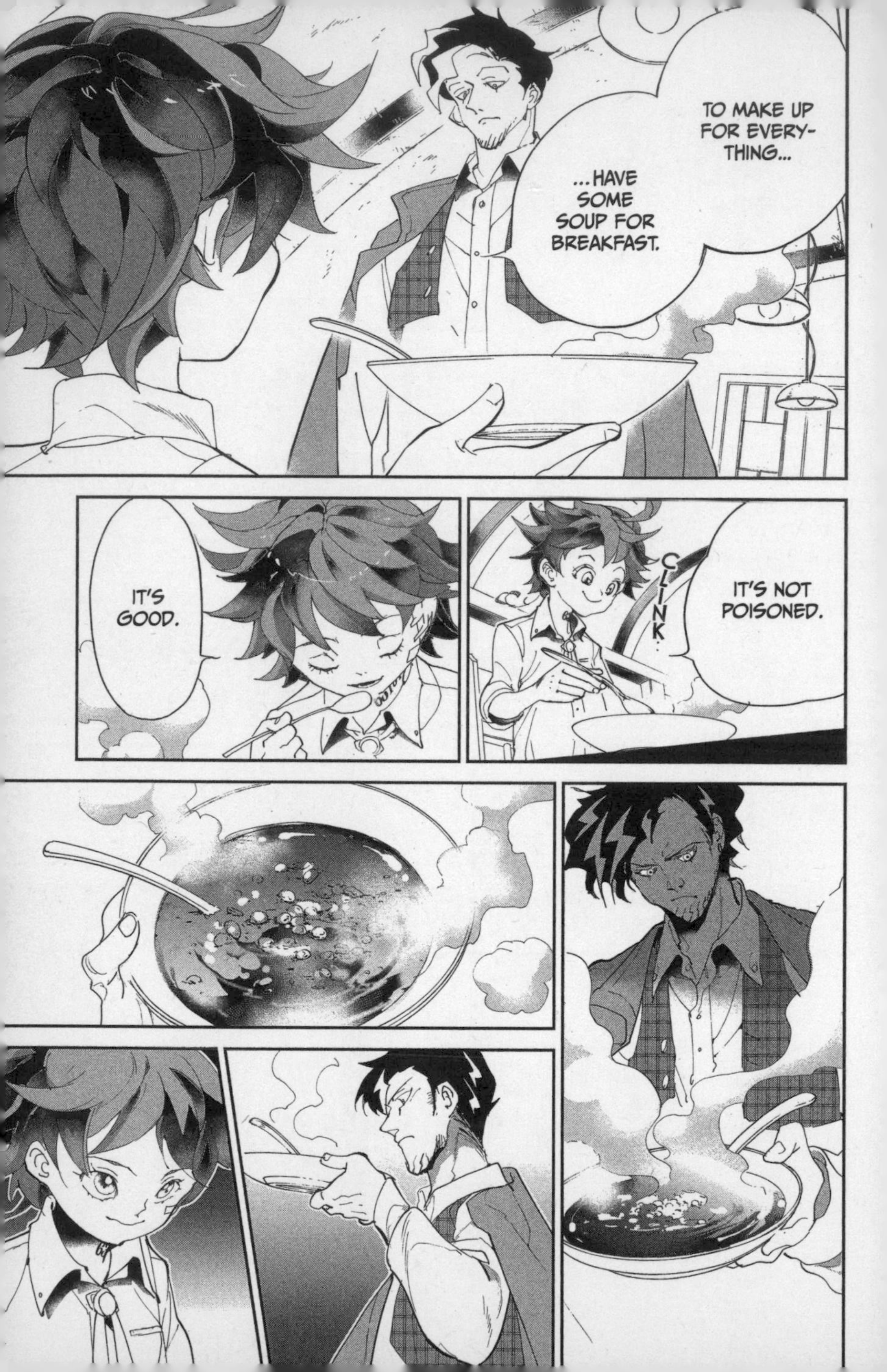
TO MAKE UP FOR EVERY-THING...
...HAVE SOME SOUP FOR BREAKFAST.
CLINK
IT'S NOT POISONED.
IT'S GOOD.

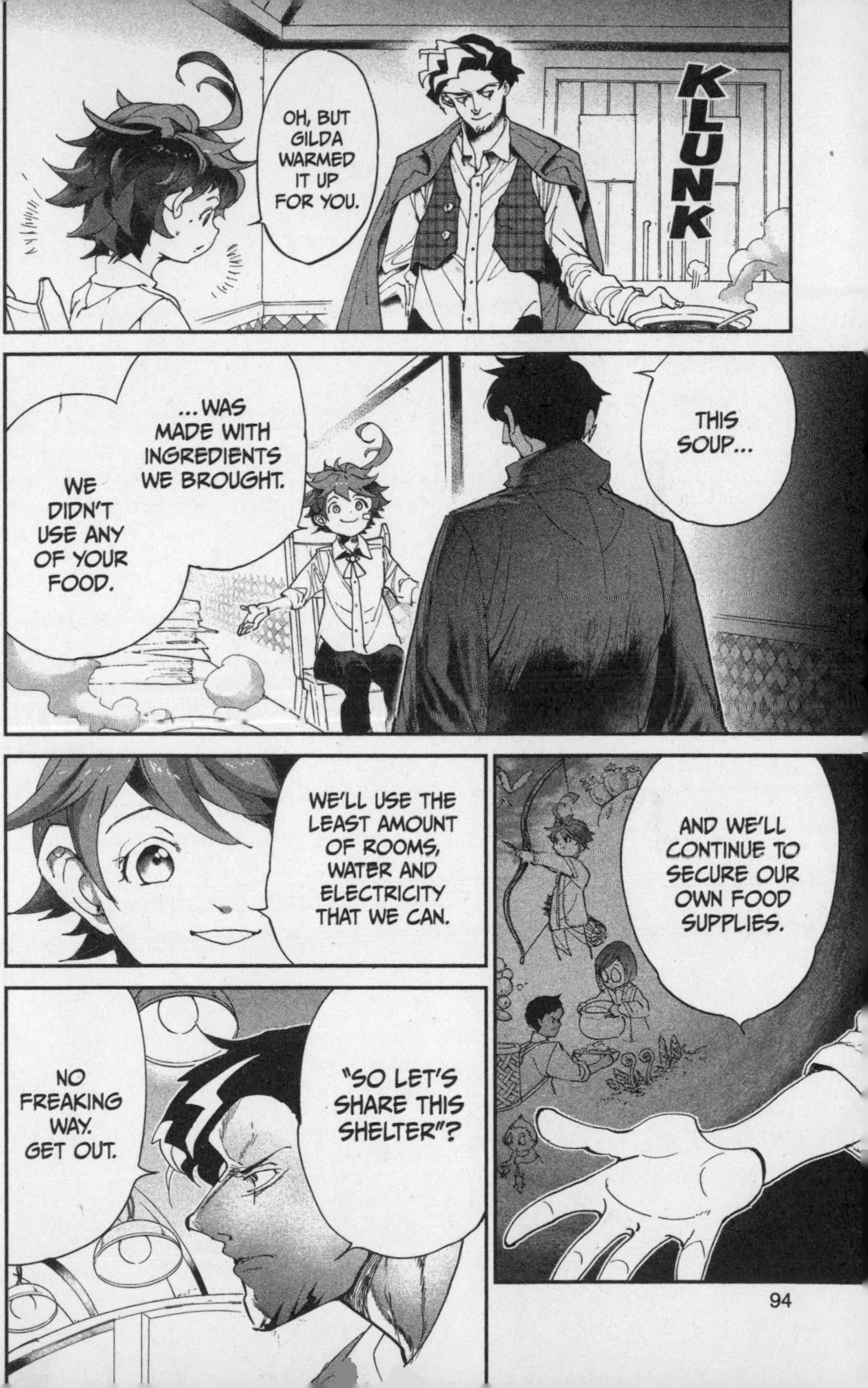
KLUNK
OH, BUT GILDA WARMED IT UP FOR YOU.
THIS SOUP...
...WAS MADE WITH INGREDIENTS WE BROUGHT.
WE DIDN'T USE ANY OF YOUR FOOD.
AND WE'LL CONTINUE TO SECURE OUR OWN FOOD SUPPLIES.
WE'LL USE THE LEAST AMOUNT OF ROOMS, WATER AND ELECTRICITY THAT WE CAN.
"SO LET'S SHARE THIS SHELTER"?
NO FREAKING WAY. GET OUT.

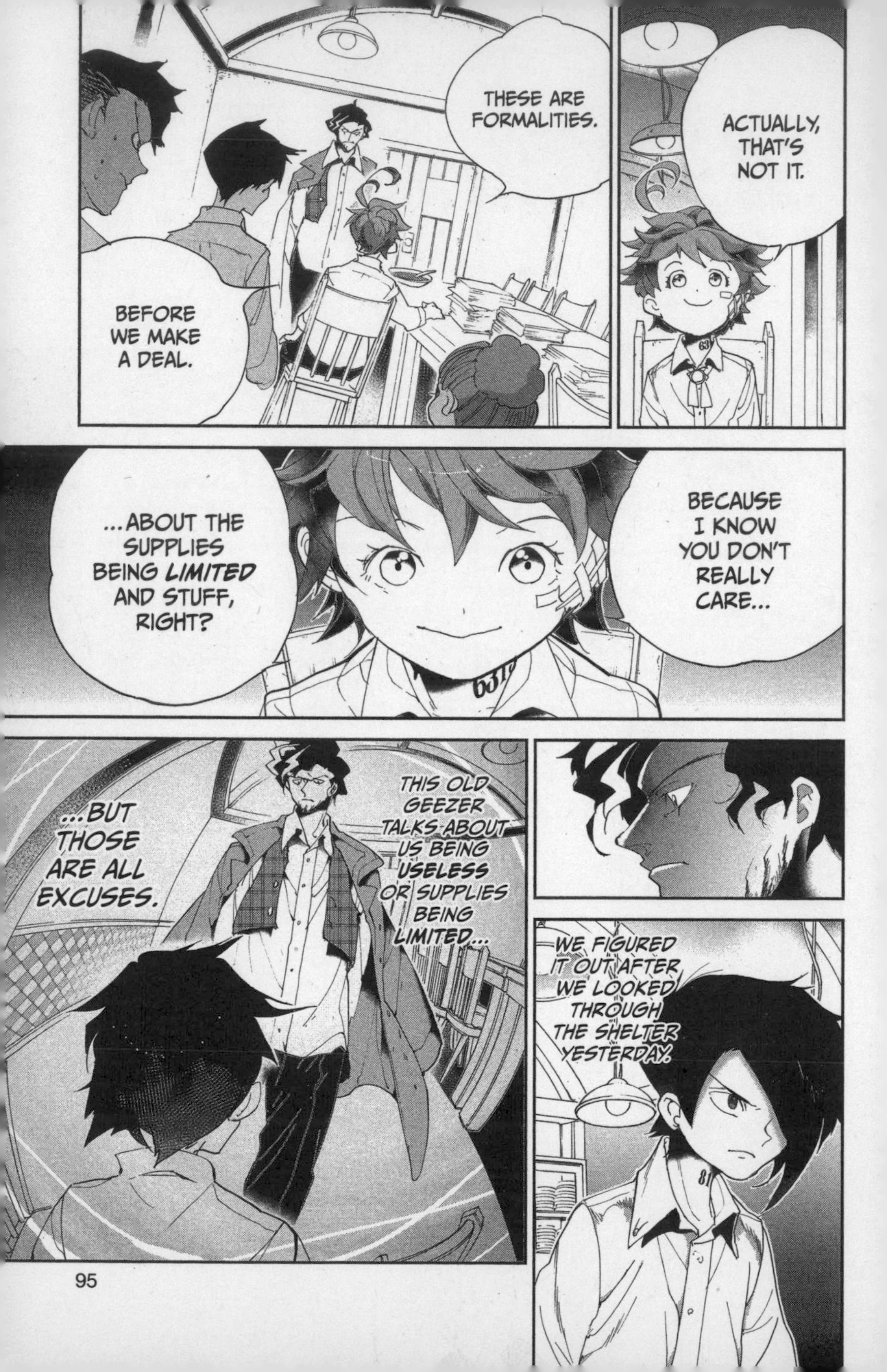
ACTUALLY, THAT'S NOT IT.
THESE ARE FORMALITIES.
BEFORE WE MAKE A DEAL.
BECAUSE I KNOW YOU DON'T REALLY CARE...
...ABOUT THE SUPPLIES BEING *LIMITED* AND STUFF, RIGHT?
WE FIGURED IT OUT AFTER WE LOOKED THROUGH THE SHELTER YESTERDAY.
THIS OLD GEEZER TALKS ABOUT US BEING USELESS OR SUPPLIES BEING LIMITED...
...BUT THOSE ARE ALL EXCUSES.

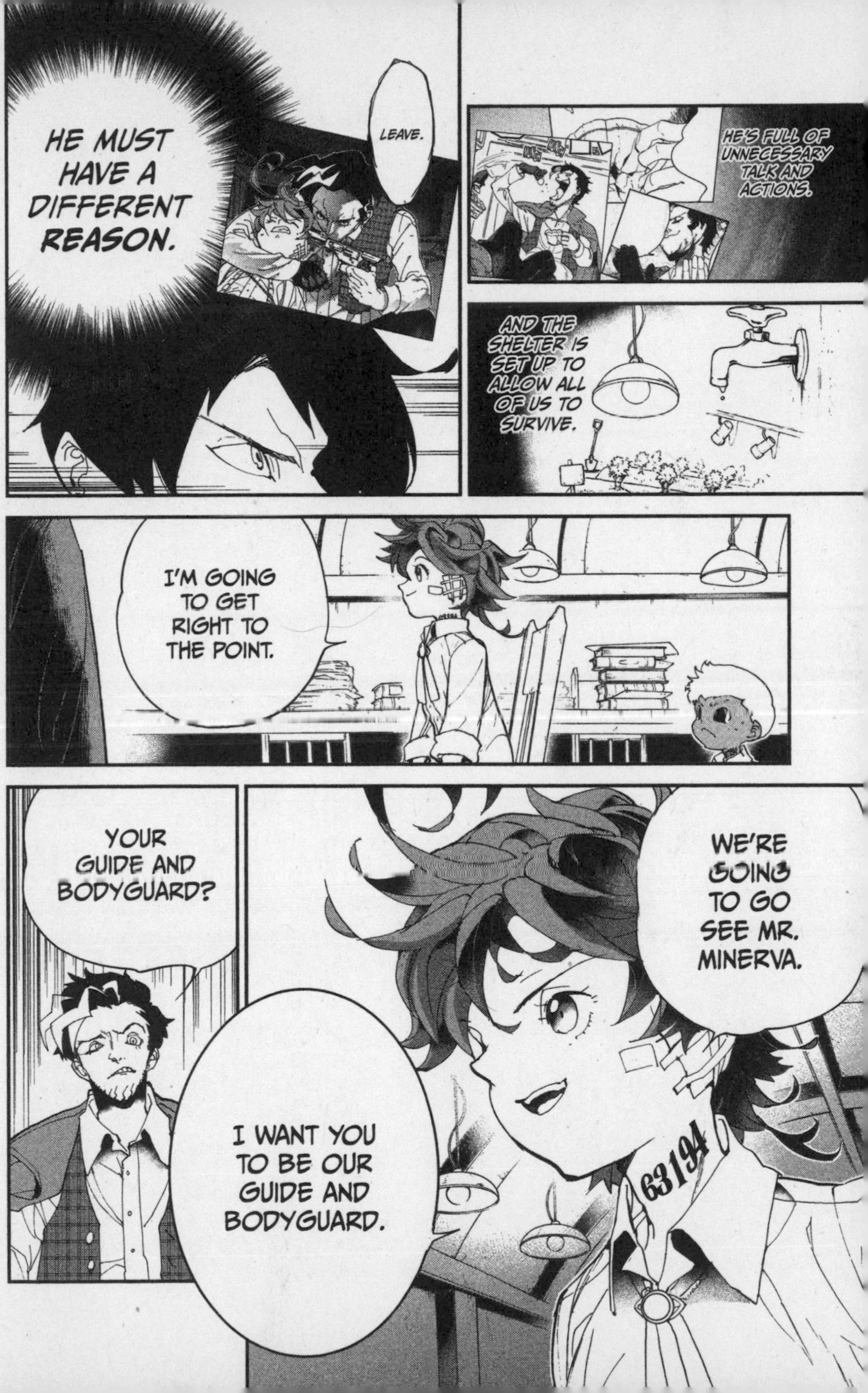
HE'S FULL OF UNNECESSARY TALK AND ACTIONS.
AND THE SHELTER IS SET UP TO ALLOW ALL OF US TO SURVIVE.
LEAVE.
HE MUST HAVE A DIFFERENT REASON.
I'M GOING TO GET RIGHT TO THE POINT.
WE'RE GOING TO GO SEE MR. MINERVA.
I WANT YOU TO BE OUR GUIDE AND BODYGUARD.
YOUR GUIDE AND BODYGUARD?
63194

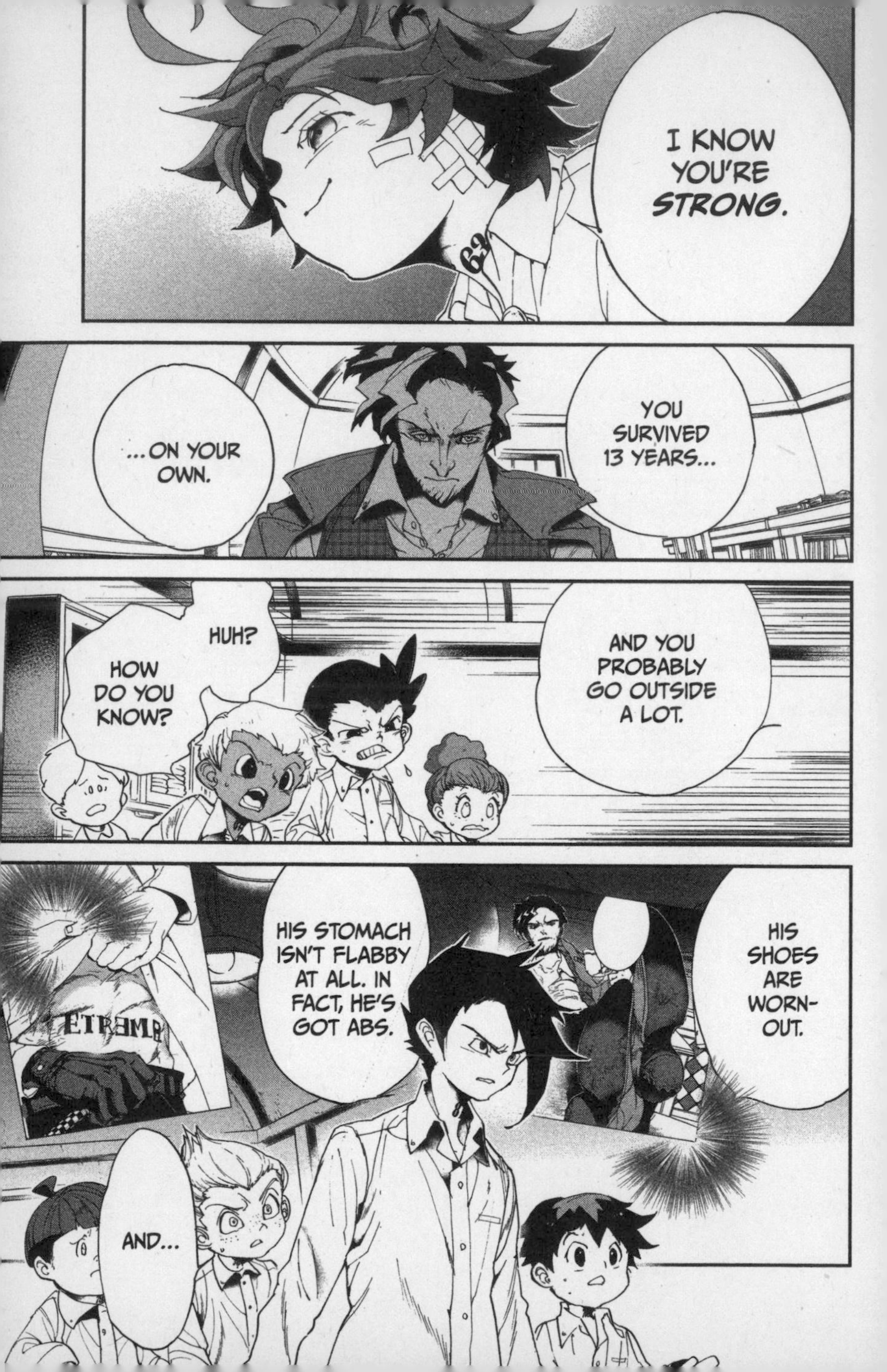
I KNOW YOU'RE STRONG.
YOU SURVIVED 13 YEARS...
...ON YOUR OWN.
AND YOU PROBABLY GO OUTSIDE A LOT.
HUH?
HOW DO YOU KNOW?
HIS SHOES ARE WORN-OUT.
HIS STOMACH ISN'T FLABBY AT ALL. IN FACT, HE'S GOT ABS.
AND...

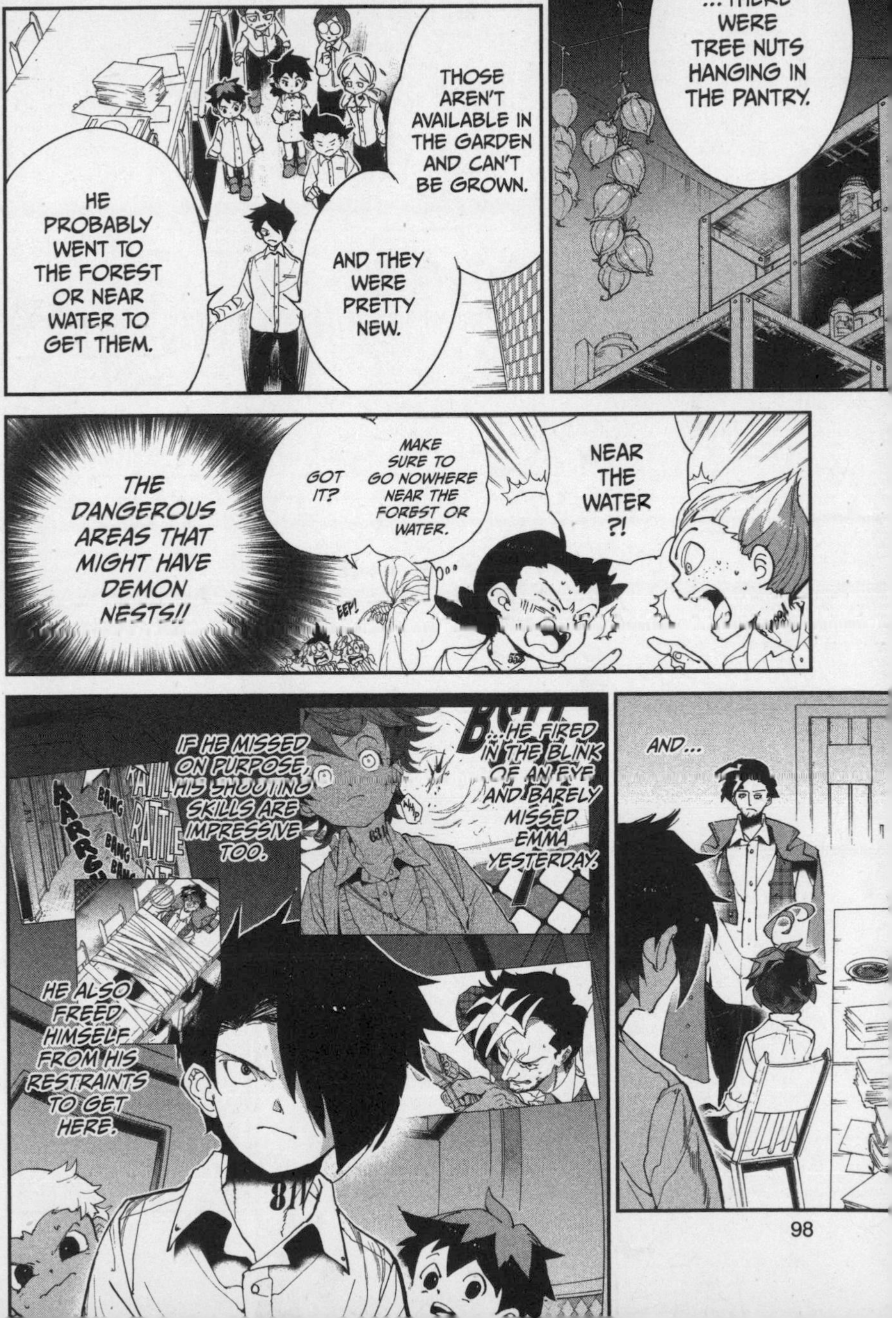
...THERE WERE TREE NUTS HANGING IN THE PANTRY.
THOSE AREN'T AVAILABLE IN THE GARDEN AND CAN'T BE GROWN.
AND THEY WERE PRETTY NEW.
HE PROBABLY WENT TO THE FOREST OR NEAR WATER TO GET THEM.
NEAR THE WATER?!
MAKE SURE TO GO NOWHERE NEAR THE FOREST OR WATER.
GOT IT?
EEP!
THE DANGEROUS AREAS THAT MIGHT HAVE DEMON NESTS!!
AND...
...HE FIRED IN THE BLINK OF AN EYE AND BARELY MISSED EMMA YESTERDAY.
IF HE MISSED ON PURPOSE, HIS SHOOTING SKILLS ARE IMPRESSIVE TOO.
RATTLE
RATTLE
BANG
BANG
HE ALSO FREED HIMSELF FROM HIS RESTRAINTS TO GET HERE.

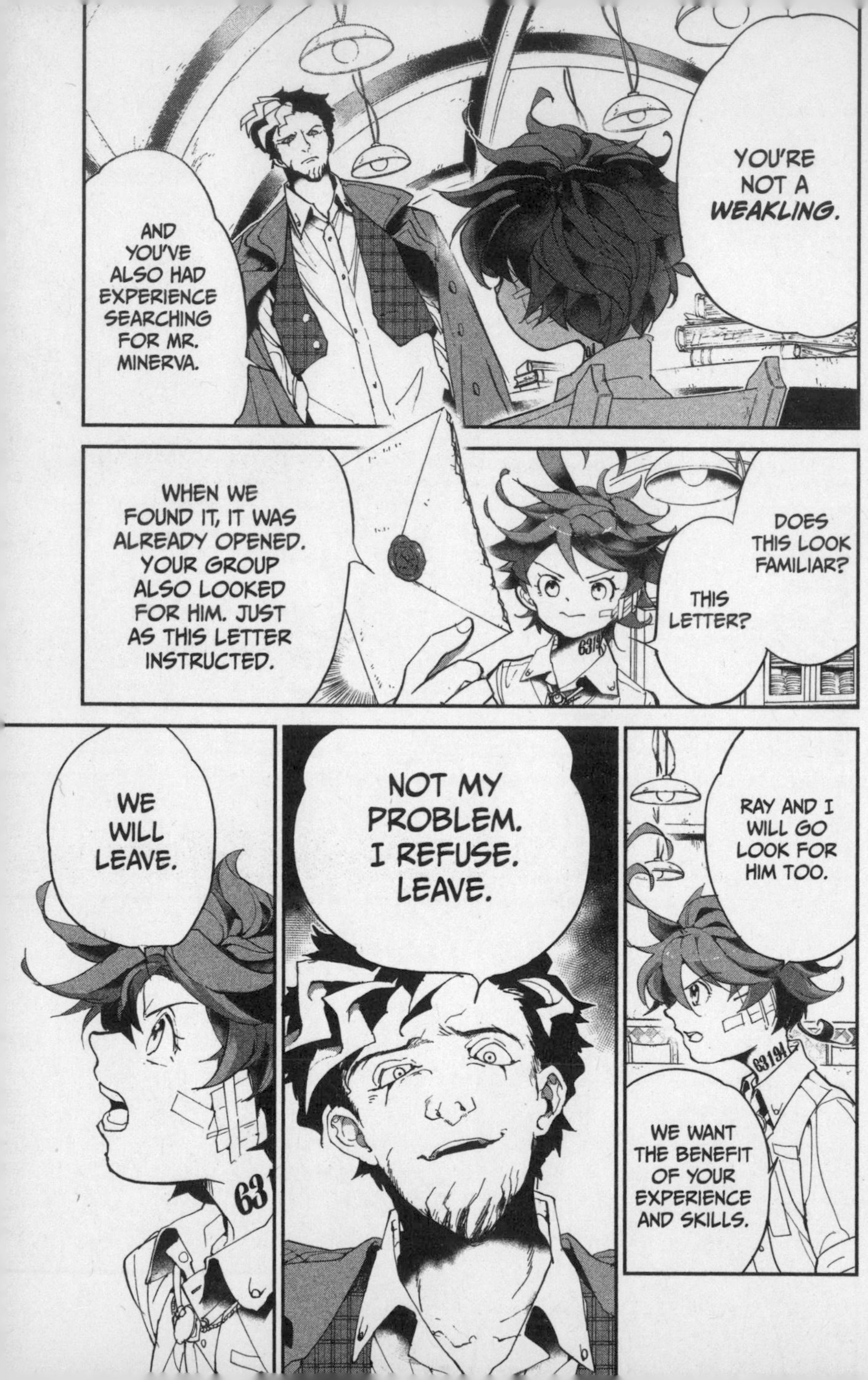
YOU'RE NOT A WEAKLING.
AND YOU'VE ALSO HAD EXPERIENCE SEARCHING FOR MR. MINERVA.
DOES THIS LOOK FAMILIAR?
THIS LETTER?
WHEN WE FOUND IT, IT WAS ALREADY OPENED. YOUR GROUP ALSO LOOKED FOR HIM. JUST AS THIS LETTER INSTRUCTED.
RAY AND I WILL GO LOOK FOR HIM TOO.
WE WANT THE BENEFIT OF YOUR EXPERIENCE AND SKILLS.
NOT MY PROBLEM. I REFUSE. LEAVE.
WE WILL LEAVE.

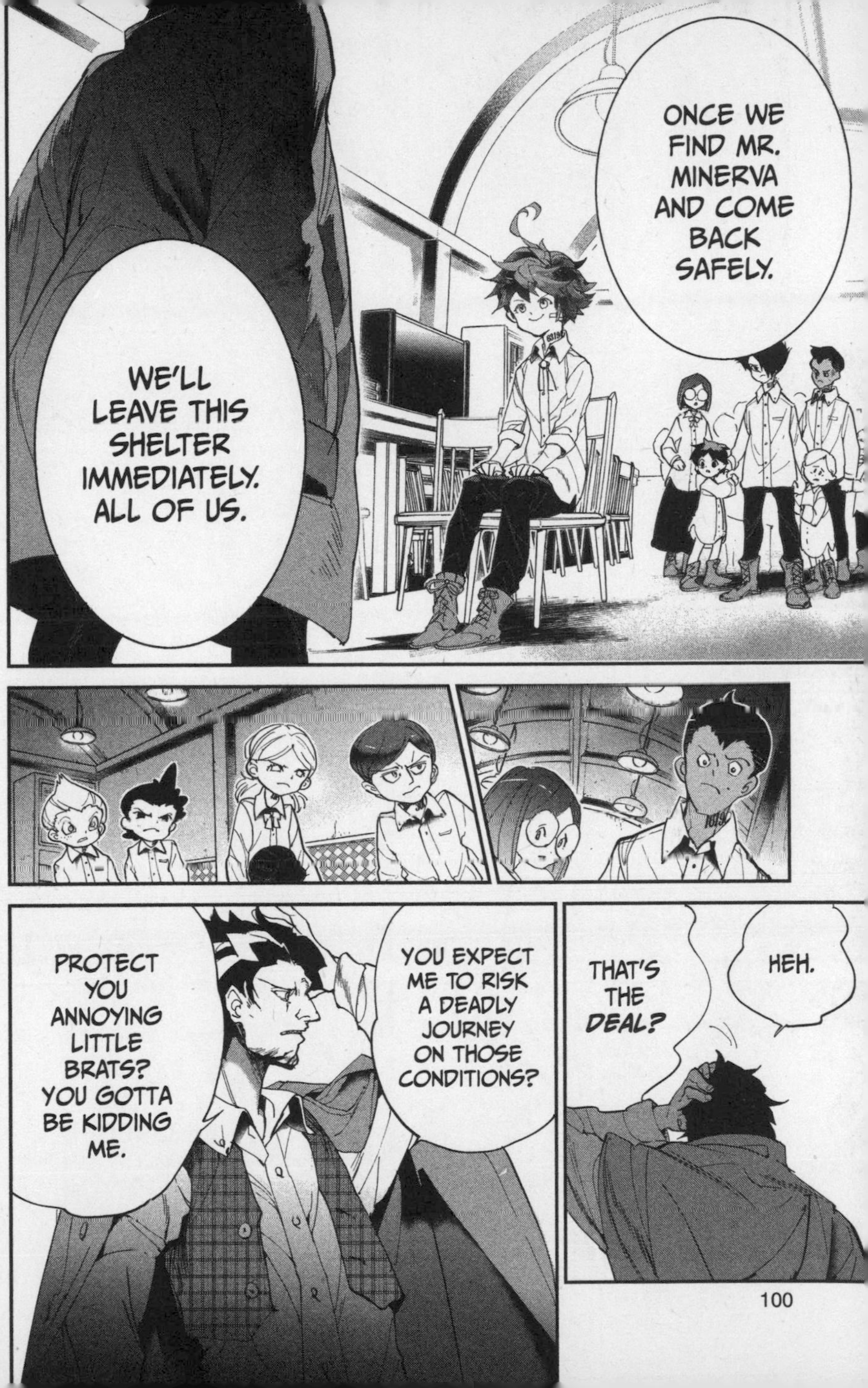
ONCE WE FIND MR. MINERVA AND COME BACK SAFELY.
WE'LL LEAVE THIS SHELTER IMMEDIATELY. ALL OF US.
HEH.
THAT'S THE *DEAL?*
YOU EXPECT ME TO RISK A DEADLY JOURNEY ON THOSE CONDITIONS?
PROTECT YOU ANNOYING LITTLE BRATS? YOU GOTTA BE KIDDING ME.

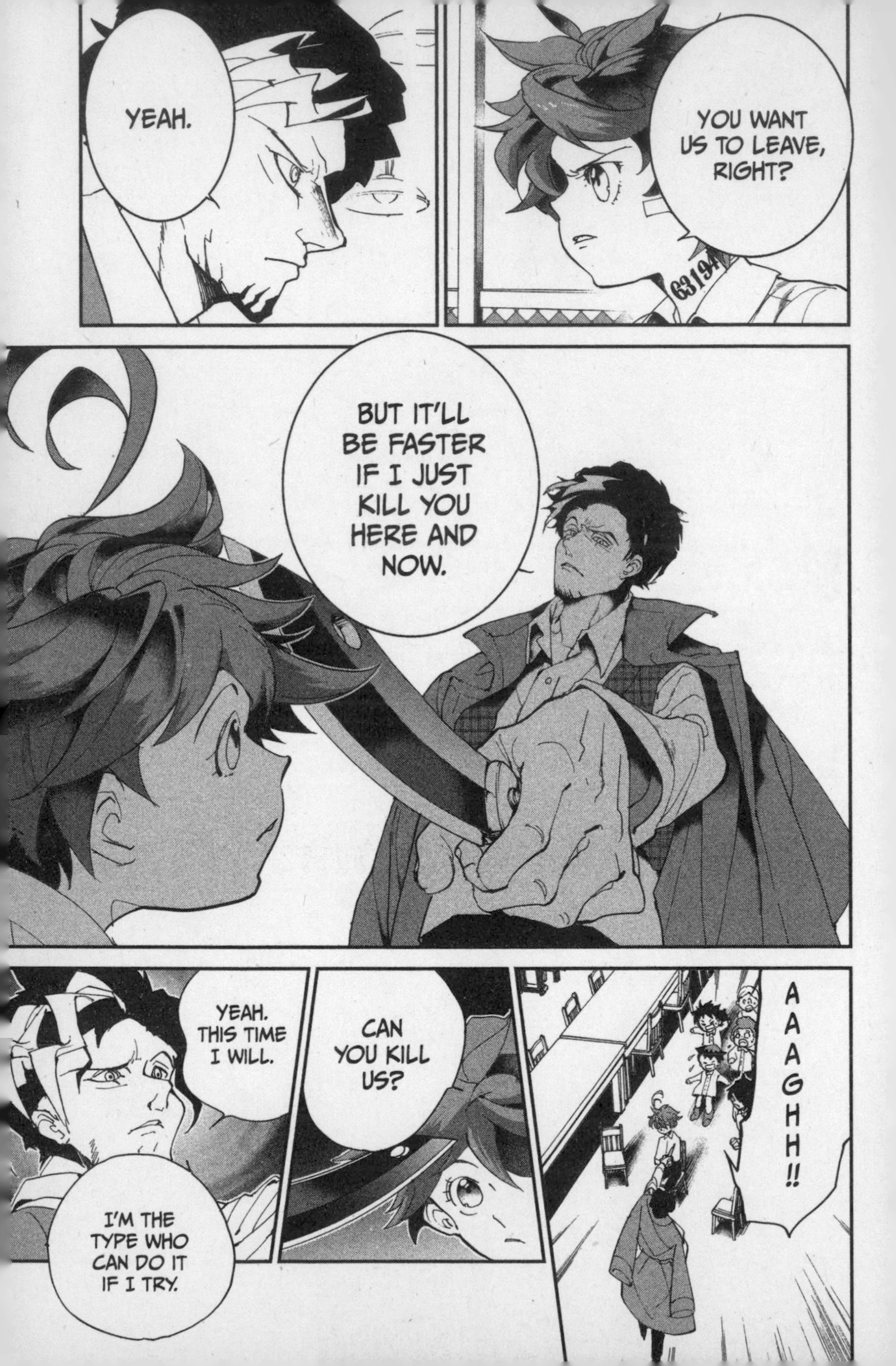
YOU WANT US TO LEAVE, RIGHT?
63194
YEAH.
BUT IT'LL BE FASTER IF I JUST KILL YOU HERE AND NOW.
AAAGHH!!
CAN YOU KILL US?
YEAH. THIS TIME I WILL.
I'M THE TYPE WHO CAN DO IT IF I TRY.

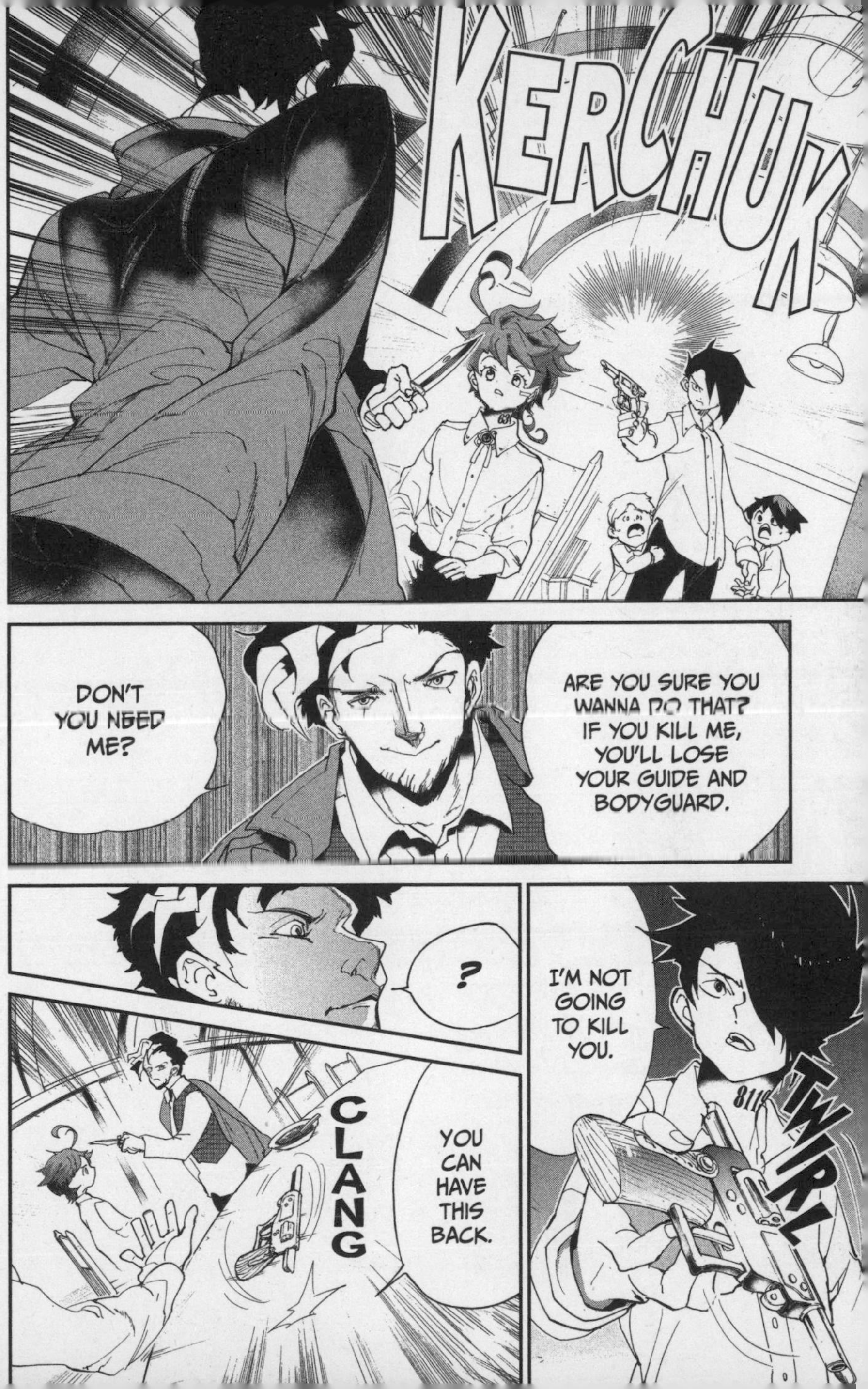
KERCHUK
ARE YOU SURE YOU WANNA DO THAT? IF YOU KILL ME, YOU'LL LOSE YOUR GUIDE AND BODYGUARD.
DON'T YOU NEED ME?
I'M NOT GOING TO KILL YOU.
TWIRL
?
YOU CAN HAVE THIS BACK.
CLANG

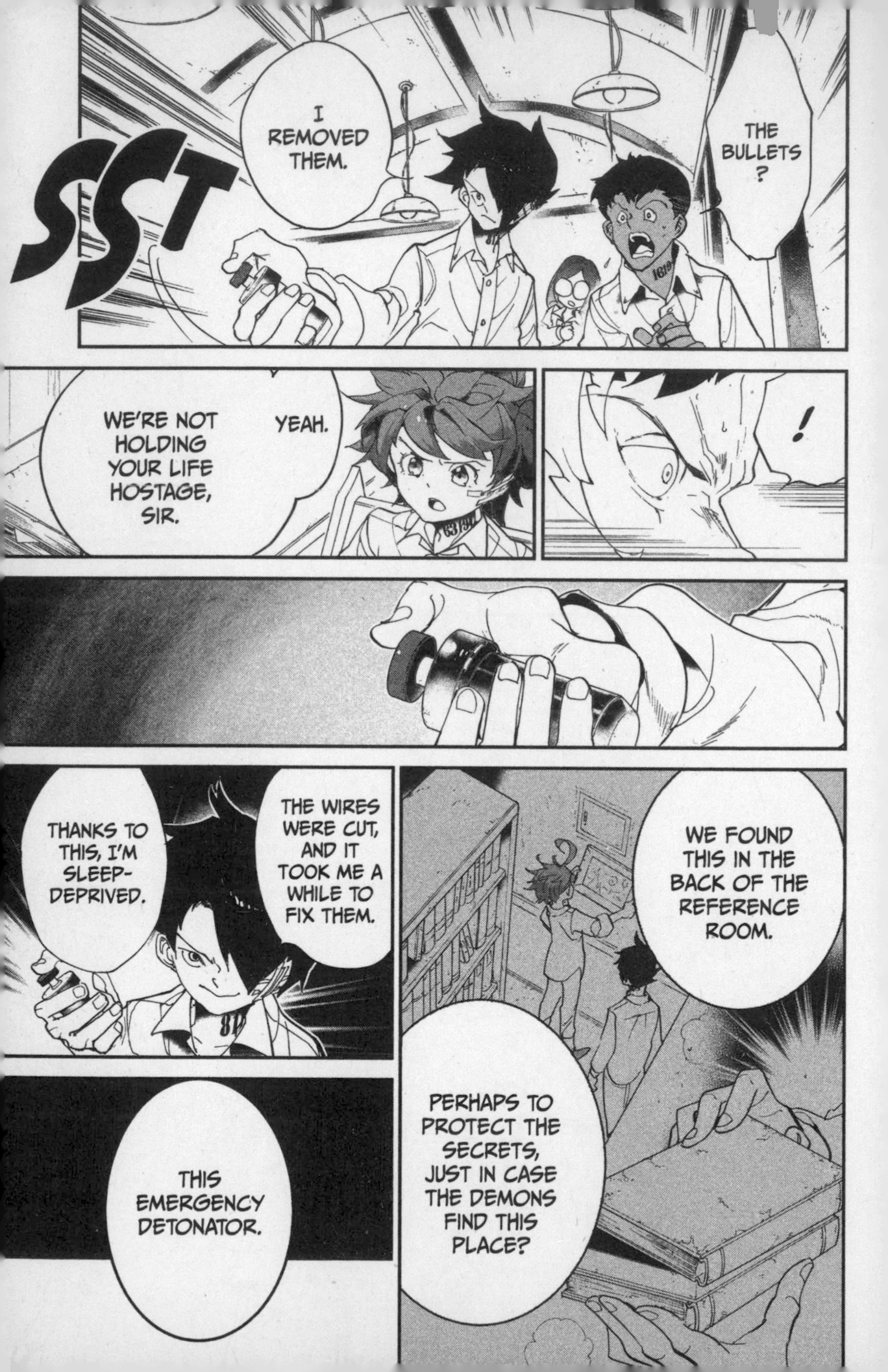
THE BULLETS?
I REMOVED THEM.
SST
!
YEAH.
WE'RE NOT HOLDING YOUR LIFE HOSTAGE, SIR.
WE FOUND THIS IN THE BACK OF THE REFERENCE ROOM.
PERHAPS TO PROTECT THE SECRETS, JUST IN CASE THE DEMONS FIND THIS PLACE?
THE WIRES WERE CUT, AND IT TOOK ME A WHILE TO FIX THEM.
THANKS TO THIS, I'M SLEEP-DEPRIVED.
THIS EMERGENCY DETONATOR.

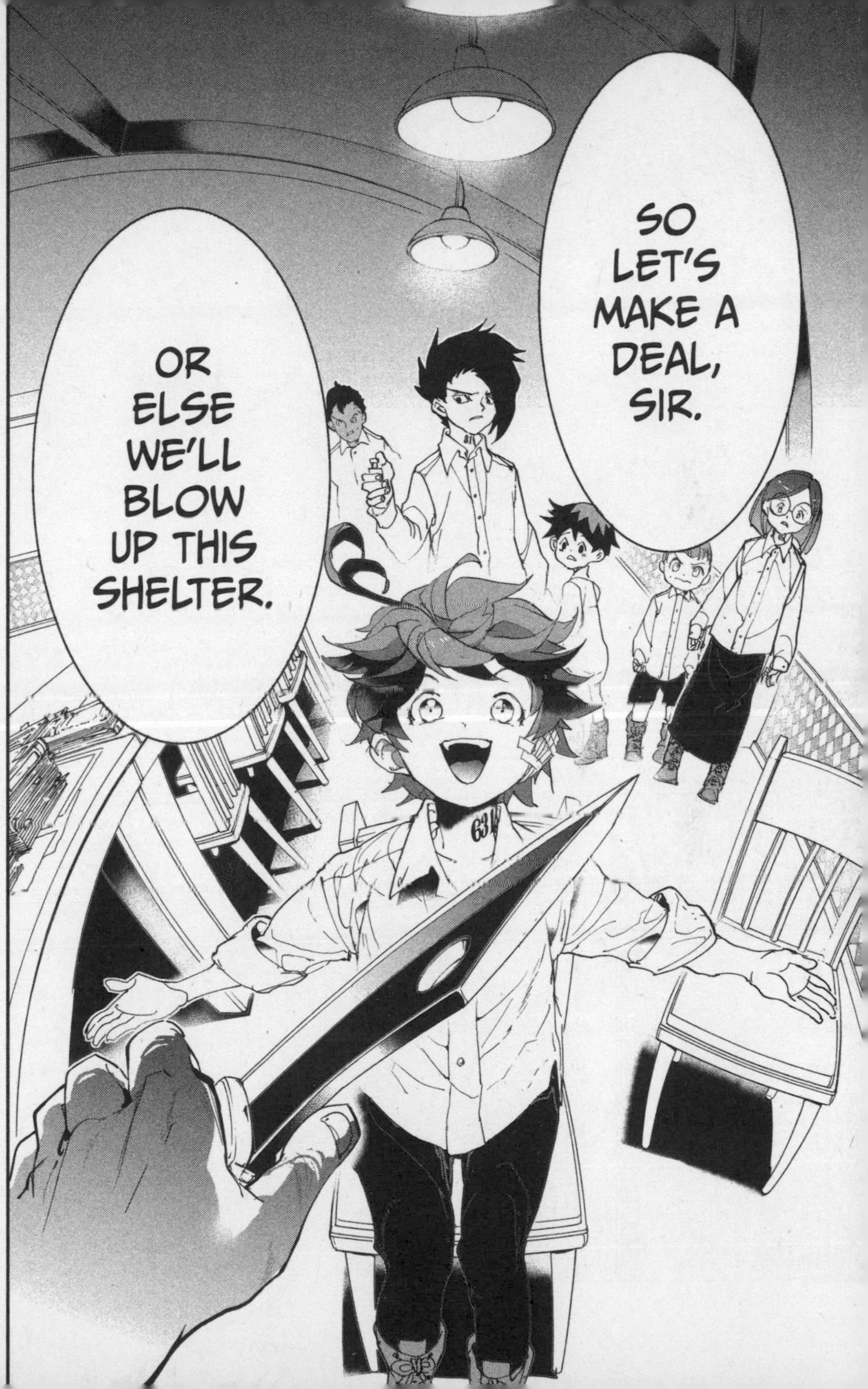
SO LET'S MAKE A DEAL, SIR.
OR ELSE WE'LL BLOW UP THIS SHELTER.

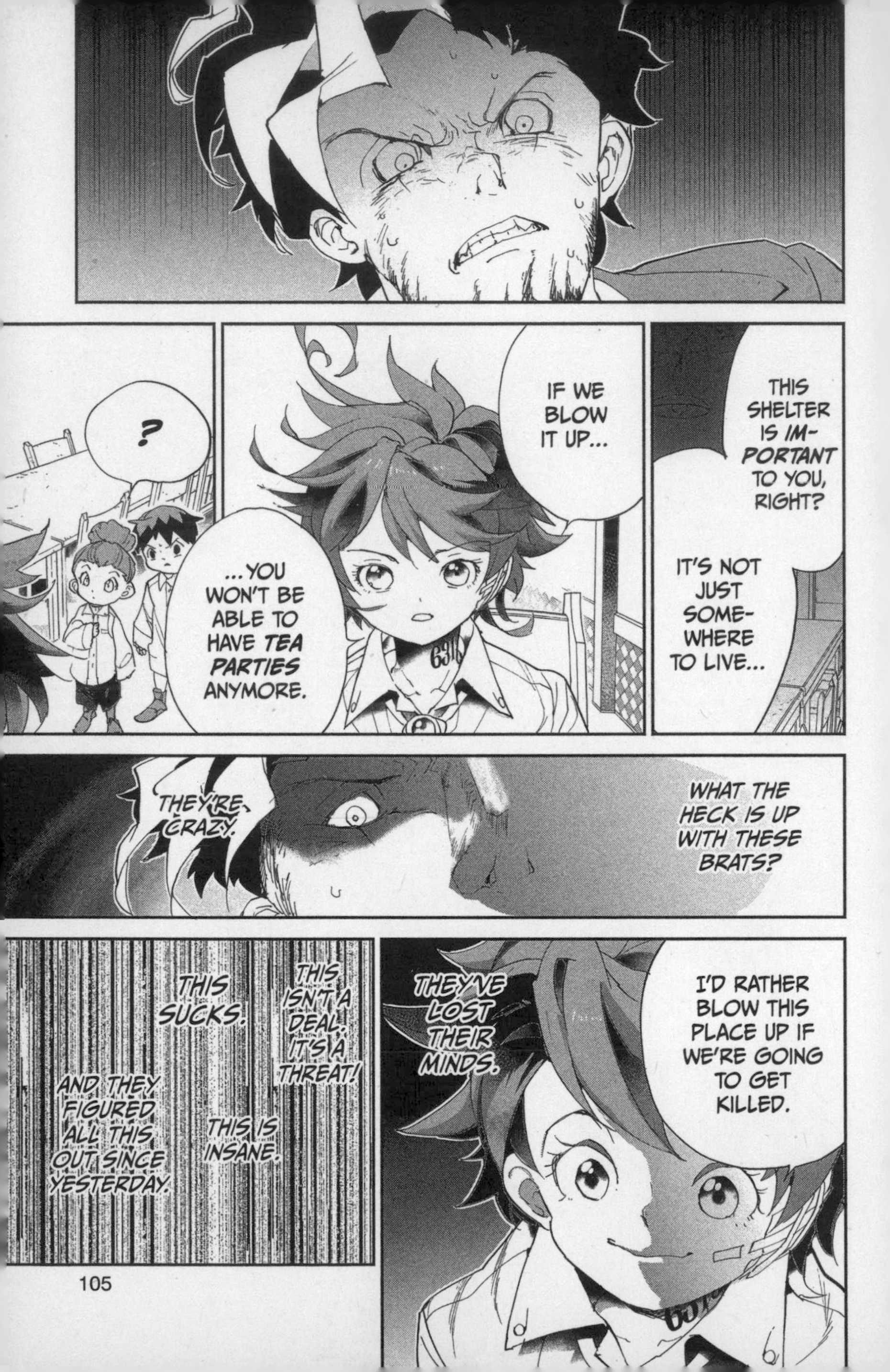
THIS SHELTER IS IMPORTANT TO YOU, RIGHT?
IT'S NOT JUST SOMEWHERE TO LIVE...
IF WE BLOW IT UP...
...YOU WON'T BE ABLE TO HAVE TEA PARTIES ANYMORE.
?
WHAT THE HECK IS UP WITH THESE BRATS?
THEY'RE CRAZY.
I'D RATHER BLOW THIS PLACE UP IF WE'RE GOING TO GET KILLED.
THEY'VE LOST THEIR MINDS.
THIS ISN'T A DEAL. IT'S A THREAT!
THIS SUCKS.
THIS IS INSANE.
AND THEY FIGURED ALL THIS OUT SINCE YESTERDAY.

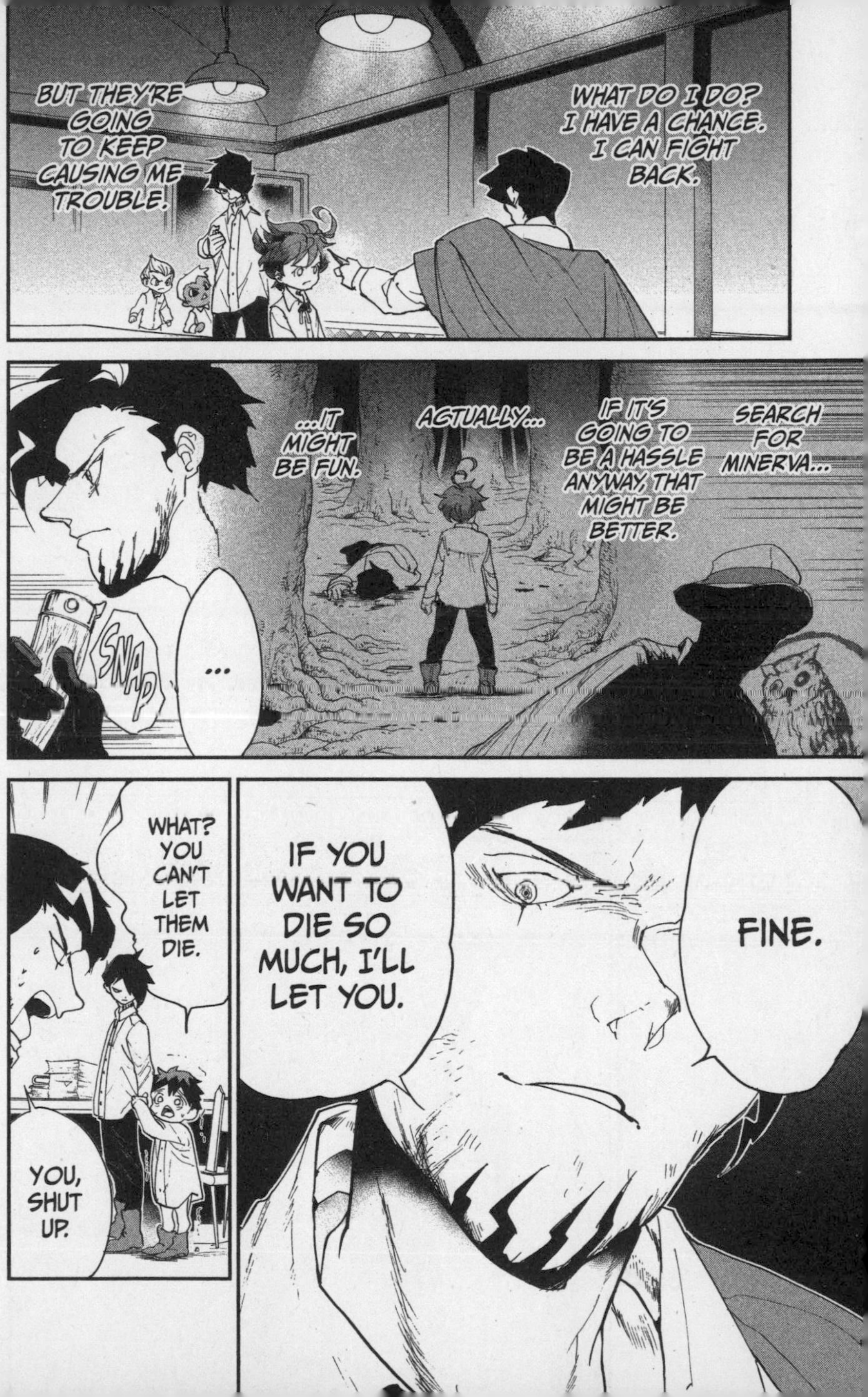
WHAT DO I DO? I HAVE A CHANCE. I CAN FIGHT BACK.
BUT THEY'RE GOING TO KEEP CAUSING ME TROUBLE.
SEARCH FOR MINERVA...
IF IT'S GOING TO BE A HASSLE ANYWAY, THAT MIGHT BE BETTER.
ACTUALLY...
...IT MIGHT BE FUN.
...
SNAP
FINE.
IF YOU WANT TO DIE SO MUCH, I'LL LET YOU.
WHAT? YOU CAN'T LET THEM DIE.
YOU, SHUT UP.

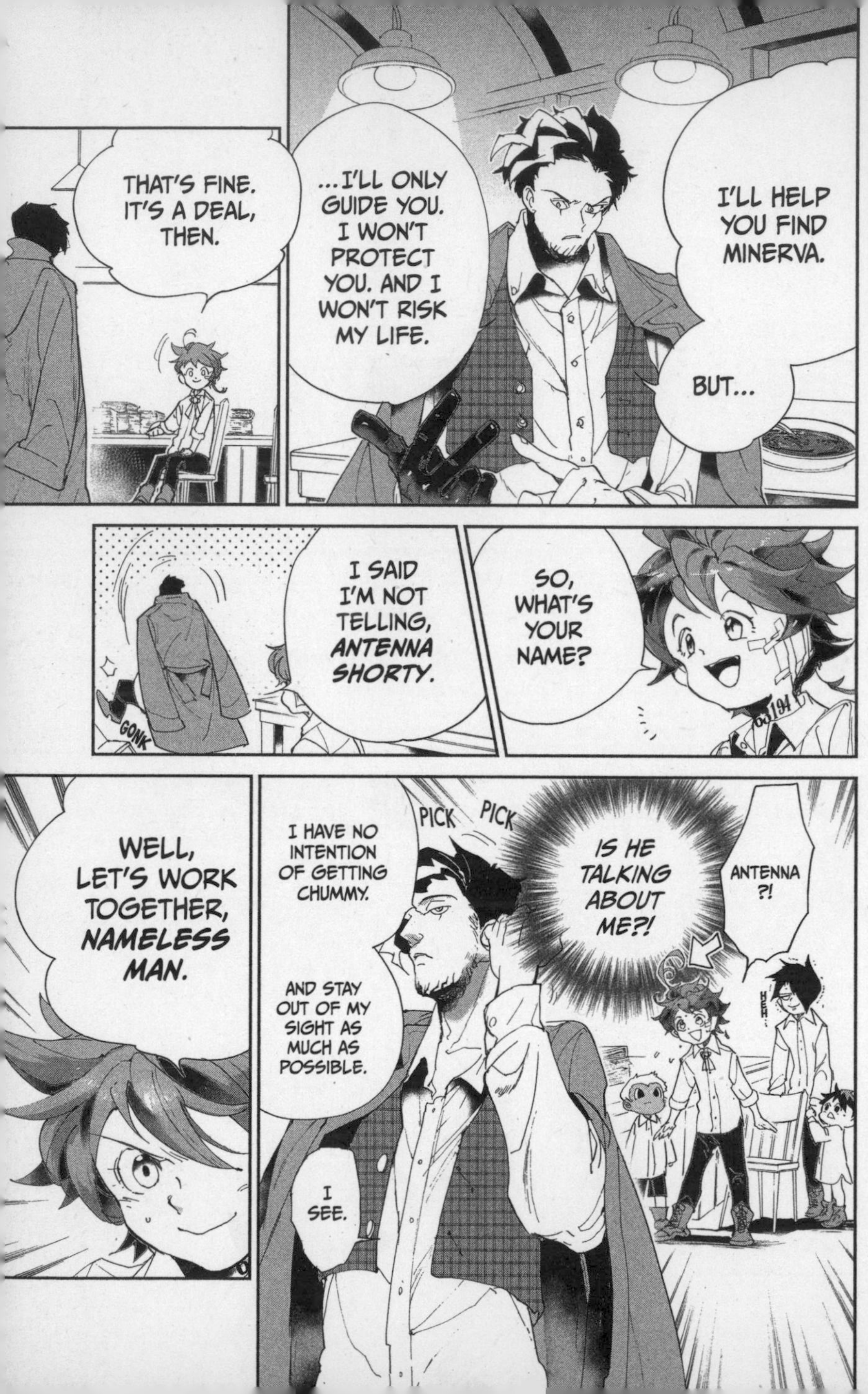
I'LL HELP YOU FIND MINERVA.
BUT...
...I'LL ONLY GUIDE YOU. I WON'T PROTECT YOU. AND I WON'T RISK MY LIFE.
THAT'S FINE. IT'S A DEAL, THEN.
SO, WHAT'S YOUR NAME?
I SAID I'M NOT TELLING, *ANTENNA SHORTY*.
GONK
ANTENNA ?!
IS HE TALKING ABOUT ME?!
PICK PICK
I HAVE NO INTENTION OF GETTING CHUMMY.
AND STAY OUT OF MY SIGHT AS MUCH AS POSSIBLE.
HEH
I SEE.
WELL, LET'S WORK TOGETHER, *NAMELESS MAN*.

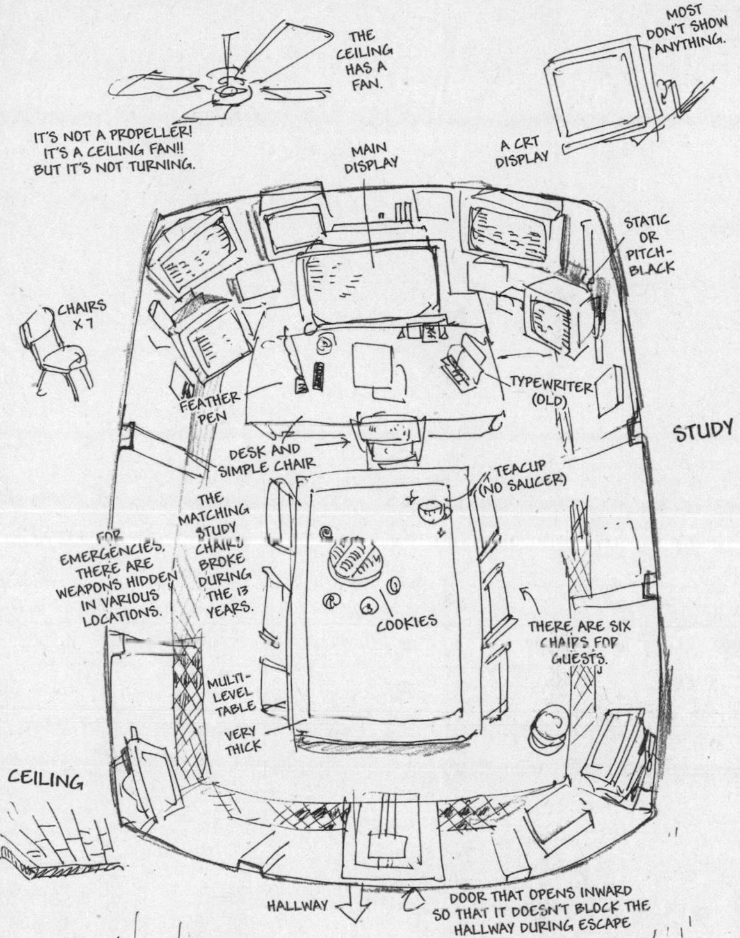
THE CEILING HAS A FAN.
MOST DON'T SHOW ANYTHING.
IT'S NOT A PROPELLER! IT'S A CEILING FAN!! BUT IT'S NOT TURNING.
MAIN DISPLAY
A CRT DISPLAY
STATIC OR PITCH-BLACK
CHAIRS X7
FEATHER PEN
TYPEWRITER (OLD)
STUDY
DESK AND SIMPLE CHAIR
TEACUP (NO SAUCER)
THE MATCHING STUDY CHAIR BROKE DURING THE 13 YEARS.
FOR EMERGENCIES, THERE ARE WEAPONS HIDDEN IN VARIOUS LOCATIONS.
COOKIES
THERE ARE SIX CHAIRS FOR GUESTS.
MULTI-LEVEL TABLE
VERY THICK
CEILING
HALLWAY
DOOR THAT OPENS INWARD SO THAT IT DOESN'T BLOCK THE HALLWAY DURING ESCAPE

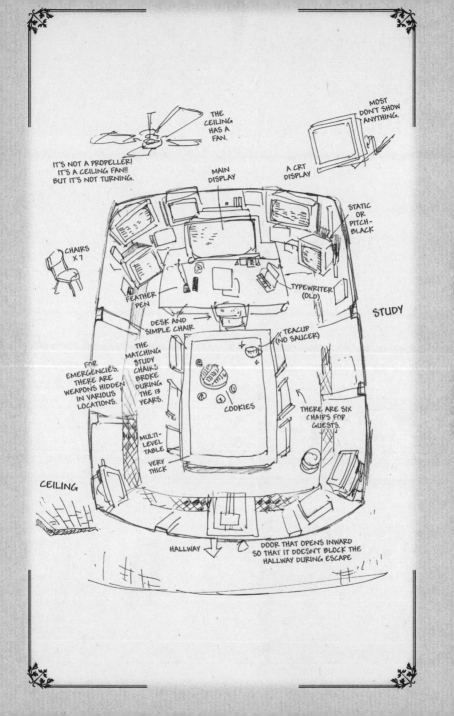

CHAPTER 58: DECISION

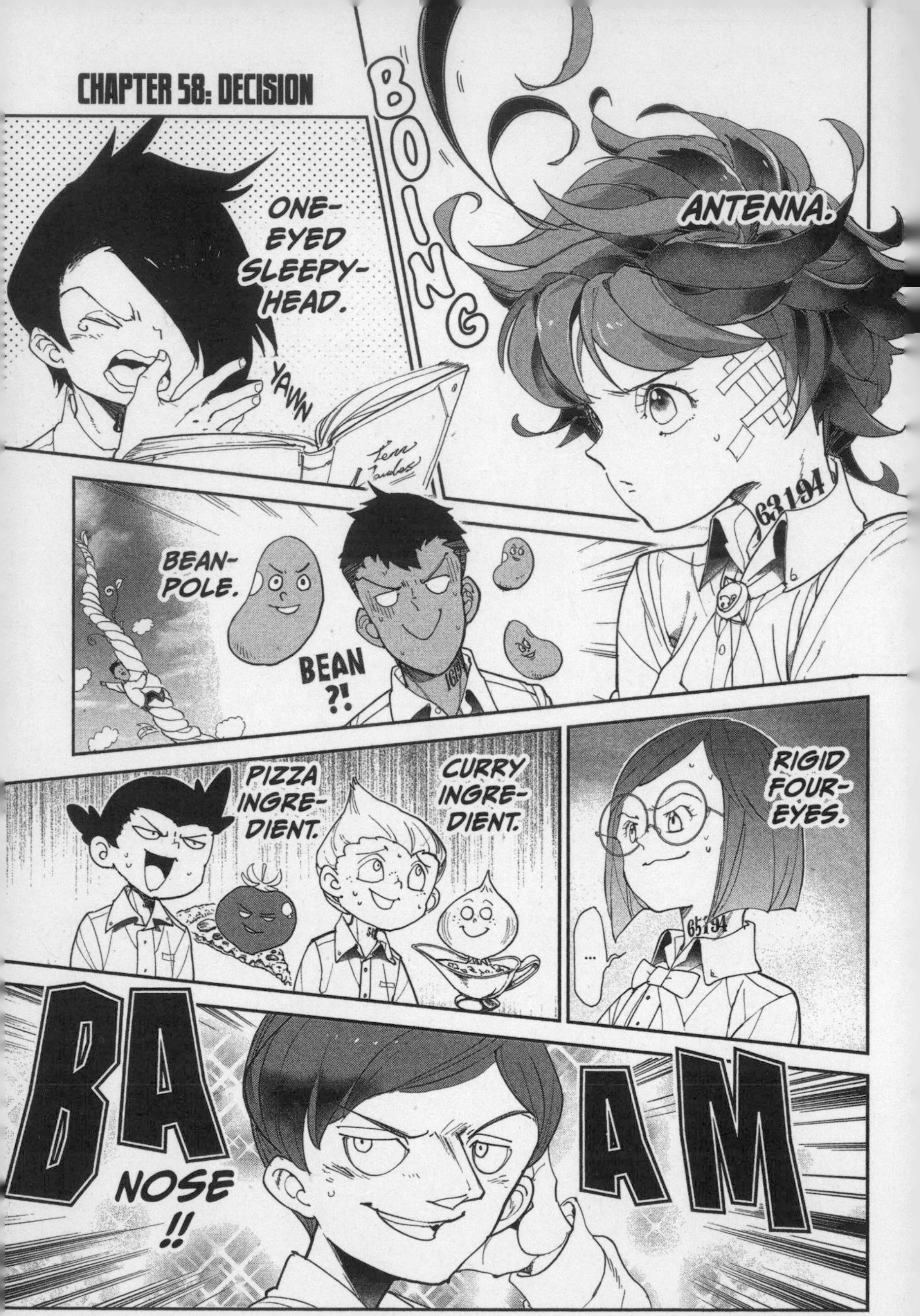
ANTENNA.
BOING
ONE-EYED SLEEPY-HEAD.
YAWN
BEAN-POLE.
BEAN ?!
RIGID FOUR-EYES.
...
CURRY INGRE-DIENT.
PIZZA INGRE-DIENT.
BA AM
NOSE !!

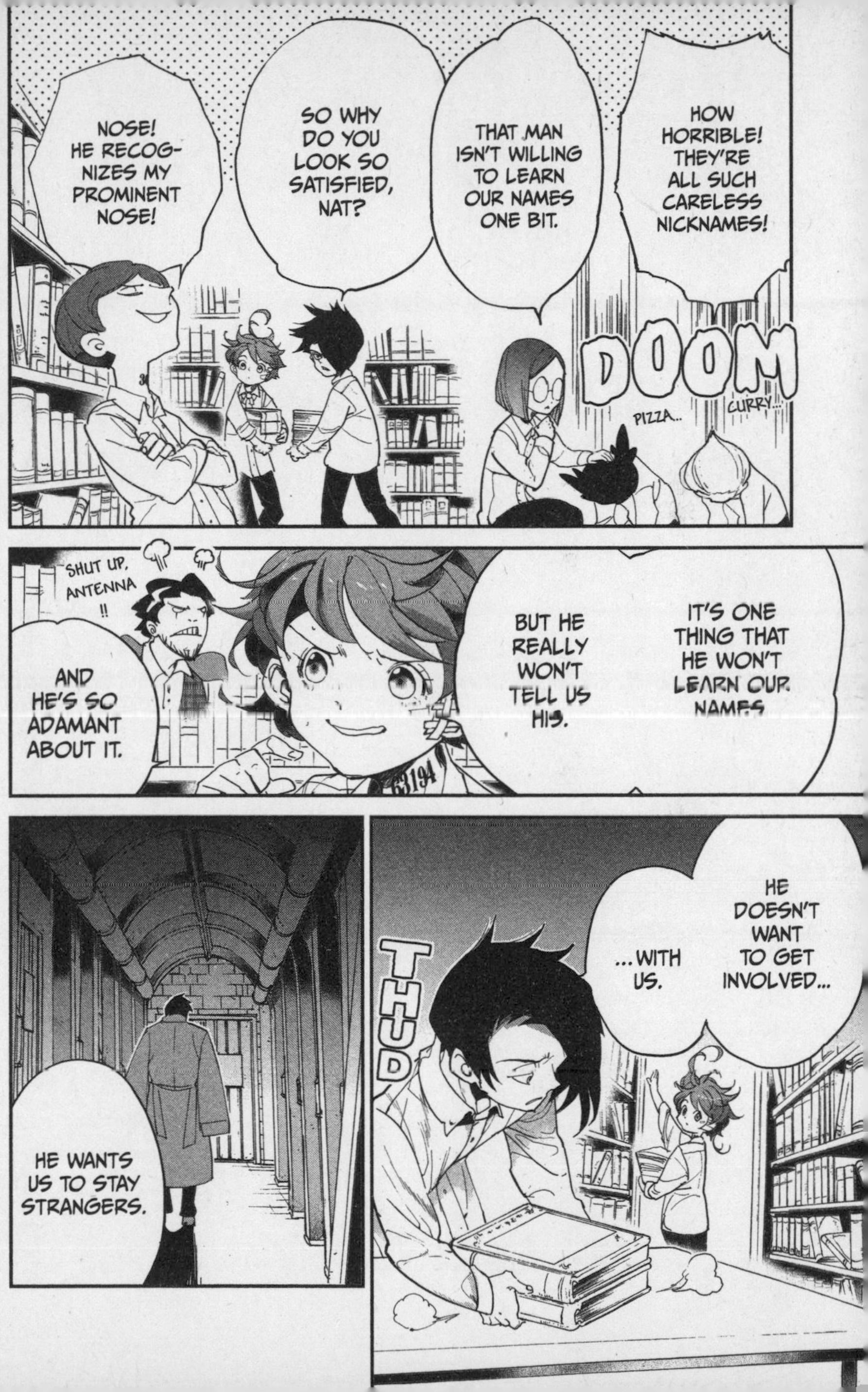
HOW HORRIBLE! THEY'RE ALL SUCH CARELESS NICKNAMES!
THAT MAN ISN'T WILLING TO LEARN OUR NAMES ONE BIT.
DOOM
CURRY...
PIZZA...
SO WHY DO YOU LOOK SO SATISFIED, NAT?
NOSE! HE RECOGNIZES MY PROMINENT NOSE!
IT'S ONE THING THAT HE WON'T LEARN OUR NAMES
BUT HE REALLY WON'T TELL US HIS.
AND HE'S SO ADAMANT ABOUT IT.
SHUT UP, ANTENNA!!
HE DOESN'T WANT TO GET INVOLVED...
...WITH US.
THUD
HE WANTS US TO STAY STRANGERS.

CHAPTER 58: DECISION

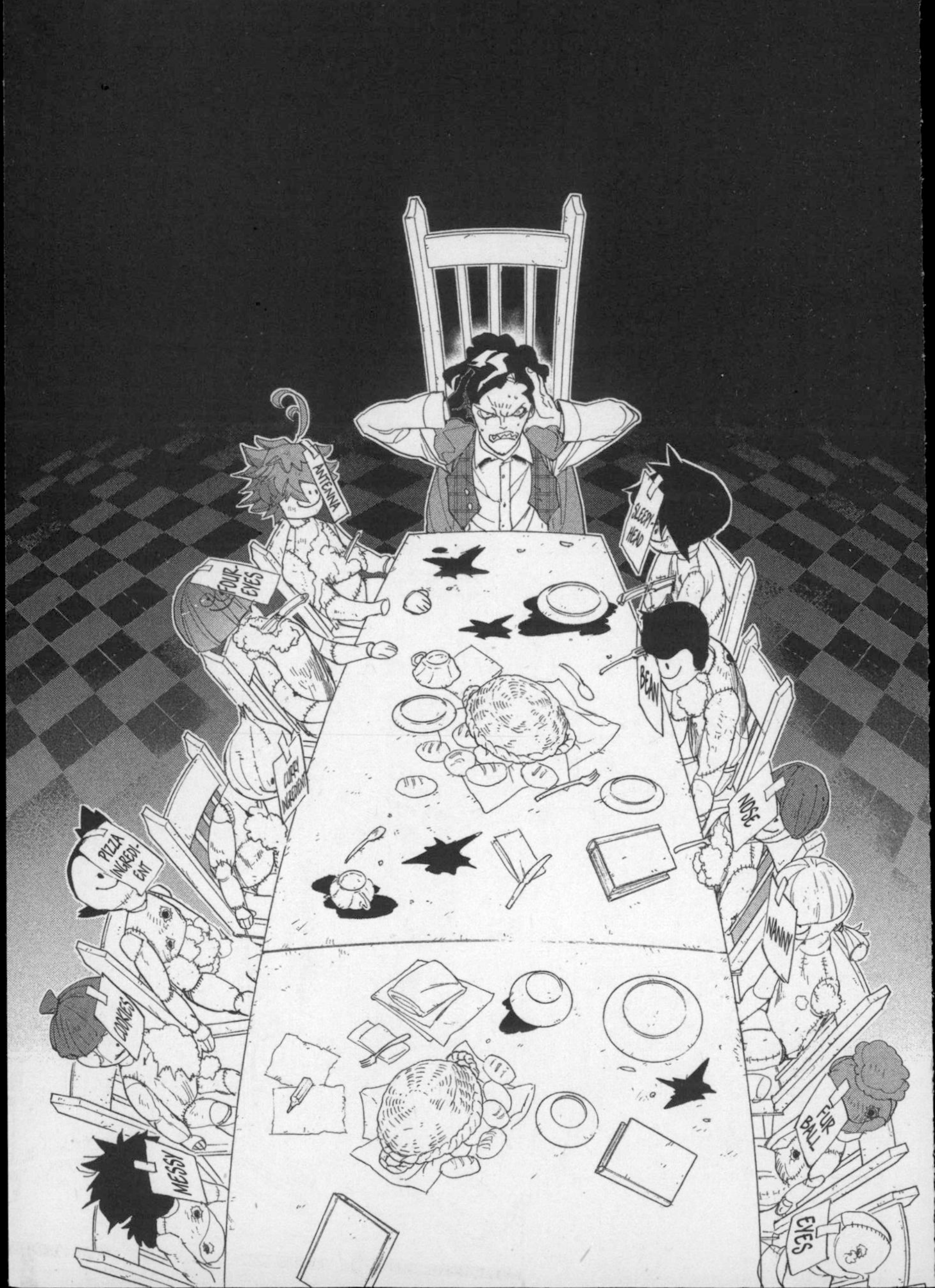
SLEEPY-HEAD
ANTENNA
FOUR-EYES
BEAN
NOSE
CURRY INGREDIENT
PIZZA INGREDI-ENT
NANNY
COOKIES
FUR BALL
MESSY
EYES

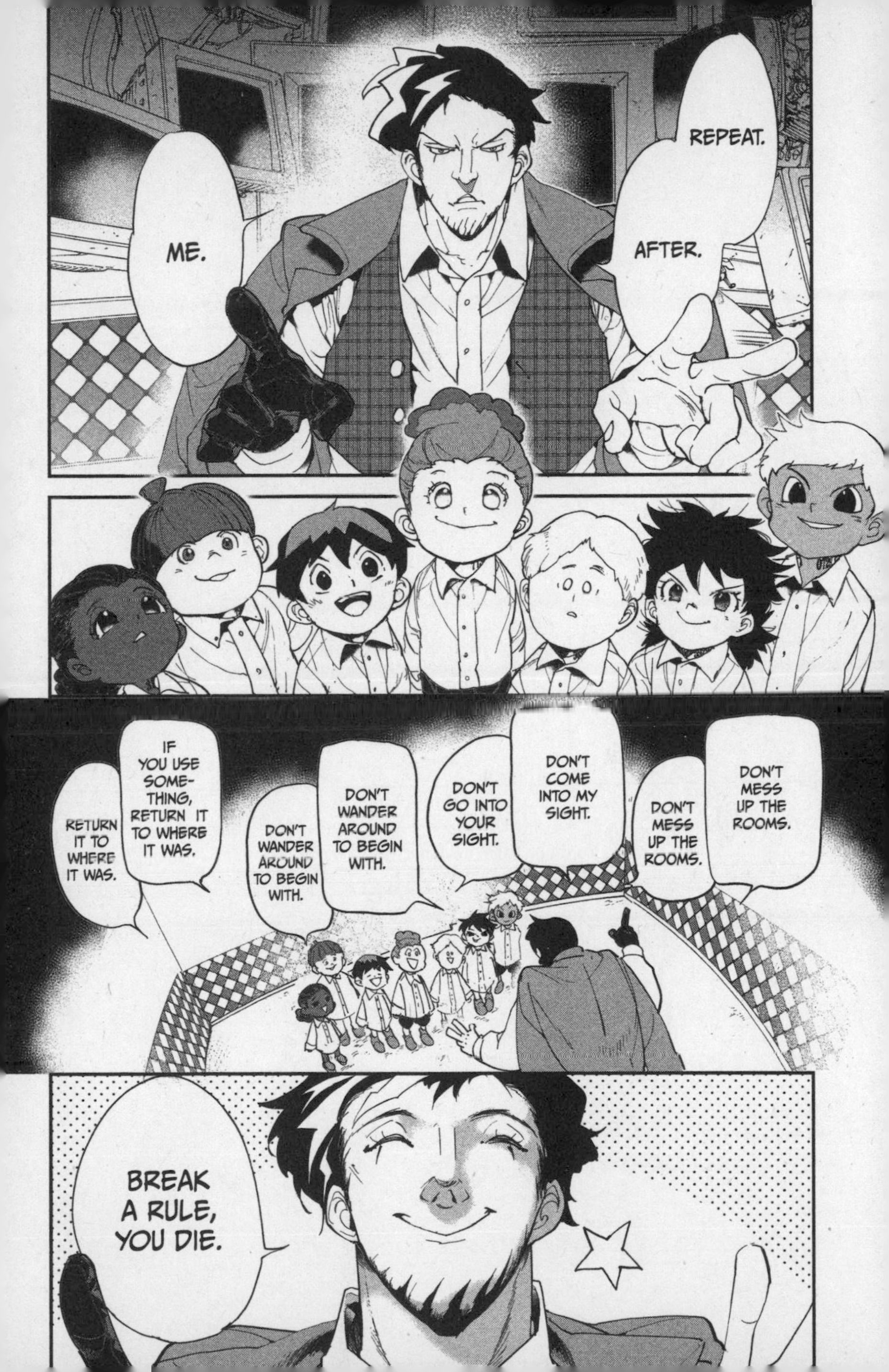
REPEAT. AFTER.
ME.
DON'T MESS UP THE ROOMS.
DON'T MESS UP THE ROOMS.
DON'T COME INTO MY SIGHT.
DON'T GO INTO YOUR SIGHT.
DON'T WANDER AROUND TO BEGIN WITH.
DON'T WANDER AROUND TO BEGIN WITH.
IF YOU USE SOME-THING, RETURN IT TO WHERE IT WAS.
RETURN IT TO WHERE IT WAS.
BREAK A RULE, YOU DIE.

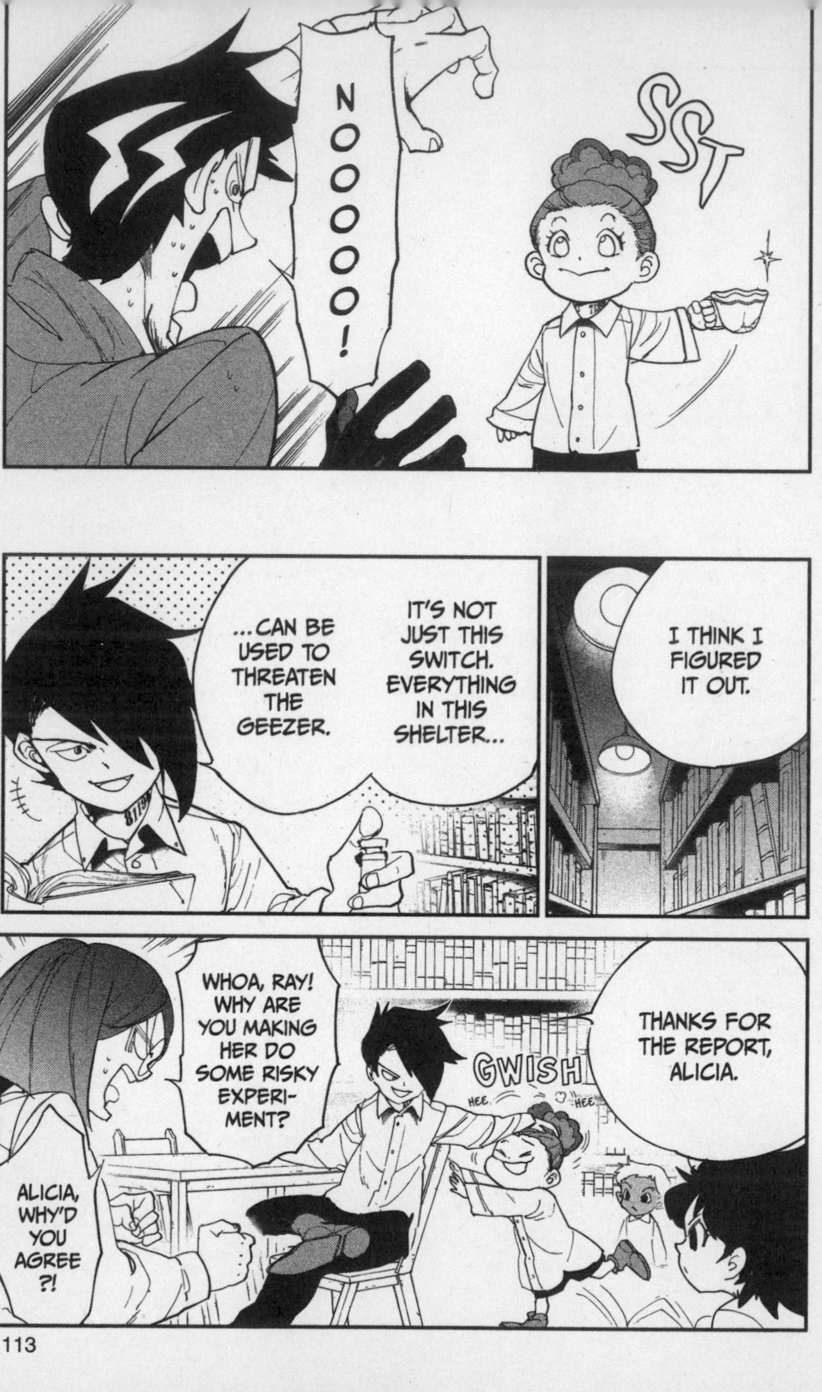
SST
NOOOOOO!
I THINK I FIGURED IT OUT.
IT'S NOT JUST THIS SWITCH. EVERYTHING IN THIS SHELTER...
...CAN BE USED TO THREATEN THE GEEZER.
THANKS FOR THE REPORT, ALICIA.
GWISH
HEE HEE
WHOA, RAY! WHY ARE YOU MAKING HER DO SOME RISKY EXPERI-MENT?
ALICIA, WHY'D YOU AGREE ?!

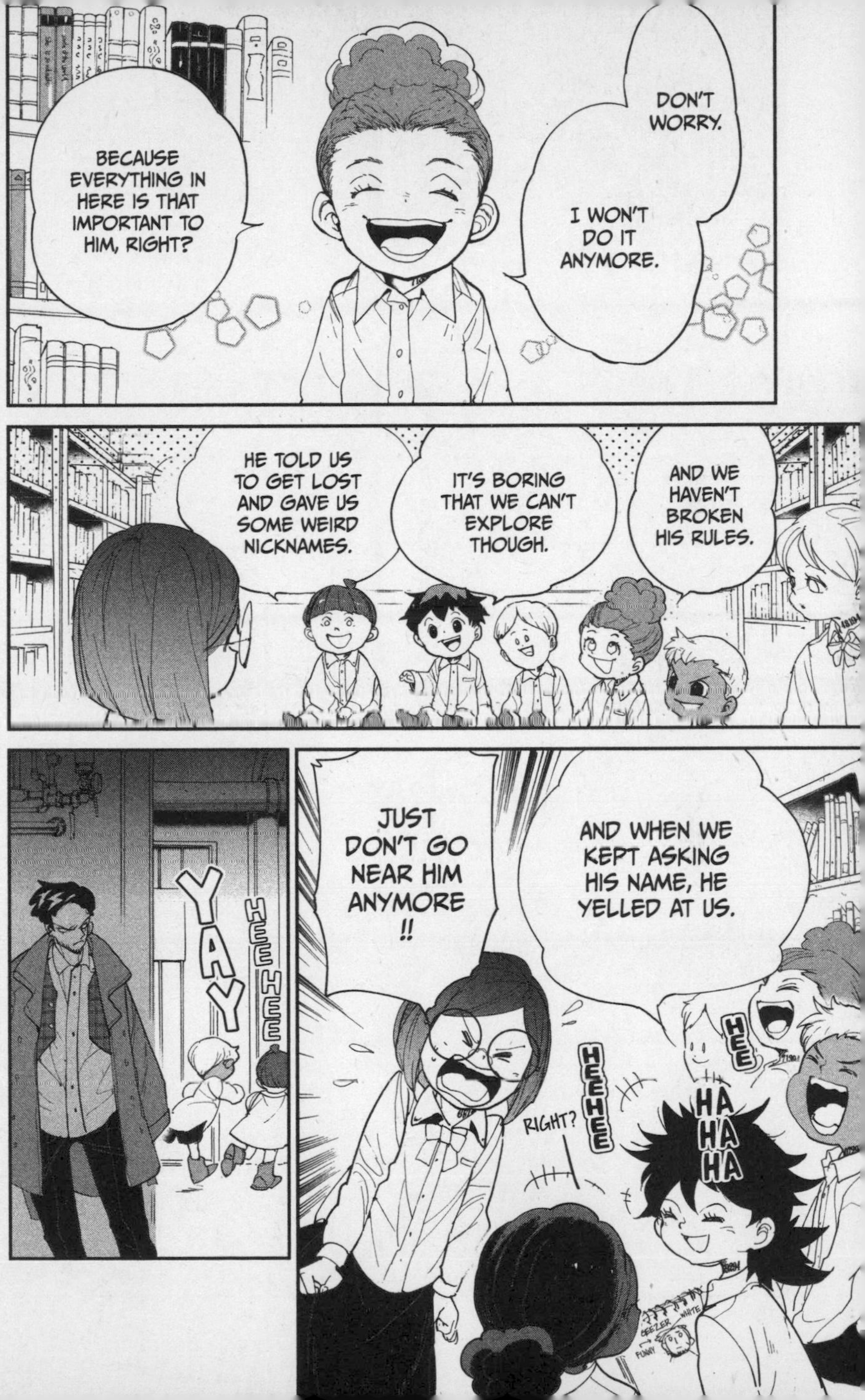
DON'T WORRY.
I WON'T DO IT ANYMORE.
BECAUSE EVERYTHING IN HERE IS THAT IMPORTANT TO HIM, RIGHT?
AND WE HAVEN'T BROKEN HIS RULES.
IT'S BORING THAT WE CAN'T EXPLORE THOUGH.
HE TOLD US TO GET LOST AND GAVE US SOME WEIRD NICKNAMES.
AND WHEN WE KEPT ASKING HIS NAME, HE YELLED AT US.
HEE
HA HA HA
HEEHEE
RIGHT?
JUST DON'T GO NEAR HIM ANYMORE!!
YAY
HEEHEE

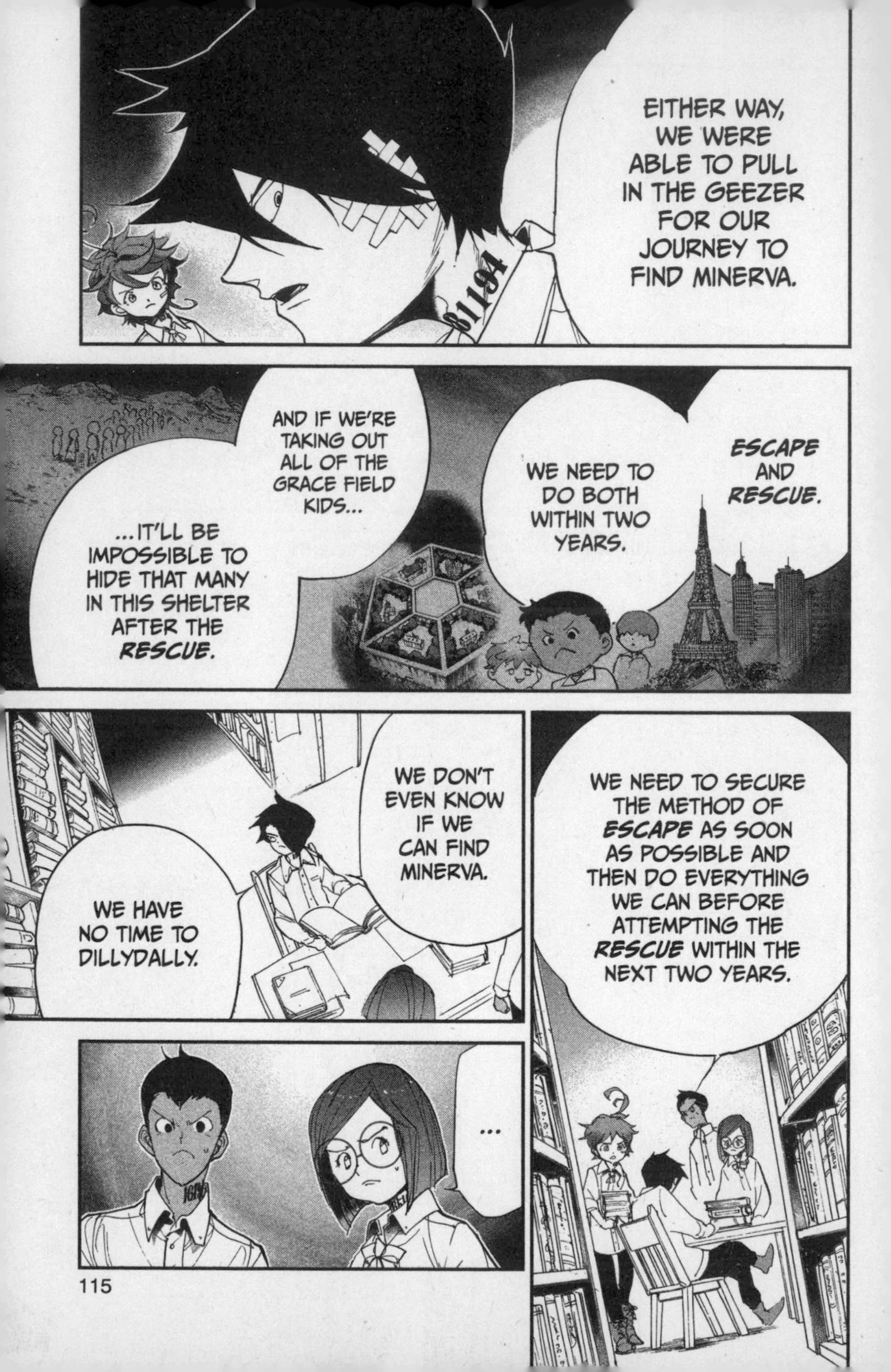
EITHER WAY, WE WERE ABLE TO PULL IN THE GEEZER FOR OUR JOURNEY TO FIND MINERVA.
ESCAPE AND RESCUE.
WE NEED TO DO BOTH WITHIN TWO YEARS.
AND IF WE'RE TAKING OUT ALL OF THE GRACE FIELD KIDS...
...IT'LL BE IMPOSSIBLE TO HIDE THAT MANY IN THIS SHELTER AFTER THE RESCUE.
WE NEED TO SECURE THE METHOD OF ESCAPE AS SOON AS POSSIBLE AND THEN DO EVERYTHING WE CAN BEFORE ATTEMPTING THE RESCUE WITHIN THE NEXT TWO YEARS.
WE DON'T EVEN KNOW IF WE CAN FIND MINERVA.
WE HAVE NO TIME TO DILLYDALLY.
...

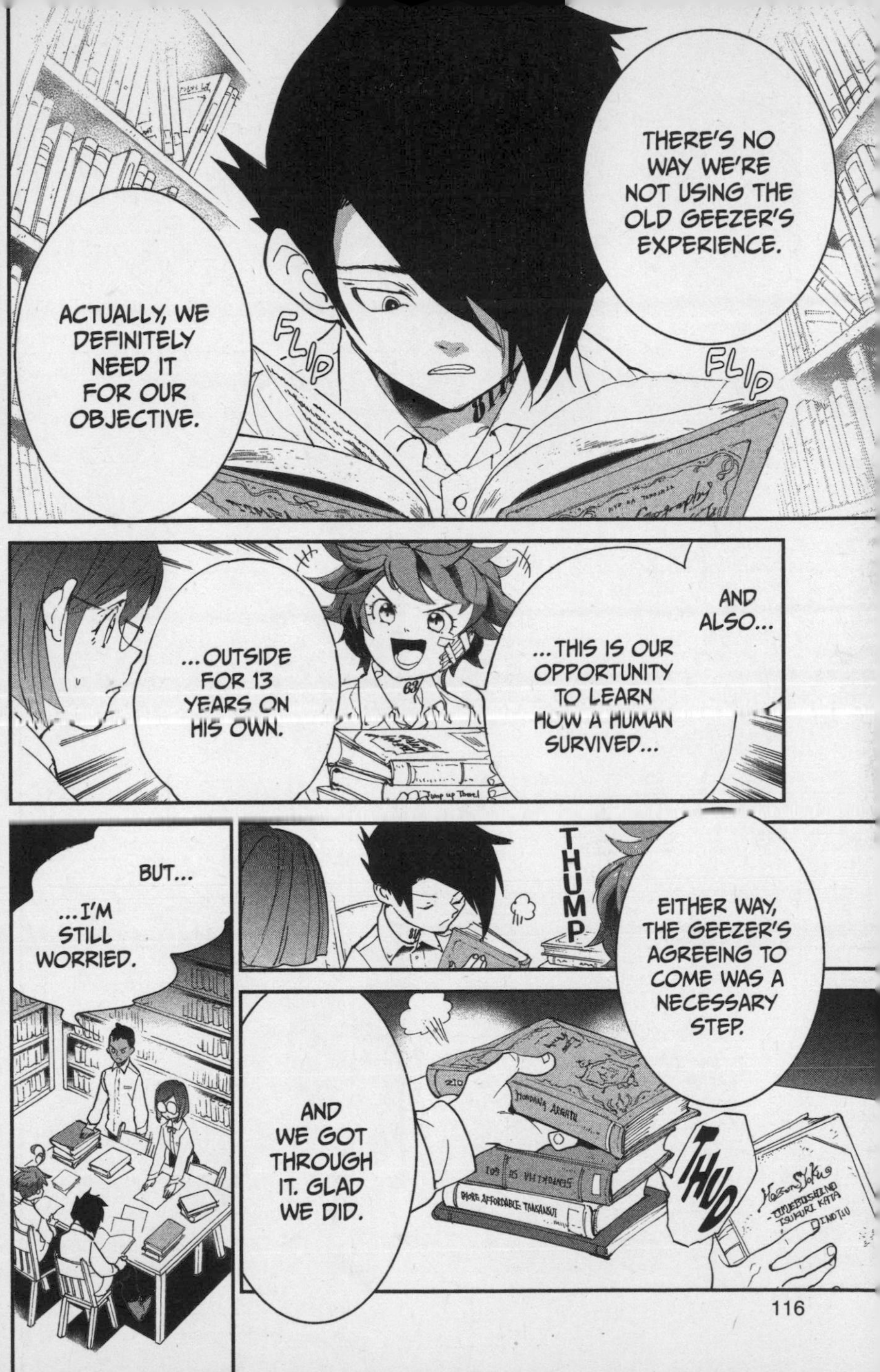
THERE'S NO WAY WE'RE NOT USING THE OLD GEEZER'S EXPERIENCE.
FLIP
FLIP
ACTUALLY, WE DEFINITELY NEED IT FOR OUR OBJECTIVE.
AND ALSO...
...THIS IS OUR OPPORTUNITY TO LEARN HOW A HUMAN SURVIVED...
...OUTSIDE FOR 13 YEARS ON HIS OWN.
THUMP
EITHER WAY, THE GEEZER'S AGREEING TO COME WAS A NECESSARY STEP.
THUD
AND WE GOT THROUGH IT. GLAD WE DID.
BUT...
...I'M STILL WORRIED.

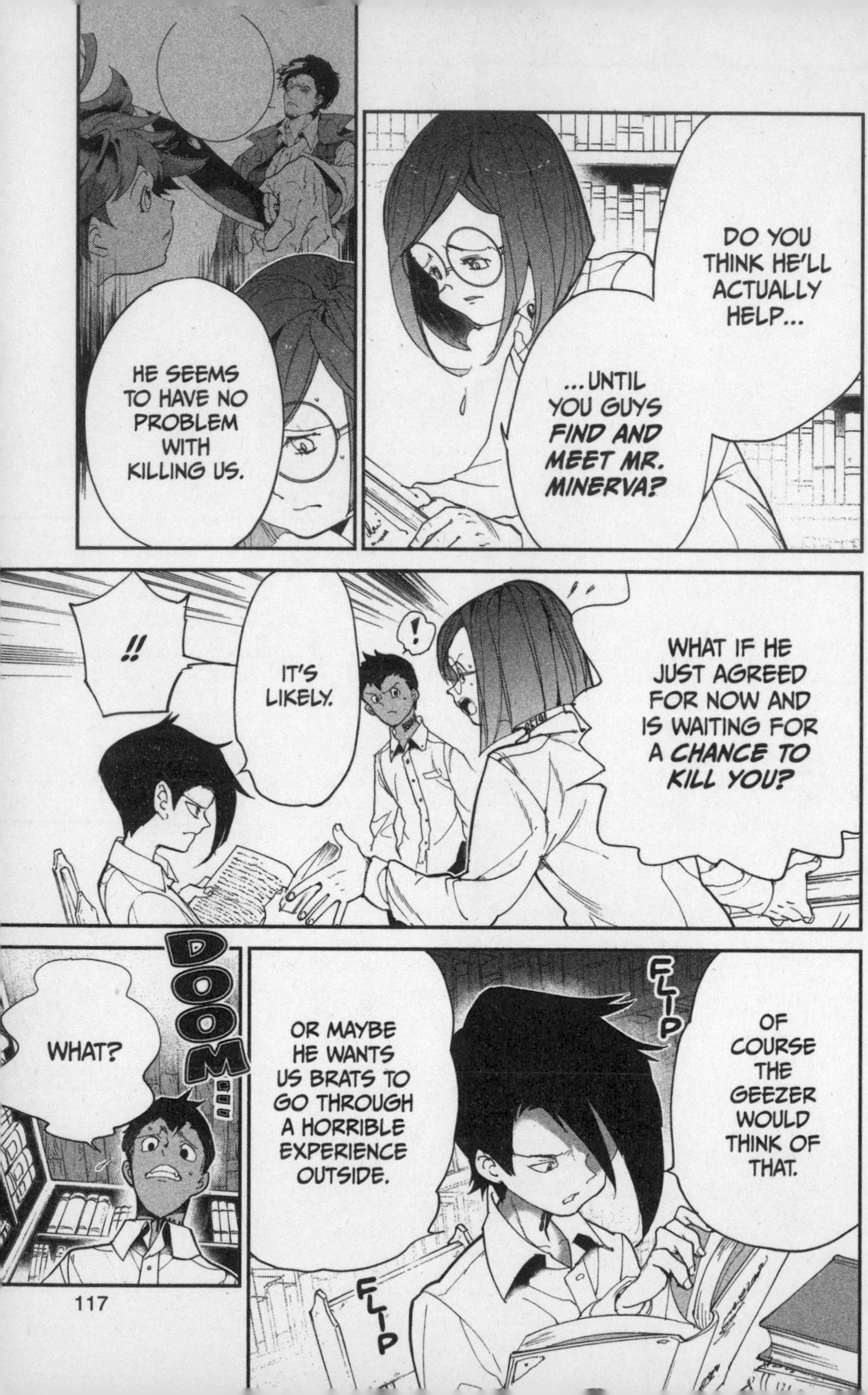
DO YOU THINK HE'LL ACTUALLY HELP...
...UNTIL YOU GUYS *FIND AND MEET MR. MINERVA?*
HE SEEMS TO HAVE NO PROBLEM WITH KILLING US.
WHAT IF HE JUST AGREED FOR NOW AND IS WAITING FOR A *CHANCE TO KILL YOU?*
!
IT'S LIKELY.
!!
FLIP
OF COURSE THE GEEZER WOULD THINK OF THAT.
OR MAYBE HE WANTS US BRATS TO GO THROUGH A HORRIBLE EXPERIENCE OUTSIDE.
FLIP
DOOM...
WHAT?

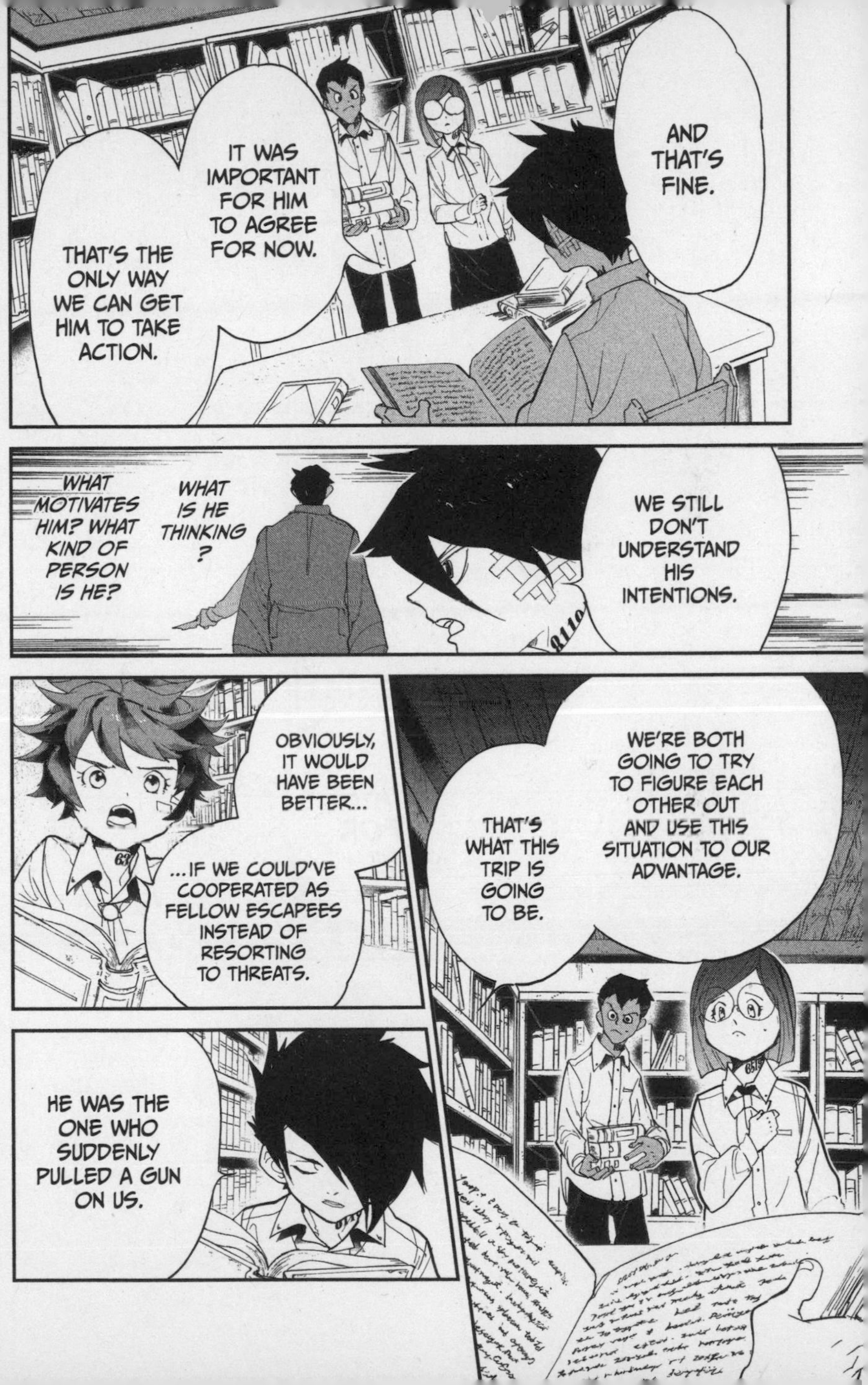
AND THAT'S FINE.
IT WAS IMPORTANT FOR HIM TO AGREE FOR NOW.
THAT'S THE ONLY WAY WE CAN GET HIM TO TAKE ACTION.
WE STILL DON'T UNDERSTAND HIS INTENTIONS.
WHAT IS HE THINKING?
WHAT MOTIVATES HIM? WHAT KIND OF PERSON IS HE?
WE'RE BOTH GOING TO TRY TO FIGURE EACH OTHER OUT AND USE THIS SITUATION TO OUR ADVANTAGE.
THAT'S WHAT THIS TRIP IS GOING TO BE.
OBVIOUSLY, IT WOULD HAVE BEEN BETTER...
...IF WE COULD'VE COOPERATED AS FELLOW ESCAPEES INSTEAD OF RESORTING TO THREATS.
HE WAS THE ONE WHO SUDDENLY PULLED A GUN ON US.

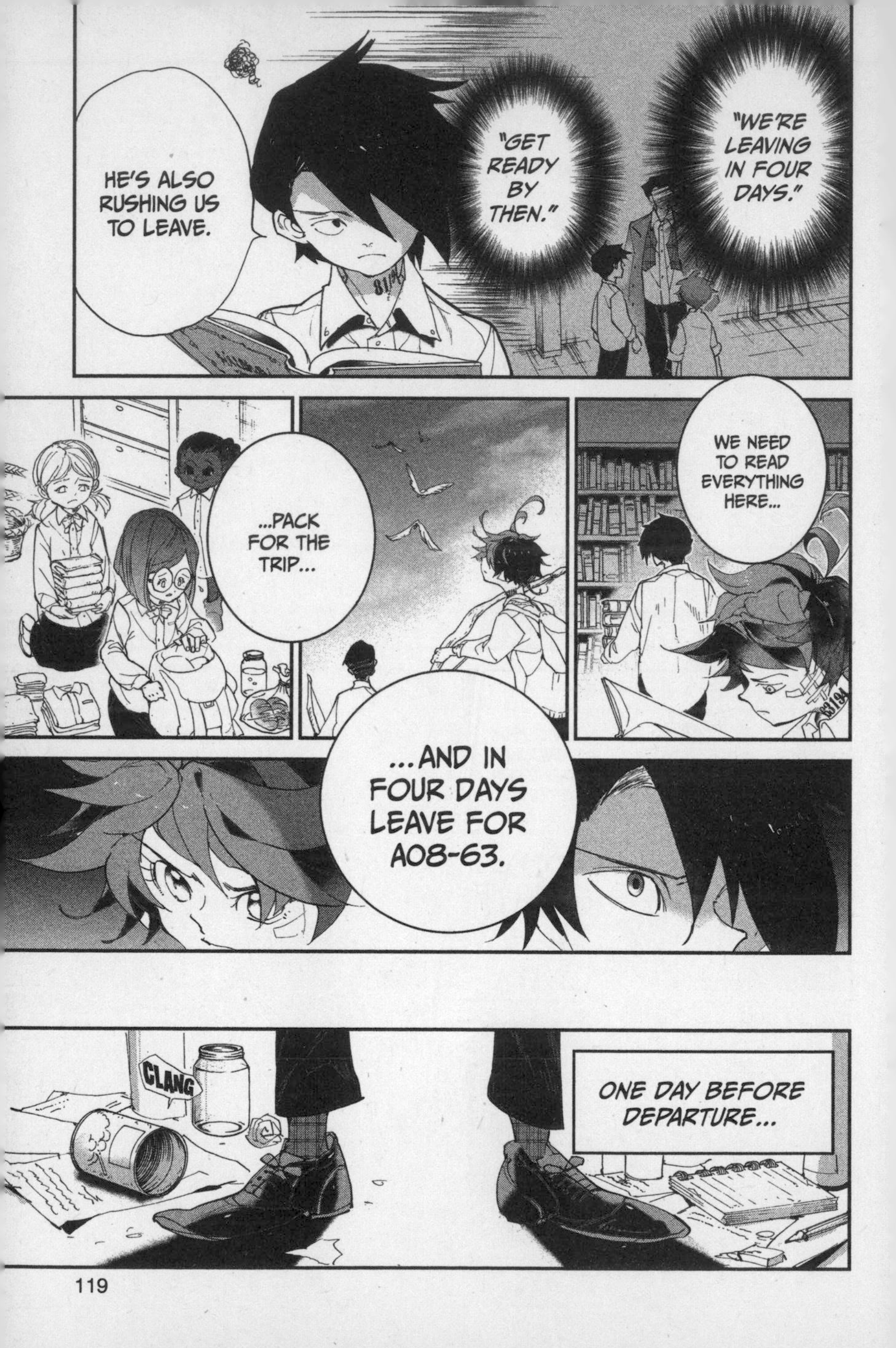
"WE'RE LEAVING IN FOUR DAYS."
"GET READY BY THEN."
HE'S ALSO RUSHING US TO LEAVE.
WE NEED TO READ EVERYTHING HERE...
...PACK FOR THE TRIP...
...AND IN FOUR DAYS LEAVE FOR A08-63.
ONE DAY BEFORE DEPARTURE...
CLANG

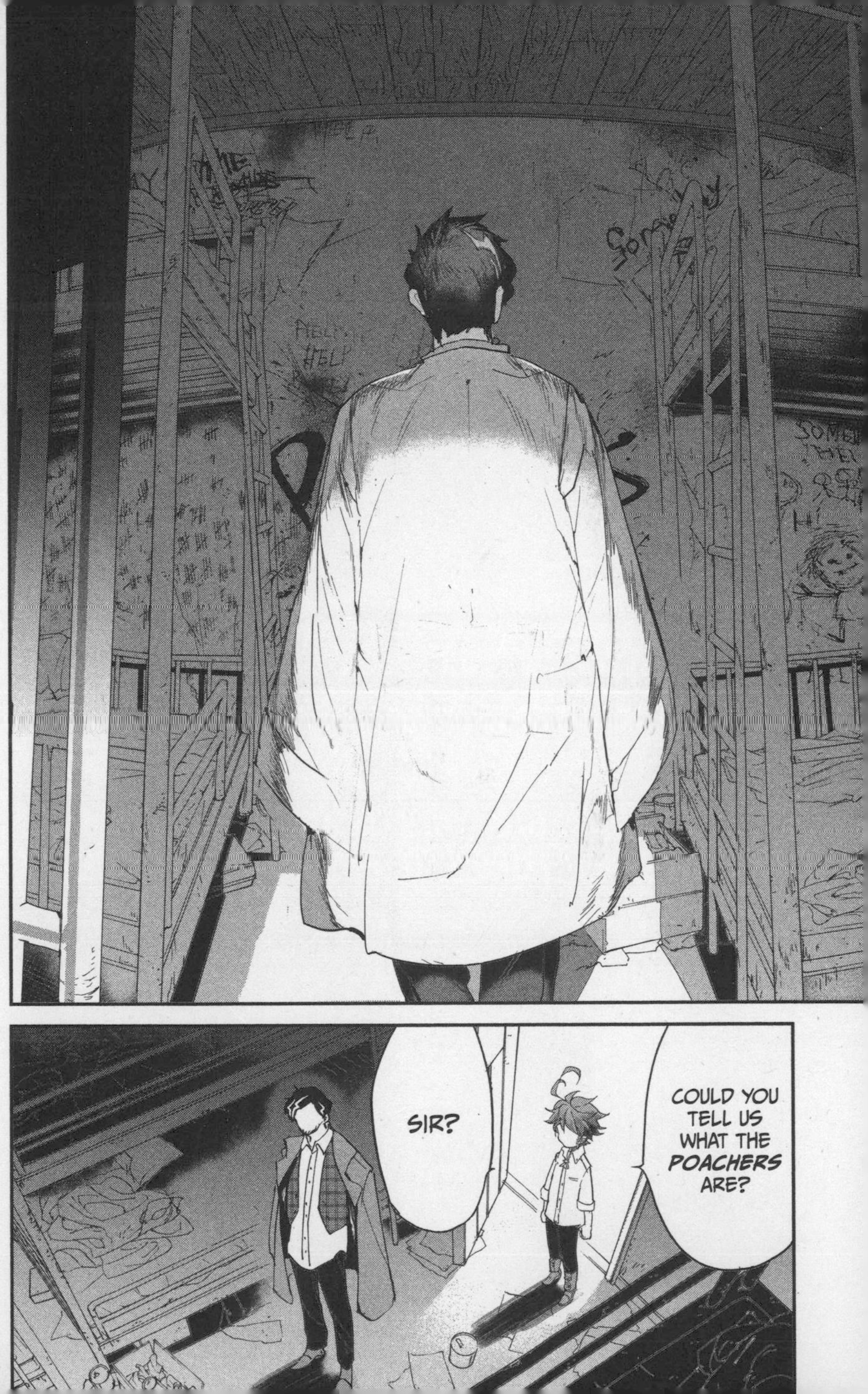
COULD YOU TELL US WHAT THE POACHERS ARE?
SIR?

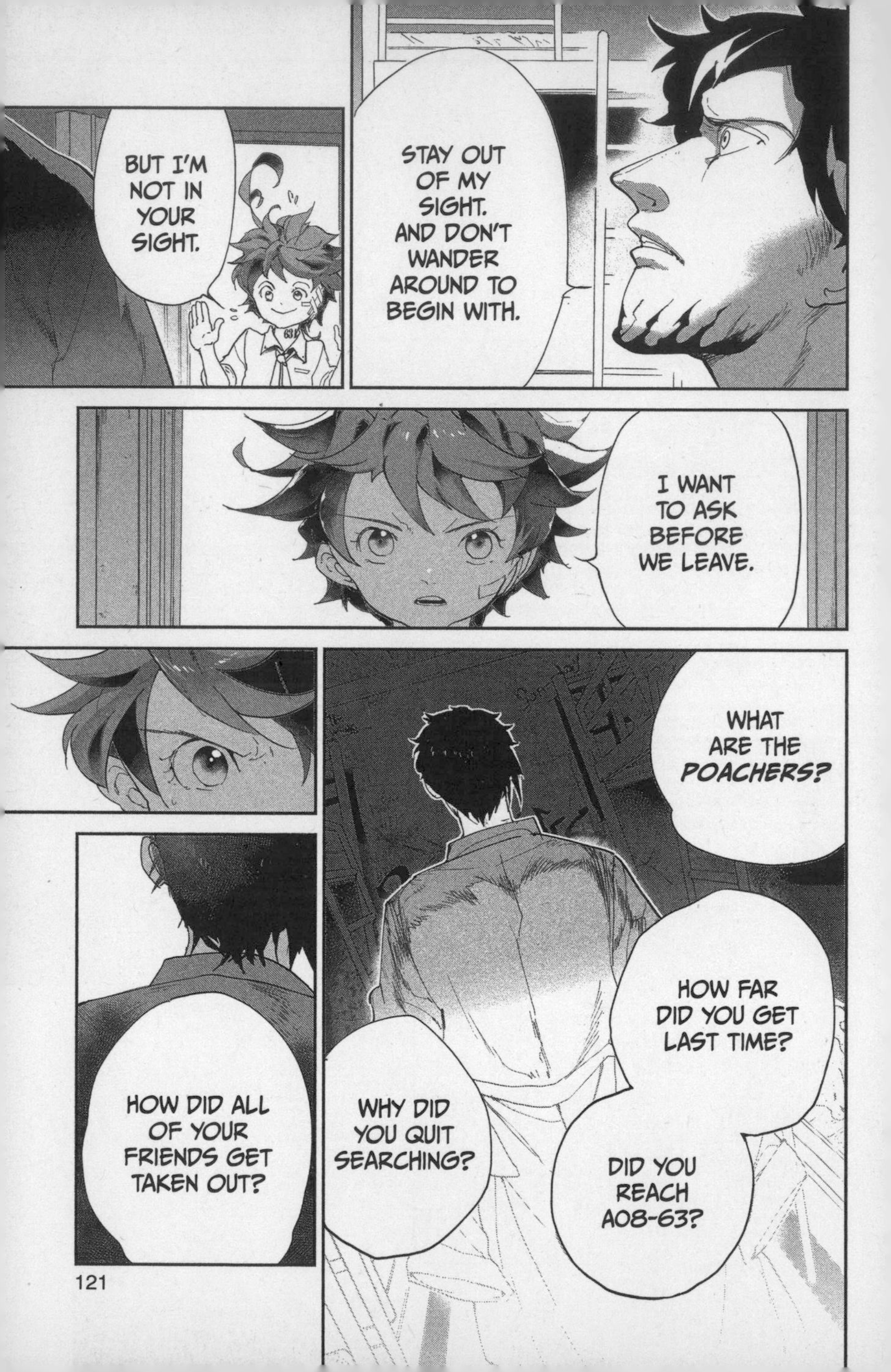
STAY OUT OF MY SIGHT. AND DON'T WANDER AROUND TO BEGIN WITH.
BUT I'M NOT IN YOUR SIGHT.
I WANT TO ASK BEFORE WE LEAVE.
WHAT ARE THE *POACHERS?*
HOW FAR DID YOU GET LAST TIME?
DID YOU REACH A08-63?
WHY DID YOU QUIT SEARCHING?
HOW DID ALL OF YOUR FRIENDS GET TAKEN OUT?

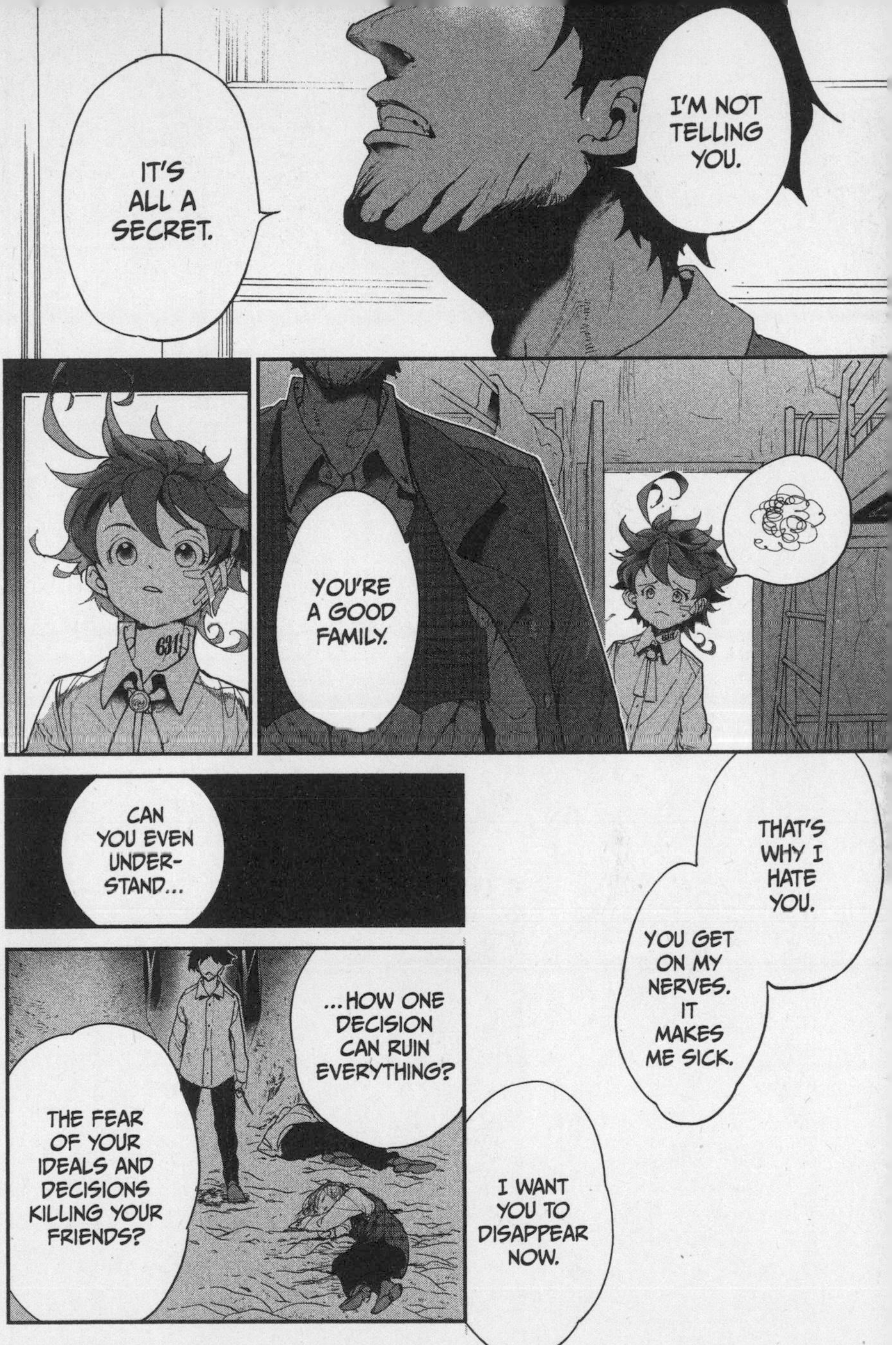
I'M NOT TELLING YOU.
IT'S ALL A SECRET.
YOU'RE A GOOD FAMILY.
THAT'S WHY I HATE YOU.
YOU GET ON MY NERVES. IT MAKES ME SICK.
CAN YOU EVEN UNDER-STAND...
...HOW ONE DECISION CAN RUIN EVERYTHING?
THE FEAR OF YOUR IDEALS AND DECISIONS KILLING YOUR FRIENDS?
I WANT YOU TO DISAPPEAR NOW.

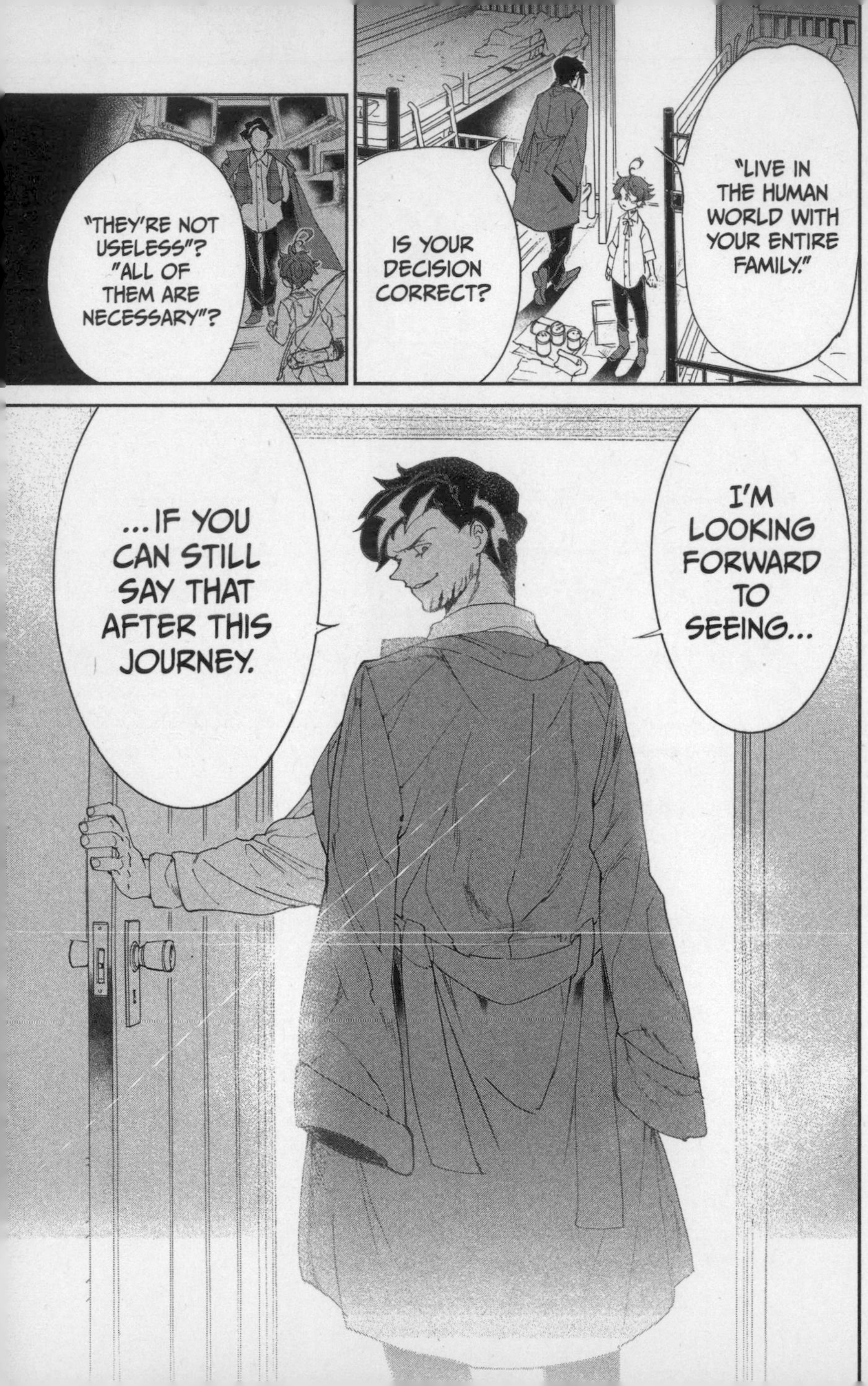
"LIVE IN THE HUMAN WORLD WITH YOUR ENTIRE FAMILY."
IS YOUR DECISION CORRECT?
"THEY'RE NOT USELESS"? "ALL OF THEM ARE NECESSARY"?
I'M LOOKING FORWARD TO SEEING...
...IF YOU CAN STILL SAY THAT AFTER THIS JOURNEY.

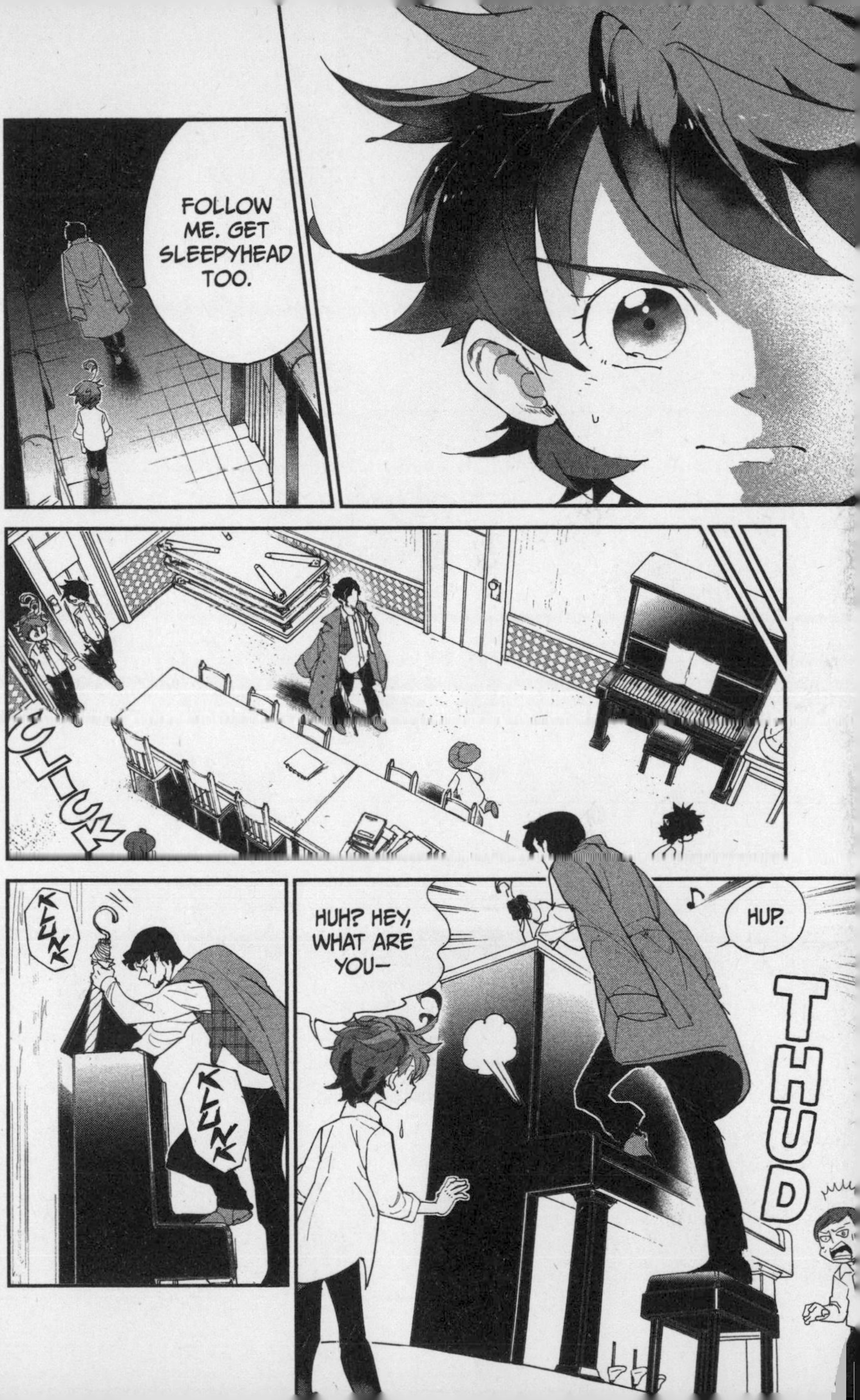
FOLLOW ME. GET SLEEPYHEAD TOO.
CLICK
HUP.
HUH? HEY, WHAT ARE YOU—
THUD
KLUNK
KLUNK

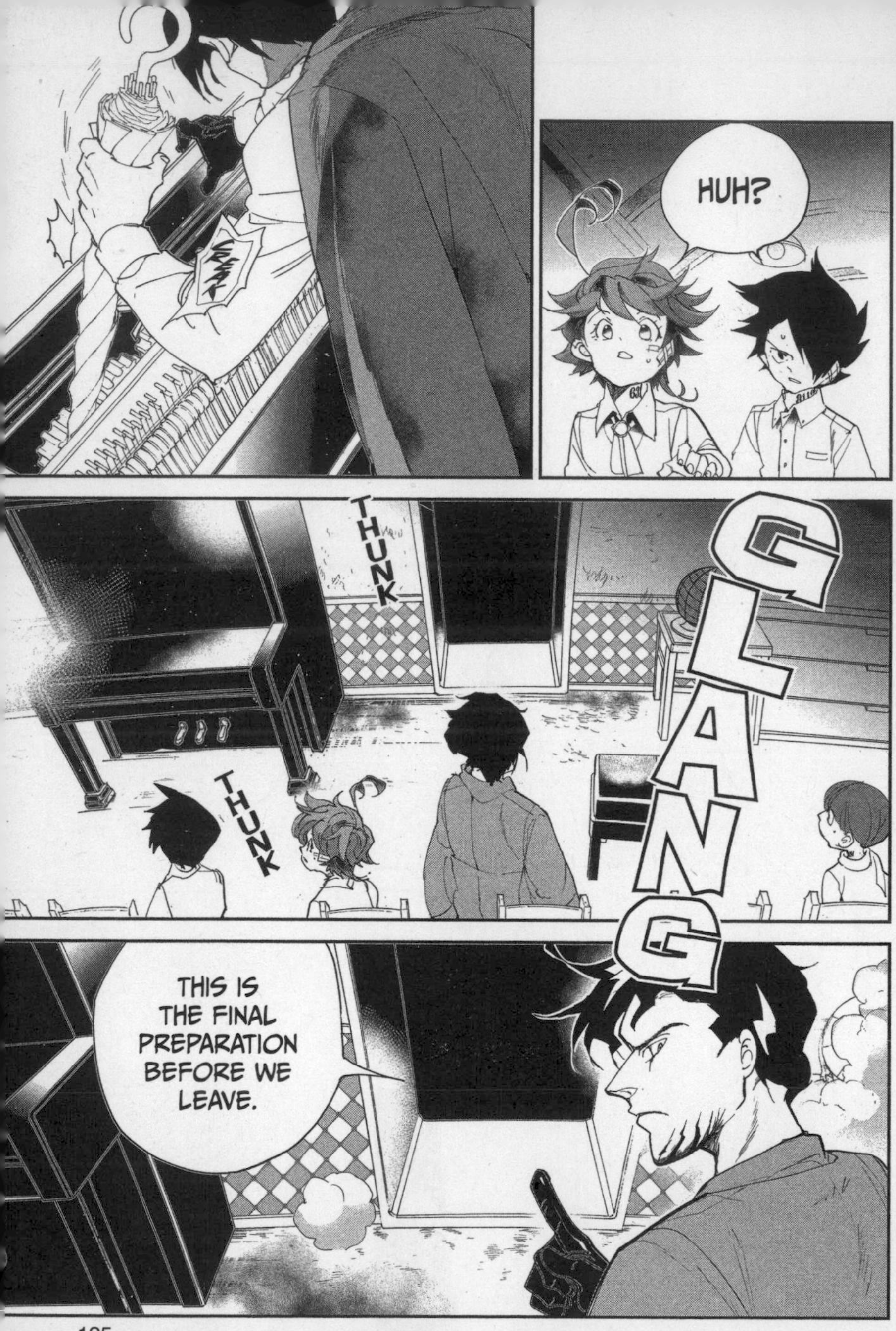
HUH?
GLANG
THUNK
THUNK
THIS IS THE FINAL PREPARATION BEFORE WE LEAVE.

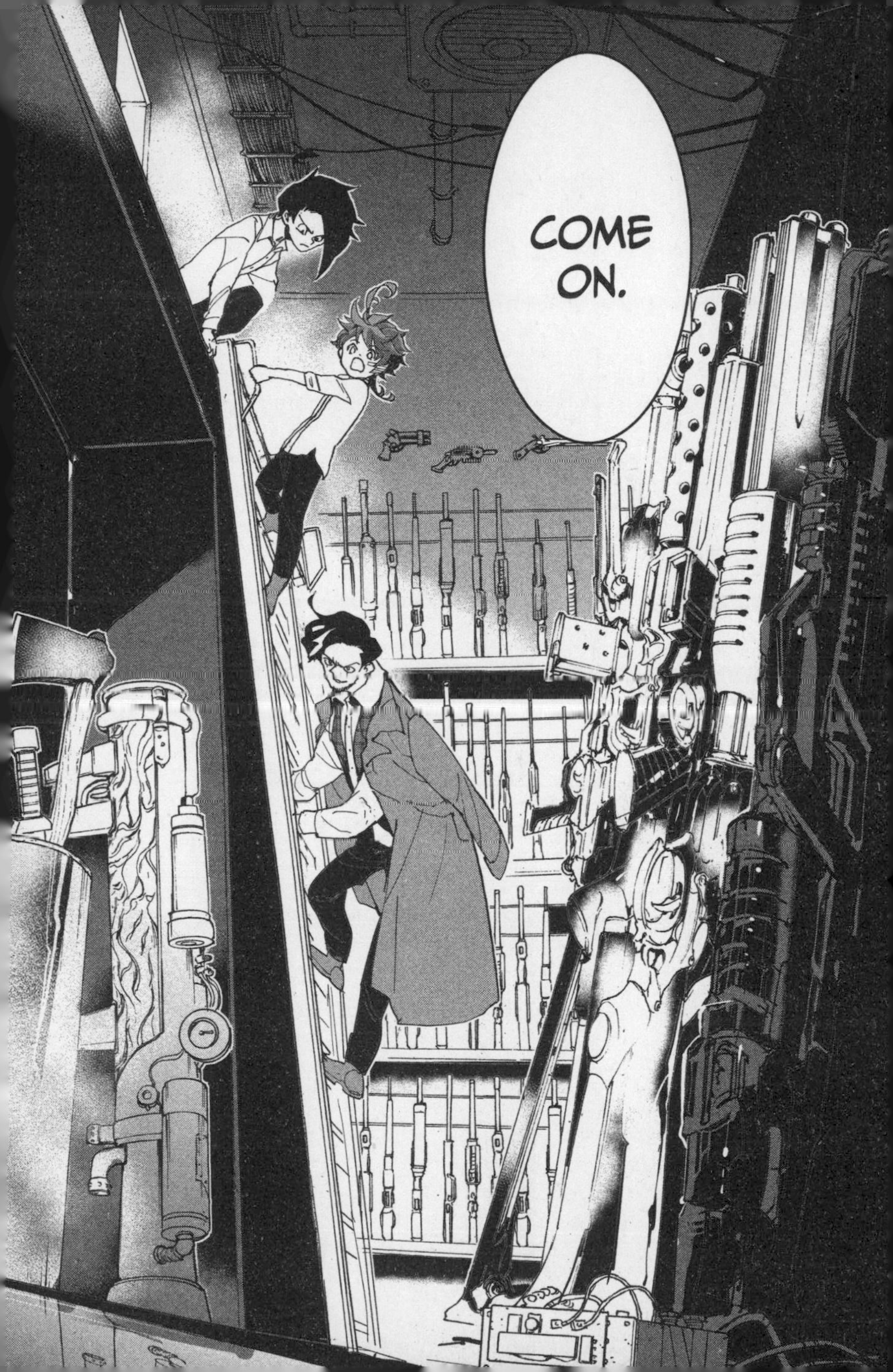
COME ON.

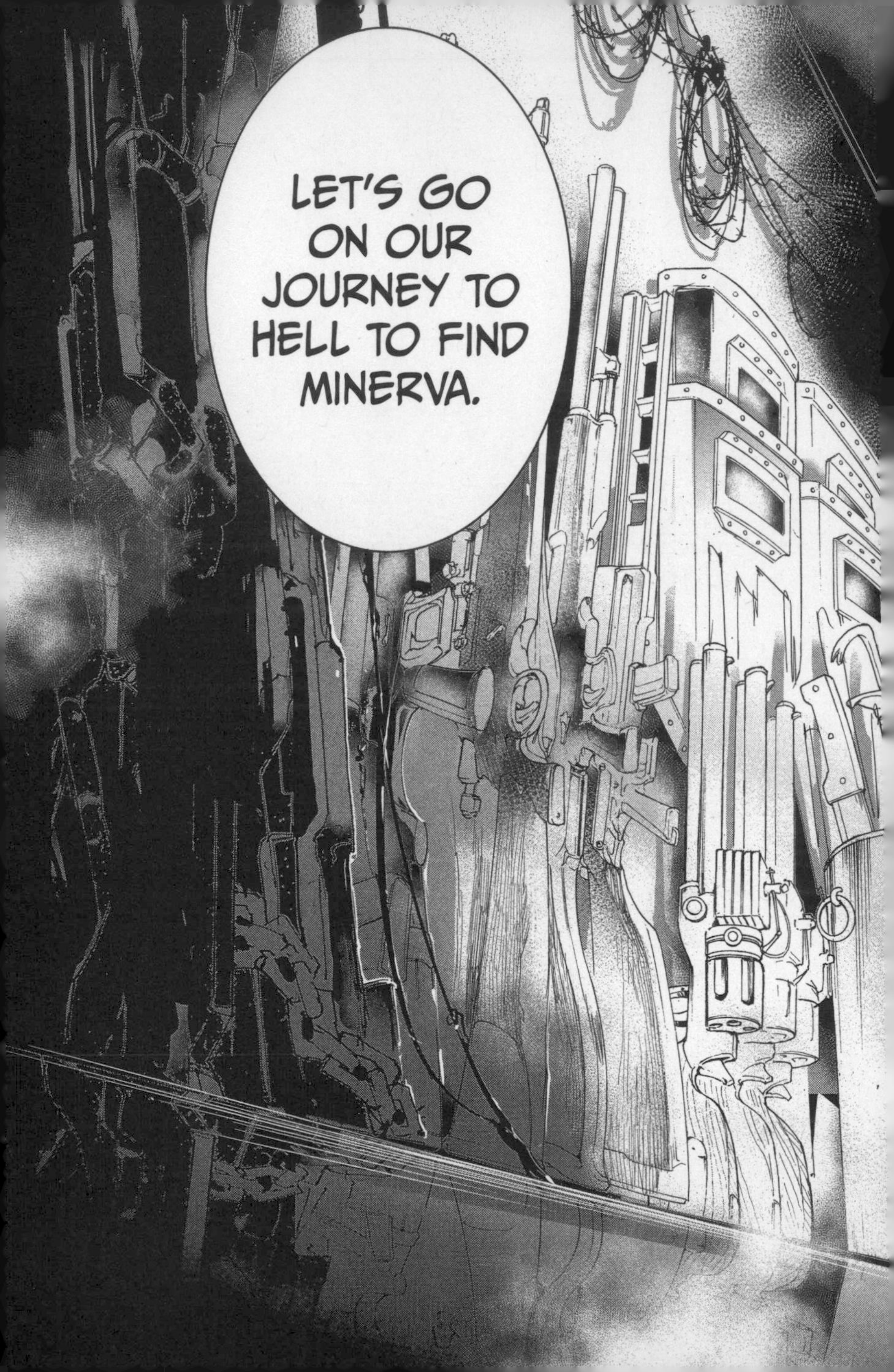
LET'S GO ON OUR JOURNEY TO HELL TO FIND MINERVA.

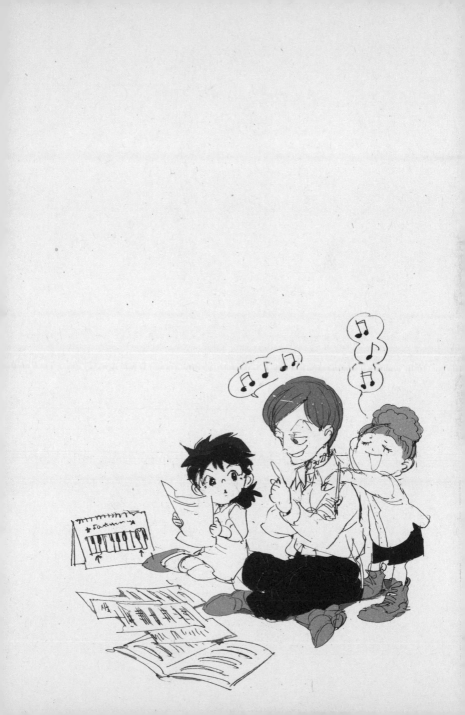

CHAPTER 59: CHOOSE YOUR WEAPON

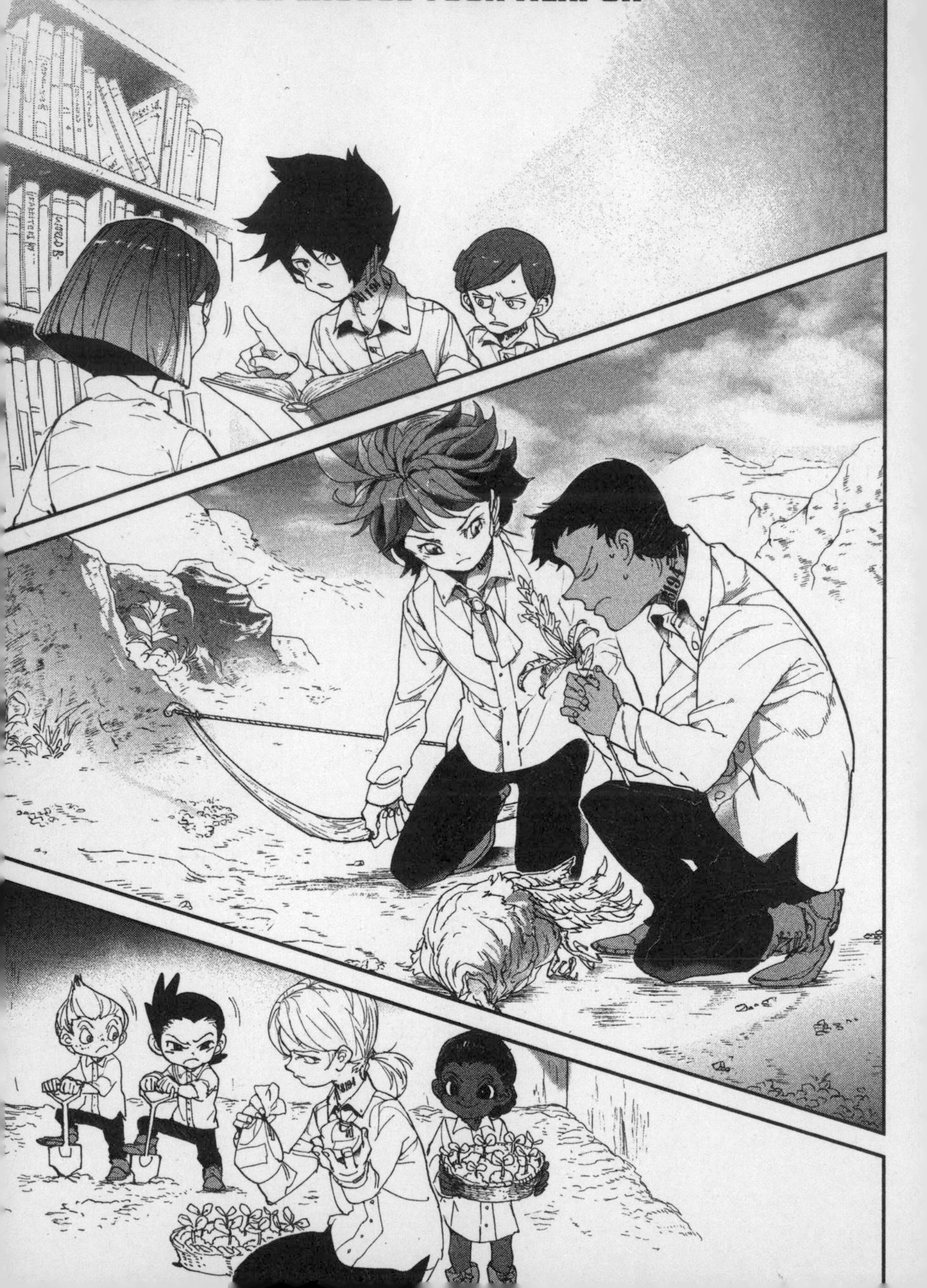

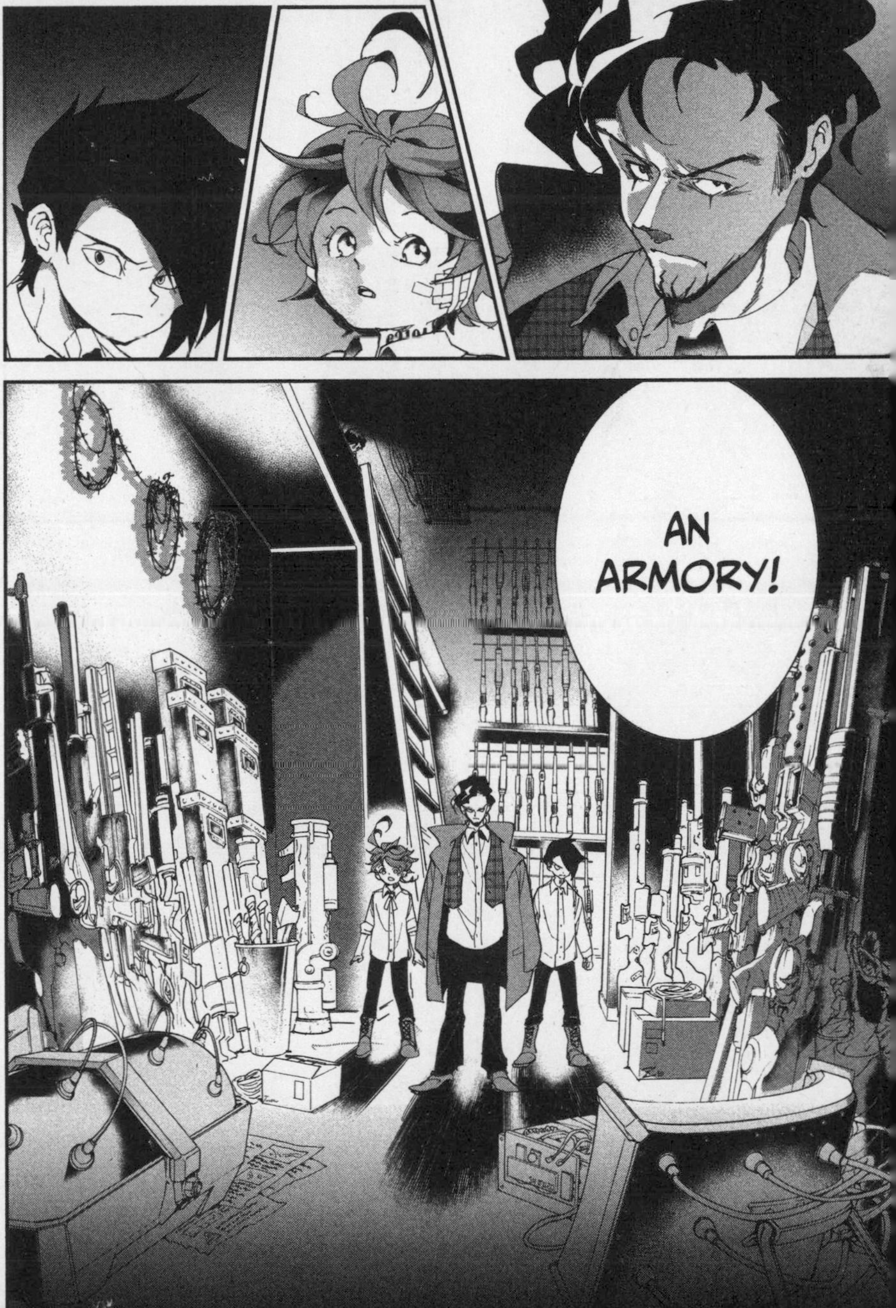
AN ARMORY!

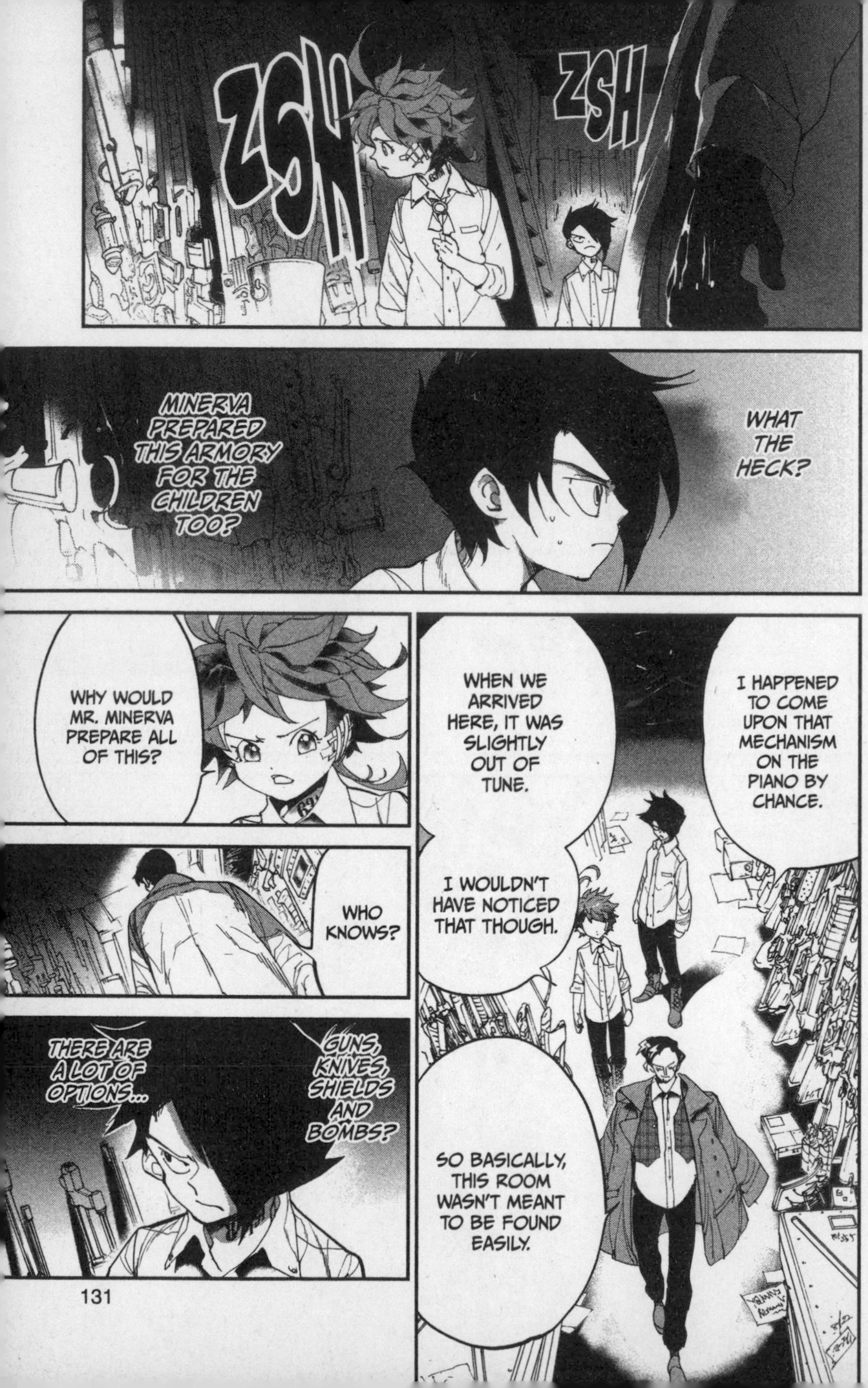

ZSH
ZSH
WHAT THE HECK?
MINERVA PREPARED THIS ARMORY FOR THE CHILDREN TOO?
I HAPPENED TO COME UPON THAT MECHANISM ON THE PIANO BY CHANCE.
WHEN WE ARRIVED HERE, IT WAS SLIGHTLY OUT OF TUNE.
I WOULDN'T HAVE NOTICED THAT THOUGH.
SO BASICALLY, THIS ROOM WASN'T MEANT TO BE FOUND EASILY.
WHY WOULD MR. MINERVA PREPARE ALL OF THIS?
WHO KNOWS?
GUNS, KNIVES, SHIELDS AND BOMBS?
THERE ARE A LOT OF OPTIONS...

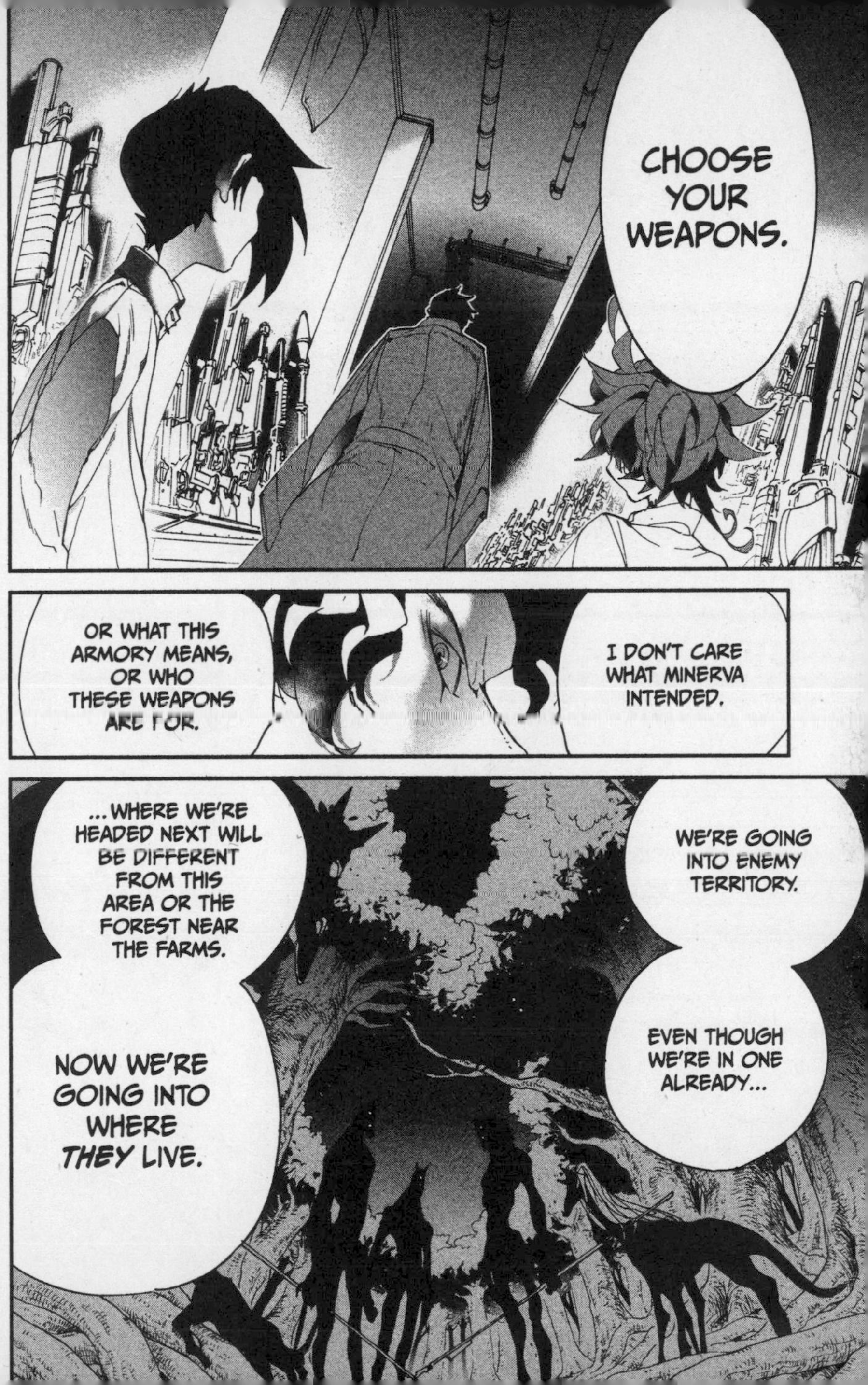
CHOOSE YOUR WEAPONS.
I DON'T CARE WHAT MINERVA INTENDED.
OR WHAT THIS ARMORY MEANS, OR WHO THESE WEAPONS ARE FOR.
WE'RE GOING INTO ENEMY TERRITORY.
EVEN THOUGH WE'RE IN ONE ALREADY...
...WHERE WE'RE HEADED NEXT WILL BE DIFFERENT FROM THIS AREA OR THE FOREST NEAR THE FARMS.
NOW WE'RE GOING INTO WHERE *THEY* LIVE.

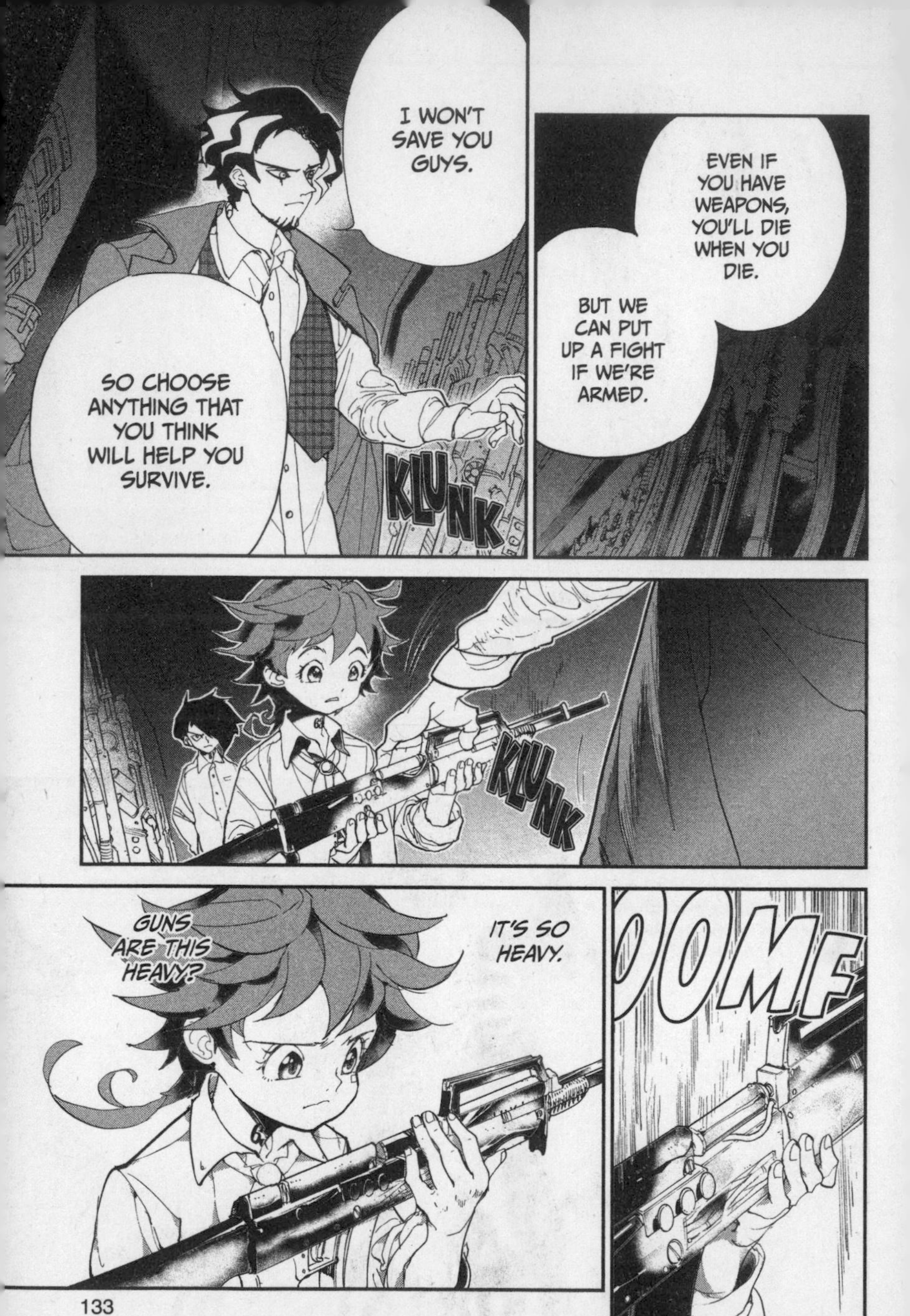
EVEN IF YOU HAVE WEAPONS, YOU'LL DIE WHEN YOU DIE.
BUT WE CAN PUT UP A FIGHT IF WE'RE ARMED.
I WON'T SAVE YOU GUYS.
SO CHOOSE ANYTHING THAT YOU THINK WILL HELP YOU SURVIVE.
KLUNK
KLUNK
OOMF
IT'S SO HEAVY.
GUNS ARE THIS HEAVY?

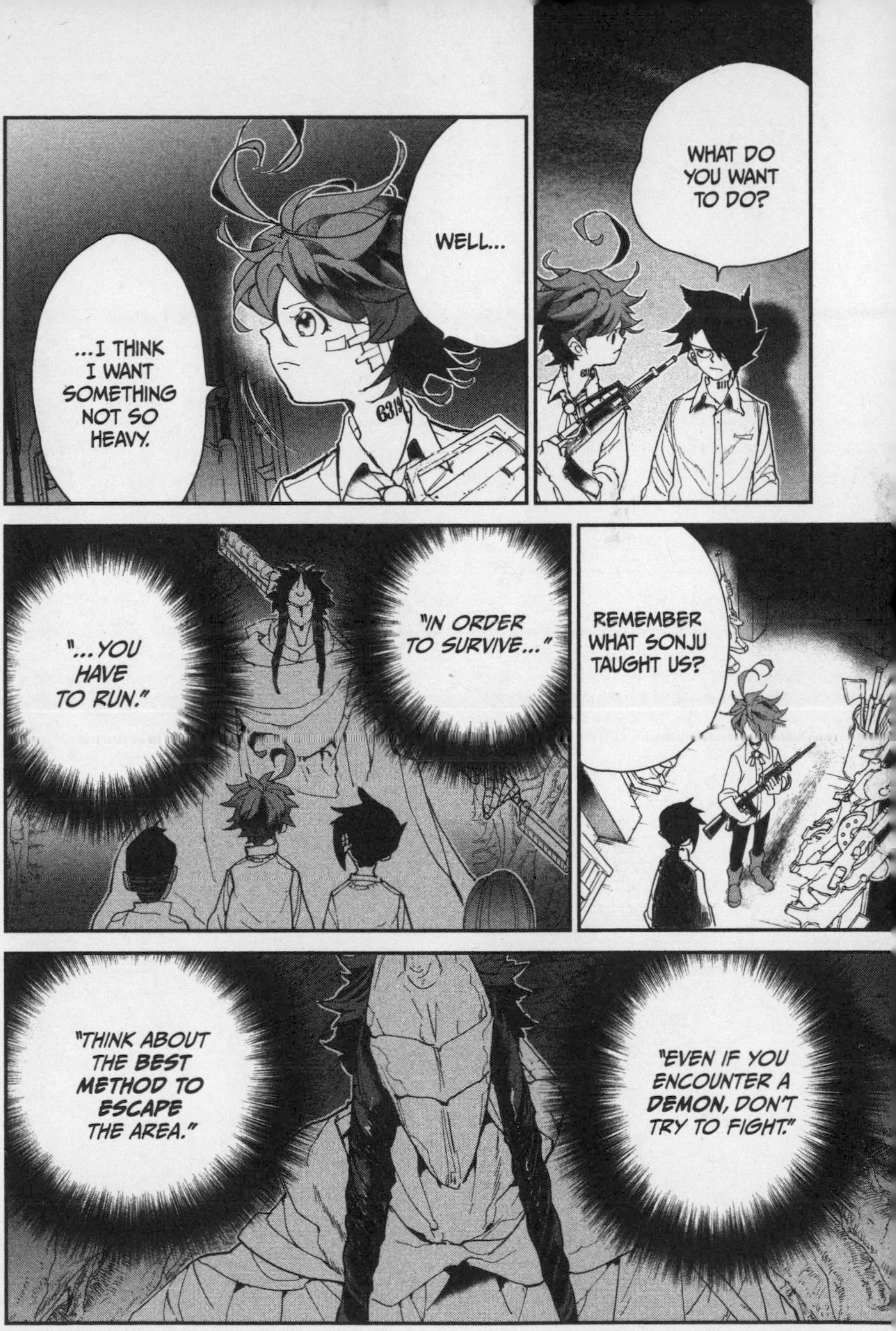
WHAT DO YOU WANT TO DO?
WELL...
...I THINK I WANT SOMETHING NOT SO HEAVY.
REMEMBER WHAT SONJU TAUGHT US?
"IN ORDER TO SURVIVE..."
"...YOU HAVE TO RUN."
"EVEN IF YOU ENCOUNTER A DEMON, DON'T TRY TO FIGHT."
"THINK ABOUT THE BEST METHOD TO ESCAPE THE AREA."

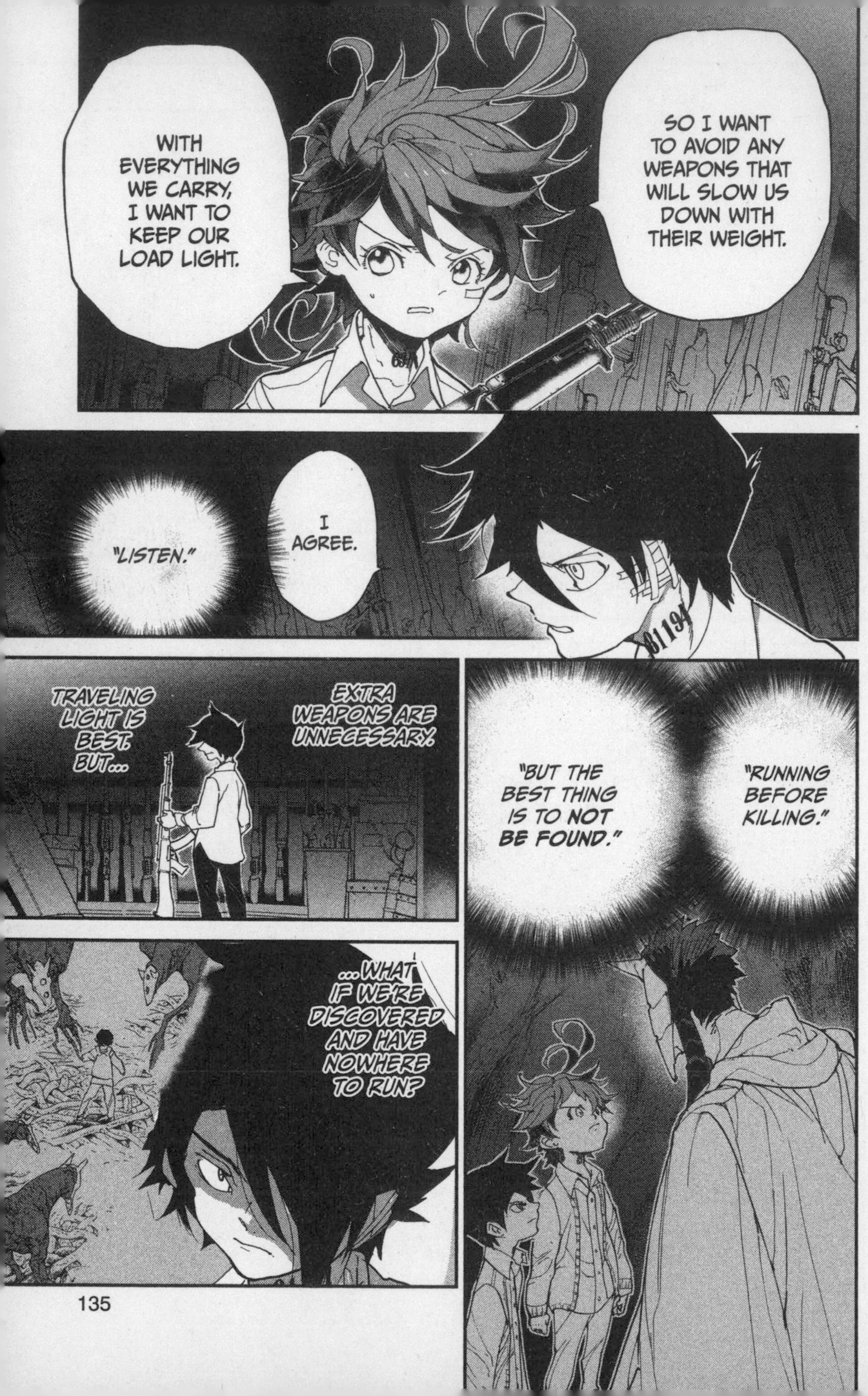

WITH EVERYTHING WE CARRY, I WANT TO KEEP OUR LOAD LIGHT.
SO I WANT TO AVOID ANY WEAPONS THAT WILL SLOW US DOWN WITH THEIR WEIGHT.
I AGREE.
"LISTEN."
"RUNNING BEFORE KILLING."
"BUT THE BEST THING IS TO NOT BE FOUND."
EXTRA WEAPONS ARE UNNECESSARY.
TRAVELING LIGHT IS BEST. BUT...
...WHAT IF WE'RE DISCOVERED AND HAVE NOWHERE TO RUN?

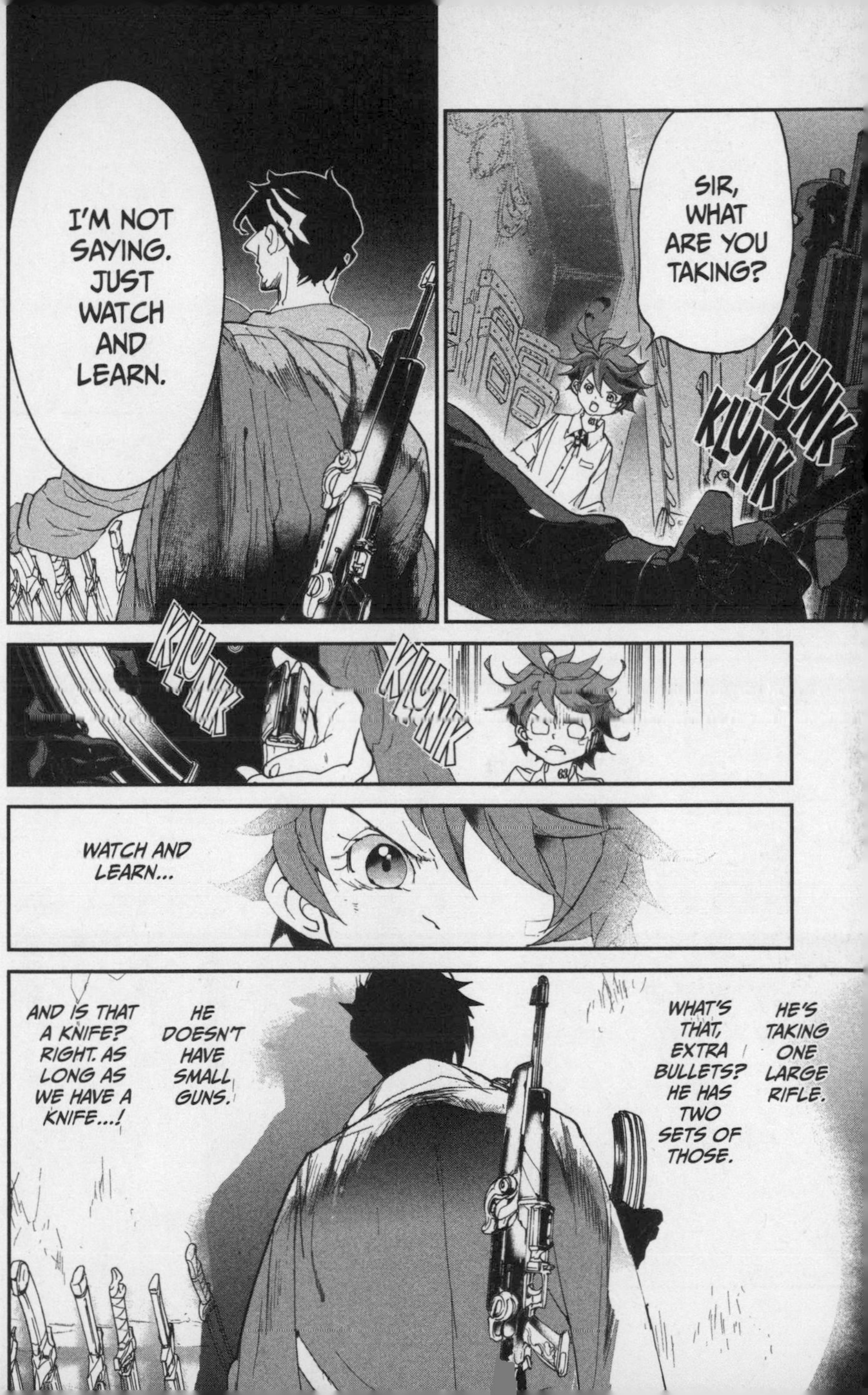
SIR, WHAT ARE YOU TAKING?
KLUNK
KLUNK
I'M NOT SAYING. JUST WATCH AND LEARN.
KLUNK
KLUNK
WATCH AND LEARN...
HE'S TAKING ONE LARGE RIFLE.
WHAT'S THAT, EXTRA BULLETS? HE HAS TWO SETS OF THOSE.
HE DOESN'T HAVE SMALL GUNS.
AND IS THAT A KNIFE? RIGHT. AS LONG AS WE HAVE A KNIFE...!

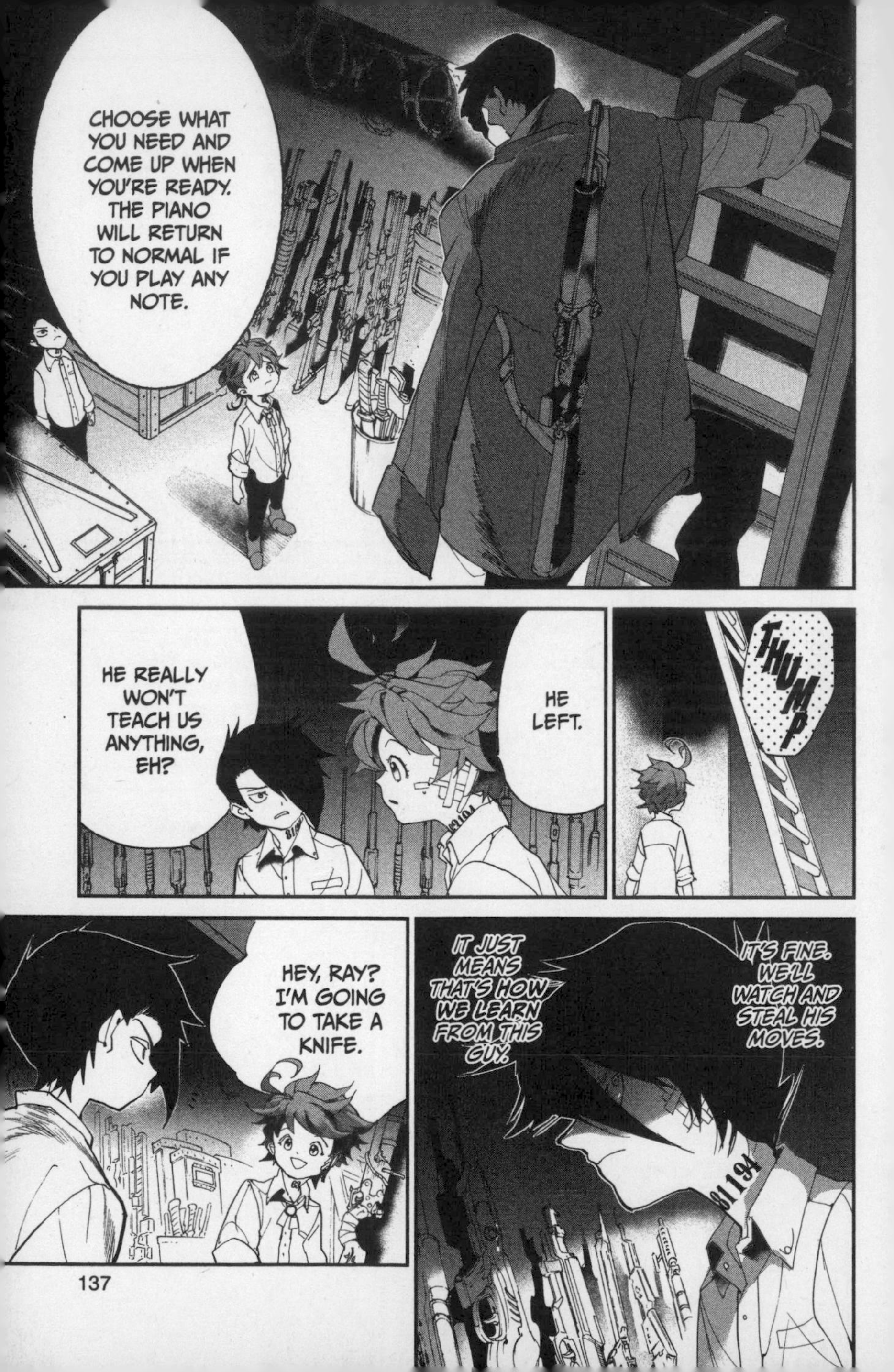
CHOOSE WHAT YOU NEED AND COME UP WHEN YOU'RE READY. THE PIANO WILL RETURN TO NORMAL IF YOU PLAY ANY NOTE.
THUMP
HE LEFT.
HE REALLY WON'T TEACH US ANYTHING, EH?
IT'S FINE. WE'LL WATCH AND STEAL HIS MOVES.
IT JUST MEANS THAT'S HOW WE LEARN FROM THIS GUY.
HEY, RAY? I'M GOING TO TAKE A KNIFE.

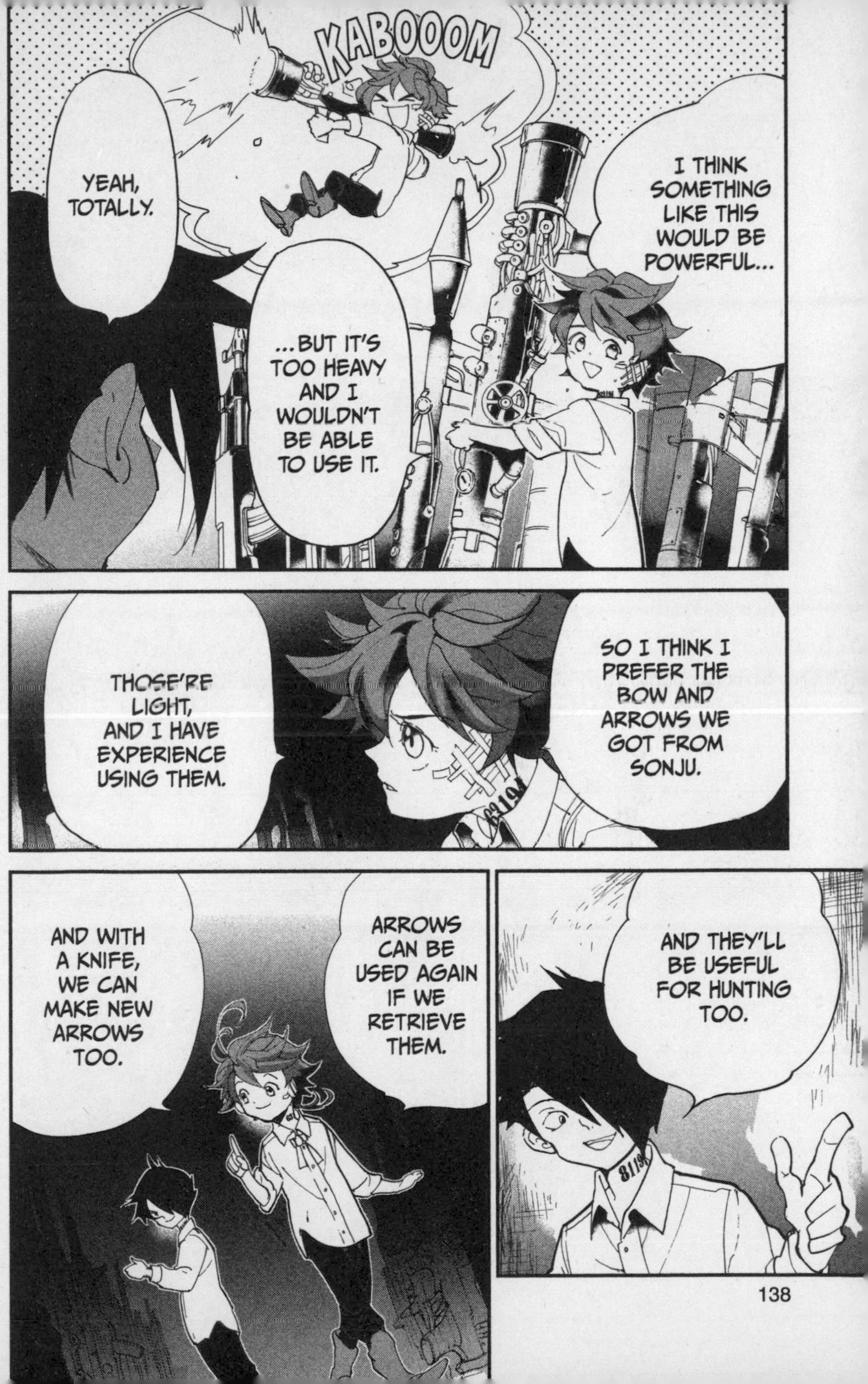
KABOOOM
I THINK SOMETHING LIKE THIS WOULD BE POWERFUL...
...BUT IT'S TOO HEAVY AND I WOULDN'T BE ABLE TO USE IT.
YEAH, TOTALLY.
SO I THINK I PREFER THE BOW AND ARROWS WE GOT FROM SONJU.
THOSE'RE LIGHT, AND I HAVE EXPERIENCE USING THEM.
AND THEY'LL BE USEFUL FOR HUNTING TOO.
ARROWS CAN BE USED AGAIN IF WE RETRIEVE THEM.
AND WITH A KNIFE, WE CAN MAKE NEW ARROWS TOO.

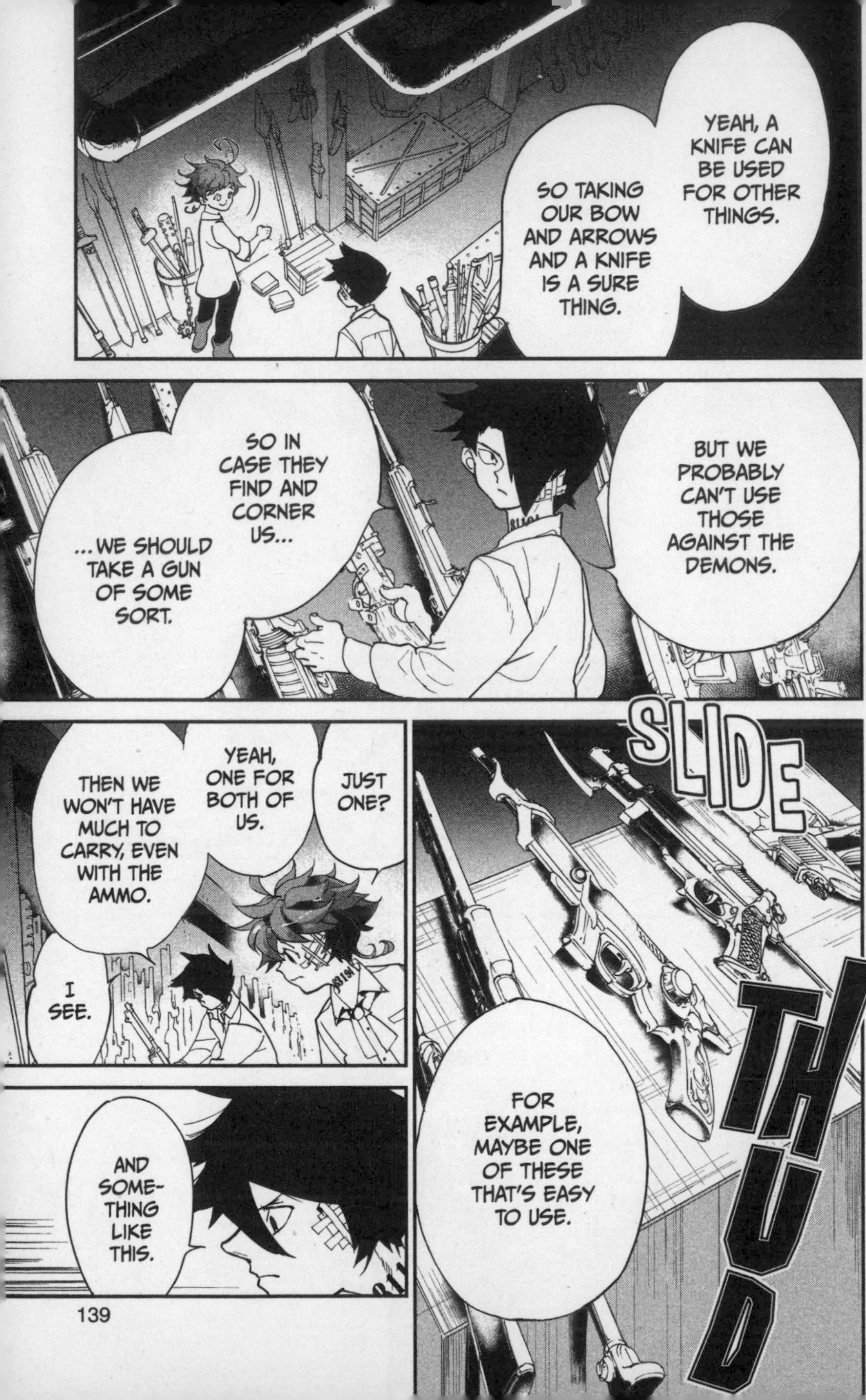
YEAH, A KNIFE CAN BE USED FOR OTHER THINGS.
SO TAKING OUR BOW AND ARROWS AND A KNIFE IS A SURE THING.
BUT WE PROBABLY CAN'T USE THOSE AGAINST THE DEMONS.
SO IN CASE THEY FIND AND CORNER US...
...WE SHOULD TAKE A GUN OF SOME SORT.
SLIDE
FOR EXAMPLE, MAYBE ONE OF THESE THAT'S EASY TO USE.
THUD
JUST ONE?
YEAH, ONE FOR BOTH OF US.
THEN WE WON'T HAVE MUCH TO CARRY, EVEN WITH THE AMMO.
I SEE.
AND SOME-THING LIKE THIS.

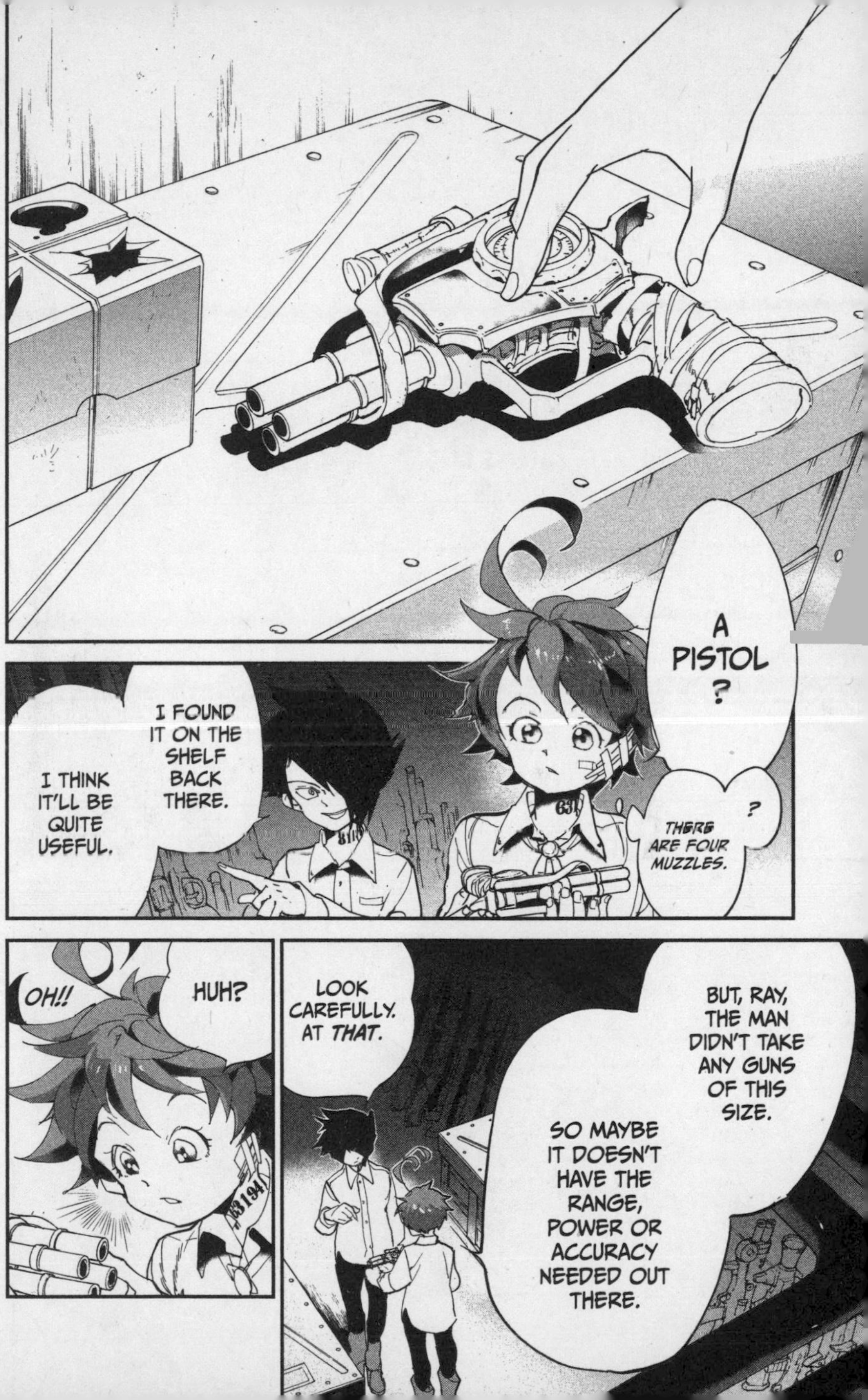
A PISTOL?
?
THERE ARE FOUR MUZZLES.
I FOUND IT ON THE SHELF BACK THERE.
I THINK IT'LL BE QUITE USEFUL.
BUT, RAY, THE MAN DIDN'T TAKE ANY GUNS OF THIS SIZE.
SO MAYBE IT DOESN'T HAVE THE RANGE, POWER OR ACCURACY NEEDED OUT THERE.
LOOK CAREFULLY. AT *THAT*.
HUH?
OH!!

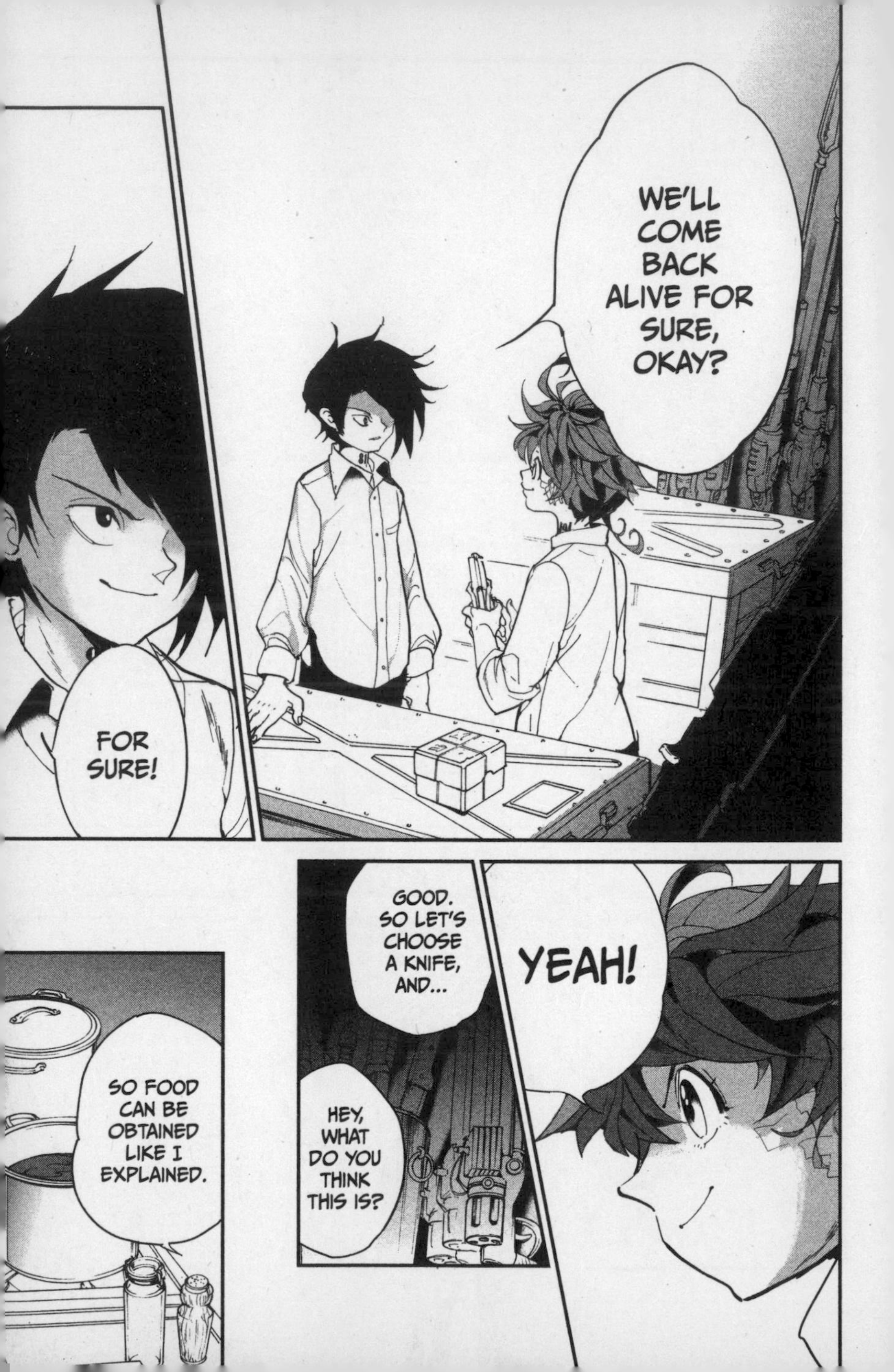
WE'LL COME BACK ALIVE FOR SURE, OKAY?
FOR SURE!
YEAH!
GOOD. SO LET'S CHOOSE A KNIFE, AND...
HEY, WHAT DO YOU THINK THIS IS?
SO FOOD CAN BE OBTAINED LIKE I EXPLAINED.

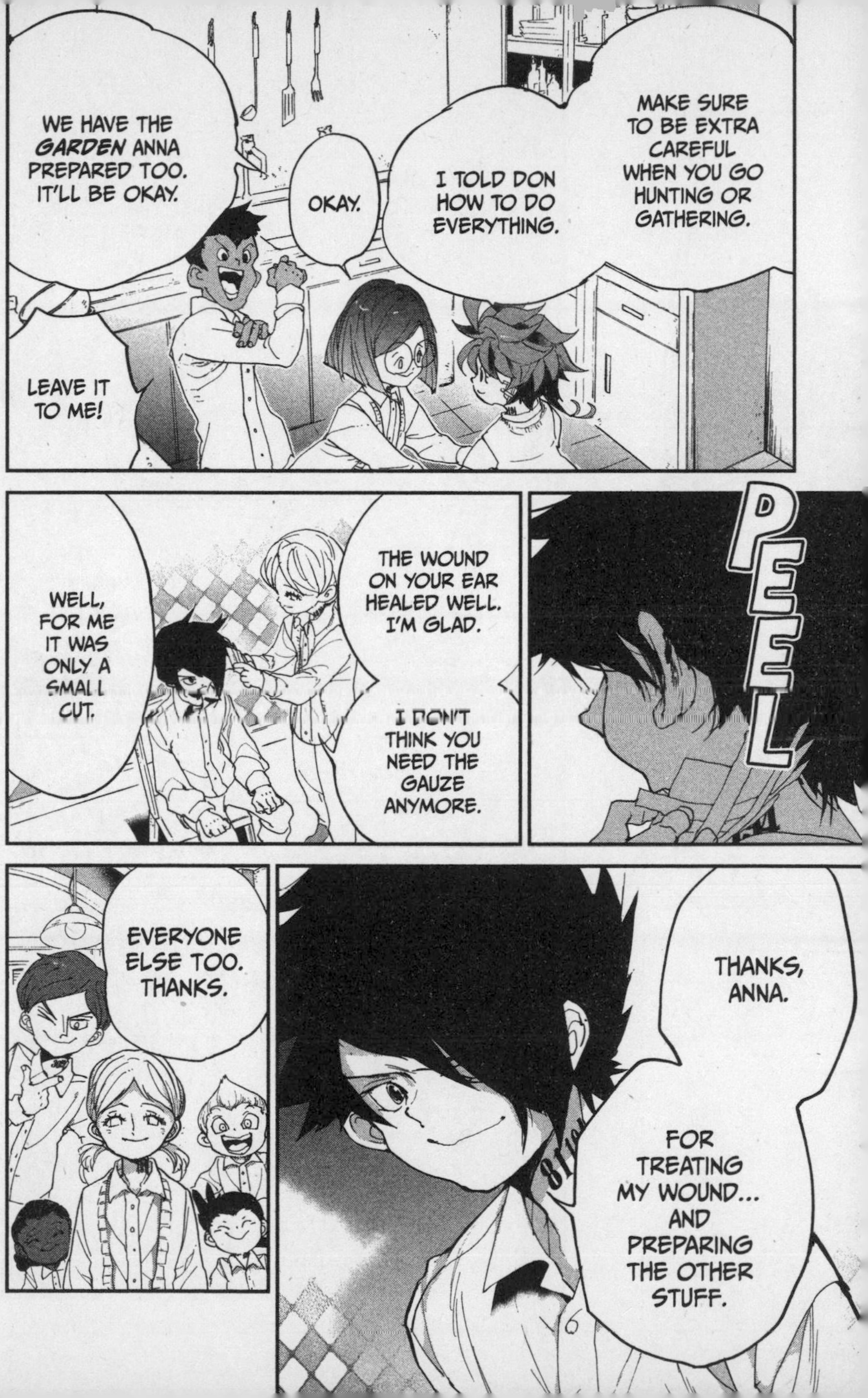
MAKE SURE TO BE EXTRA CAREFUL WHEN YOU GO HUNTING OR GATHERING.
I TOLD DON HOW TO DO EVERYTHING.
OKAY.
WE HAVE THE GARDEN ANNA PREPARED TOO. IT'LL BE OKAY.
LEAVE IT TO ME!
PEEL
THE WOUND ON YOUR EAR HEALED WELL. I'M GLAD.
I DON'T THINK YOU NEED THE GAUZE ANYMORE.
WELL, FOR ME IT WAS ONLY A SMALL CUT.
THANKS, ANNA.
FOR TREATING MY WOUND... AND PREPARING THE OTHER STUFF.
EVERYONE ELSE TOO. THANKS.

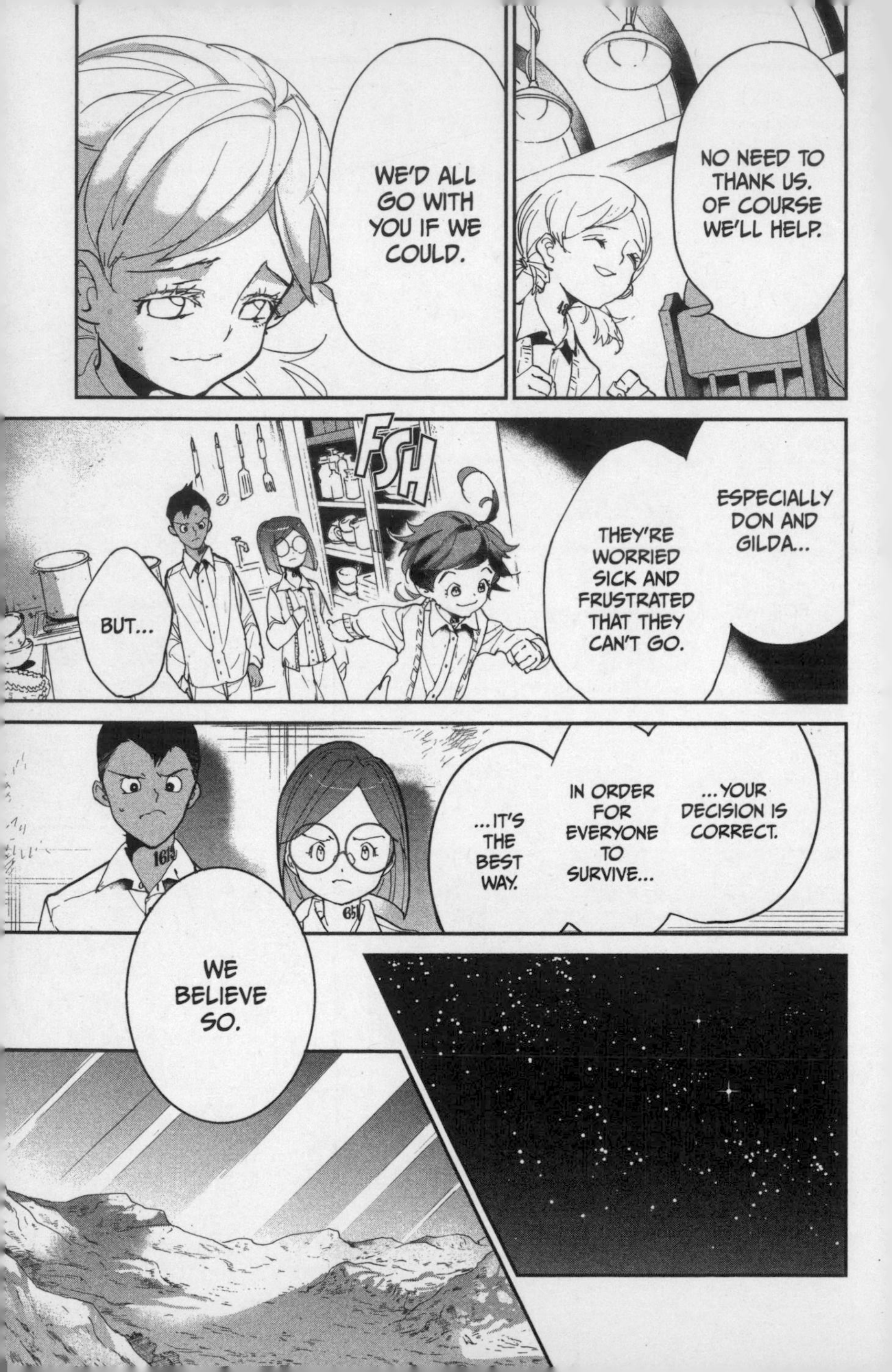
NO NEED TO THANK US. OF COURSE WE'LL HELP.
WE'D ALL GO WITH YOU IF WE COULD.
ESPECIALLY DON AND GILDA...
THEY'RE WORRIED SICK AND FRUSTRATED THAT THEY CAN'T GO.
FSH
BUT...
...YOUR DECISION IS CORRECT.
IN ORDER FOR EVERYONE TO SURVIVE...
...IT'S THE BEST WAY.
WE BELIEVE SO.

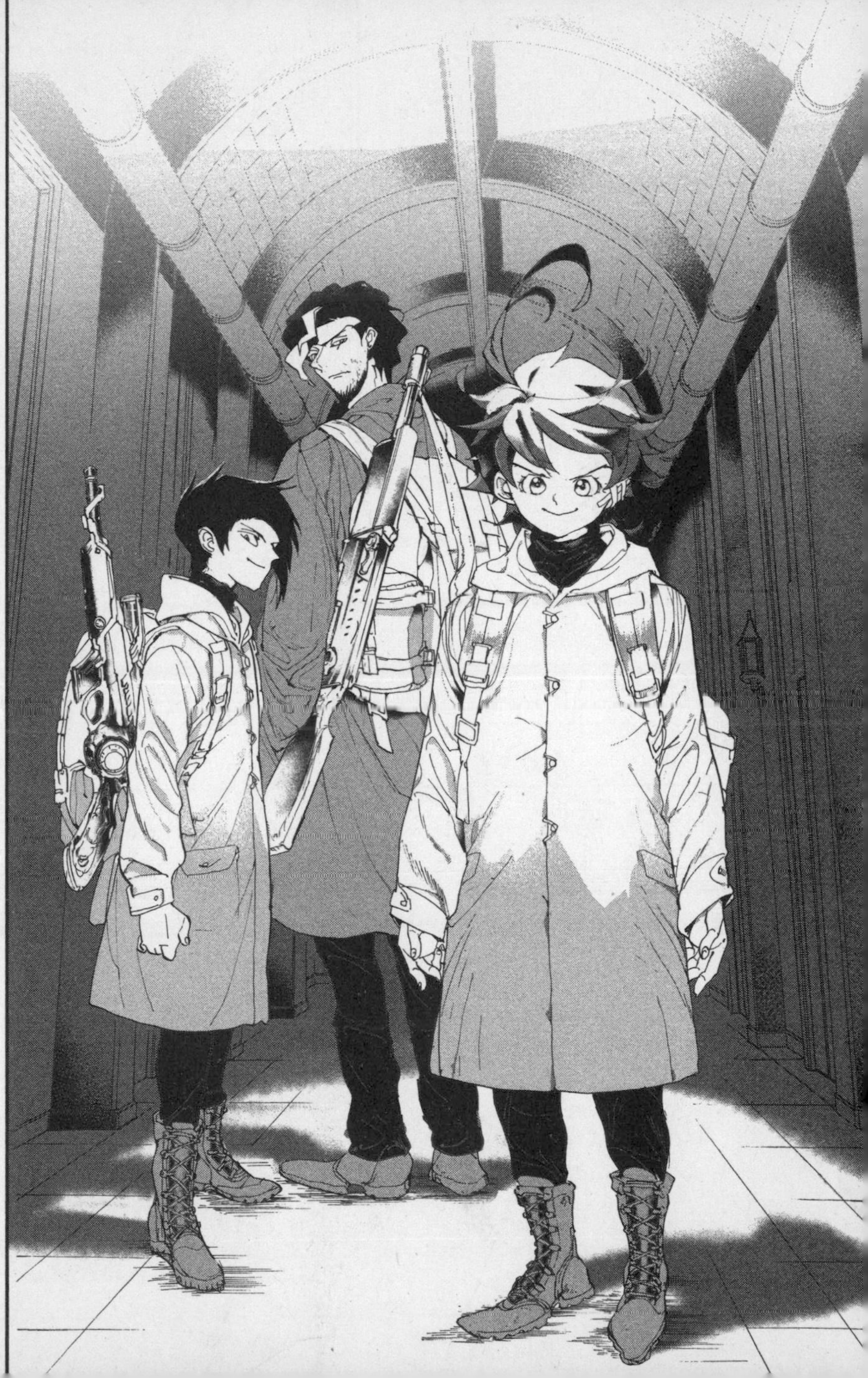

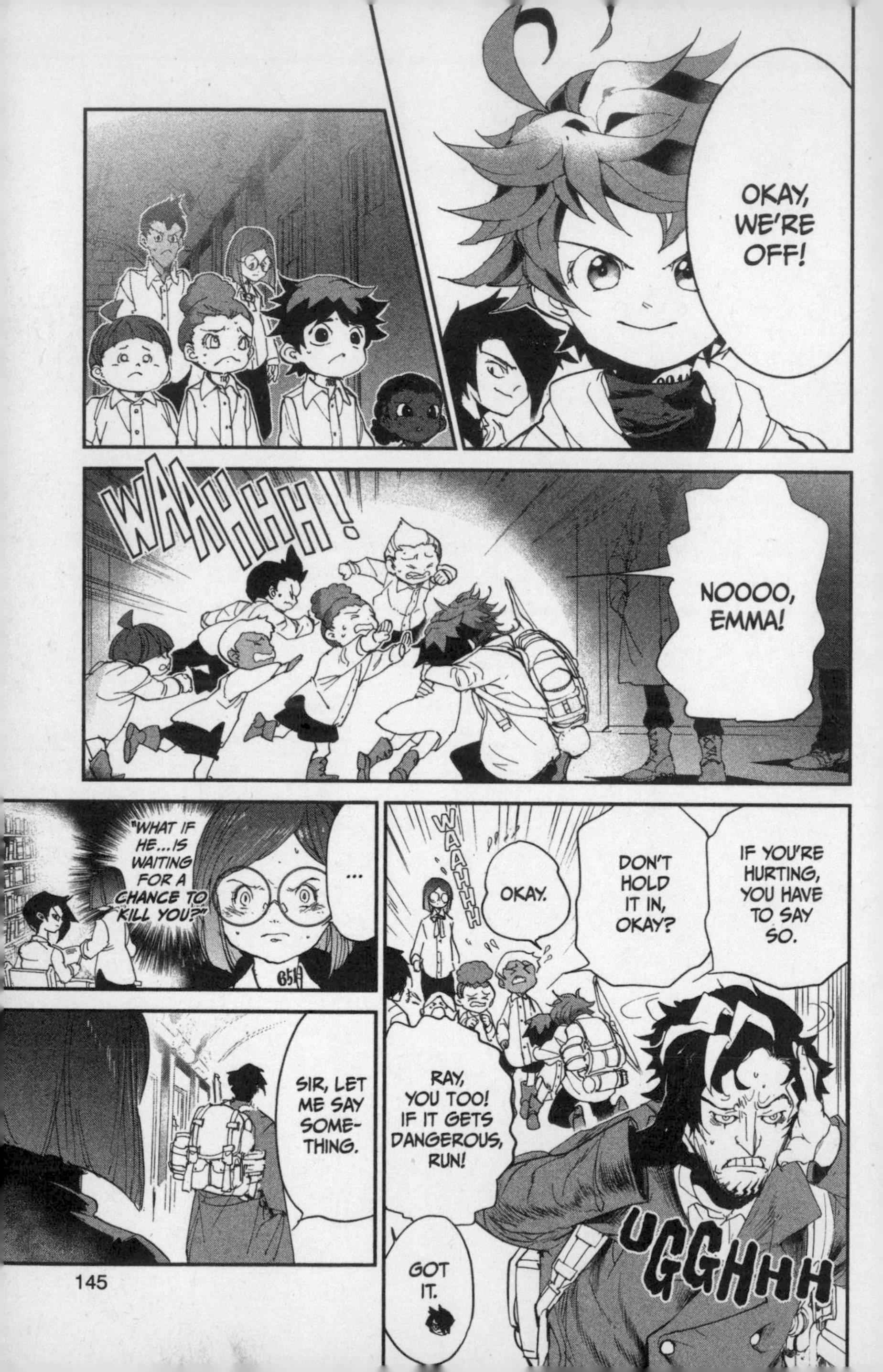
OKAY, WE'RE OFF!
NOOOO, EMMA!
WAAHHHH!
IF YOU'RE HURTING, YOU HAVE TO SAY SO.
DON'T HOLD IT IN, OKAY?
OKAY.
WAAHHHH
RAY, YOU TOO! IF IT GETS DANGEROUS, RUN!
GOT IT.
UGGHHH
...
"WHAT IF HE...IS WAITING FOR A CHANCE TO KILL YOU?"
SIR, LET ME SAY SOME-THING.

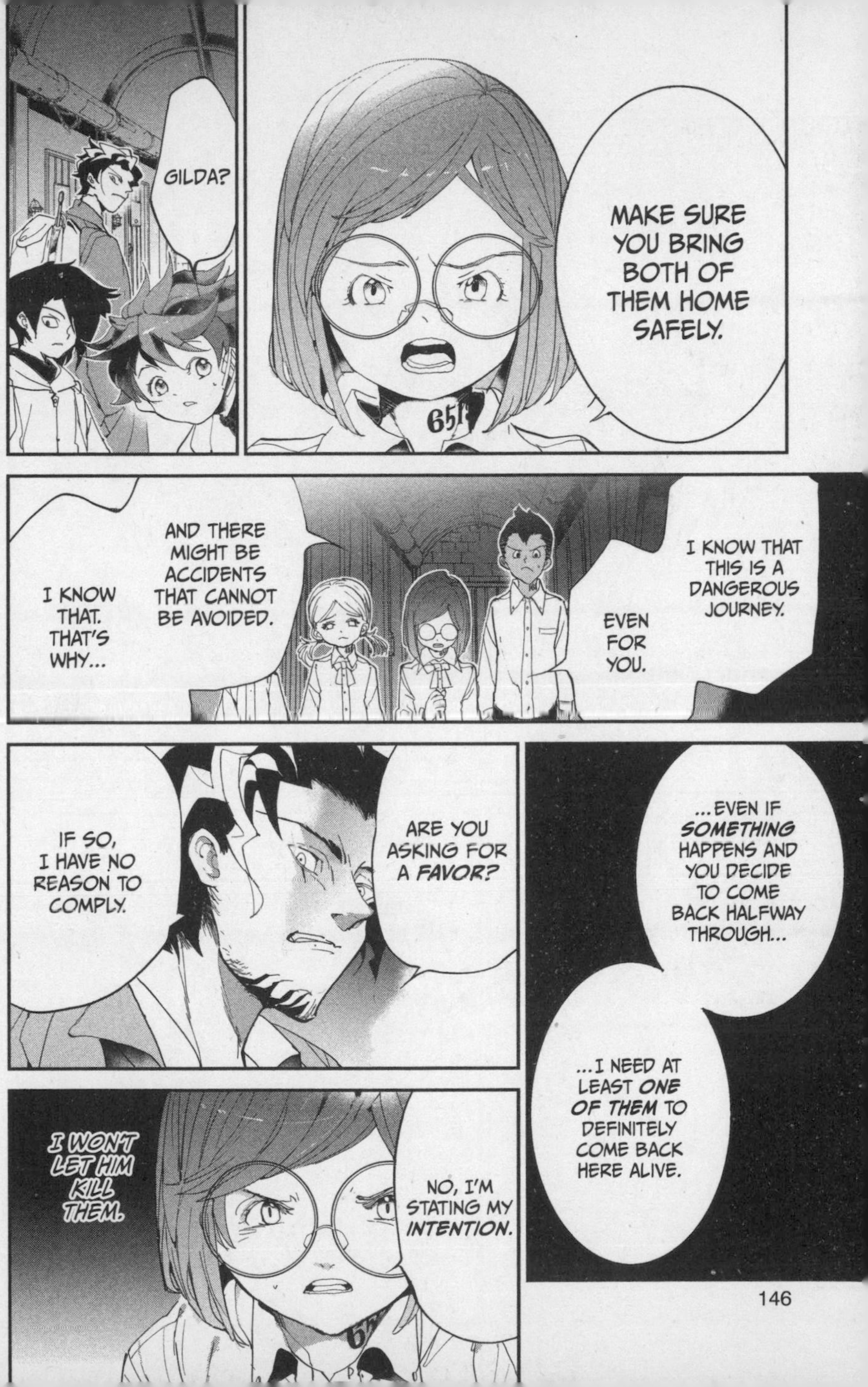
MAKE SURE YOU BRING BOTH OF THEM HOME SAFELY.
GILDA?
I KNOW THAT THIS IS A DANGEROUS JOURNEY.
EVEN FOR YOU.
AND THERE MIGHT BE ACCIDENTS THAT CANNOT BE AVOIDED.
I KNOW THAT. THAT'S WHY...
...EVEN IF *SOMETHING* HAPPENS AND YOU DECIDE TO COME BACK HALFWAY THROUGH...
...I NEED AT LEAST *ONE OF THEM* TO DEFINITELY COME BACK HERE ALIVE.
ARE YOU ASKING FOR A *FAVOR?*
IF SO, I HAVE NO REASON TO COMPLY.
NO, I'M STATING MY *INTENTION.*
I WON'T LET HIM KILL THEM.

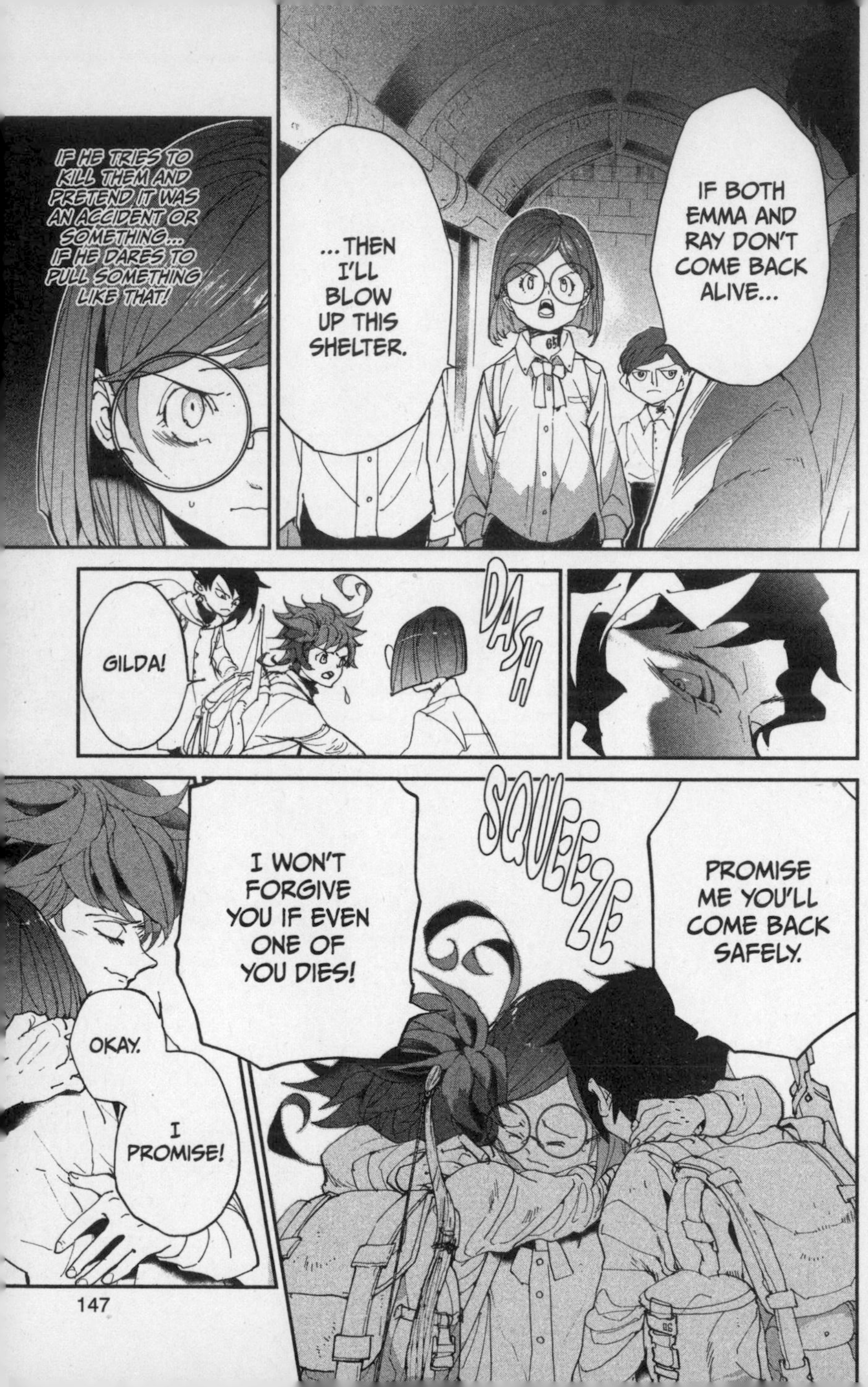
IF BOTH EMMA AND RAY DON'T COME BACK ALIVE...
...THEN I'LL BLOW UP THIS SHELTER.
IF HE TRIES TO KILL THEM AND PRETEND IT WAS AN ACCIDENT OR SOMETHING... IF HE DARES TO PULL SOMETHING LIKE THAT!
DASH
GILDA!
SQUEEEZE
PROMISE ME YOU'LL COME BACK SAFELY.
I WON'T FORGIVE YOU IF EVEN ONE OF YOU DIES!
OKAY.
I PROMISE!

SIDE STORY 6

MORE "IF IT WAS NORMAN"...

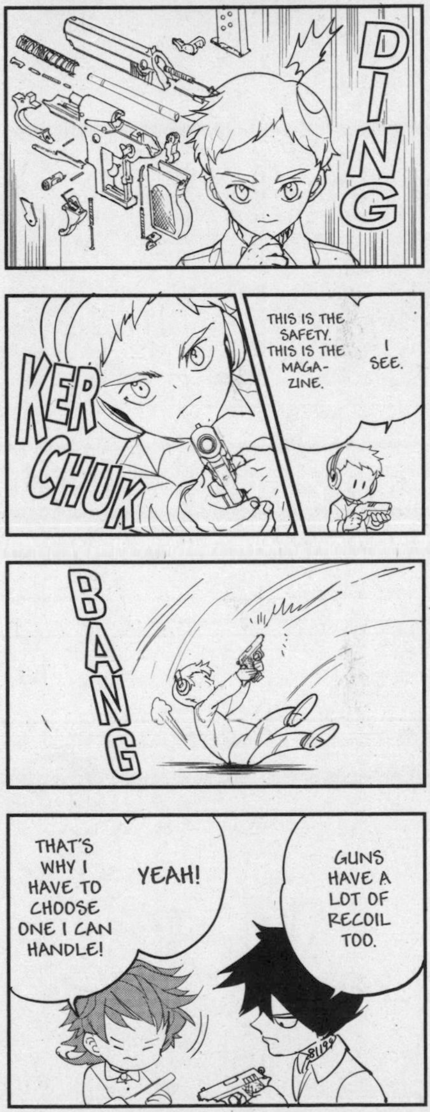
DING
THIS IS THE SAFETY. THIS IS THE MAGAZINE.
I SEE.
KERCHUK
BANG
GUNS HAVE A LOT OF RECOIL TOO.
YEAH!
THAT'S WHY I HAVE TO CHOOSE ONE I CAN HANDLE!

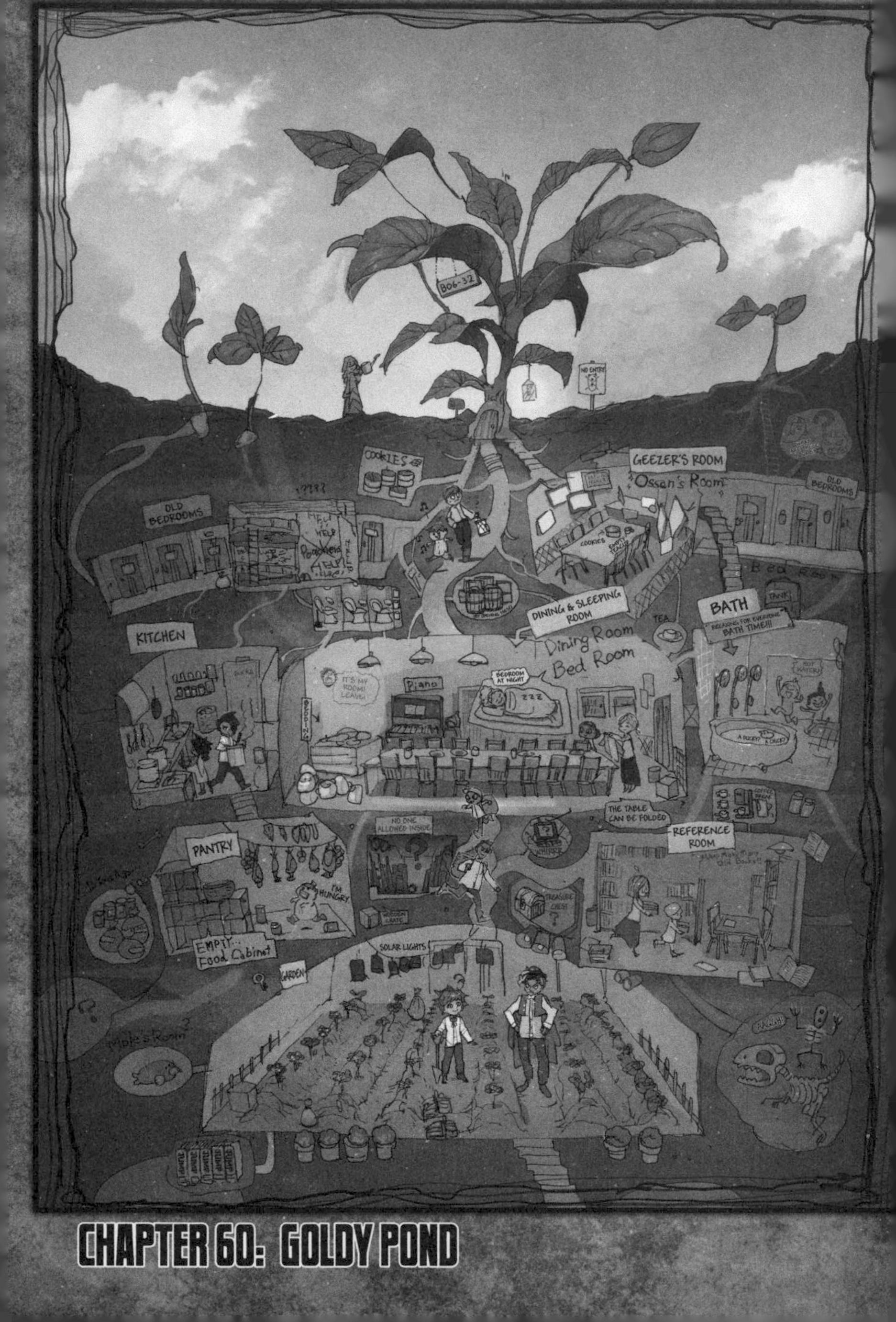

B06-32
NO ENTRY
COOKIES
GEEZER'S ROOM
Ossan's Room
OLD BEDROOMS
OLD BEDROOMS
Bed Room
DINING & SLEEPING ROOM
BATH
RELAXING FOR EVERYONE BATH TIME!!!
TANK
TEA
KITCHEN
Dining Room
Bed Room
IT'S MY ROOM! LEAVE!
Piano
BEDDING
BEDROOM AT NIGHT
ZZZ
HOT WATER!
THE TABLE CAN BE FOLDED
NO ONE ALLOWED INSIDE
PANTRY
I'M HUNGRY
REFERENCE ROOM
TREASURE CHEST
EMPTY... Food Cabinet
SOLAR LIGHTS
GARDEN
Mole's Room

CHAPTER 60: GOLDY POND

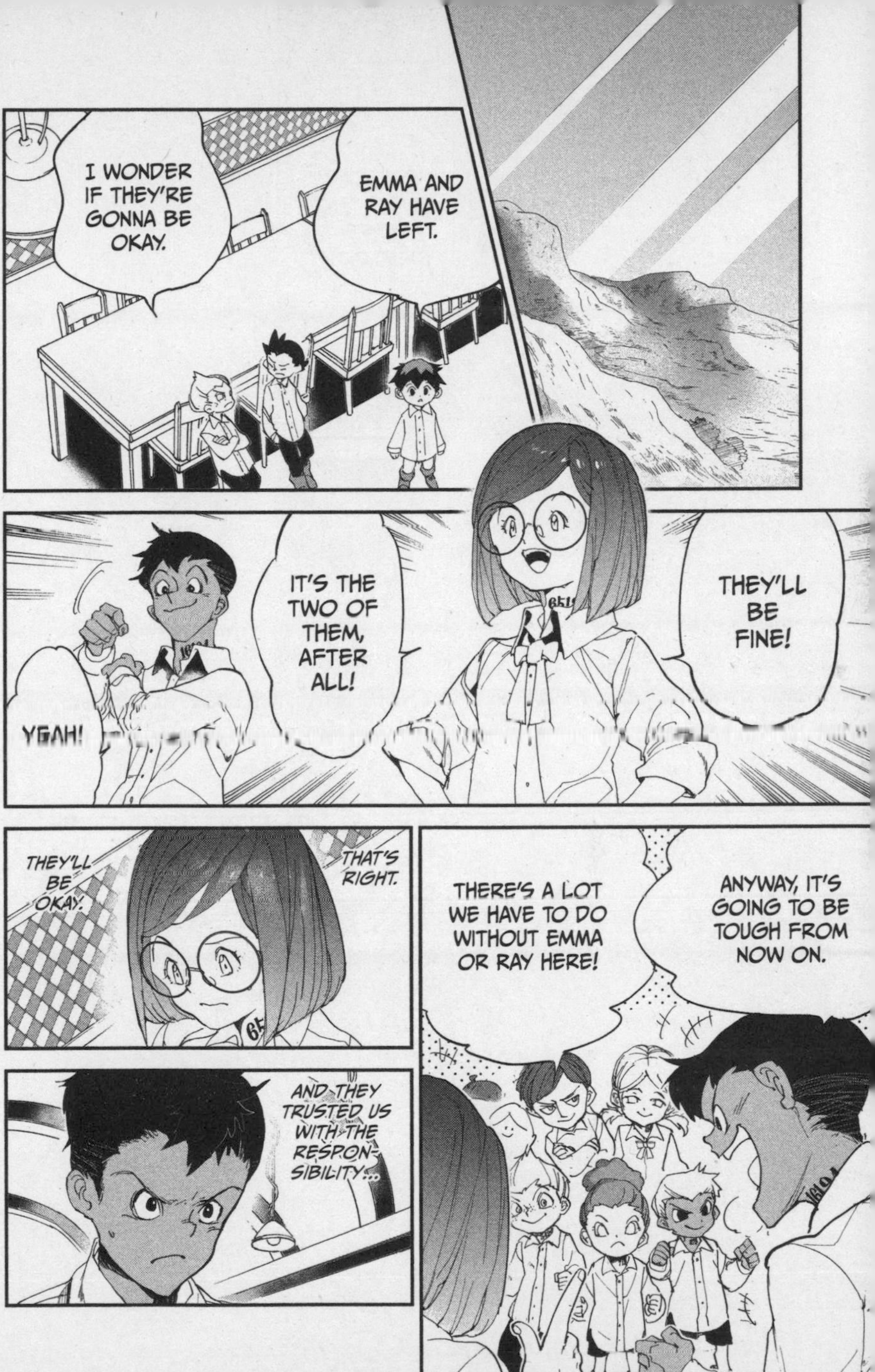
EMMA AND RAY HAVE LEFT.
I WONDER IF THEY'RE GONNA BE OKAY.
THEY'LL BE FINE!
IT'S THE TWO OF THEM, AFTER ALL!
YEAH!
ANYWAY, IT'S GOING TO BE TOUGH FROM NOW ON.
THERE'S A LOT WE HAVE TO DO WITHOUT EMMA OR RAY HERE!
THAT'S RIGHT.
THEY'LL BE OKAY.
AND THEY TRUSTED US WITH THE RESPON-SIBILITY...

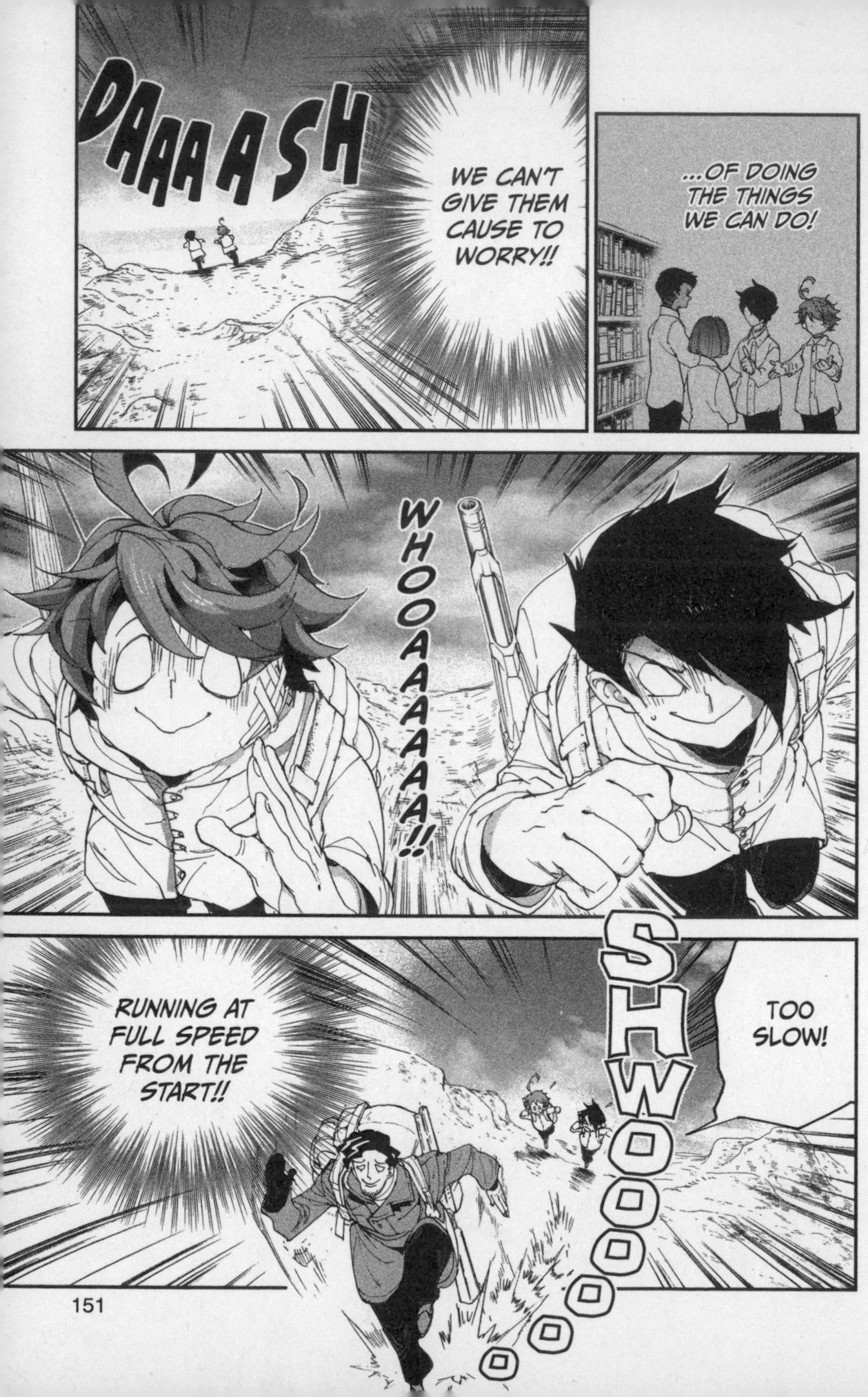
...OF DOING THE THINGS WE CAN DO!
DAAAASH
WE CAN'T GIVE THEM CAUSE TO WORRY!!
WHOOAAAAAAAA!!
SHWOOOOOOOO
TOO SLOW!
RUNNING AT FULL SPEED FROM THE START!!

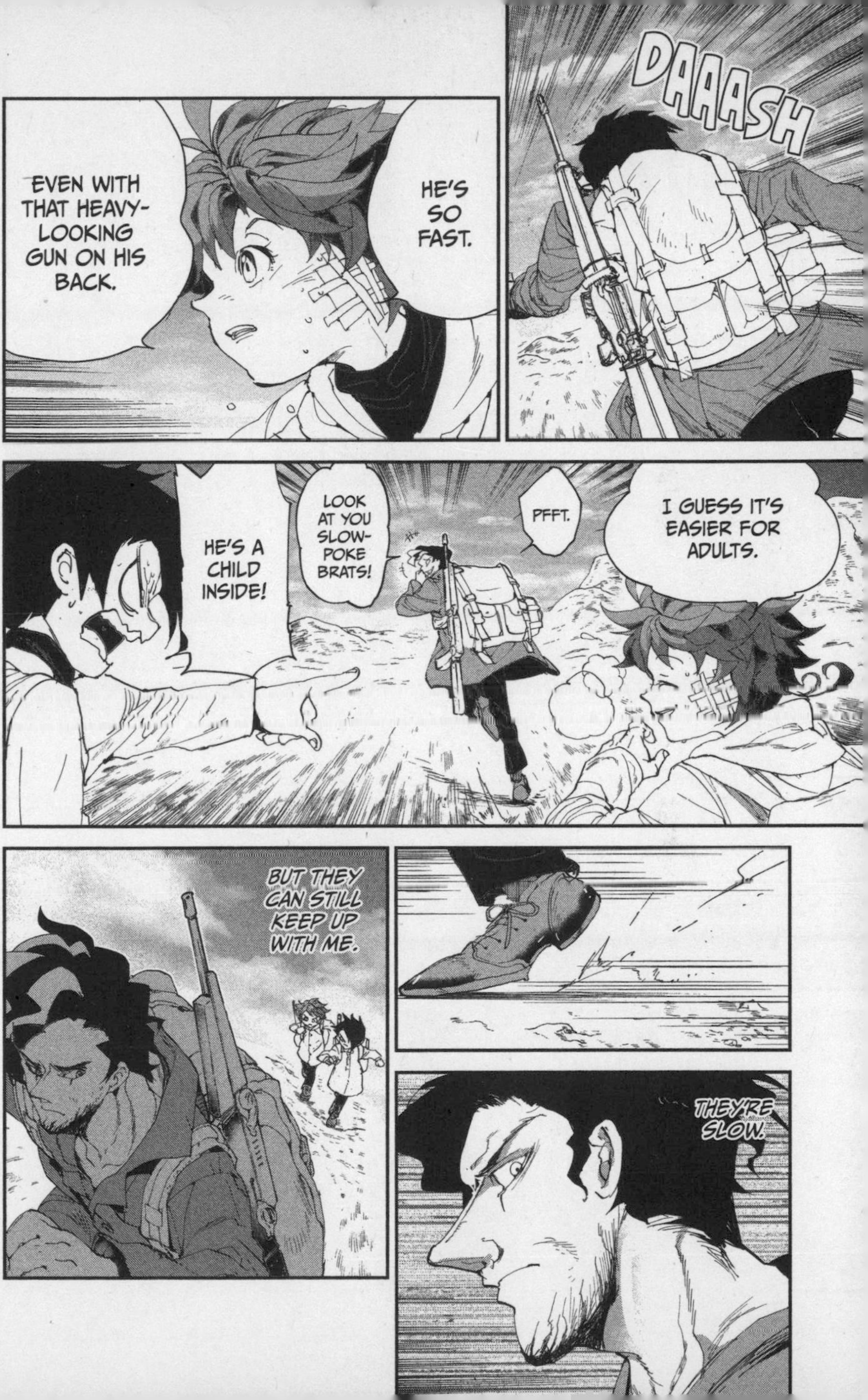
DAAASH
HE'S SO FAST.
EVEN WITH THAT HEAVY-LOOKING GUN ON HIS BACK.
I GUESS IT'S EASIER FOR ADULTS.
PFFT.
LOOK AT YOU SLOW-POKE BRATS!
HE'S A CHILD INSIDE!
THEY'RE SLOW.
BUT THEY CAN STILL KEEP UP WITH ME.

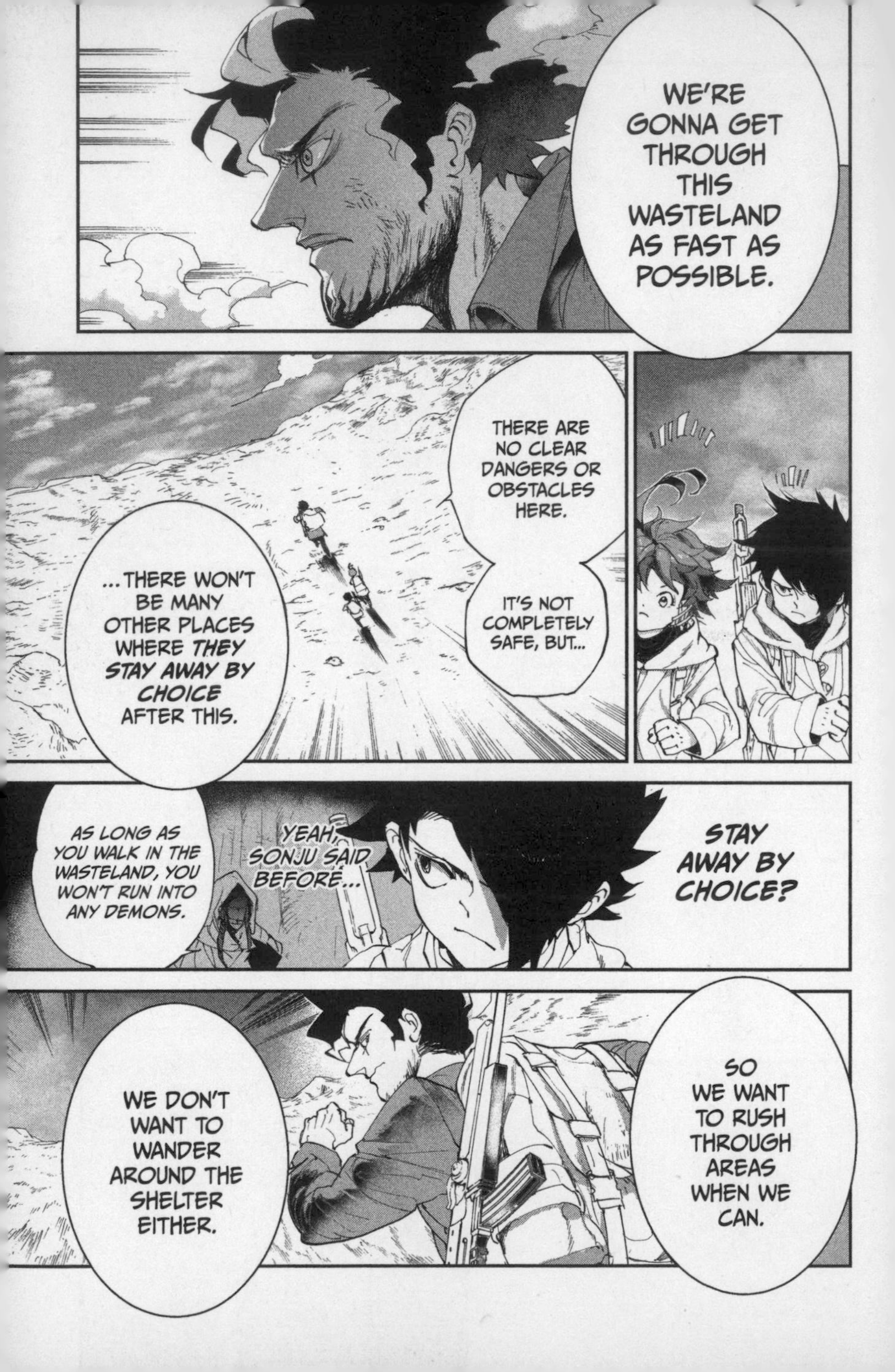
WE'RE GONNA GET THROUGH THIS WASTELAND AS FAST AS POSSIBLE.
THERE ARE NO CLEAR DANGERS OR OBSTACLES HERE.
IT'S NOT COMPLETELY SAFE, BUT...
...THERE WON'T BE MANY OTHER PLACES WHERE *THEY STAY AWAY BY CHOICE* AFTER THIS.
STAY AWAY BY CHOICE?
YEAH, SONJU SAID BEFORE...
AS LONG AS YOU WALK IN THE WASTELAND, YOU WON'T RUN INTO ANY DEMONS.
SO WE WANT TO RUSH THROUGH AREAS WHEN WE CAN.
WE DON'T WANT TO WANDER AROUND THE SHELTER EITHER.

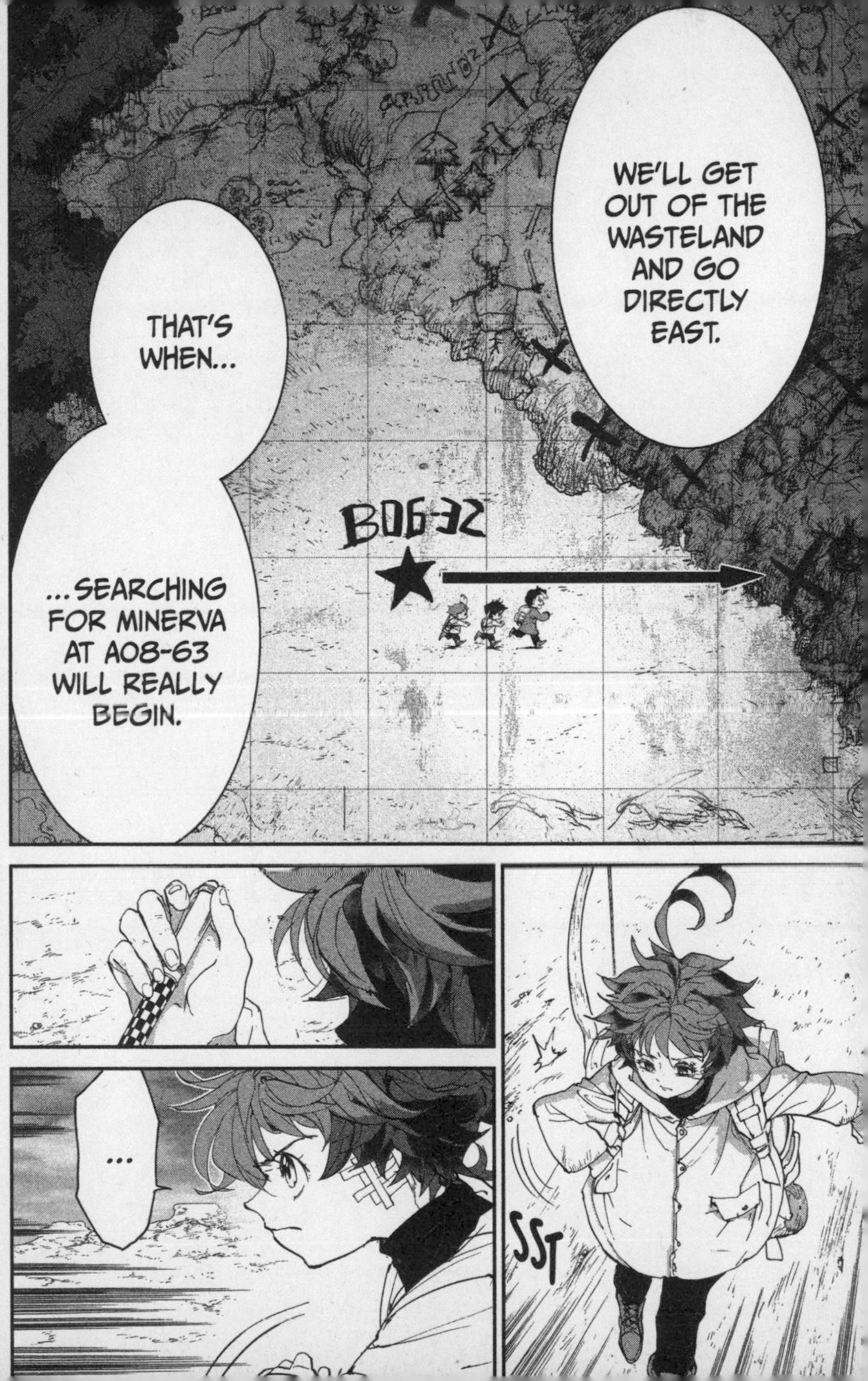
WE'LL GET OUT OF THE WASTELAND AND GO DIRECTLY EAST.
THAT'S WHEN...
...SEARCHING FOR MINERVA AT A08-63 WILL REALLY BEGIN.
B06-32
SST
...

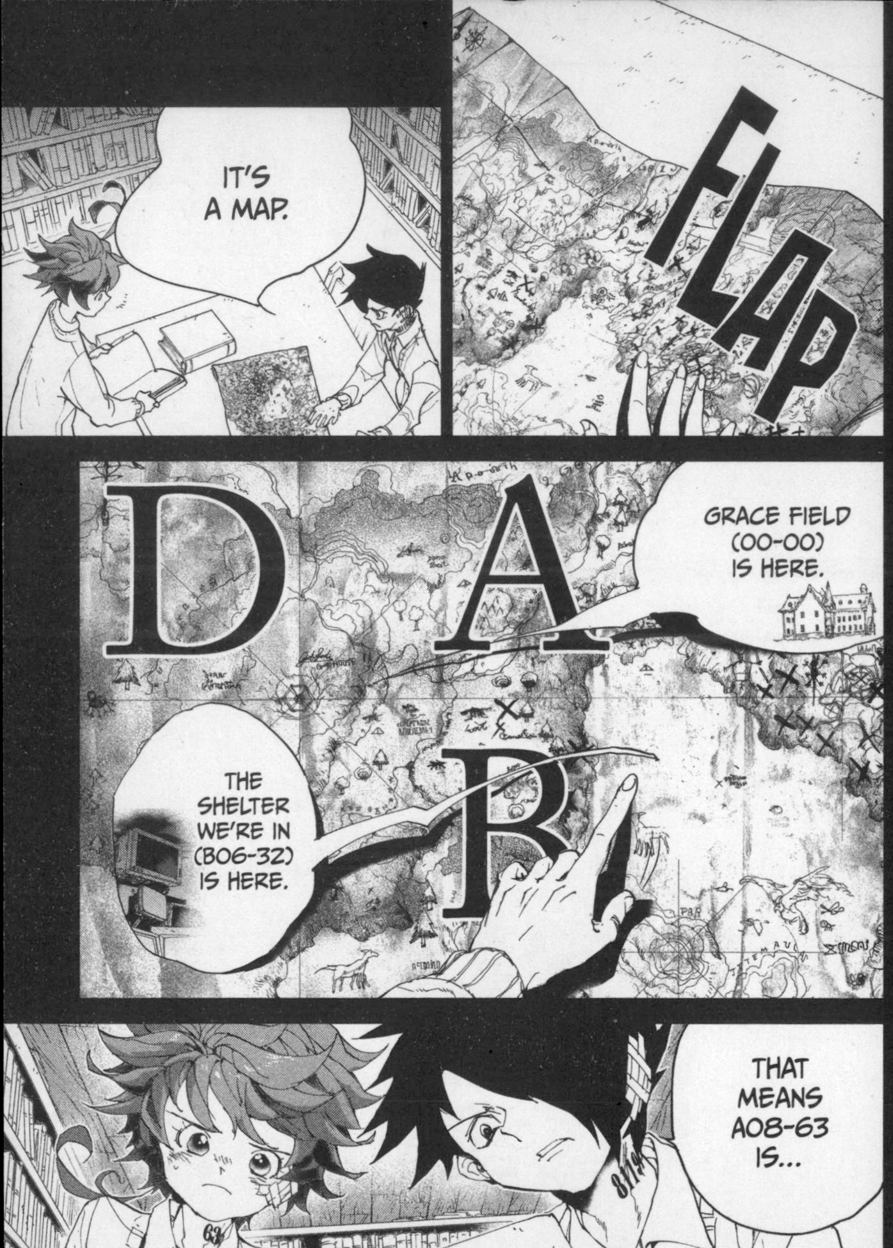
FLAP
IT'S A MAP.
D
A
B
GRACE FIELD (00-00) IS HERE.
THE SHELTER WE'RE IN (B06-32) IS HERE.
THAT MEANS A08-63 IS...

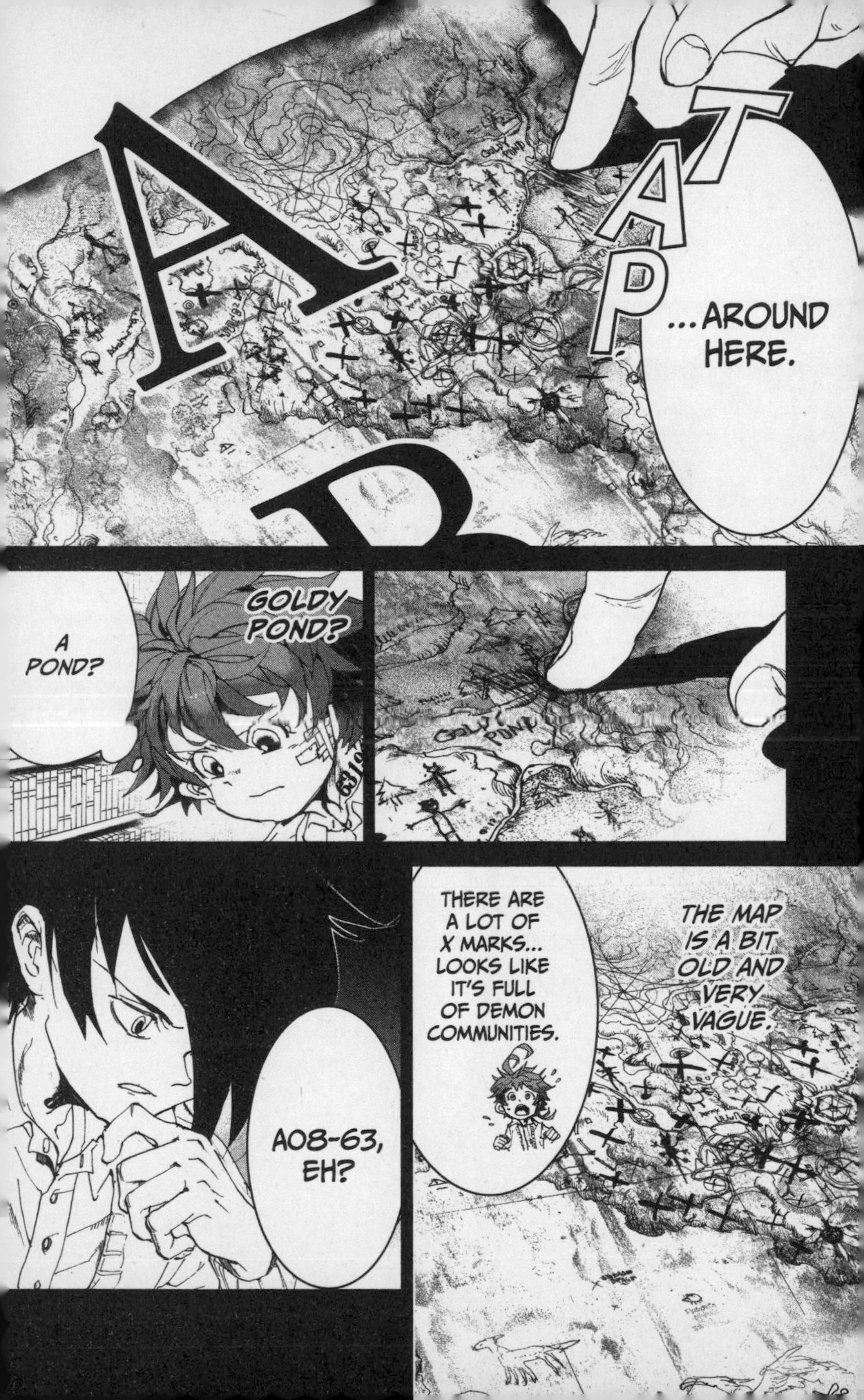
TAP
...AROUND HERE.
GOLDY POND?
A POND?
THE MAP IS A BIT OLD AND VERY VAGUE.
THERE ARE A LOT OF X MARKS... LOOKS LIKE IT'S FULL OF DEMON COMMUNITIES.
A08-63, EH?

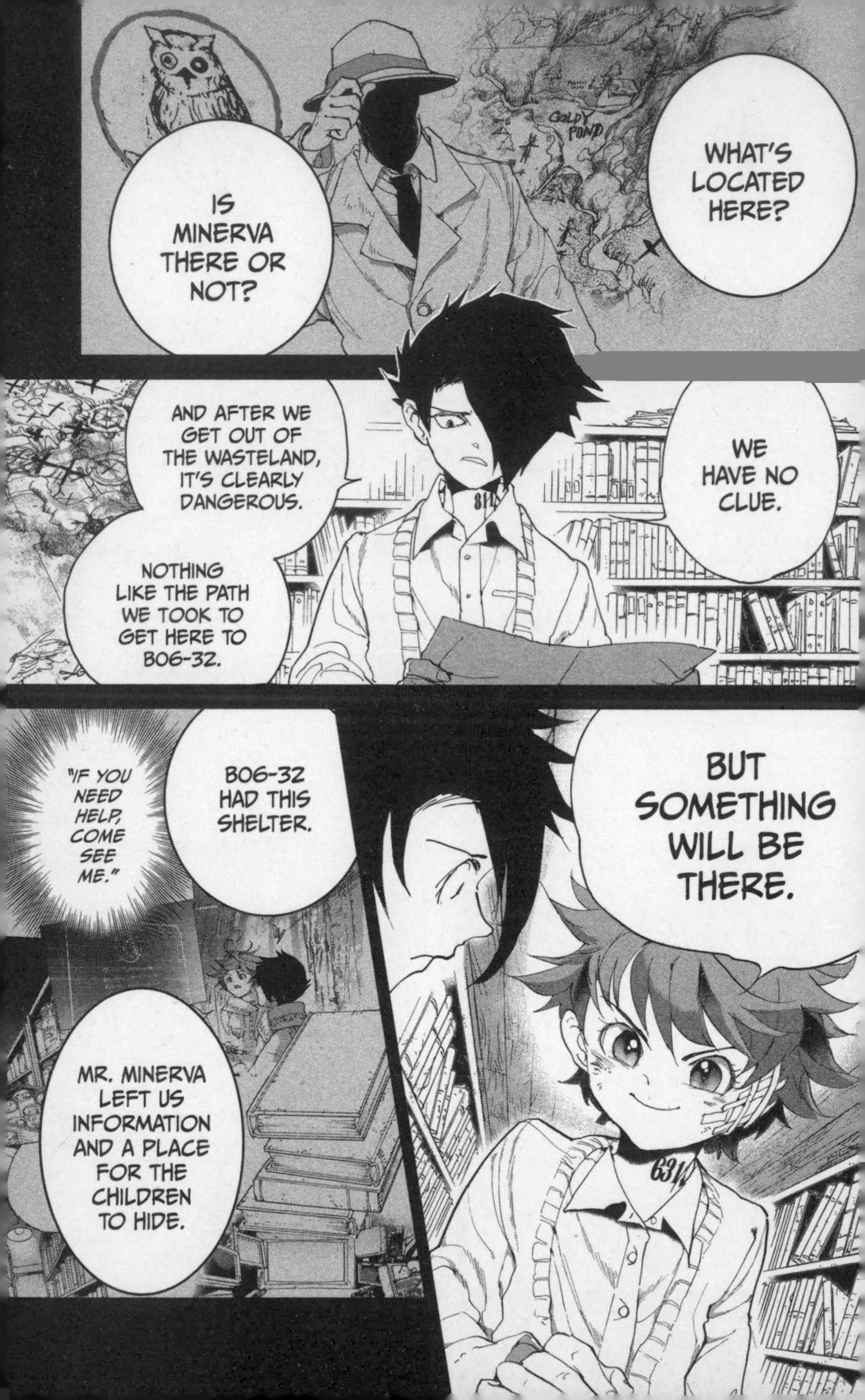
WHAT'S LOCATED HERE?
GOLDY POND
IS MINERVA THERE OR NOT?
WE HAVE NO CLUE.
AND AFTER WE GET OUT OF THE WASTELAND, IT'S CLEARLY DANGEROUS.
NOTHING LIKE THE PATH WE TOOK TO GET HERE TO B06-32.
BUT SOMETHING WILL BE THERE.
B06-32 HAD THIS SHELTER.
"IF YOU NEED HELP, COME SEE ME."
MR. MINERVA LEFT US INFORMATION AND A PLACE FOR THE CHILDREN TO HIDE.

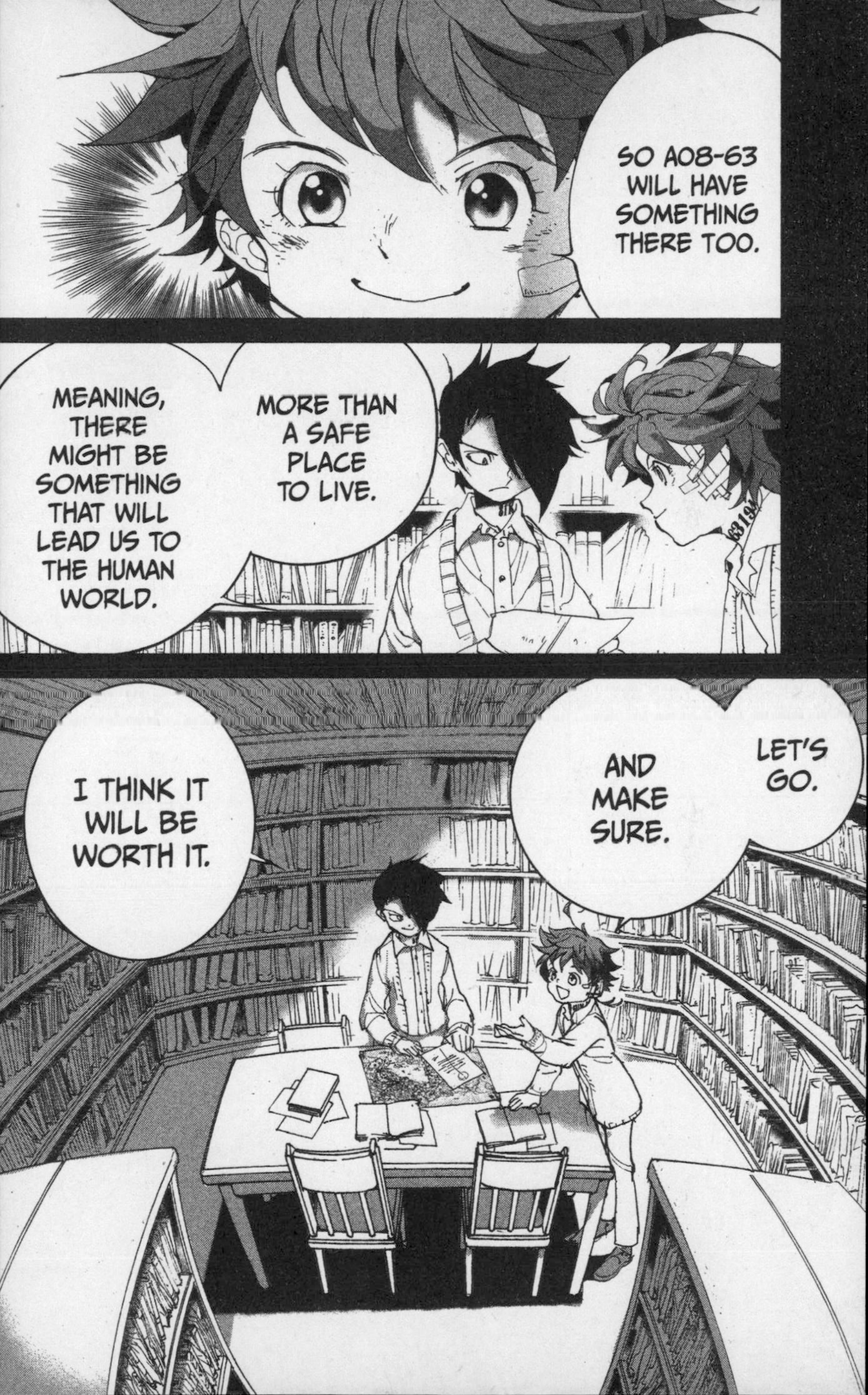
SO A08-63 WILL HAVE SOMETHING THERE TOO.
MORE THAN A SAFE PLACE TO LIVE.
MEANING, THERE MIGHT BE SOMETHING THAT WILL LEAD US TO THE HUMAN WORLD.
LET'S GO.
AND MAKE SURE.
I THINK IT WILL BE WORTH IT.

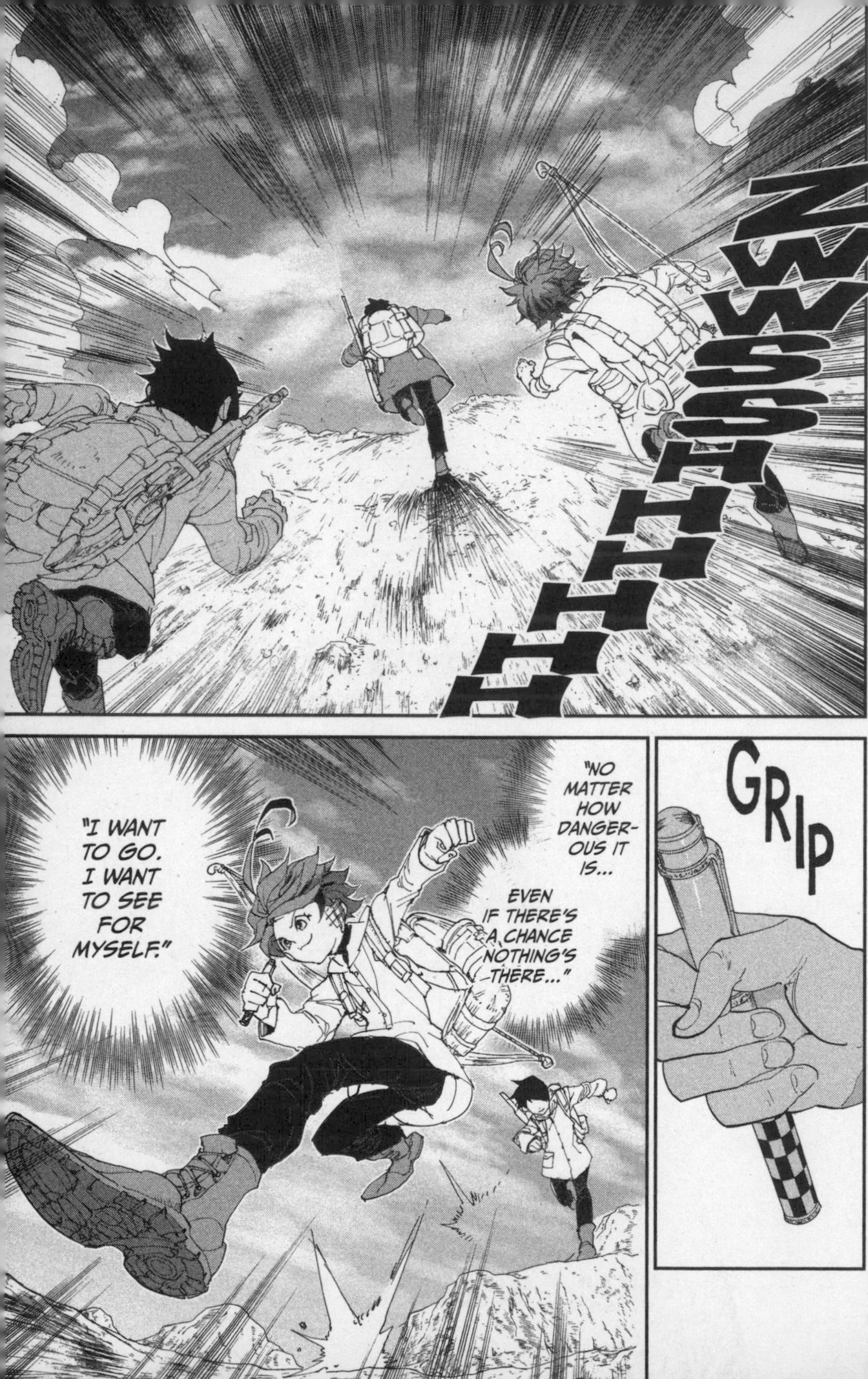
ZWWSSHHHHHH
GRIP
"NO MATTER HOW DANGER-OUS IT IS...
EVEN IF THERE'S A CHANCE NOTHING'S THERE..."
"I WANT TO GO. I WANT TO SEE FOR MYSELF."

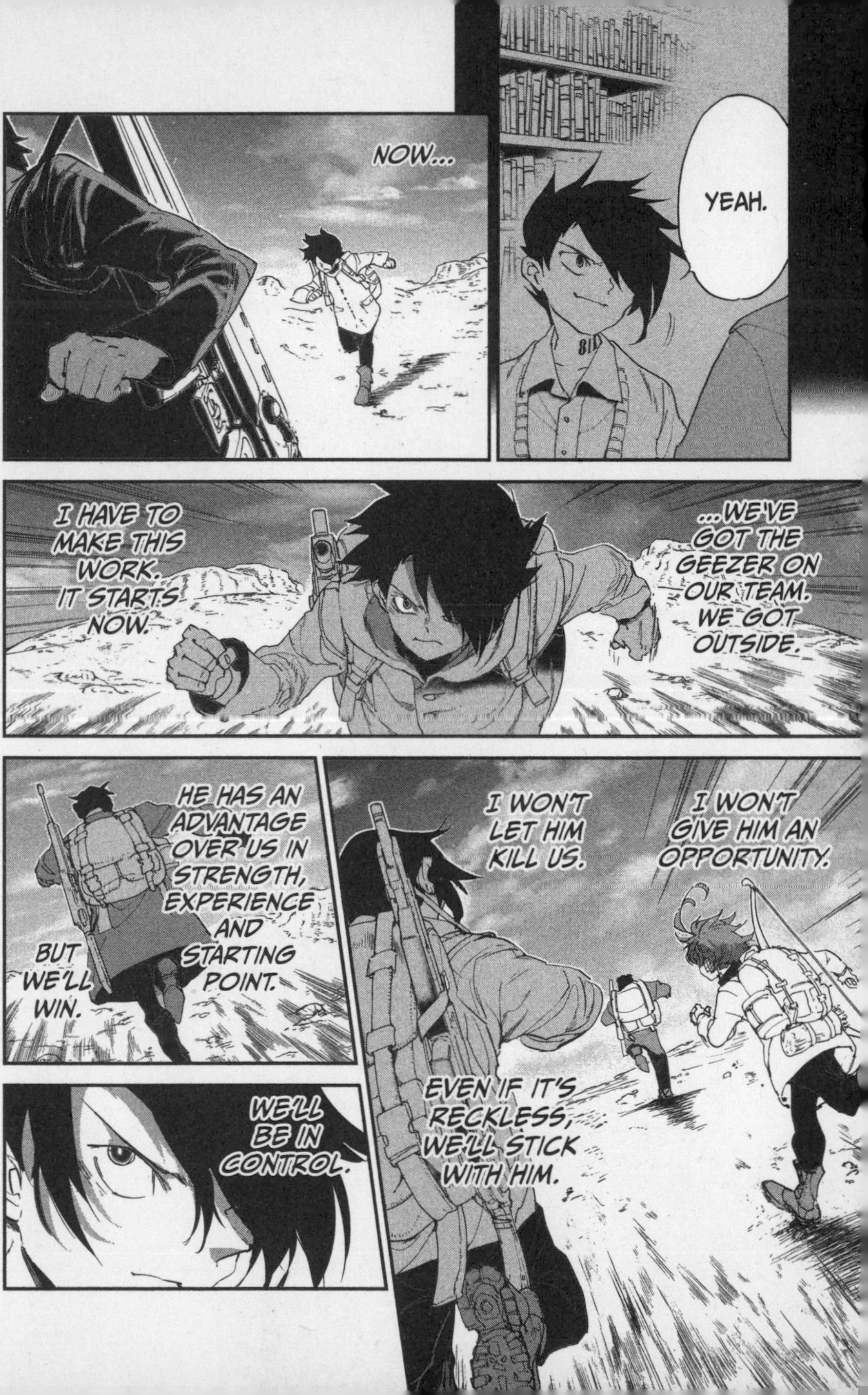
YEAH.
NOW...
...WE'VE GOT THE GEEZER ON OUR TEAM. WE GOT OUTSIDE.
I HAVE TO MAKE THIS WORK. IT STARTS NOW.
I WON'T GIVE HIM AN OPPORTUNITY.
I WON'T LET HIM KILL US.
EVEN IF IT'S RECKLESS, WE'LL STICK WITH HIM.
HE HAS AN ADVANTAGE OVER US IN STRENGTH, EXPERIENCE AND STARTING POINT.
BUT WE'LL WIN.
WE'LL BE IN CONTROL.

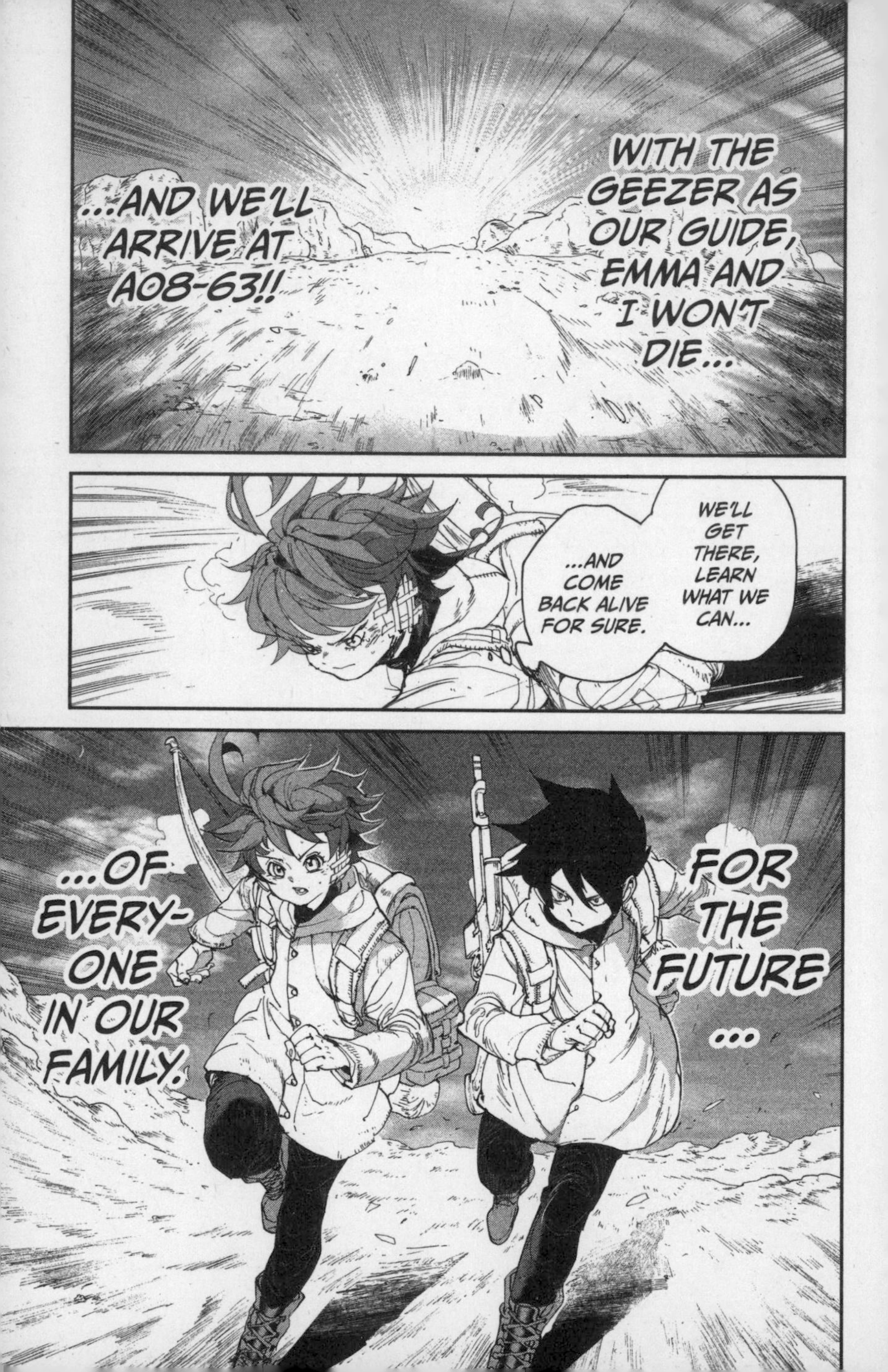
WITH THE GEEZER AS OUR GUIDE, EMMA AND I WON'T DIE...
...AND WE'LL ARRIVE AT A08-63!!
WE'LL GET THERE, LEARN WHAT WE CAN...
...AND COME BACK ALIVE FOR SURE.
FOR THE FUTURE ...
...OF EVERY-ONE IN OUR FAMILY.

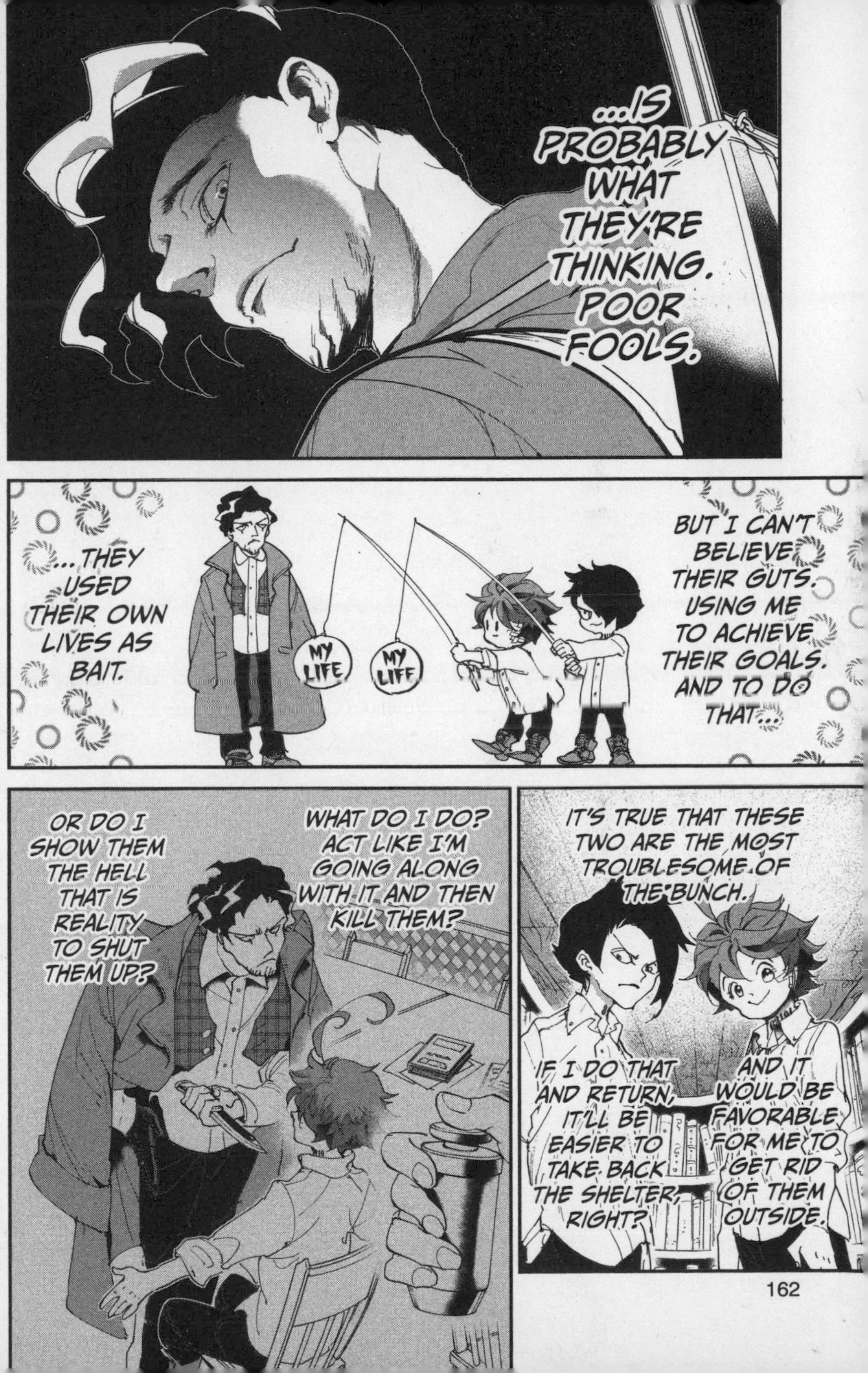
...IS PROBABLY WHAT THEY'RE THINKING. POOR FOOLS.
BUT I CAN'T BELIEVE THEIR GUTS. USING ME TO ACHIEVE THEIR GOALS. AND TO DO THAT...
...THEY USED THEIR OWN LIVES AS BAIT.
MY LIFE
MY LIFE
IT'S TRUE THAT THESE TWO ARE THE MOST TROUBLESOME OF THE BUNCH.
AND IT WOULD BE FAVORABLE FOR ME TO GET RID OF THEM OUTSIDE.
IF I DO THAT AND RETURN, IT'LL BE EASIER TO TAKE BACK THE SHELTER, RIGHT?
WHAT DO I DO? ACT LIKE I'M GOING ALONG WITH IT AND THEN KILL THEM?
OR DO I SHOW THEM THE HELL THAT IS REALITY TO SHUT THEM UP?

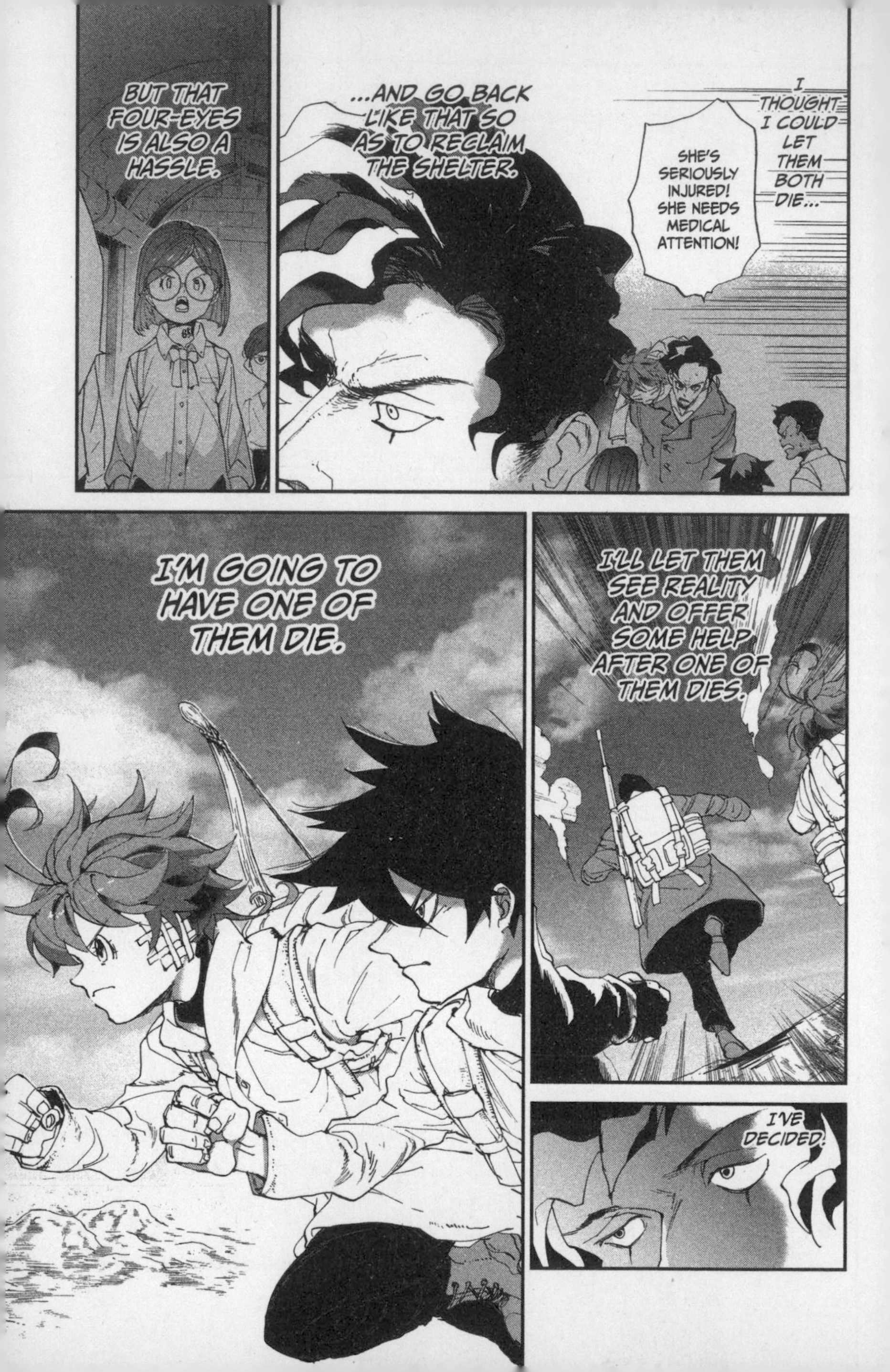
I THOUGHT I COULD LET THEM BOTH DIE...
SHE'S SERIOUSLY INJURED! SHE NEEDS MEDICAL ATTENTION!
...AND GO BACK LIKE THAT SO AS TO RECLAIM THE SHELTER.
BUT THAT FOUR-EYES IS ALSO A HASSLE.
I'LL LET THEM SEE REALITY AND OFFER SOME HELP AFTER ONE OF THEM DIES.
I'VE DECIDED.
I'M GOING TO HAVE ONE OF THEM DIE.

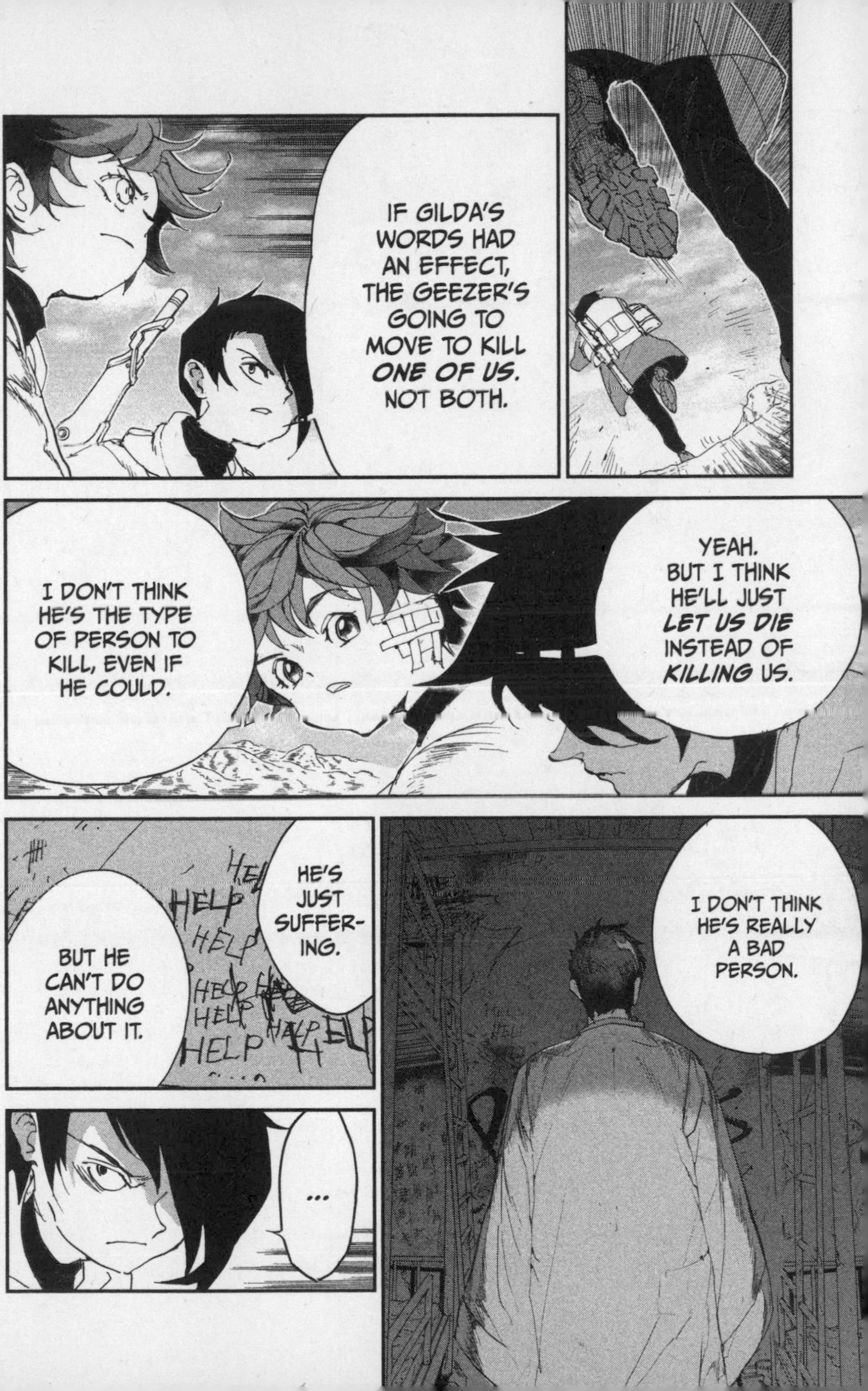
IF GILDA'S WORDS HAD AN EFFECT, THE GEEZER'S GOING TO MOVE TO KILL *ONE OF US.* NOT BOTH.
YEAH. BUT I THINK HE'LL JUST *LET US DIE* INSTEAD OF *KILLING* US.
I DON'T THINK HE'S THE TYPE OF PERSON TO KILL, EVEN IF HE COULD.
I DON'T THINK HE'S REALLY A BAD PERSON.
HE'S JUST SUFFER-ING.
BUT HE CAN'T DO ANYTHING ABOUT IT.
...

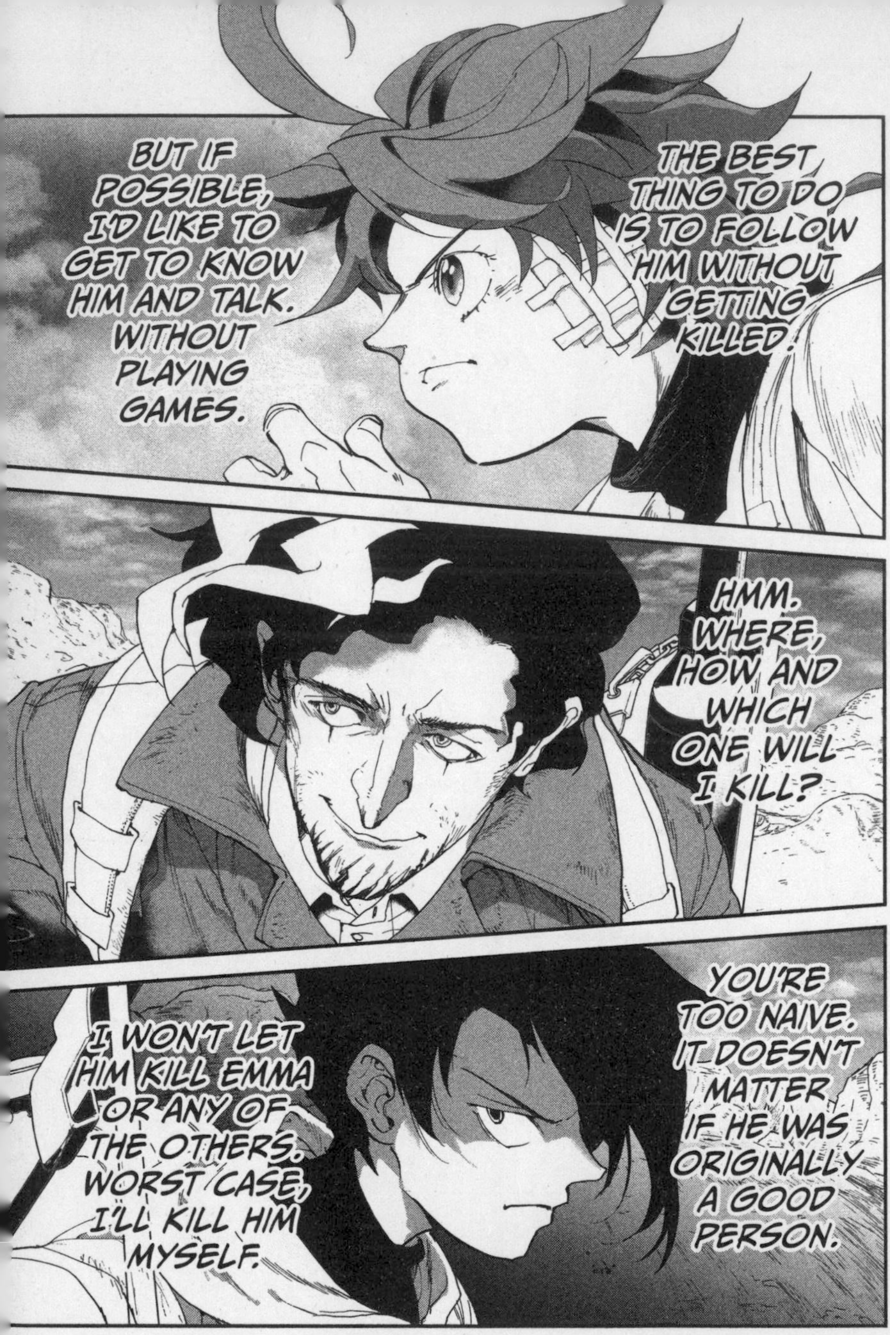
THE BEST THING TO DO IS TO FOLLOW HIM WITHOUT GETTING KILLED.
BUT IF POSSIBLE, I'D LIKE TO GET TO KNOW HIM AND TALK. WITHOUT PLAYING GAMES.
HMM. WHERE, HOW AND WHICH ONE WILL I KILL?
YOU'RE TOO NAIVE. IT DOESN'T MATTER IF HE WAS ORIGINALLY A GOOD PERSON.
I WON'T LET HIM KILL EMMA OR ANY OF THE OTHERS. WORST CASE, I'LL KILL HIM MYSELF.

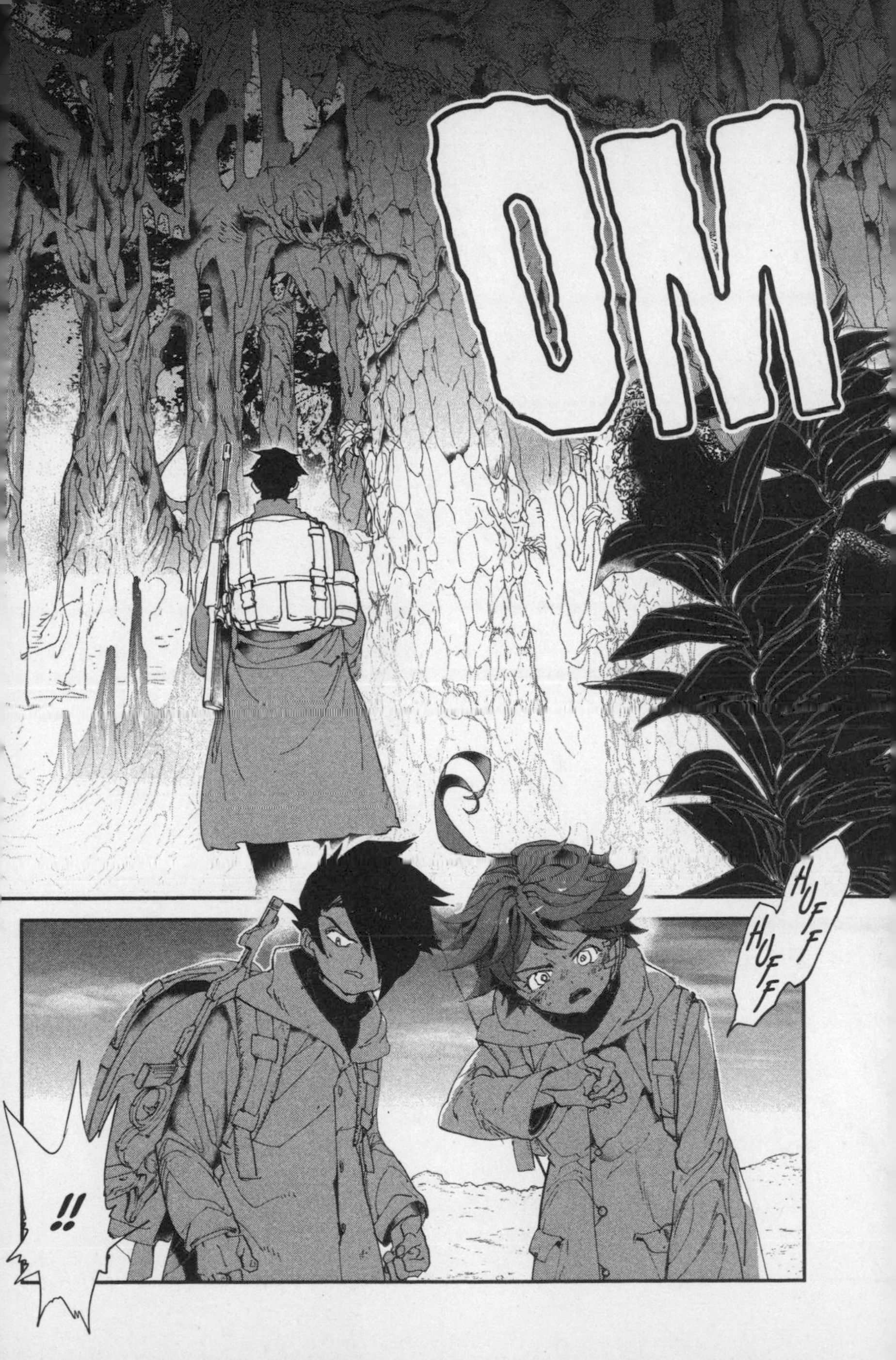
OM
HUFF HUFF
!!

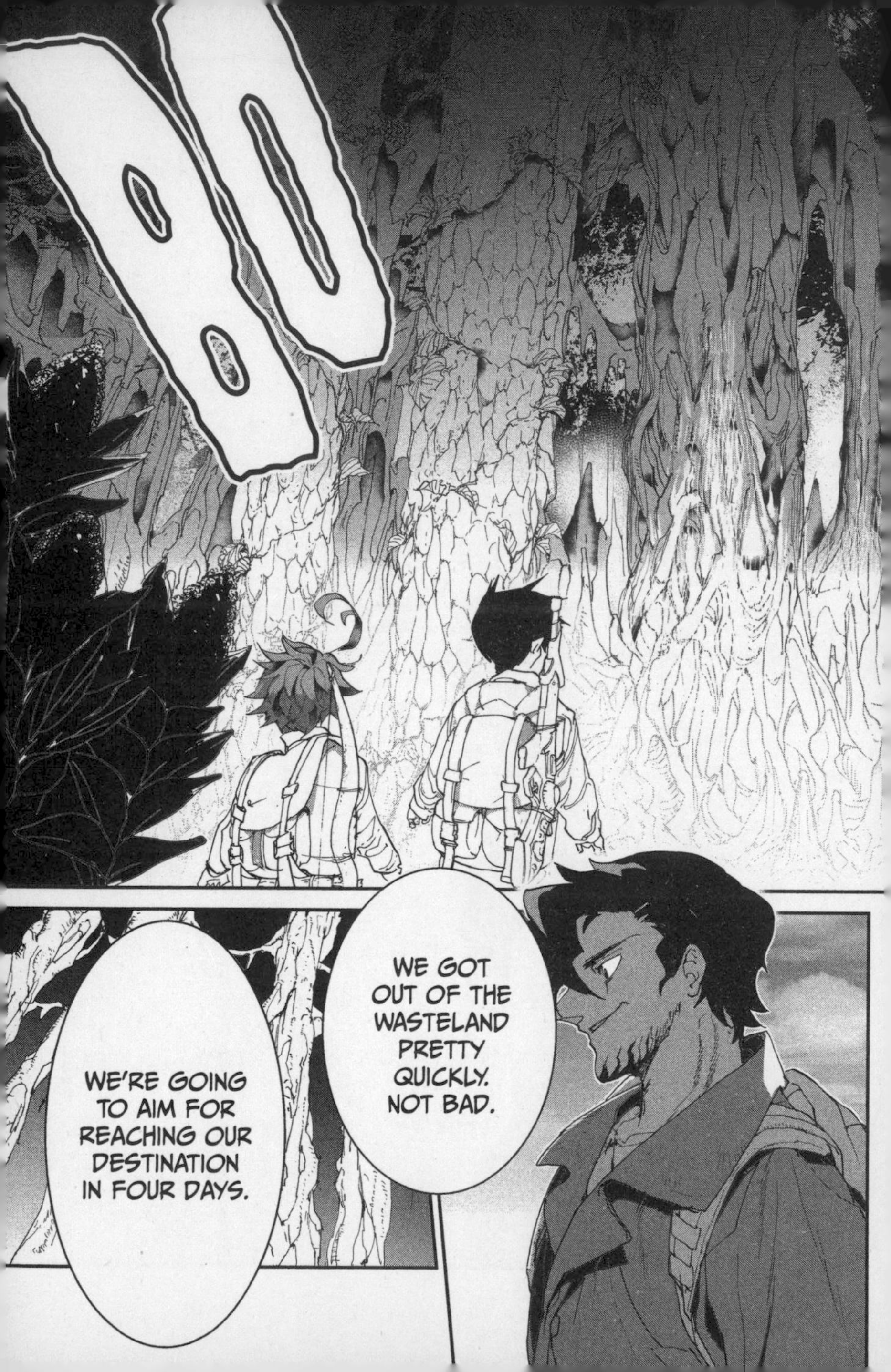
WE GOT OUT OF THE WASTELAND PRETTY QUICKLY. NOT BAD.
WE'RE GOING TO AIM FOR REACHING OUR DESTINATION IN FOUR DAYS.

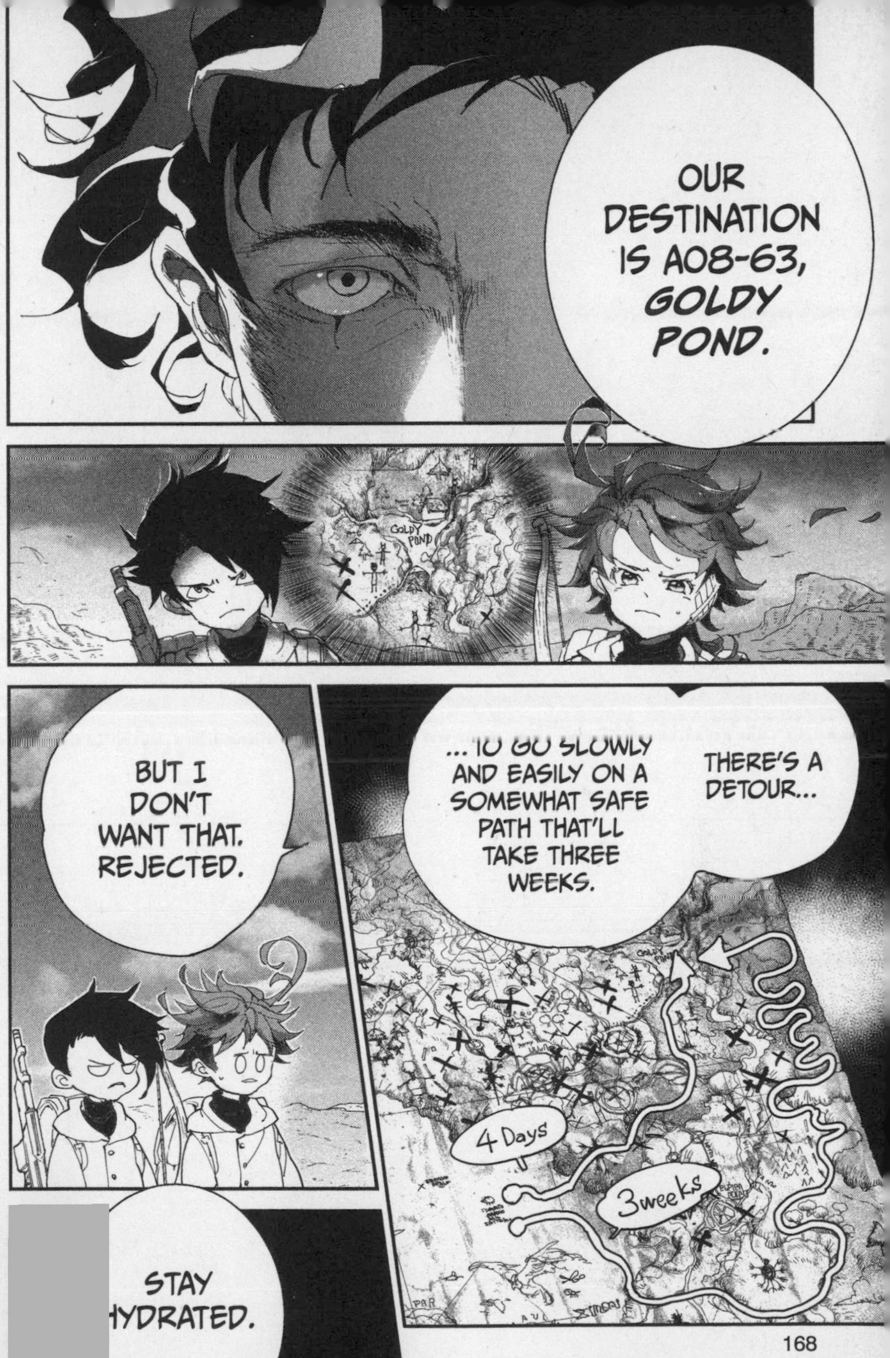
OUR DESTINATION IS A08-63, GOLDY POND.
GOLDY POND
THERE'S A DETOUR...
...TO GO SLOWLY AND EASILY ON A SOMEWHAT SAFE PATH THAT'LL TAKE THREE WEEKS.
GOLDY POND
4 Days
3weeks
BUT I DON'T WANT THAT. REJECTED.
STAY HYDRATED.

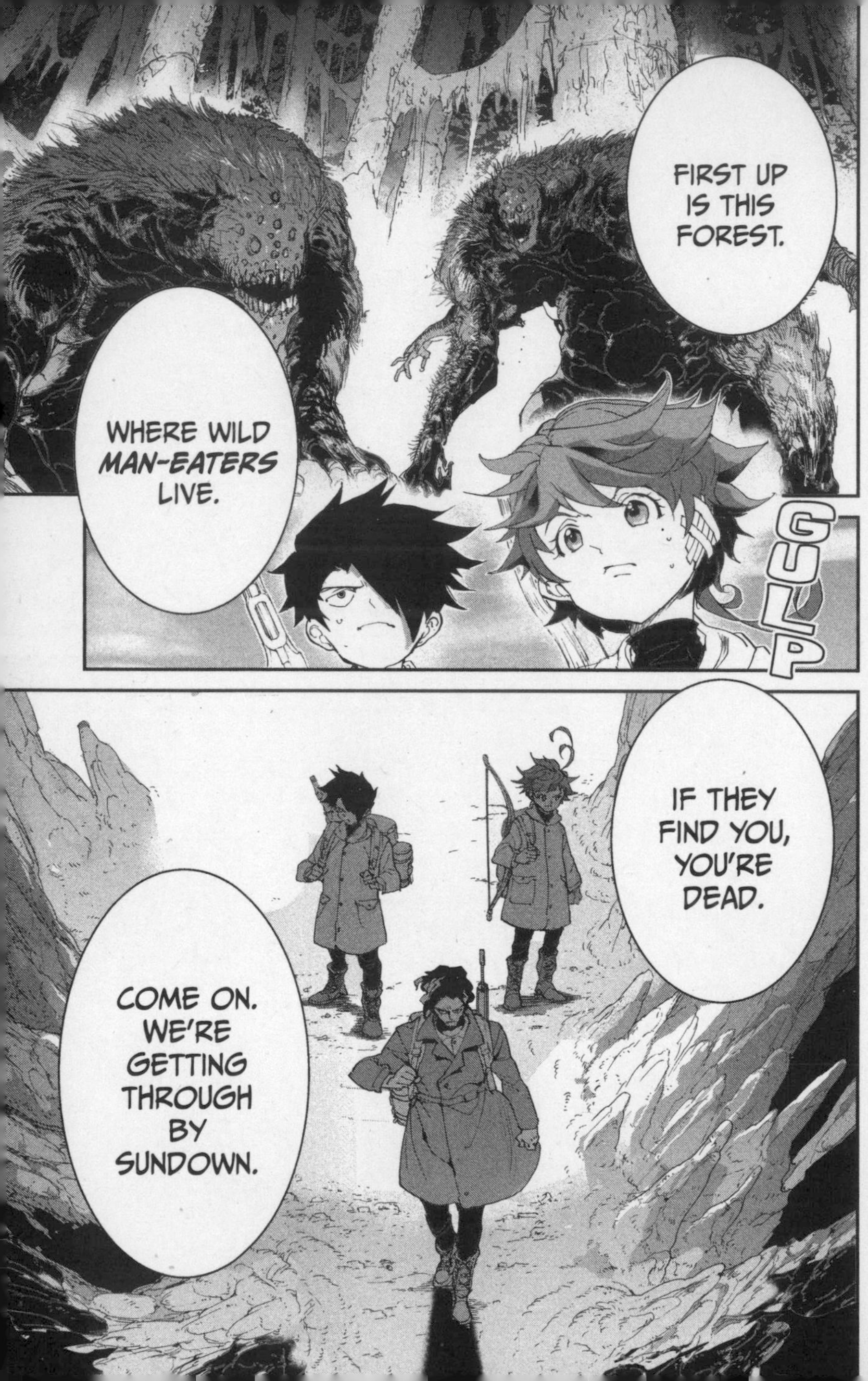
FIRST UP IS THIS FOREST.
WHERE WILD *MAN-EATERS* LIVE.
GULP
IF THEY FIND YOU, YOU'RE DEAD.
COME ON. WE'RE GETTING THROUGH BY SUNDOWN.

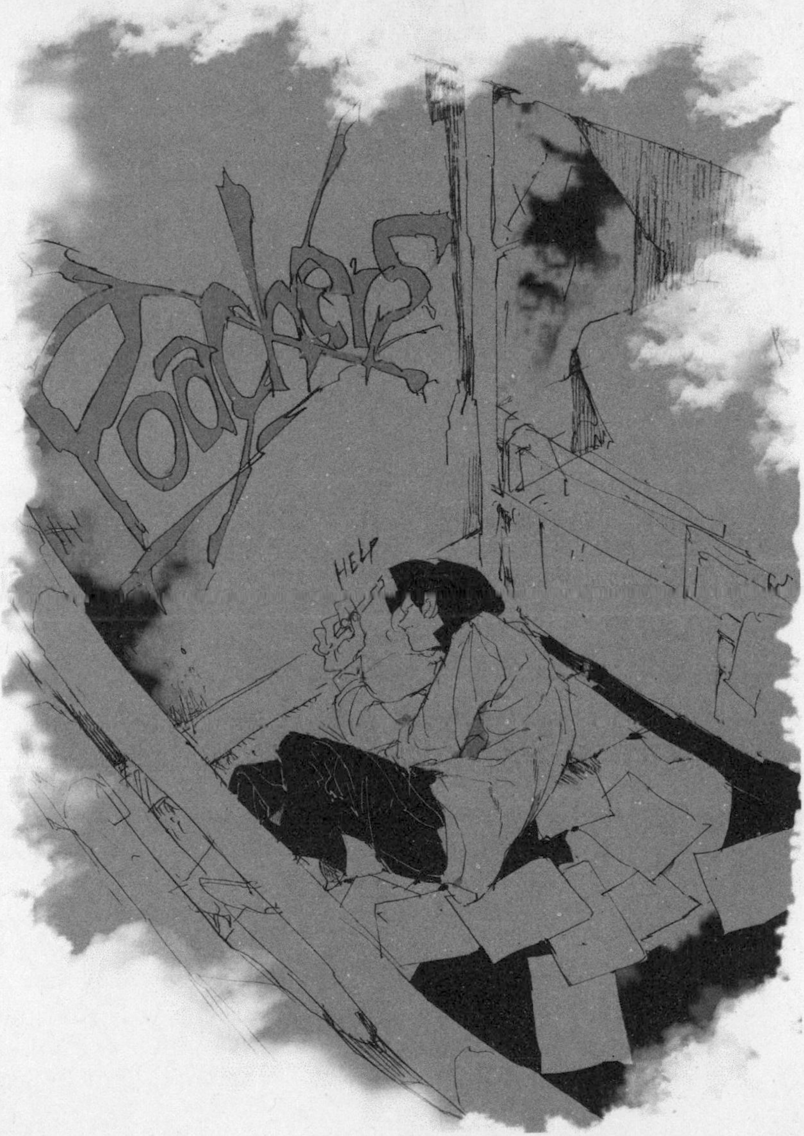
Poachers
HELP

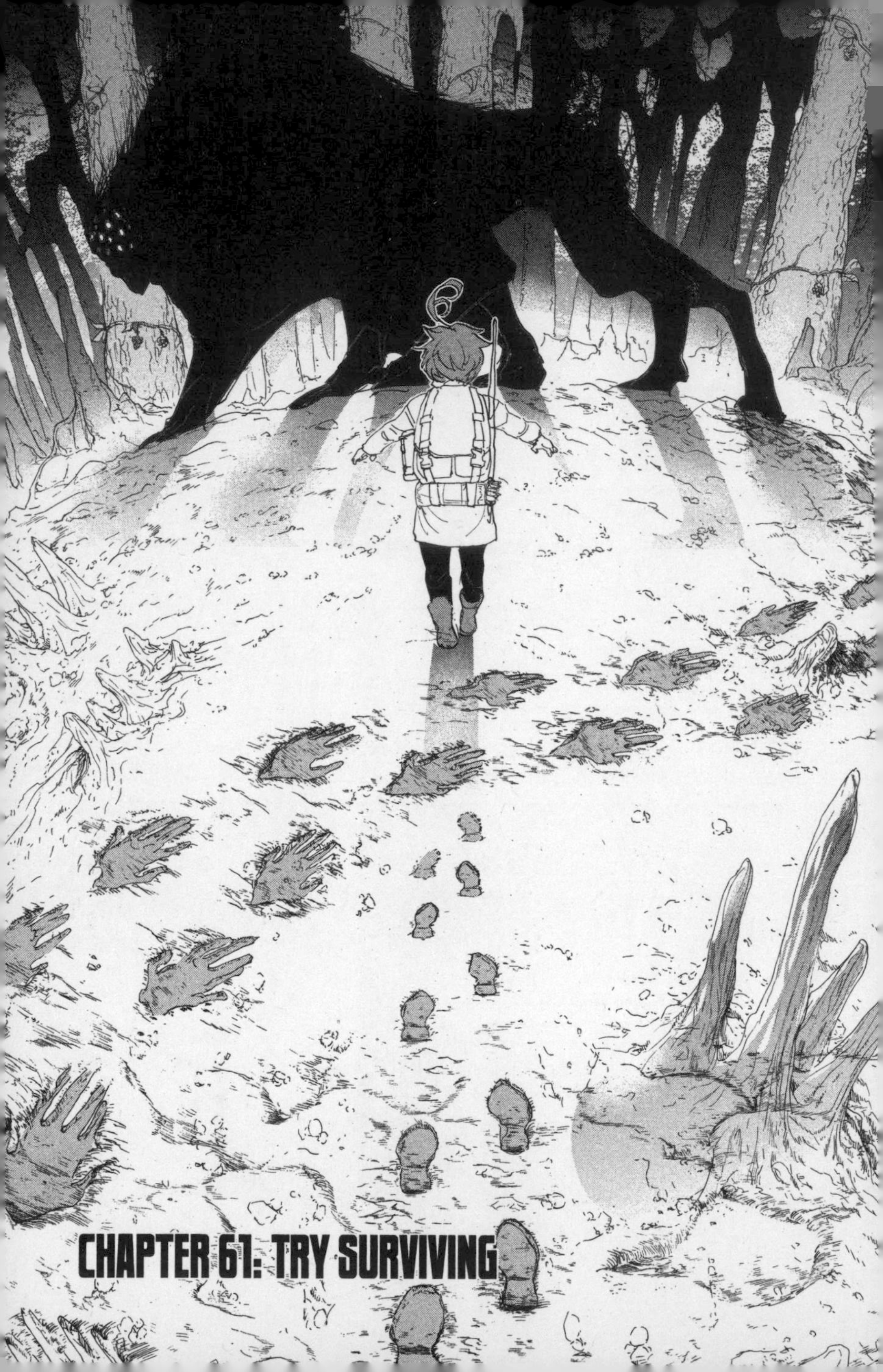
CHAPTER 61: TRY SURVIVING

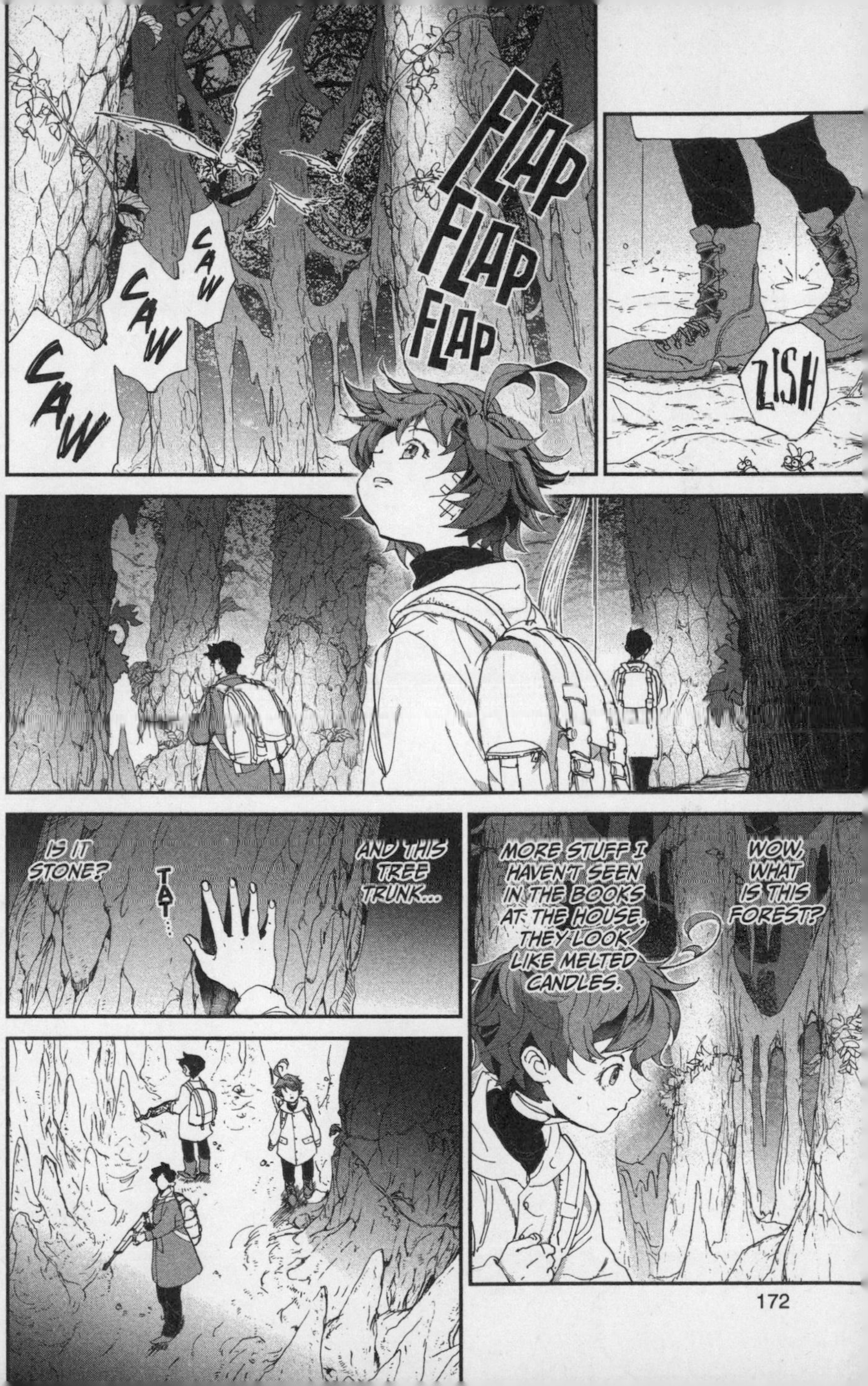
ZISH
FLAP
FLAP
FLAP
CAW
CAW
CAW
CAW
WOW, WHAT IS THIS FOREST?
MORE STUFF I HAVEN'T SEEN IN THE BOOKS AT THE HOUSE. THEY LOOK LIKE MELTED CANDLES.
AND THIS TREE TRUNK...
TAT...
IS IT STONE?

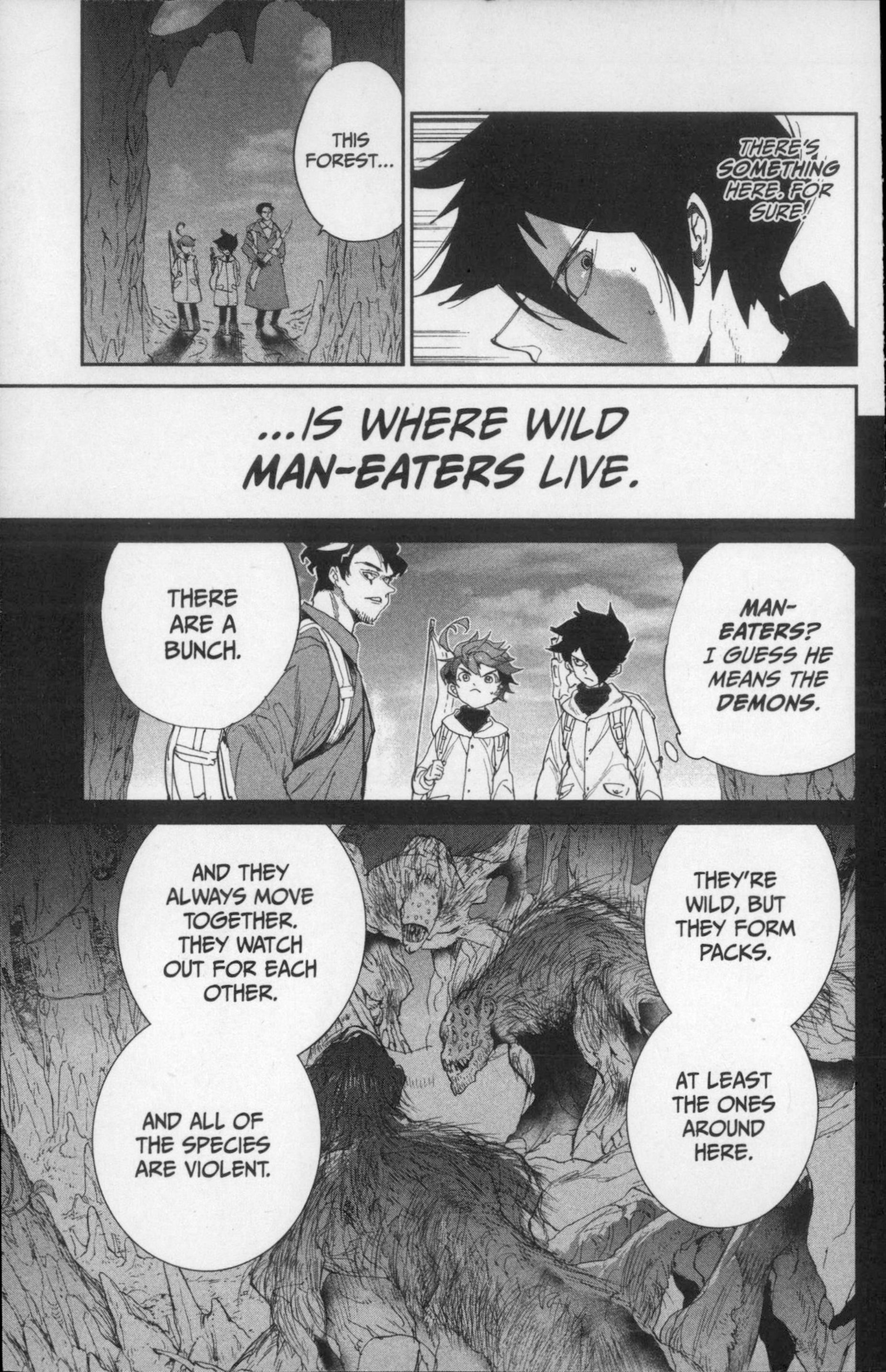
THERE'S SOMETHING HERE. FOR SURE!
THIS FOREST...
...IS WHERE WILD MAN-EATERS LIVE.
MAN-EATERS? I GUESS HE MEANS THE DEMONS.
THERE ARE A BUNCH.
THEY'RE WILD, BUT THEY FORM PACKS.
AND THEY ALWAYS MOVE TOGETHER. THEY WATCH OUT FOR EACH OTHER.
AT LEAST THE ONES AROUND HERE.
AND ALL OF THE SPECIES ARE VIOLENT.

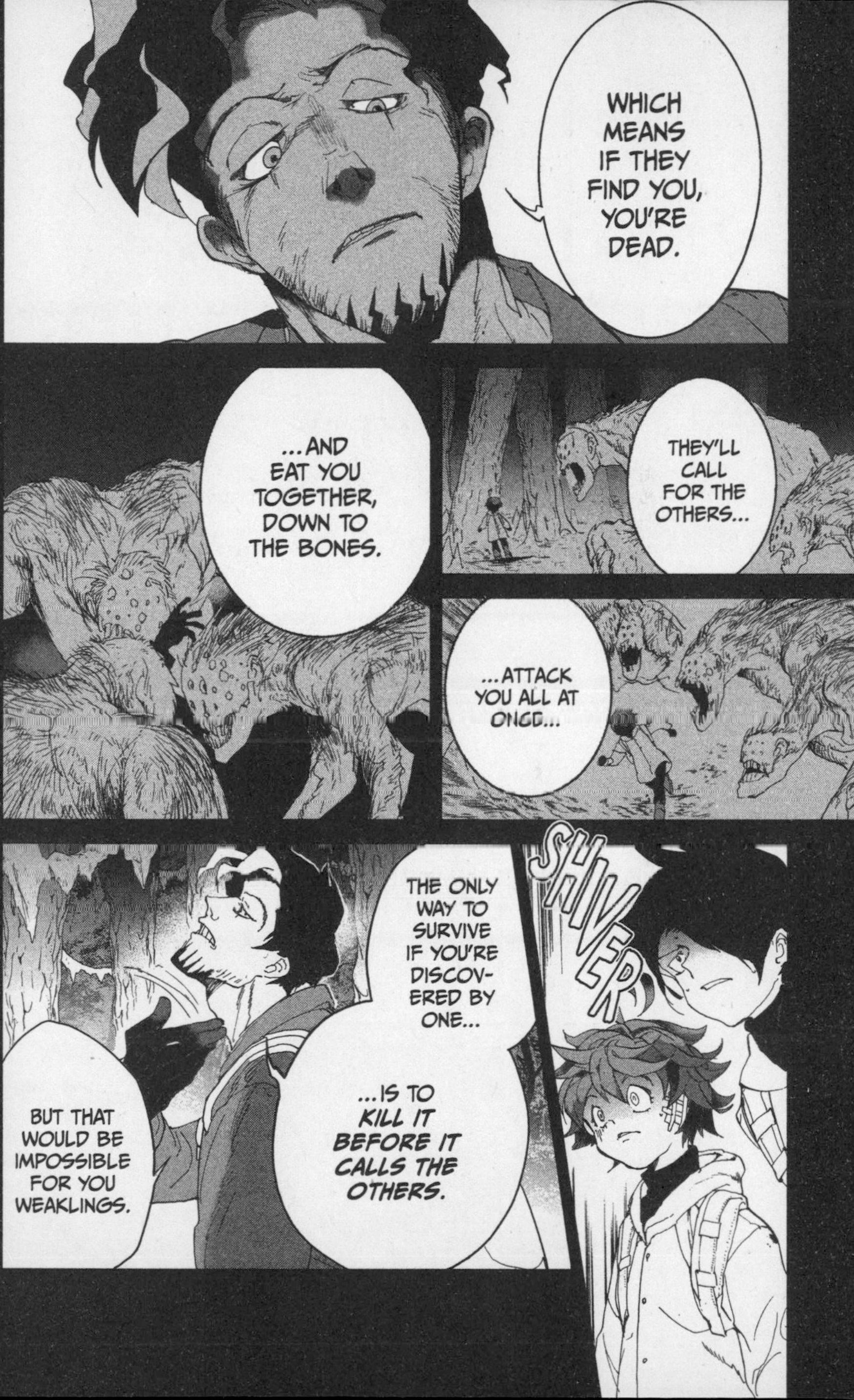
WHICH MEANS IF THEY FIND YOU, YOU'RE DEAD.
THEY'LL CALL FOR THE OTHERS...
...ATTACK YOU ALL AT ONCE...
...AND EAT YOU TOGETHER, DOWN TO THE BONES.
SHIVER
THE ONLY WAY TO SURVIVE IF YOU'RE DISCOVERED BY ONE...
...IS TO *KILL IT BEFORE IT CALLS THE OTHERS.*
BUT THAT WOULD BE IMPOSSIBLE FOR YOU WEAKLINGS.

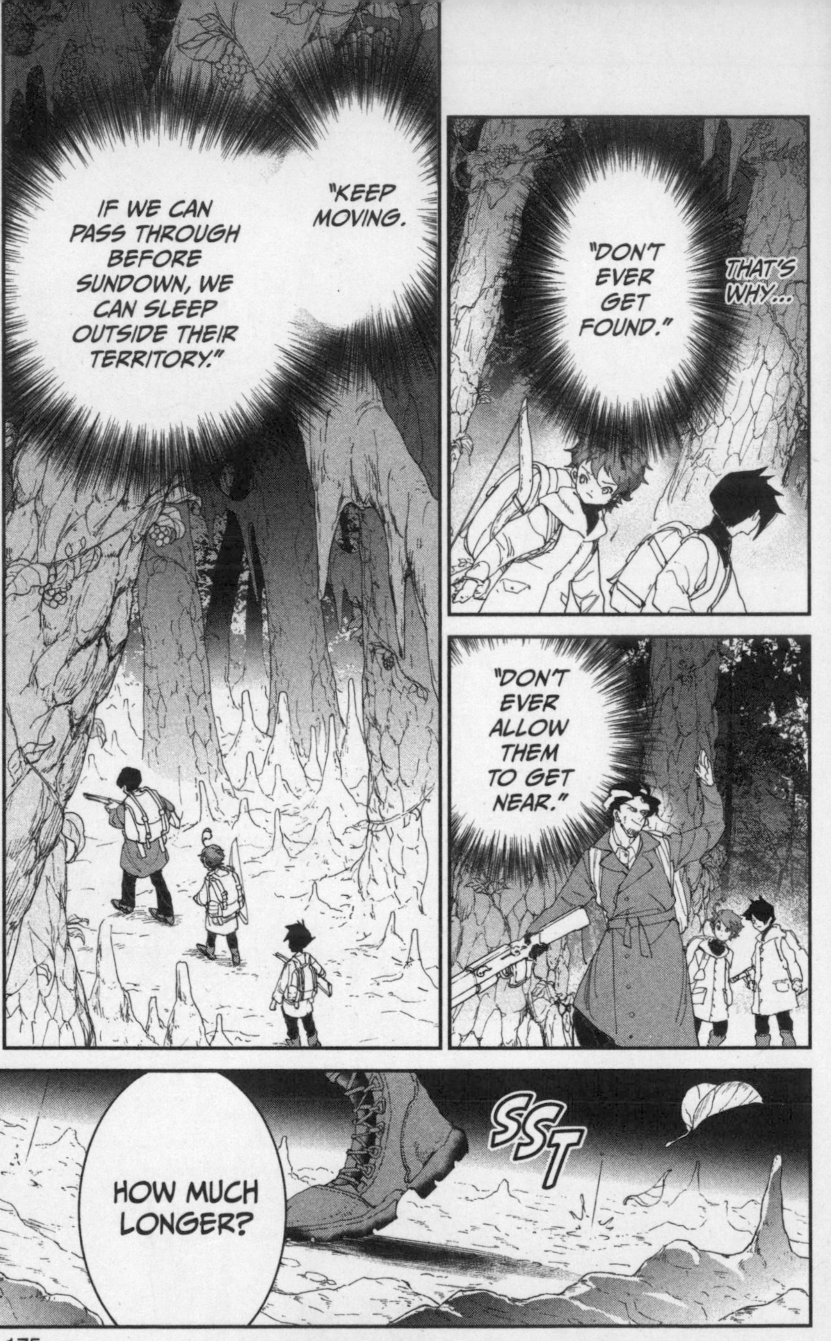
THAT'S WHY...
"DON'T EVER GET FOUND."
"DON'T EVER ALLOW THEM TO GET NEAR."
"KEEP MOVING.
IF WE CAN PASS THROUGH BEFORE SUNDOWN, WE CAN SLEEP OUTSIDE THEIR TERRITORY."
SST
HOW MUCH LONGER?

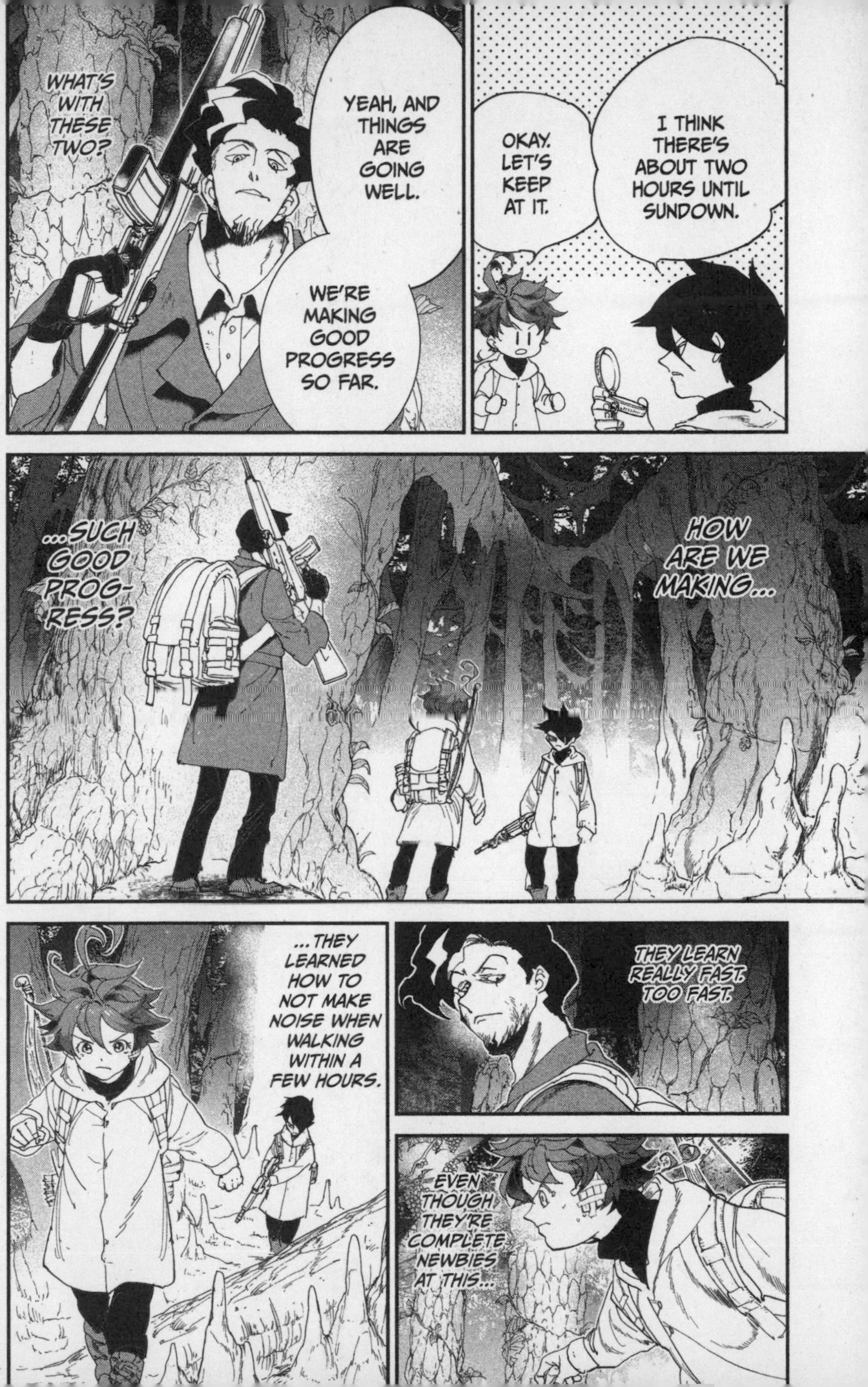
I THINK THERE'S ABOUT TWO HOURS UNTIL SUNDOWN.
OKAY. LET'S KEEP AT IT.
YEAH, AND THINGS ARE GOING WELL.
WHAT'S WITH THESE TWO?
WE'RE MAKING GOOD PROGRESS SO FAR.
HOW ARE WE MAKING...
...SUCH GOOD PROG-RESS?
THEY LEARN REALLY FAST. TOO FAST.
EVEN THOUGH THEY'RE COMPLETE NEWBIES AT THIS...
...THEY LEARNED HOW TO NOT MAKE NOISE WHEN WALKING WITHIN A FEW HOURS.

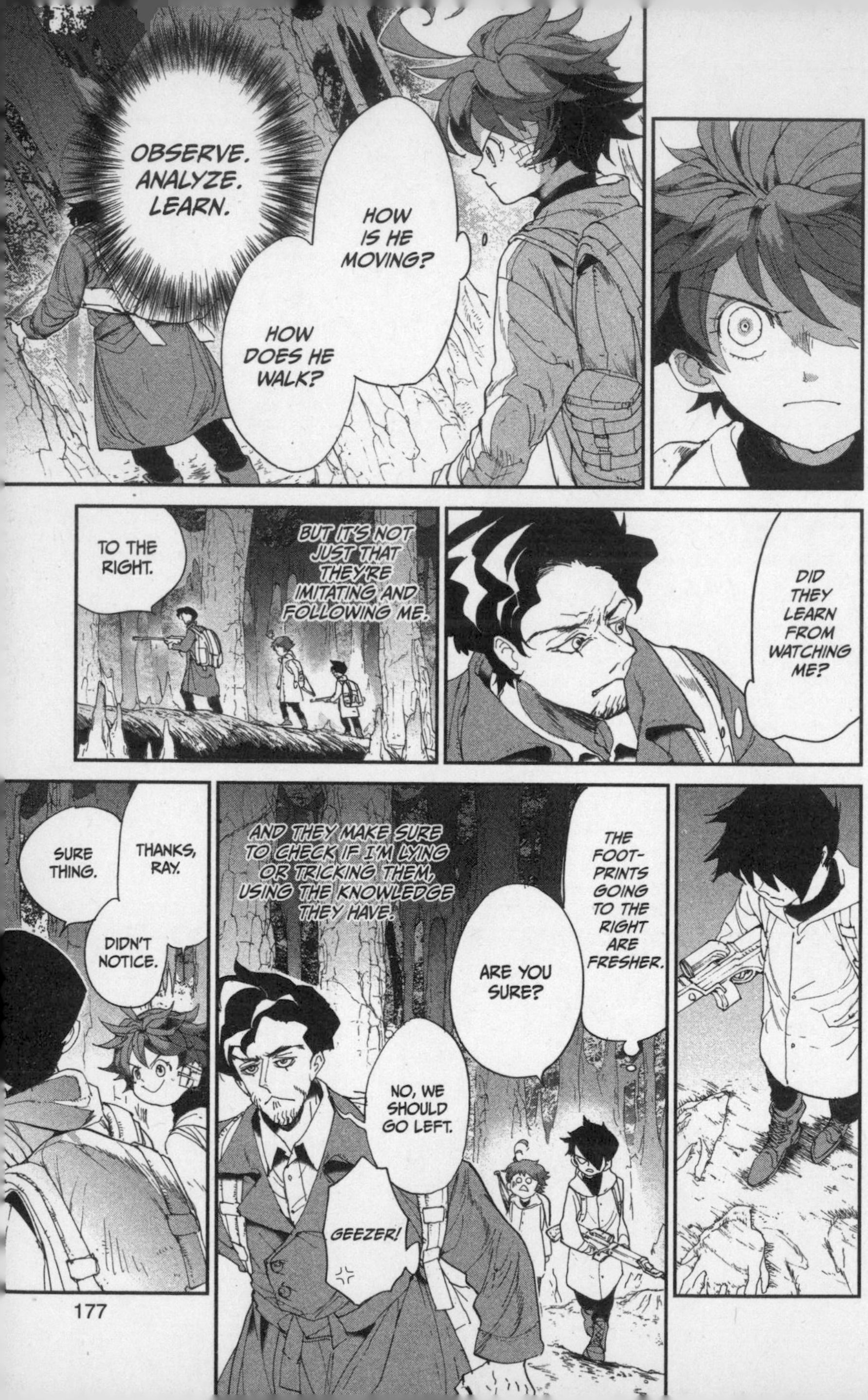
HOW IS HE MOVING?
HOW DOES HE WALK?
OBSERVE. ANALYZE. LEARN.
DID THEY LEARN FROM WATCHING ME?
BUT IT'S NOT JUST THAT THEY'RE IMITATING AND FOLLOWING ME.
TO THE RIGHT.
THE FOOT-PRINTS GOING TO THE RIGHT ARE FRESHER.
AND THEY MAKE SURE TO CHECK IF I'M LYING OR TRICKING THEM, USING THE KNOWLEDGE THEY HAVE.
ARE YOU SURE?
NO, WE SHOULD GO LEFT.
GEEZER!
THANKS, RAY.
SURE THING.
DIDN'T NOTICE.

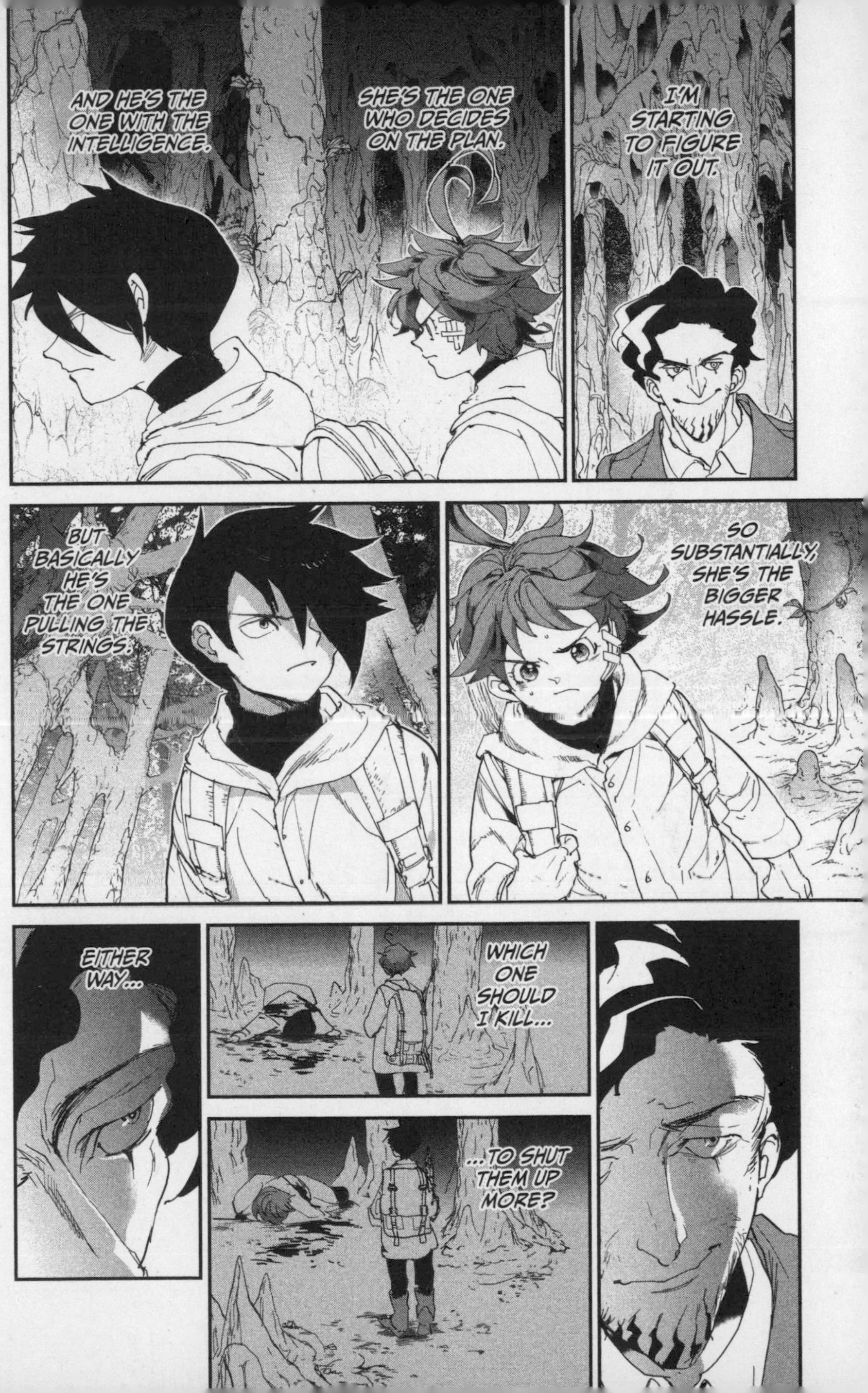
I'M STARTING TO FIGURE IT OUT.
SHE'S THE ONE WHO DECIDES ON THE PLAN.
AND HE'S THE ONE WITH THE INTELLIGENCE.
SO SUBSTANTIALLY, SHE'S THE BIGGER HASSLE.
BUT BASICALLY HE'S THE ONE PULLING THE STRINGS.
WHICH ONE SHOULD I KILL...
...TO SHUT THEM UP MORE?
EITHER WAY...

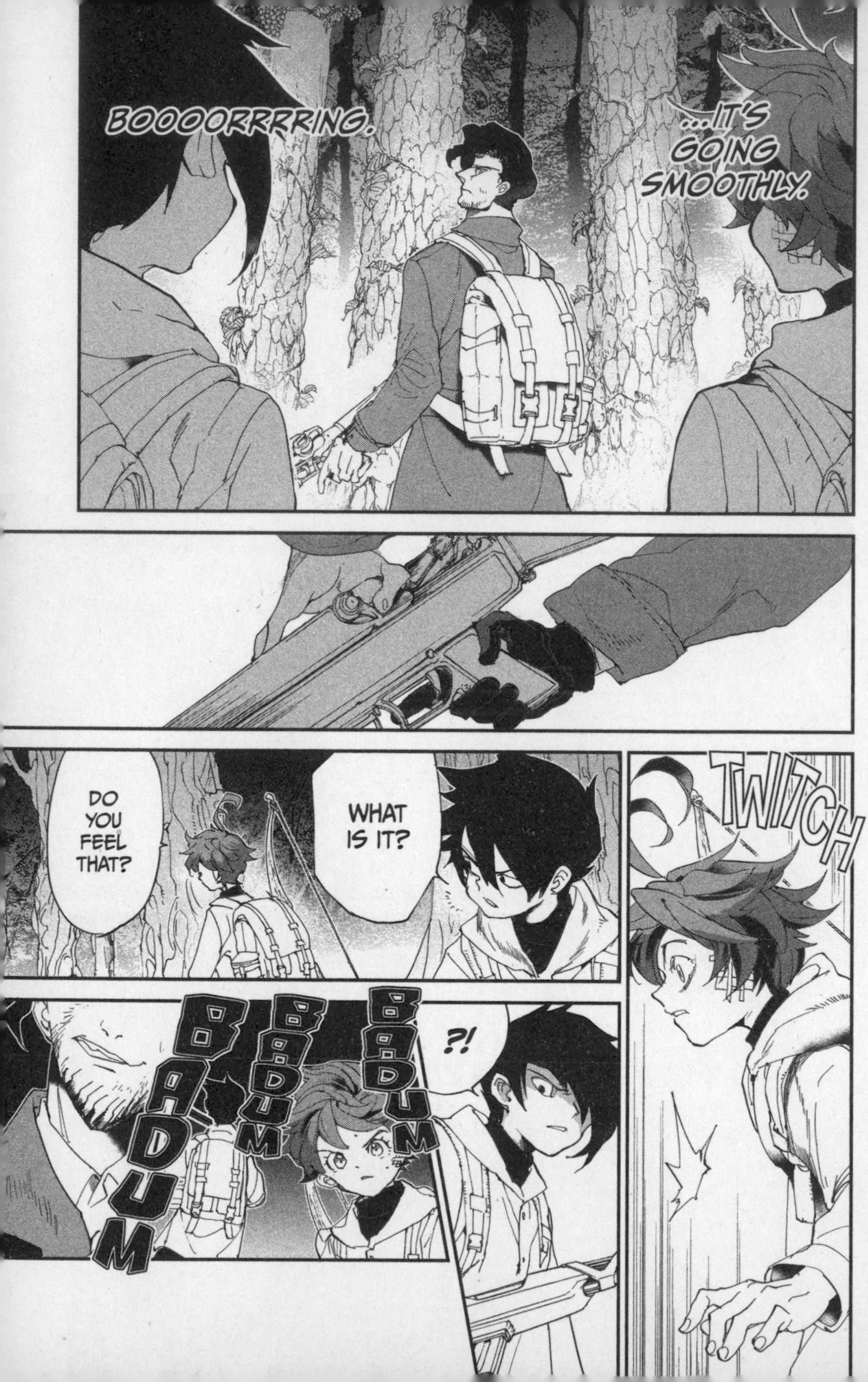
...IT'S GOING SMOOTHLY.
BOOOORRRRING.
TWITCH
WHAT IS IT?
DO YOU FEEL THAT?
?!
BADUM
BADUM
BADUM

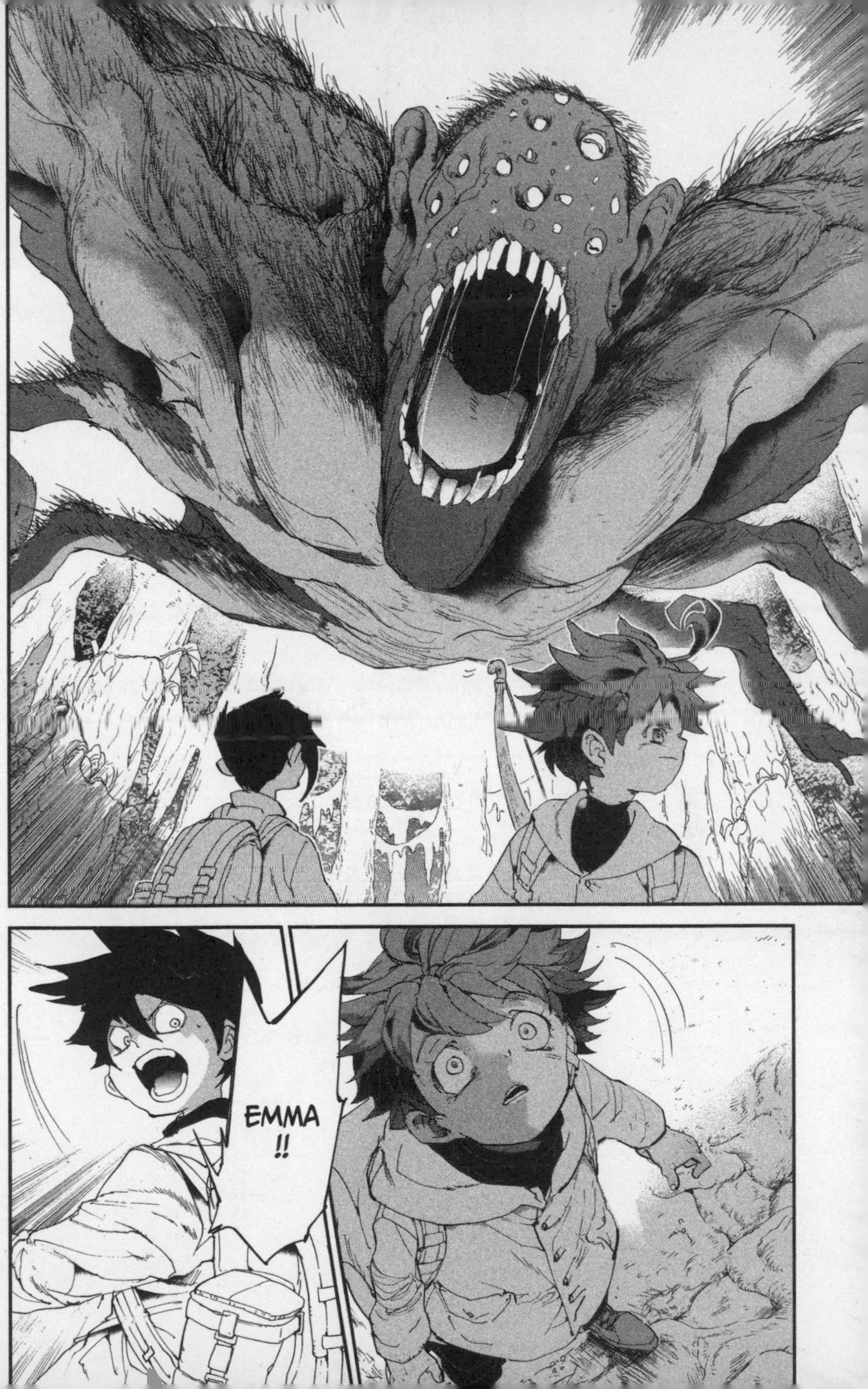
EMMA
!!

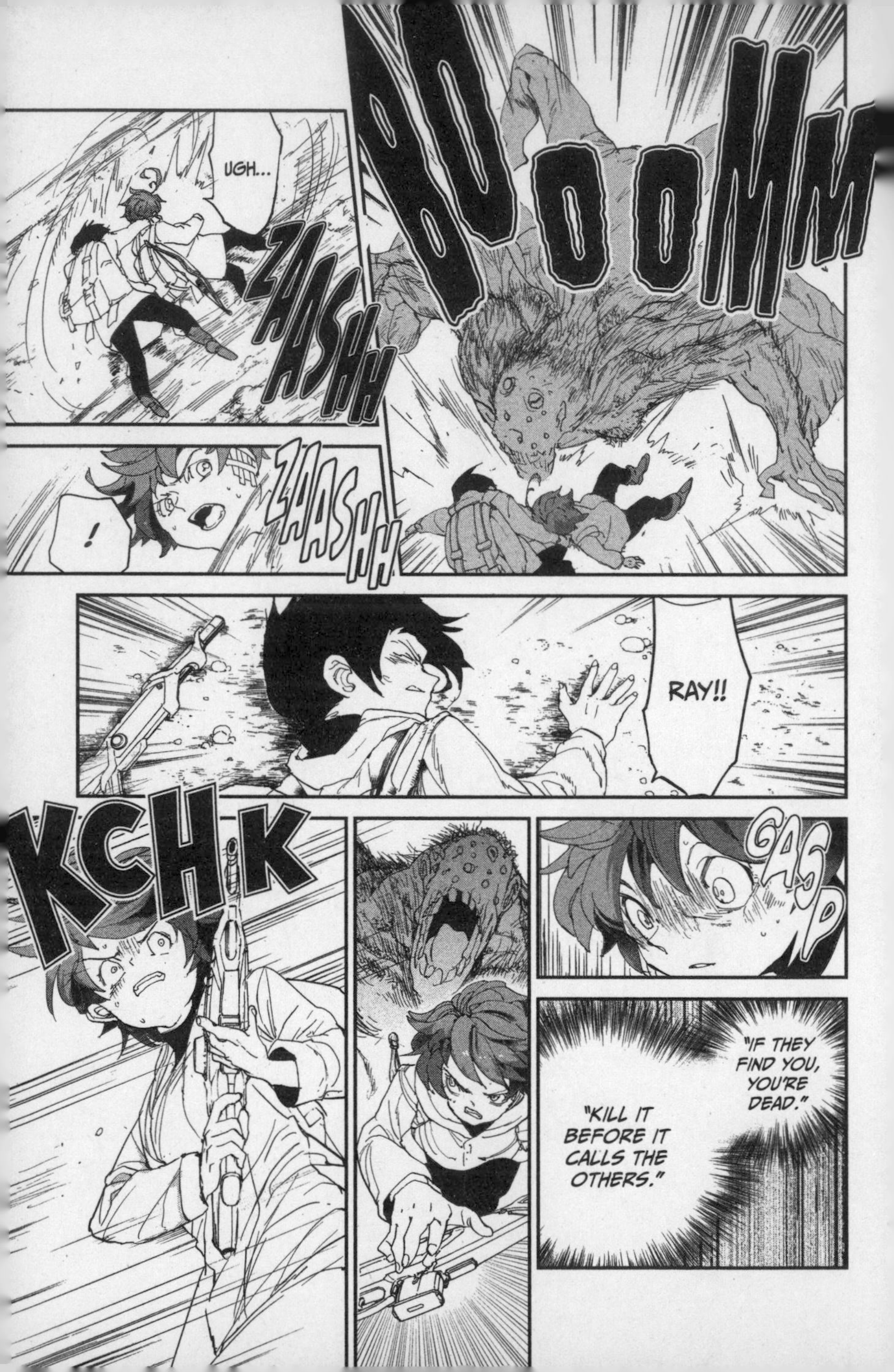

BOOOMM
UGH...
ZAASHH
!
ZAASHH
RAY!!
GASP
"IF THEY FIND YOU, YOU'RE DEAD."
"KILL IT BEFORE IT CALLS THE OTHERS."
KCHK

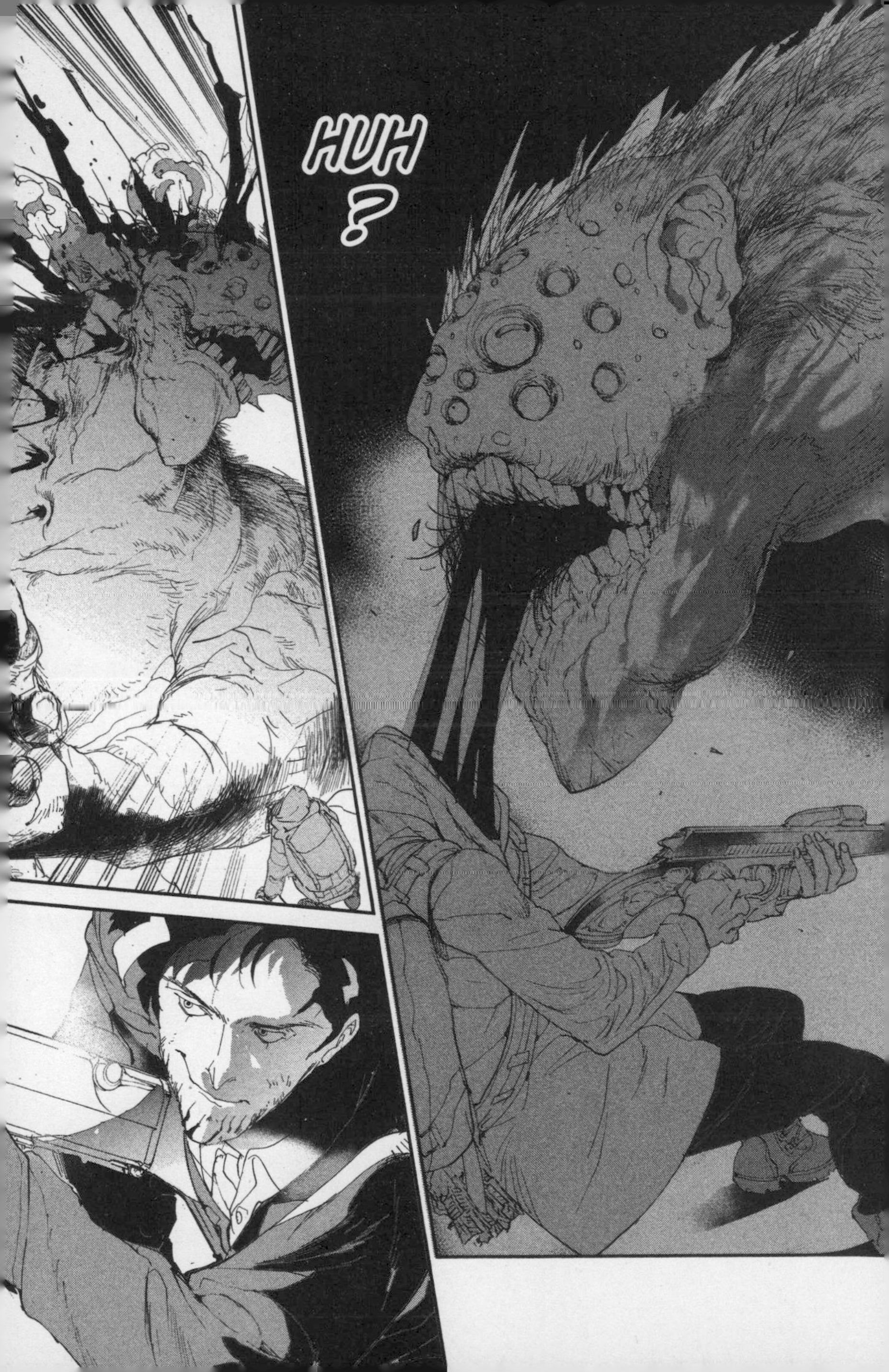
HUH
?

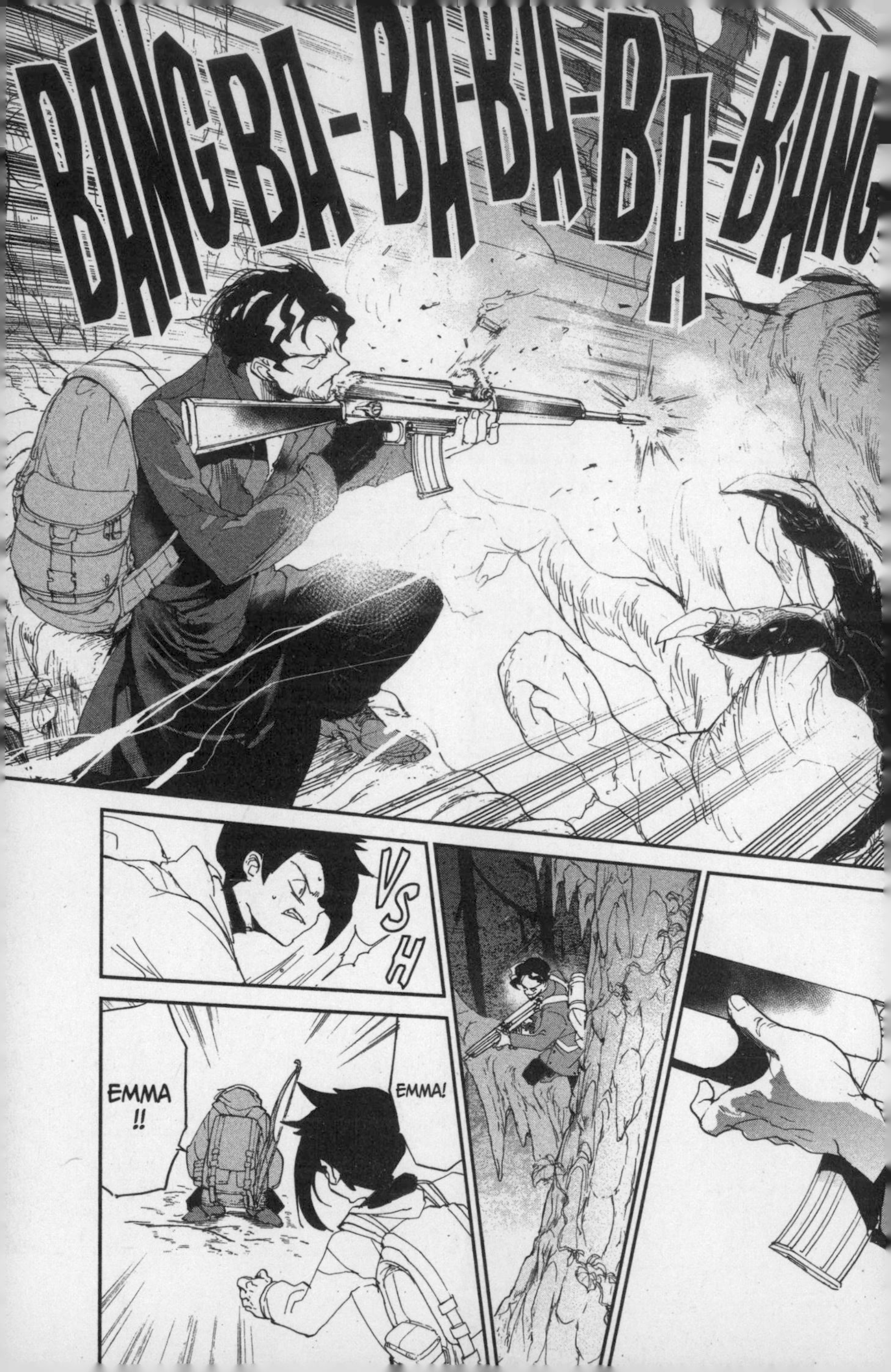
BANG BA-BA-BA-BA-BANG
VSH
EMMA!
EMMA !!

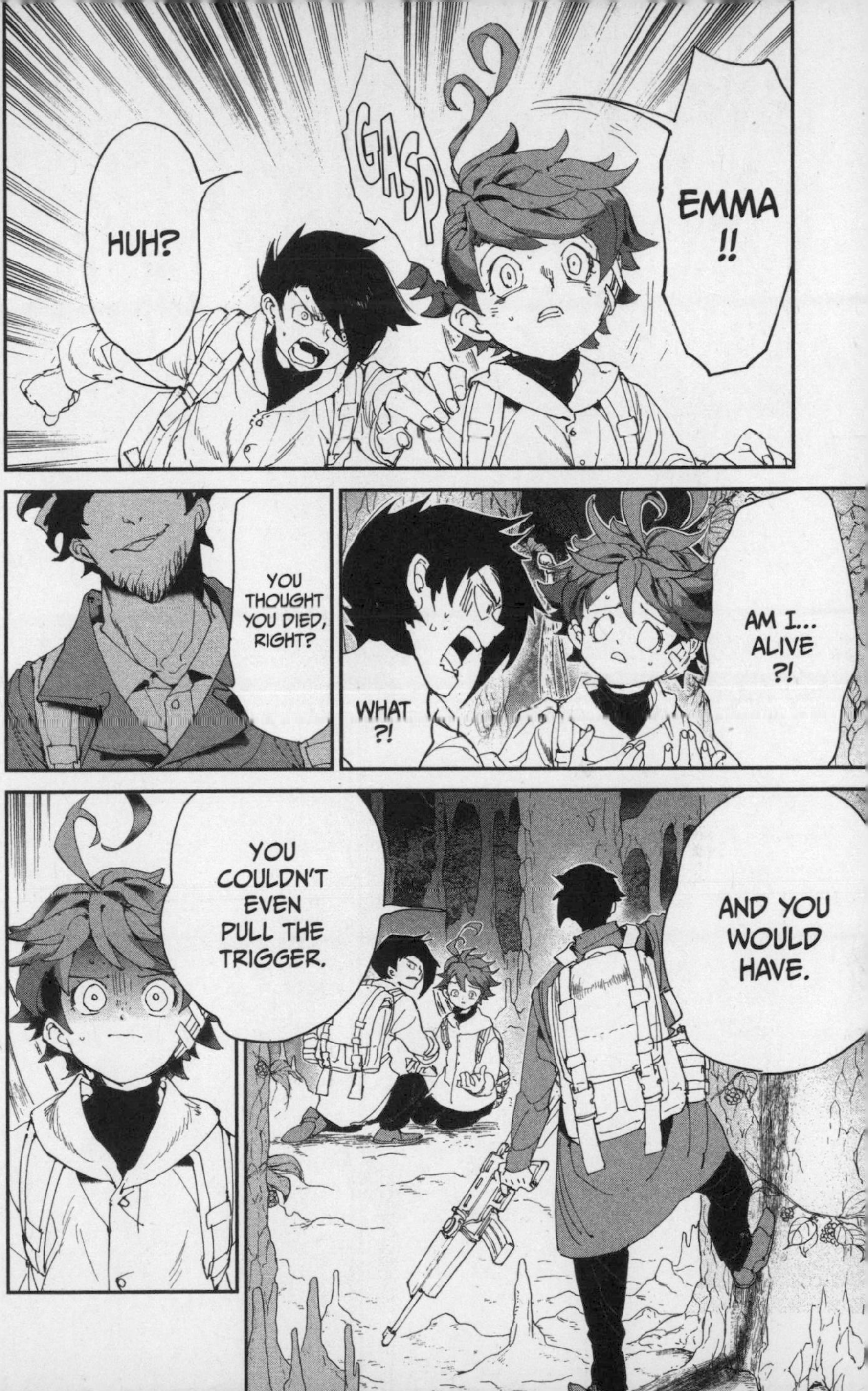
EMMA !!
GASP
HUH?
AM I... ALIVE ?!
WHAT ?!
YOU THOUGHT YOU DIED, RIGHT?
AND YOU WOULD HAVE.
YOU COULDN'T EVEN PULL THE TRIGGER.

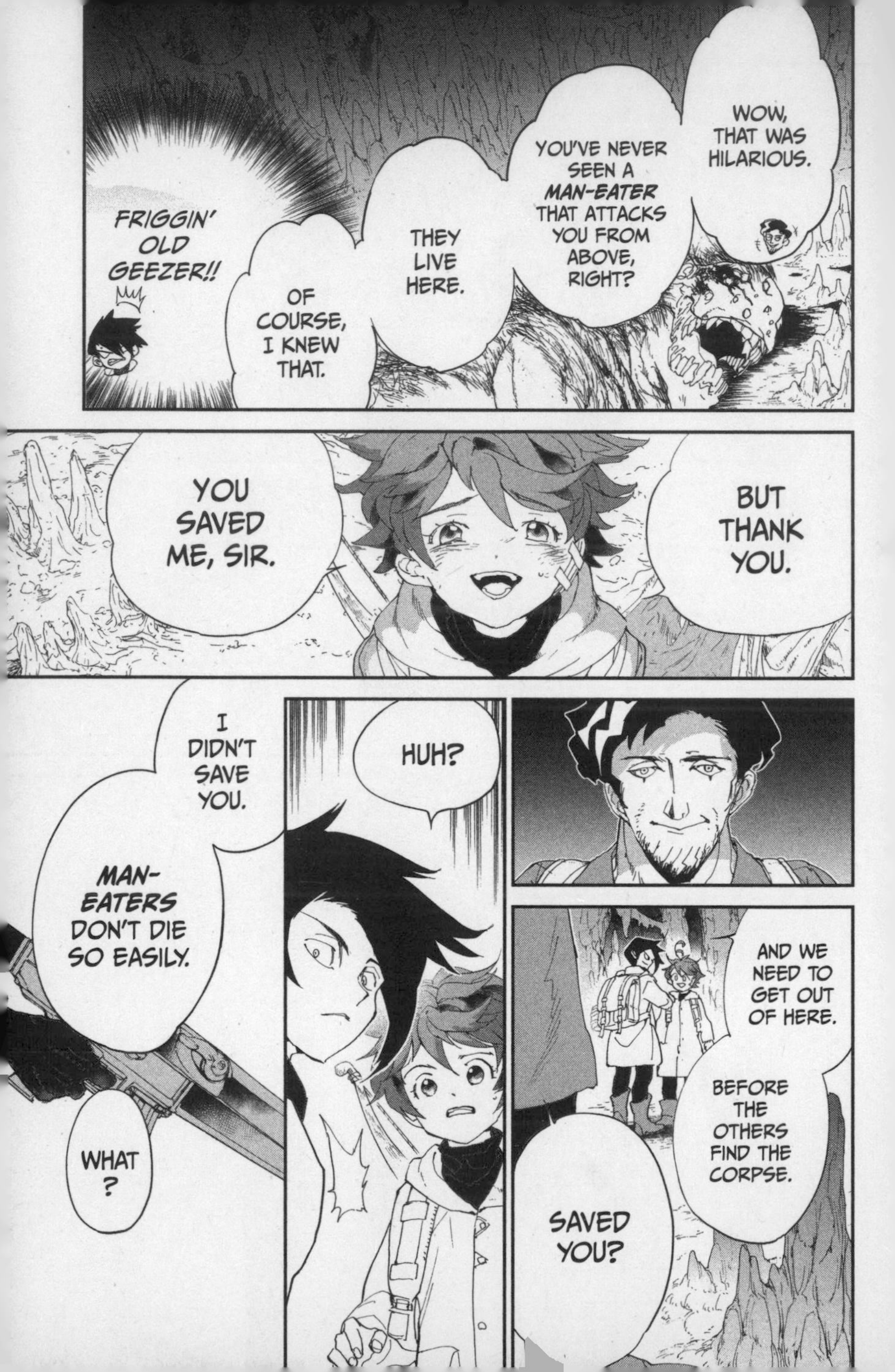
WOW, THAT WAS HILARIOUS.
YOU'VE NEVER SEEN A *MAN-EATER* THAT ATTACKS YOU FROM ABOVE, RIGHT?
THEY LIVE HERE.
OF COURSE, I KNEW THAT.
FRIGGIN' OLD GEEZER!!
BUT THANK YOU.
YOU SAVED ME, SIR.
I DIDN'T SAVE YOU.
HUH?
MAN-EATERS DON'T DIE SO EASILY.
WHAT?
SAVED YOU?
AND WE NEED TO GET OUT OF HERE.
BEFORE THE OTHERS FIND THE CORPSE.

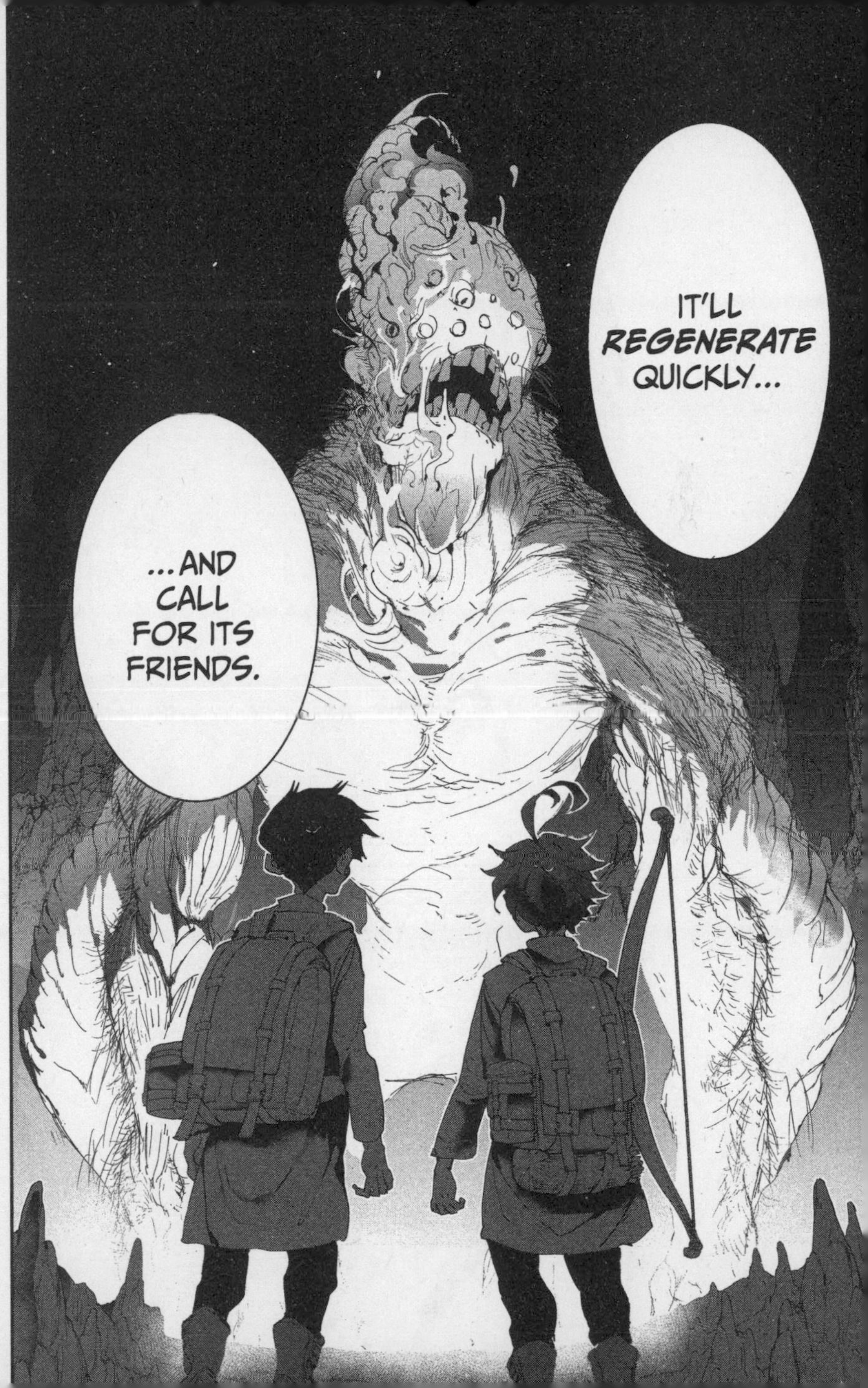
IT'LL REGENERATE QUICKLY...
...AND CALL FOR ITS FRIENDS.

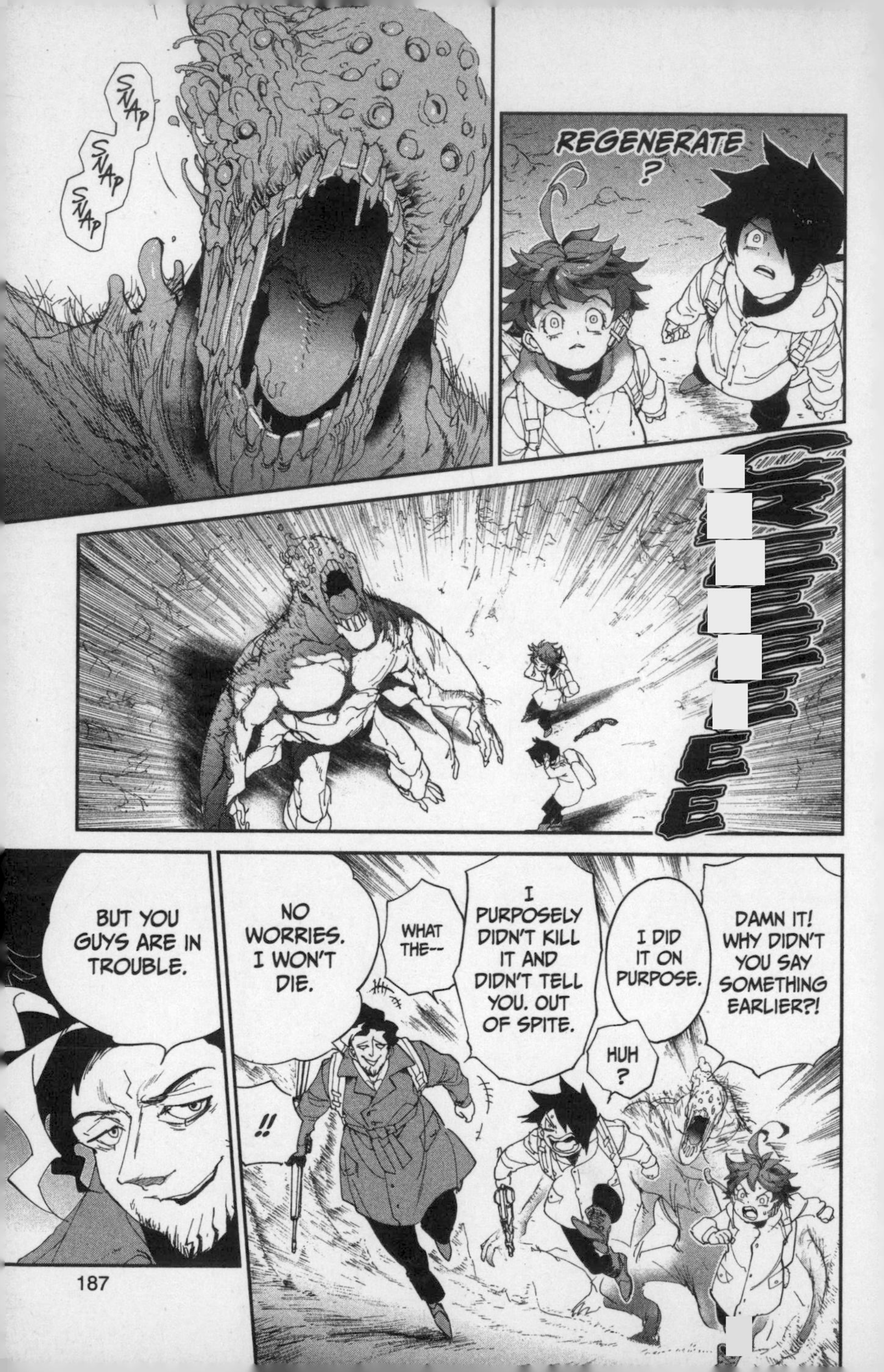
REGENERATE?
SNAP
SNAP
SNAP
DAMN IT! WHY DIDN'T YOU SAY SOMETHING EARLIER?!
I DID IT ON PURPOSE.
HUH?
I PURPOSELY DIDN'T KILL IT AND DIDN'T TELL YOU. OUT OF SPITE.
WHAT THE--
NO WORRIES. I WON'T DIE.
!!
BUT YOU GUYS ARE IN TROUBLE.

THEY DIDN'T GET TO EAT YOU. YOU ATTACKED ONE OF THEIR OWN. THEY'RE PISSED.

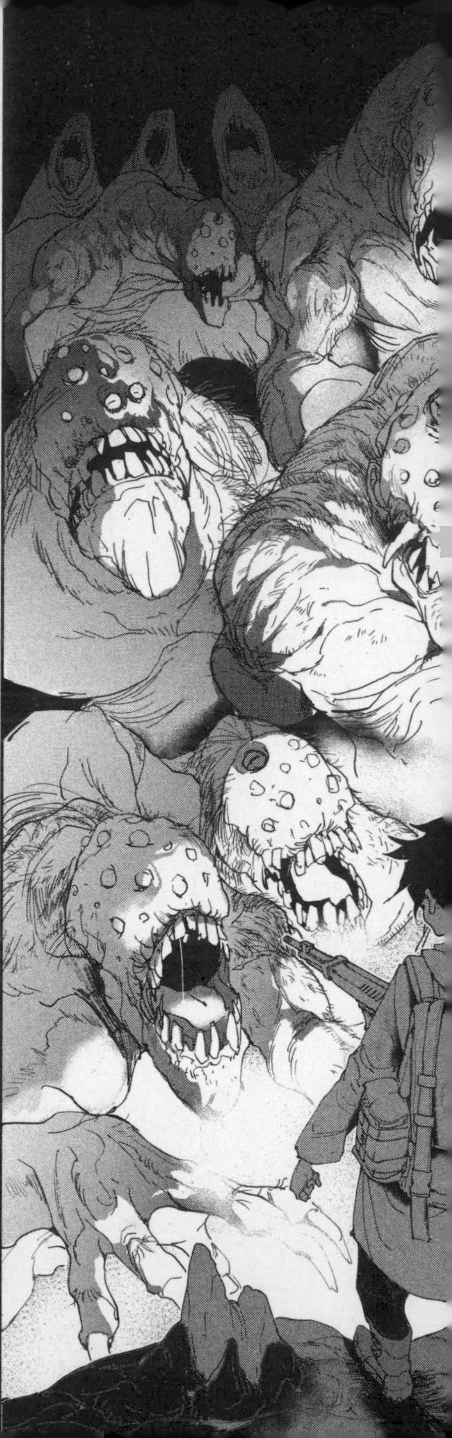

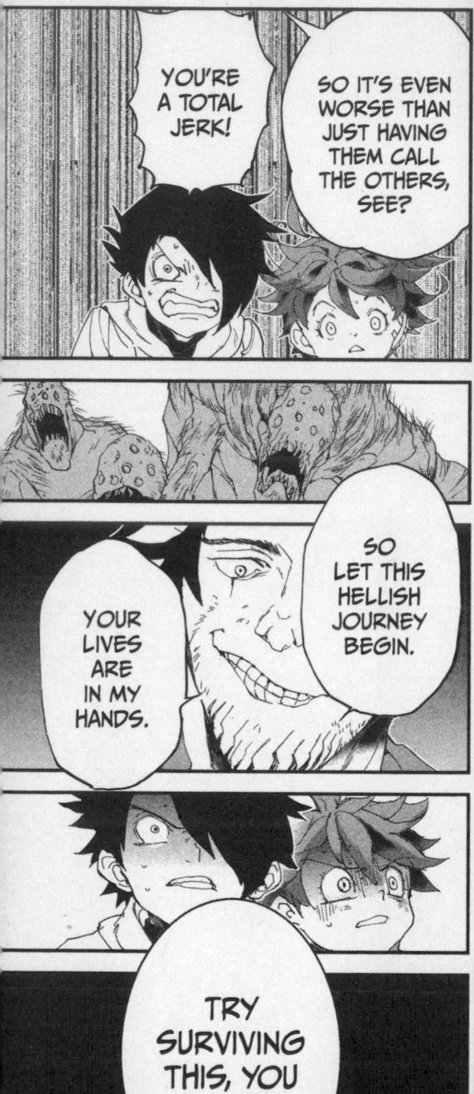
SO IT'S EVEN WORSE THAN JUST HAVING THEM CALL THE OTHERS, SEE?
YOU'RE A TOTAL JERK!
SO LET THIS HELLISH JOURNEY BEGIN.
YOUR LIVES ARE IN MY HANDS.
TRY SURVIVING THIS, YOU BRATS.

TO BE CONTINUED...

THE PROMISED NEVERLAND SIDE SCENE 014

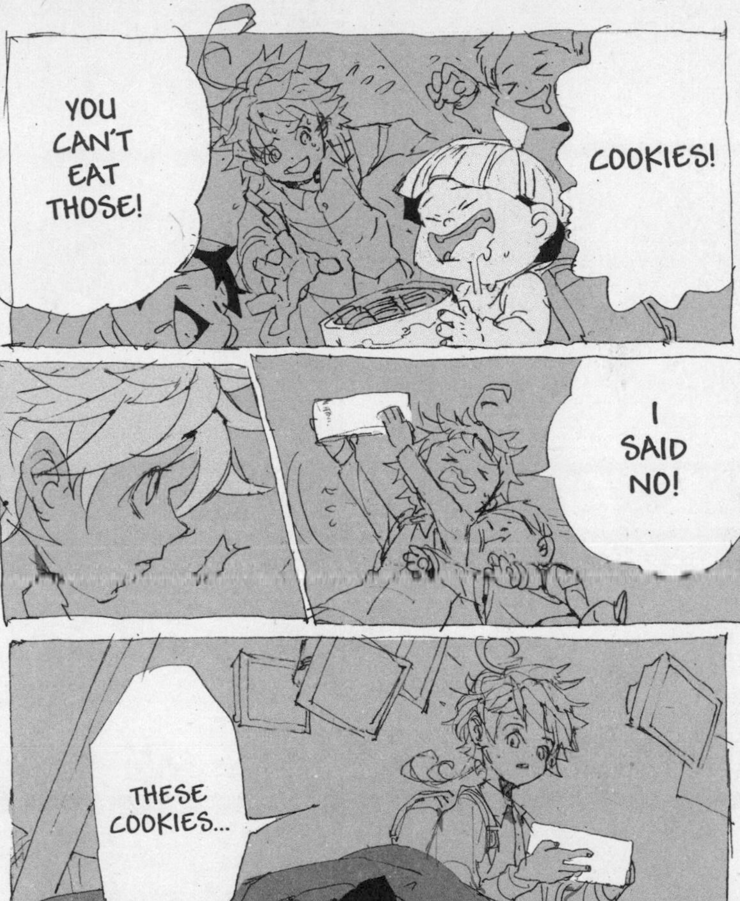
COOKIES!
YOU CAN'T EAT THOSE!
I SAID NO!
THESE COOKIES...

YOU'RE READING THE **WRONG WAY!**

1
2
1
3
4
2
5
6
3
7
8
4
9
5
142

The Promised Neverland **reads from right to left, starting in the upper-right corner. Japanese is read from right to left, meaning that action, sound effects and word-balloon order are completely reversed from English order.**

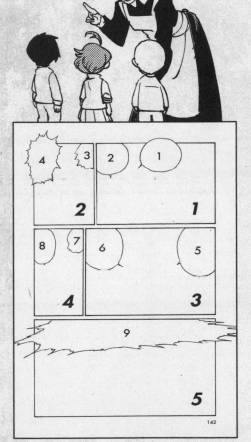